THE
BILL JAMES
PLAYER RATINGS
BOOK
1995

A FIRESIDE BOOK
Published by Simon & Schuster

New York   London   Toronto   Sydney   Tokyo   Singapore

FIRESIDE
Rockefeller Center
1230 Avenue of the Americas
New York, NY 10020

FIRESIDE and colophon are registered trademarks
of Simon & Schuster Inc.

Designed by Irving Perkins Associates

Manufactured in the United States of America

1   3   5   7   9   10   8   6   4   2

Library of Congress Cataloging-in-Publication Data is available.

ISBN 0-684-80089-6

ACKNOWLEDGMENTS

Well, thank you, thank you; I never dreamed that I would win, so I don't know quite what to say . . . I have so many people to thank.

I suppose I should start with the screenwriter, John Sickels, who gave me such strong material to put myself into. The director, Bill Rosen, was a joy to work with from beginning to end, and the producer, Gillian Sowell, brought all of the elements together with no egos and no misunderstandings.

John Dewan, second-unit director, thanks . . . the lighting director, Don Zminda . . . cameraman Ross Schaufelberger . . . all of the gang from Screen Talent and Tactics; you were all fabulous to work with. I need to thank Liz Darhansoff, who believed in me even when I got turned down for that razor blade commercial in '76, and Chuck Verrill, who has given me such strong career guidance in recent years.

And, of course, everything is for Susan, who had to be two parents for three children during all of those weeks I was on location in Kentucky, and for Rachel, Isaac, and Reuben. I hope that someday, when they're bigger, maybe they'll go to Blockbuster and rent the tape, and then maybe they'll understand why Daddy couldn't always be there. This will be on my mantel forever, and I thank you all.

This book is for Kent Earl
Because he works so cheerfully
Helping others to enjoy the games

CONTENTS

INTRODUCTION

This book was written with the lights out. This book is written (or was written, if you prefer) in September and October 1994, finished November 16, 1994. It is unclear, during most of this time, what sort of baseball season we will have in 1995. We might have what could be called a completely ordinary season—that is, the union and the owners might somehow settle their disagreements like gentlemen, open the camps, and let the players report back to the playgrounds in mid-February.

Hey, it could happen. The Arabs and Israelis are trying to work things out. The Protestants and Catholics are talking in Northern Ireland.

We might have, on the other hand, what could be called a complete disaster. In a moment, I will do what I can to sort out the possibilities. First, I need to say a word about the effects of this uncertainty on the book you hold in your hands.

I normally try, in annual editions of this book, to tell you a little bit about everybody who played in the major leagues last year or who might reasonably be expected to play in the major leagues this year. The unsettled labor situation makes it all but impossible to guess accurately who might play in the major leagues in 1995.

We might have no baseball at all, in which case all such efforts are doomed to failure.

We might have a scab league, with the real major leaguers holding out, and the rosters of the 28 teams filled by anonymous minor league journeymen, or, indeed, by a class of players well below them, by college baseball stars of 1989 who didn't get drafted by the pros.

We might have some combination of those two things, a league with 100 or 200 recognized players breaking with their union and returning to the game, but most players still holding out.

Although it is now clear that a third league cannot launch until 1996, if it gets started at all, this did not become clear until early November, after 98 percent of this book was already at the publishers.

So what should I do? How should I deal with the vast number of players who *might* play in the major leagues in 1995?

What I decided to do was to increase the number of players in this book in two ways. First, I shrunk the comments about players, which were 75-80 words last year, to 60-65 words. This allowed me to deal with a few more players in the same space. Second, I added to the book this year a section of one-line comments, which appear near the back of the book.

The one-line comments—I think there are about 250 of them—concern players who would not *ordinarily* be expected to play in the major leagues this year, but who might because of the unusual circumstances. They're guys who played in Japan last year, guys who were cut in spring training a year or two ago, Triple-A veterans who got a couple of cups of coffee in 1990 and 1992, and young players who need a year of Triple-A, but might be able to skip it if they are willing to break ranks.

There is a disadvantage in doing this, which is that it may make the player you are looking for harder to find. The thing I always liked about the organization of this book was that players were easy to find. If you hear about Phil Leftwich and Ron Tingley, you might not know anything about either one, but you could count on the fact that Phil Leftwich would be found between Craig Lefferts and Dave Leiper, and Ron Tingley would be found between Mike Timlin and Lee Tinsley.

Well, this is no longer true. If you hear about a young player and he's not in one place, he might still be found in the other. It's a tradeoff: The player you are looking for may be harder to find, but there is a better chance that he's here somewhere.

As to what we should most expect to happen . . . there is a gap of at least two months between when I write this and when you read it, and in those two months it is likely that the crawl of events may reach beyond me in at least some respects, and thus that I will wind up speculating on outcomes that are already decided before you read this. If so, I ask your indulgence, and perhaps, if I'm lucky, a few paragraphs of this might still be interesting. If the situation remains unresolved, let me try to help you understand it, as best I can.

Let us begin by making an inventory of the unresolved questions that create this quagmire. I count fifteen questions which outline the discussion we should be having, if only sportswriters and TV commentators were capable of having a discussion, rather than telling us how angry we are supposed to be about the whole thing. I would put these questions into order, except that there isn't any order they go in; they'll all have to be resolved simultaneously as events unfold. The key questions are:

1. Will the players' union give in, and accept the salary cap?
2. Will the owners give up, and abandon the salary cap?
3. Will the owners open their books?
4. Will there be a compromise?
5. Will the owners unilaterally impose a salary cap if no agreement is reached?
6. Will the small markets and large markets reach agreement on revenue sharing?
7. Will the owners attempt to start the 1995 season with replacement players?
8. Will the minor leaguers, the Triple-A players, be willing to fill in for the major leaguers?
9. If the Triple-A players don't agree to come up to play in the majors, who would they get?
10. Will the public accept substitute players as "real" major leaguers?
11. Will the union break?
12. Will the fans come back after a strike?
13. Will Congress act to repeal the anti-trust exemption if the owners hold tough?
14. Will some team be forced into bankruptcy?
15. Will there be a third league?

Three points about this list of questions. First, the answer to each of these questions is unknown, by definition. History is a trial of unknown questions; these are the issues which are currently being tried. If we could agree on the answers to these questions, we wouldn't be having this strike.

Second, in each of these larger questions, there are hundreds of smaller questions yet to be addressed. The question "Will the union break?" is a question about each of the individual players who make up the union. Would Terry Pendleton break with the union, and report to camp? Would Jay Buhner? Would Tony Pena?

Third, the outcome of the struggle depends not merely on all of those thousands of unknown "little answers," but on the timing of the relationships among them, and in particular, on *what breaks first*. The exact moment at which Terry Pendleton would break with the union and return to the Braves will never matter if something else breaks first.

With that, a few thoughts about what the answers to each of these questions *might* be:

1. Will the players' union give in, and accept the salary cap?

There is no point at which the players will vote to surrender because they will conclude that they have lost as much money as they can stand to lose, so it's time to give up and accept the salary cap. The players' union *will* surrender, in my opinion, if

a. The owners open the books and persuade the players that the teams are actually losing money, or
b. The Players' Association perceives itself as being in danger of *losing* the battle. If the leaders of the Players' Association start getting messages from their members that they have gone as far as they're willing to go, one would expect the union leaders to adjust their strategy, and accept a dignified retreat in preference to the breakup of the union.

So the answer to this question depends on the leadership's perception of the 11th question: Will the union break? As long as they are convinced it won't, they're not going to accept a salary cap, or whatever scheme is offered to replace it.

2. Will the owners give up, and abandon the salary cap?

I have never been able to think along with the owners, so my insight into their plans deserves to be lightly regarded. However, by last July it was apparent to me that the owners intended to have a strike. The owners, regardless of how backward-looking they may be, regardless of how out of touch, cannot believe that the players' union will fracture under a little pressure. There is too much history which shows too plainly that this is not going to happen. Since the owners *intended* to cause a strike, knowing that it would not be a short strike, they obviously must be prepared to have a *long* strike.

So it has been apparent to me since July that we were going to have a long strike.

Now, the question is, do the owners have some reason to give the players what they want in February or March, if they would not in September?

That depends on two of the other questions—but the short answer is that as long as nothing else changes, they don't. If Congress acts to remove the anti-trust exemption, that might force them to move. If the third league gets a TV contract, that might force them to move.

The thing is, they *can* give up the salary cap, without there being any actual movement in the strike. The salary cap is as much pretext as cause. So if they give up the salary cap, it might be a big, loud "So what?"

3. Will the owners open their books?

The key here is why the owners are so resistant to sharing their financial data. If the owners did open the books, and if the books did show what the owners say would be revealed (that the business is unprofitable), then this would *help* them in their negotiating position, since the union would be much more likely to accept salary restraints if they were genuinely convinced there was a problem.

Since the owners refuse to do what it would be in their interest to do if they were telling the truth, it must be assumed that they are less than candid. And if that's so, they're *not* going to open the books to reveal this.

4. Will there be a compromise?

There can only be a compromise if there is a desire on both sides to reach an agreement. Every indication we have had from the owners is that they *don't* want an agreement; what they want is a fight.

I could be completely wrong, but as I see it, the owners had to know last July that they couldn't win a big ugly fight with a six-week strike. Therefore, they must be counting on winning it with a *longer* fight, a fight carrying on into the 1995 season. They want to break the union, or they want to force the union to back down. They had to know that they couldn't do that in September. Their first chance to do it will be in March. So there is a good chance that there will not be a compromise before March 15.

5. Will the owners unilaterally impose a salary cap if no agreement is reached?

The union is convinced that this announcement will be made before you read these words. The owners will unilaterally impose a salary cap. Those guys know more about it than I do, but I'm not really convinced that that's what's going to happen, because I'm not convinced that the owners really *care* about the salary cap. I think what the owners want is a big fight, which the players lose. The salary cap is the chip on their shoulder, the putative cause of the fight.

And if so, then management's "announcement" may not be a salary cap, but something much more sweeping than that. They may announce the end of arbitration, unlimited free agency after four seasons, maximum salaries by service class, financial compensation to small-market teams losing free agents, or any number of other alterations to the working arrangement. The package would probably include some features that management could point to and claim that they were dealing fairly with the players, such as an increase in the minimum salary, but the total effect, if put into practice, would be to drive salaries down dramatically over a period of years.

6. Will the small markets and large markets reach agreement on revenue sharing?

There are several ways of looking at this issue. One is that baseball is having a tri-partite negotiation—small market owners, big market owners, players. If this is an accurate representation of the problem, then one would assume that the big market/small market problem has to be the first one solved, since the players have to make a single agreement with all the owners.

Another way of looking at it is that while the big market/small market split is no doubt real, it has nothing to do with the labor negotiation. The players cannot solve a problem among the owners—in fact, it's a very strange argument to have mixed into a labor negotiation. Suppose there were a strike in the auto industry. Would you expect Ford to say to the UAW, "You've got to help us work out this problem with General Motors; then we'll talk about a contract." That is a separate problem that has to be solved separately, before or after the contract with the union.

Perhaps the most accurate way of looking at it, however, is to say that the small market owners have shut baseball down until they get what they want. They don't care where it comes from. They can get what they need from the big market owners, or they can get it from the players.

If that is the most accurate way of looking at the issue, then the "solution" to the situation will probably be that the small market owners will eventually get *some* concessions from both parties—some from the players, some from the big market owners.

This is a gloomy thought, because such a compromise is by its nature almost impossible to arrange. If everything depends on the small market owners, then the structure of the solution does not parallel the structure of the negotiation. The *negotiation* has the players on one side of the table, and all of the owners on the other side. The *solution* has the small market owners on one side of the table, and the big market owners on the other side, with the players. But you could never persuade the big market owners to accept this, because they would perceive it as a weakening of their position. Their thinking is, "We've got to stay united. Our strength is in a unified position." And by so saying, they make it all but impossible to reach the logical compromise.

7. Will the owners attempt to start the 1995 season with replacement players?

I assume that they will. Why wouldn't they? They promised last year not to use "scabs" or replacement players to break the strike, and they didn't do so last

September, which would have caused obvious problems.

But are they supposed to say, ''These guys don't want to play, they're the only people in the world who can play baseball, therefore we'll just shut down indefinitely''? That's certainly not what I would do if I were an owner.

8. Will the minor leaguers, the Triple-A players, be willing to wear the major league uniforms?

The great majority of the Triple-A players will *not* work as strike-breakers.

Baseball players are not stupid and not short-sighted, as a rule. There is tremendous loyalty to the union among major league players, or at least there has been, up to now. Most Triple-A players at any moment have been up to the majors a couple of times, and have been around the major leaguers in spring training, as minor league teammates, and at other times. They have agents, the same agents who represent the major league players.

It has always been understood, among the players, that anyone who broke with the union would have a very difficult time staying in the game. You remember what happened to the umpires who came to the majors during their strike a few years ago, the scab umpires? They were ostracized by the other umpires, and had very difficult working conditions for the rest of their careers. The other umpires would not speak to them, would not eat with them, would not travel with them, wouldn't support them in on-field controversies, and immediately reported any failure or transgression on their part to the league offices.

Ratchet that up about five notches, and you've got an idea of what would happen to a Triple-A player who crossed the line. The first guy who crosses the line is going to lead the league in being hit with the pitch, and we're not talking off-speed stuff. A middle infielder who crossed the picket line couldn't possibly get out of the way fast enough to avoid a collision at second base, and he'd better be prepared to spend the rest of his career dressing in a small closet somewhere. And this persecution would follow the player not merely while he was in the majors, but the rest of his career in baseball, or even the rest of his life. He's not getting invited to any reunions.

The loyalty of baseball players to the union
   a. Has probably dissipated somewhat over time, and is probably not now as strong as it was in the Marvin Miller era, and
   b. Has no doubt been sapped significantly by the strike.

How much of the loyalty to the union has been dissipated is unknown, and cannot be known to anyone until it becomes apparent to everyone. This is one of the issues being tried in this contest. It's not like football; the football players never did have any strong loyalty to their union. But even assuming that the union is ready to break, it is much more likely that the first people to break with the union will be the people who have strength within the system, much more likely Frank Thomas than Kerry Taylor.

9. If the Triple-A players don't agree to come up to play in the majors, who would they get?

So 90 percent of the Triple-A players are not going to work as strike-breakers—but *somebody* will. If the club owners announce that they're opening the camps on February 15 and they're going to make a team out of whoever shows up, I guarantee you that *somebody* will show up to play baseball and make $110,000 a year.

The best candidates would be players whose careers are over, or almost over. A guy who spent eight years in the minors, got a couple of weeks in the majors, and was released last May—he's a great candidate to show up in spring training. There are any number of guys like that around, and if 10 percent of them are willing to put on a uniform, that's a starting place.

There are good players, or pretty good players, who have been trapped in the minors just by bad timing and bad luck. I have mentioned most of them in this book—Jeff Manto, Russ Morman, Greg Pirkl, Sherman Obando, Mike Twardoski. The difference between them and guys like Gary Varsho, Mark Carreon, and Billy Hatcher is just luck—and they know it.

So what happens if you are a major league executive, and you go to one of those players, and you say, ''OK, kid, this is your chance. We'll pay you $200,000 to play in the major leagues this year, and we'll guarantee the whole contract—but you've got to report to camp by February 20.'' It seems unlikely to me that *all* of those players will say ''No.'' Some of them will take the money and run.

Beyond that, the next class is the young players who
   a. Played A Ball or Rookie Ball last year, and
   b. *Aren't* moving up.

The guys who *are* moving up, the Ken Griffeys of the next generation—they mostly know that their time is going to come, anyway, and also I'm not sure that the clubs would *want* to poison their careers by putting them in such a difficult position.

I would be surprised if all 28 teams could completely fill out a roster with these three classes of players, so beyond that you've got the amateurs and the semi-pro players, and guys who played college ball but didn't get drafted.

But clearly, the clubs can put teams together, if

they choose to do so. I assume that they will choose to do so.

10. Will the public accept substitute players as "real" major leaguers?

Maybe I phrased that wrong: Can the substitute players be *sold* to the public as major leaguers?

And the answer is that yes, they unquestionably can, if the owners will get off their butt and do it. I would ask you to consider the example of *American Gladiators*, Bill Clinton's favorite TV show. The creators of that show, when they started, not only didn't have any athletes, they didn't even have a *sport*. They took a combination of obstacle courses and war games, and constructed a kind of made-for-TV sport.

Then they recruited *athletes*, people who had obvious physical attributes which qualified them as athletes.

The press is going to have a tendency to make fun of the replacement athletes, to make jokes about them, the drift of which is that they are really no more athletes than you and I. Of course, this is literally untrue—no matter how much the quality of play slips, those guys are still going to be vastly better athletes than the typical man on the street.

But baseball executives, over the years, have sometimes been inclined to sit back and expect the public to come out because they always have. They will need to *sell* their players.

11. Will the union break?

One has to assume that, at some point, some players will break with the union. The question is, who?

I think we can sort players, for our present purpose, into four groups, which are:

    a. Young stars,
    b. Established players,
    c. Fading players, and
    d. Fringe players.

The last two groups are alike, in that their time is very short, and for that reason they are paying a heavy price for the strike. If Tom Glavine loses a third of a season to a strike, that's 2 or 3 percent of his career. But an older player, like Gary Gaetti or Harold Reynolds, is within a few months of the end of his career. The prospect of losing another two months to a strike, to such a player, may very well mean the loss of the rest of his career.

But will those players break with the union? I doubt it. They have a long history with the union. They have put away a lot of money, because of the union's good work.

The fringe players, I think, will not break with the union, because their position is so weak.

So who will break first? The young stars. The players who came up three to six years ago, who have played well, and who are just now beginning to earn big money. They'll be the ones who will break with the union, because

    a. Their position within the game is strong, and
    b. Their loyalty to the union is comparatively weak.

12. Will the fans come back after a strike?

As we all know, they always have. Two things are different about this strike, which are the cancellation of the World Series, and the fact that the teams are heading into the winter, the time when they normally sell season tickets, with no baseball to sell. This latter factor, if it continues for another couple of months, would have to affect the number of tickets sold to some extent.

One of the most common stories filed by journalists whenever there is a strike is that the fans are terribly angry, they're being mistreated, and they *should* stay angry and stay away after the strike ends, but being such a bunch of saps, they of course will come running right back to the park.

What I've never been able to understand about this is why, exactly, I was supposed to be so furious. If my neighbors Sam and Julie have a fight, should I be angry at them because they were angry at each other? I know some fans do get quite upset about the work stoppage, but hell, this is America; there are people who are angry about almost anything. I doubt that intense anger about a baseball strike is really very common, and it probably indicates emotional instability in those afflicted.

13. Will Congress act to repeal the anti-trust exemption if the owners hold tough?

Not now.

There is broad, bipartisan agreement that the anti-trust exemption makes no sense. A resolution to remove the owners' anti-trust exemption was introduced in the Senate by Orrin Hatch (Republican, Utah, among the most conservative members of Congress) and Howard Metzenbaum (Democrat, Ohio, among the most liberal). A similar resolution was introduced in the House by Mike Synar (Democrat, Oklahoma) and Jim Bunning (Republican, once threw a perfect game). Anti-trust law, while in practice it is often unpopular, is in theory favored both by Democrats, because they believe it protects the interests of organized labor, and by Republicans, because they believe it promotes free market competition. The anti-trust exemption for baseball, which rests on the flight of fancy that baseball is a sport, and therefore not a business, has no natural political protection.

But the new Republican Congress has a list of projects as long as your arm that they have promised to work on in their first 100 days. The longer the strike continues, the less attention it receives in the national press. Both Howard Metzenbaum and Mike Synar are no longer in Congress, Metzenbaum having retired and Synar having been defeated. It just does not seem likely that baseball will be able to force its way onto the agenda.

To go back to point A . . . anti-trust legislation is intended to prevent a large corporation or a powerful individual from taking over a business, and pushing around everybody else who is in that business or who wants to be in that business. In a 1922 decision of the Supreme Court, written by Oliver Wendell Holmes, it was decreed that baseball was a sport, not a business, and therefore that baseball was exempt from anti-trust legislation. This exemption was affirmed, and arguably expanded, in two subsequent Supreme Court decisions—*Toolson* v. *New York*, 1952, and *Flood* v. *Kuhn*, 1972.

It is a truism among educated baseball fans that baseball's anti-trust exemption is a strange and unjustifiable circumstance at best, and a hindrance to labor relations at the worst. The exemption is based upon the utterly absurd logic that since baseball is a sport, it therefore is not a business.

Now, baseball *is* a sport; indeed, it is more of a sport than it is a business, as is evident to anyone who really thinks about the subject. I am wearing a blue shirt. Holmes' dictum is analogous to saying that because it is a shirt, it is *not* a blue object. My shirt, of course, can be both a shirt *and* blue, and baseball can be (and is) both a sport *and* a business.

But rolling the subject around in my head in recent weeks, I finally was able to understand what Holmes was thinking when he wrote this unfortunate decision. What he was trying to say was that baseball must be *free* to do what it needs to do as a sport. It must be *free* of the financial pressures that afflict businesses. It must be able to make its internal decisions based on what it needs to do as a sport—not on what it needs to do as a business. If we subject baseball to anti-trust law, Holmes was thinking, we may be forcing economic pressures upon the game which will force the sporting interest to the rear.

The irony of this decision, of course, is that freeing baseball from anti-trust action has enabled the economic interest of the game to rage unchecked, pushing the sporting interest out of the picture. So the *effect* of Holmes' decision has been exactly the opposite of his intention. If Holmes had lived another 75 years and remained on the Court, he would no doubt have recognized this. But life is limited, and thus the progress of understanding in each generation is limited.

Also, I may be a minority of one, but I'm not convinced that the owners are all that terrified about the prospect of losing the anti-trust exemption, or that they have any reason to be frightened about it. Football and basketball don't have the anti-trust exemption. They seem to get along all right. I once had a very interesting discussion with two learned economists about the effects on baseball of removing the anti-trust exemption. Both men had researched the subject and had very strong opinions about what the effects would be, but their two opinions were diametrically opposed.

In 1990, when the winners of the last expansion derby were announced (Miami and Denver), a congressman from Tennessee was so angry about the fact that Memphis didn't get a team that he introduced a bill to remove the anti-trust exemption. I had a national radio show at the time, so we called the guy up and got him on the show. I asked him what the effects of his legislation would be, if it was adopted. He didn't have a clue. I asked him what his legislation would do, and he said It would force baseball teams to obey anti-trust law, and I said Well, are they violating anti-trust law now, and he said No, not that I know of.

Well, I said, what *exactly* would your legislation do?

He said it would force baseball to obey the anti-trust law.

The truth is that *nobody* knows what the effects of removing the anti-trust exemption would be, and no one can possibly know, because it would depend on factors that are yet to be determined. Anti-trust law is a very strange animal, and no one is really sure *what* is prohibited and what isn't. Practices which are common in one business are prohibited in other businesses, based on interpretations of law by Justice Department attorneys, interpretations that would have to be illuminated at length before they could be described as arcane.

The practical outcome of removing baseball's anti-trust exemption would depend entirely on how that action was interpreted by the Justice Department. If Congress specifically acted to *remove* the anti-trust exemption, the Justice Department would have to infer from that action that Congress intended for certain activities of professional baseball to be curtailed—but which activities, specifically? A Justice Department under a Democratic president would probably come up with a very different answer than a Justice Department under a Republican president—and we don't *know* which we would have. If baseball had no current labor problems, would the issue get shuffled to a back burner? Or, once the Justice Department began to take action in regard to baseball, would that action be carried forward by its own momentum?

No one can possibly know the answers to these questions.

14. Will some team be forced into bankruptcy?

Many teams now claim, and have claimed for years, that they are losing money. While expenses are sharply reduced by the strike, they're not eliminated. If a strike continues for another year, one would have to assume that there is a possibility that some team could go bankrupt.

While it is *unlikely* that a team will go bankrupt during a strike, the signficance of such an event, if it did occur, could scarcely be overstated. The danger inherent in this situation is that the system could simply break—indeed, it may already be broken. Taking the machine as a whole—the union, the teams, the leagues, the agents, the players, the TV contract, the fan base—if any piece of that system breaks, it becomes vastly more difficult to put the machine back together and get it running again. And as difficult as it has been to keep this machine running anyway, if something broke we would have to be concerned about the possibility that it might become impossible to fix.

History will show you many parallels for comparable failures.

15. Will there be a third league?

The intention to start a third league in 1996 has been announced.

I see no reason why this league should not succeed.

The argument that is offered by baseball men and baseball fans against a new league is that there is a shortage of players. For reasons I have explained at other times, I believe that this is a fatuous argument. I think that if the major leagues expanded immediately to 250 teams, in 20 years there would be no difference whatsoever in the quality of play.

However, let's assume for the sake of argument that the opposite is true, that the players really *aren't* there. Even so, how many businesses fail because of a shortage of qualified workers? I suppose that it must happen, but it would certainly be the exception, rather than the rule. New businesses fail because of a shortage of customers, because of an inability to produce their product at a reasonable price, or because of an inability to sell their product to the public.

Is there a shortage of customers here? Obviously there is not. There are numerous major league cities, like Buffalo, New Orleans, Tampa, Indianapolis, Washington, and Phoenix, which have no major league teams. Looking at the attendance figures in the established markets, we see that attendance has grown by leaps and bounds in the last fifteen years, making it difficult to get a good ticket in many places. Does it not seem reasonable that New York, which supported three teams from 1903 to 1957, might do so again? Does it not seem reasonable that Boston, St. Louis, and Philadelphia, which were two-team markets for many years, might still support a second team, or that other cities might have moved into that class in the last thirty years? If the "customers" are considered to be TV networks, rather than individuals, the conclu-

sion is the same. With several alliances formed in the effort to create new networks, the demand for televised games should grow tremendously in the next fifteen years. Organized baseball cannot sell its product to *all* of those networks.

The problem for the new league, it seems to me, is that

    a. In order to establish credibility as a major league product, it may have to attract some big-name players,

    b. In order to attract big-name players, the league may have to increase its salary structure too rapidly.

If the money coming in doesn't follow quickly enough behind the money committed, the league could fall into the gap.

But the great potential in organized sports as a commercial product is the willingness of the press, the willingness of people like me, to provide free advertising. If the new owners are patient, the press will build their stars for them. I have always believed that it is foolish for new sports franchises to pay big money for established stars, because what you're doing, really, is investing in old publicity, when *new* publicity is available to you at a fraction of the price. Some of you may be old enough to remember how the press loved Julius Erving, when he was in the old ABA. The fact that he *wasn't* competing against the other big stars made him shine all the brighter. The press built a myth around him—and the ABA owners were able to make a lot of money out of that myth.

The league *could* fail for a hundred reasons—internal squabbling, external lawsuits, financial backers whose eyes are bigger than their pocketbooks. There is no reason why it *must* fail.

The conservative impulse of the traditional baseball fan, the fan who only wants for things to be "normal" again—I am as prone to this feeling as any of you. I grew into a baseball world in which there were Yankees and Dodgers and Giants and Red Sox and Tigers and Cardinals. I have only half assimilated the Blue Jays and Mariners into my psychic network, and I am just beginning to work on the Marlins and Rockies. I am really not ready for the Tampa Bay Lizards, the Washington Bureaucrats, the New Orleans Cajuns, and the Buffalo Coffee Whiteners.

But on the other hand, the people who run baseball now are not exactly doing a tremendous job of it. Was it Roger Angell who said that the owners have never met a bad idea they didn't like? These gentlemen have given us three divisions, World Series games lasting until Halloween, and 25 years of unnecessary labor strife. I'm sure you have your own complaints about them, or if you don't you're different from any baseball fan I ever knew. Maybe it's time to give somebody else a chance?

*   *   *

Well, I hope some of that is useful, somehow. There are a few things I need to explain in this intro every year, such as the meanings of terms. From this point on, for those of you who wish to get on with your lives, this article will be strongly reminiscent of the introductory article in last year's *Player Ratings Book*. The terms used include:

MLE, *or* **Major League Equivalent.** This is a method by which minor league batting statistics are translated into major league equivalents. Billy Ashley hit .345 with 37 homers and 105 RBI in 107 games for Albuquerque last year: What would be the equivalent performance with the Dodgers?

The answer is, .283 with 21 homers, 63 RBI—a pretty good season.

If you don't believe that I can actually do this accurately, there is absolutely nothing I can say here that will convince you otherwise, so I normally don't try. All I can say is, take last year's book, and look at the MLEs that were in that book, and compare that to what the players actually did in the major leagues. Or hold on to this year's book, and drag it out in October, and see how I did. I simply ask you to check it out. I am confident that you will gradually come to trust the method.

An MLE is not a prediction, except in that the past tends to predict the future. MLEs predict how a player will hit in the major leagues exactly as well as past major league performance predicts future major league performance. If a player hit .280 last year, he'll tend to hit around .280 again this year—but he might hit .240, or he might hit .310. MLEs are exactly the same. If a guy had an MLE of .280, he'll tend to hit about .280 in the majors—but it might be .240, or it might be .310.

Another term that I will use occasionally is **secondary average.** Secondary average is *not* an overall indicator of how good a hitter someone is. Secondary average is a shorthand way of consolidating the *other* things that a hitter does, other than hit for average. The formula is extra bases on hits, plus walks, plus stolen bases, divided by at bats.

The normal secondary average is about the same as the normal batting average. The National League batting average last year was .267; the secondary average was .263. The Dodgers and Braves played 114 games each. The Dodgers had a higher batting average, .270 to .267—but the Braves had a higher secondary average, .277 to .257, and for that reason the Braves scored more runs, 542 to 532.

If the book says that a player has hit .236 but has a secondary average of .379, this is just a somewhat more precise way of saying that even if he hits .236, the player will help his team score runs. If a player hits .300 but has a secondary average of .137, then he's *not* doing a lot to help the offense, despite his good batting average. Kirk Gibson last year hit .276; so did Joe Girardi. The two players had an identical number of at bats (330) and an identical number of hits (91)—but while Girardi had a secondary average of .161, Gibson had a secondary average of .405. For that reason, Gibson had 50 percent more runs scored (71-47), and more than twice as many RBI (72-34). This will essentially always happen. Given two players with the same batting average and comparable playing time, if one of them has a much higher secondary average than the other he will also drive in and score many more runs.

Another term I should explain is **Rule V,** or **Rule 5.** The agreement under which major league teams operate allows each team to protect 40 players. After a player has been in organized baseball for a couple of years, he must be placed on the 40-man roster, or he can be purchased by another team, under Rule 5. The team that drafts him, however, must carry him on their 25-man roster, their major league active roster. If they decide not to, they must offer him back to his original team, at a fraction of the price they paid for him a few months earlier.

There is a major league Rule 5 draft, and there is also a minor league Rule 5 draft. It's a kind of gambit, usually used by a weak organization to strengthen their talent base. When they draft a player they are saying, in essence, "You may not think this guy is one of your 40 best players, but we think he is one of our 25 best." It is normally used to draft a young player who is perceived as having talent, but who for some reason isn't playing very well. The organization that drafts him is gambling that they might be able to get him straightened out.

For some players, I will show **projected 1995** batting stats. I wouldn't want you to take these projections too seriously. God doesn't talk to me about baseball statistics; hell, Oral Roberts doesn't even return my phone calls. I don't have any special insight into what a player is going to do next, other than the fact that I can read and adjust minor league batting statistics more accurately than anyone else can. Otherwise, it's a simple matter of projecting that a player will do in 1995 about what he has done before—a little better if he is still young, a little worse if he's getting old and starting to vote for Republicans. If a player is getting older, we project him to lose speed; if he's still young, we project him to add power.

I do these projections with John Dewan of STATS

Inc.; we've run them for years in an annual reference book. There are no projections for several groups of players—several groups, who taken together could be described as "most of them." There are no projections for pitchers, because I don't know how to project pitchers, who are unpredictable by nature. There are no projections for players who will probably spend most of the season in the minor leagues. There are no projections for players who have retired, and there are no projections for players in those cases when I simply don't trust the projection. In many cases, I'm going to know something about a player that the computer which creates the projections doesn't know. If that causes me to believe that the projection may be misleading, then it doesn't make sense for me to run the projection anyway.

When I have a projection, when that projection seems reasonable to me, then I print the projection. But if the player has spent this long winter lifting weights and running marathons, I won't know that until April, when he starts hitting unexpected home runs. If he has spent the winter lifting pizzas, I won't know that, either.

This leads into a general question, which is, how do I decide what information to run about each player?

What I try to do is choose the best available three lines of information about each player. For some players, we might have as many as nine lines of data to choose from. Those would include:

1992 Minor League Performance
1992 Major League Performance
1993 Minor League Performance
The 1993 MLE (Major League Equivalent)
1993 Major League Performance
1994 Minor League Performance
The 1994 MLE
1994 Major League Performance
Projected 1995 Major League Performance

Actually, there are more than that to choose from, because sometimes a player plays with two or three minor league teams in one season. Suppose that a player plays for both Syracuse and Knoxville. In that case, what shows above as one option is actually three: 1994 Syracuse, 1994 Knoxville, and 1994 combined minor league performance.

I try to choose among those options, keeping this in mind:

1. This is not a reference book. If you want to know every stat in Charles Johnson's minor league career, there are books for that. I can't do that here, so it's futile to try. I need to choose the three best lines to describe the players' major league skills.

2. Major league performance is preferred to minor league performance.

3. I don't like to run data in samples so small that skills are not reliably measured.

4. I don't run stats from A Ball if there is any good alternative.

The players are evaluated on a dollar scale. The best player in baseball, who I still believe is Barry Bonds, is worth $100. Players who have retired or have been released and clearly aren't coming back have no value. Everybody else is somewhere between zero and $100.

These values are entirely relative. Barry Bonds is worth $100, so what is Ken Griffey, Jr., worth? $99. What is Bernie Williams worth? $41.

That $41 is still quite a bit. The great majority of players are valued at less than $50; only the very good players, proven quality players, are over $50. Here's the way the scale works:

$71-100	The best players in baseball
$51-70	All-Stars
$41-50	Very good players, minor stars
$31-40	Quality regulars
$21-30	Run-of-the-mill regulars, good platoon players
$10-20	Role players
Under $10	Players who probably won't be on a roster

At $41, Bernie Williams has 90 percent of the baseball world looking up at him. He ranks below Larry Walker ($78), Robin Ventura ($68), Mo Vaughn ($59), Sammie Sosa ($53), and John Smoltz ($46), but ahead of Mike Stanley and Danny Tartabull ($38 each), Jose Vizcanio ($32), Paul Sorrento ($28), and J. T. Snow ($24). And J. T. Snow, at $24, is still above the median.

The values are subjective; there is no "formula" which creates them. The value structure that I used this year is the same that I have used for the last two seasons. The structure assumes that a roster spot is worth about $15. The last man on the roster, if he is in the majors all year, has a value of about $15. Anybody below $15 is somebody that I figure most likely isn't going to be on a roster for the full season.

Of course, if there's a scab league, everything's going to be scrambled. If that happens, there will be some player that I have tagged at $7 who is going to play every day and hit .285. The values look *forward*, not backward. I am attempting to guess what players will do next year, not evaluating them based on what they did last year.

The values do not imitate any specific game except baseball. There are many "shadow games" that are based on baseball, such as Rotisserie, Strat-O-Matic, APBA, Fantasy Games, Earl Weaver Baseball, and the Winter Game. They're all based on baseball, but they all give different approximations of a player's performance.

This poses a question: What game should I evaluate? Should I give a player extra value because he's a base stealer, and a rotisserie manager needs base stealers? Should I give closers extra value because some games place a premium on saves?

There is only one answer to this: *The sum of all other images of the game of baseball must be the original game.* I evaluate players based on their value in real baseball. I assume that however it is that you come to be interested in baseball, you will want to know who the players are, particularly the young players, and whether they're any good. It is my job, as the author of this book, to find out who every player in baseball is, where he came from, what he does well and what he does poorly, and to make an educated guess about what kind of a career he is going to have from now on.

I have, as I see it, three basic responsibilities in writing the player comments.

1. To do my research,
2. To tell the truth, and
3. To make it as entertaining as I can.

If you are playing a game that needs a *different* value, a value weighted toward saves or RBI or intentional walks, it's on you to look out for that.

I don't claim to know more about every player than you do. If you're a Florida Marlins fan, you're going to know more about the Marlins' players than I do. What I claim is what I said above: that I'll do my research, and tell you honestly what I think. That's all.

And, of course, I'm going to make an error once in a while. Somewhere in this book there is a switch hitter who is identified as a right-handed batter, a six-foot-two-inch pitcher who is described as six-foot-seven, and a Bosnian diplomat who is described as a Boston laundromat. I take full responsibility for the accuracy of everything in the book, and I apologize for any such mistakes. I work hard to avoid those mistakes, and I will assure you that there are very few of them.

My sources:

1. *John Sickels*. John works with me; it's his job to round up media guides, index articles about young players, and provide me with files of information about each player. John also wrote draft comments for about 30 percent of the players in the book, and many times things that he wrote remained in the final book in some slightly altered form.

2. *STATS Inc.* STATS Inc. is the nation's largest and finest resource for statistical information about baseball. I work with STATS on dozens of different projects, and almost every stat in this book comes, in one way or another, from the home office in Chicago.

3. *Personal observation.* I go to games, I watch them on TV, and I make notes. I visit ballparks, minor league and major league and miscellaneous, and sometimes talk to managers and media people. Whatever I hear, I make a note of it.

4. *Friends.* I know dozens of people who live and breathe baseball, and I talk to them. The things that they know are of great value to me.

5. *Media guides.* We collect the media guides from all 28 teams, and these are invaluable.

6. *Baseball America.* I don't work regularly with *Baseball America*, although I do write an article for them once in a while. *BA* is what *The Sporting News* used to be—the best source of information about minor league players. John Sickels reads and indexes all of their articles, so that when we need to find out something about some guy who played well in a half-season at Osceola, we can find the article.

7. *The Baseball Weekly*, from *USA Today*. Provides the other half of the picture that *The Sporting News* used to provide—the minutes and minutiae of major league baseball.

As to how all of this information is processed, I have been writing baseball books for a long time. I used to do what is called sabermetrics, which is a type of original baseball research. I did thousands of studies of baseball-related questions over a period of ten-plus years. Which elements of a pitcher's record predict future success? Which is a better predictor of next year's won-lost record: a pitcher's ERA, or his won-lost record? Who lasts longer, a power pitcher or a finesse pitcher? A left-hander or a right-hander? What type of pitcher does well on artificial turf?

I don't do many of those studies anymore, and don't publish the ones I do; I retired from that in 1988. But I still know the things that I learned in doing that, and I still use that information to evaluate players. A few of the key things that I know:

1. The number of runs a team scores is essentially a function of two things: the number of men on base, and the team slugging percentage. Nothing else significantly changes the number of runs a team will score.

2. The batting average is important, but it's not the whole game. It is not uncommon for a .250 hitter to contribute more runs to his team than a .300 hitter.

3. A player's offensive contribution can only be evaluated in the context of his defensive contribution, and vice versa. A shortstop who puts 60 runs on the scoreboard is worth more than a left fielder who creates 75 runs.

4. A player's hitting or pitching statistics are very heavily colored by the park in which he plays. An ERA of 5.00 in Colorado is equivalent to an ERA of 3.89 in Candlestick Park.

5. The best predictor of future success by a pitcher

is his strikeout-to-walk ratio. In last year's book, I wrote this paragraph:

> Make a list of pitchers with good strikeout/walk ratios but poor overall records—Mark Clark, Kevin Tapani, Greg Swindell, Doug Drabek, Rheal Cormier, even Melido Perez. You'll find that their overall record, as a group, will be better next year than it was this year. Do the opposite—pitchers with good records but bad strikeout/walk ratios—and check them next year. You'll see that, as a group, they've collapsed.

The six pitchers that I mentioned by name had posted a cumulative 1993 record of 53-71 (.427), and an ERA of 4.33. Last year they posted a cumulative record of 54-31 (.635), and cut their ERA, despite the ballooning ERAs leaguewide, to 4.01. And that will always happen. Pitchers with good strikeout/walk ratios but poor records will always, as a group, improve dramatically in the subsequent season. To watch in 1995: Pedro Astacio, Kevin Brown, Erik Hanson, Denny Neagle, Scott Sanders, and Tom Urbani.

6. Power pitchers are vastly more durable and more consistent than finesse pitchers. Never bet on a finesse pitcher to sustain success, even when he has it. Always bet on a power pitcher; you'll load the odds in your favor.

7. Career length for batters is essentially a function of ability. Career length for a pitcher is primarily a function of two things: his ability to stay healthy, and how many strikeouts he gets.

8. An individual player may reach his peak at any age between 21 and 37, but any *group* of players will reach their peak value, as a group, at age 27. The only exceptions to this are a) knuckleballers, b) Tommy John–type pitchers, and c) those who are pre-selected because they had their best years at some other age.

9. In evaluating a young player, the first thing you want to know is his age. Suppose you've got two rookies of the same ability: a 23-year-old and a 25-year-old. Suppose they each hit 15 home runs, same batting average and RBI. The 23-year-old can expect to hit, in his career, about 60 percent more home runs than the 25-year-old. A rookie who comes up at the age of 20 and hits .240 is a far better gamble, in the long run, than a rookie who comes up at age 26 and hits .300.

It's not that *all* young players improve; they don't. Many players level off about age 23. The key is that *some young players improve dramatically*. A 25-year-old player (non-pitcher) will never improve dramatically; a 22-year-old often will.

10. A pitcher's won-lost record in an individual season doesn't mean much of anything.

There are a lot of other things that I believe as a consequence of my research or somebody else's, more minor things that may come into play in this comment or that one, but that aren't systematically important. Much of this is just entrenched skepticism. Whenever you read about a young player who is fast but doesn't steal bases, the inevitable next line is that he'll steal 40 bases a year once he learns to use his speed. Nine times in 10, it's not going to happen.

You will wonder, sometime before the end of the book, "What exactly is a Grade A prospect?" The term "Grade A prospect" means that *the balance of information that can be known about this young player at this time is overwhelmingly positive*. What the term Grade A prospect does *not* mean is that the guy is going to be a star, and especially what it does not mean is that he is going to be a superstar. Many Grade A prospects will go on to become major league stars, but many will not. What we're saying with the term is that *there is no apparent reason* why this player should not become a star. When we look at his future, we don't see a limit.

The players identified as Grade A prospects in the first edition of this book, two years ago, included Wilfredo Cordero, Mike Piazza, Jeff Conine, Tim Salmon, Pedro Martinez, and Jim Thome, all of whom are now well on their way toward stardom. They also included Dmitri Young, Sam Militello, Melvin Nieves, Alan Embree, Kevin Rogers, and Tavo Alvarez, all of whom you can now get for the price of the phone call, overstating the situation just a little bit. Grade A prospects aren't sure things; they're just good gambles.

The term "Grade B prospect" means that what we know about the player is mostly good, but with something that bothers you. A Grade B prospect is an exciting young player who strikes out too much, or a player who has hit extremely well in the minors, but started a year late.

There are Grade B prospects who will go on to become major league stars. Bob Gibson, evaluated at age 24, would have been a Grade B prospect. Tom Glavine was a Grade B prospect. The term is *not* meant at all to say that the player *won't* be a major league star—only that there is something here to worry about.

The term "Grade C prospect" means that there is a more or less even mix of information that makes you think that the player *will* be a good major league player, and information that makes you think that he won't.

The critical thing is the relationship between age and ability—where is the player at this age, compared to where he should be if he's going to be a good player?

A Grade A prospect is a player who tears up the Eastern League when he is 21.

A Grade B prospect is a player who tears up the Eastern League when he is 22.

A Grade C prospect is a player who tears up the

Eastern League when he is 23 or 24. You look at the record and say, "Gee, he looks great . . . but if he's really that good, why is he in the Eastern League at age 24? Shouldn't he be in the majors by now?"

A Grade A prospect is a player who hits .320 in the Texas League at age 21.

A Grade B prospect is a player who hits .275 in the Texas League at age 21.

A Grade C prospect is a player who hits .250 in the Texas League at age 21.

These are over-simplifications, of course. It's all a balancing act, and many times I really don't have the space, in a 65-word comment, to explain *why* I have classified the guy the way I have. You've always got multiple seasons to deal with—one good, one not so good, one that you don't know what to do with. But it is usually obvious, in practice, how a player should be classified. Of the hundreds of players who were classified as Grade A, Grade B, Grade C, Grade D, or no prospect in this book, in only a handful of cases was it difficult to decide where to put a player. I believe that anyone else, using the same system, would have classified most players the same way I did.

Can a Grade C prospect go on to become a major league star? Sure, it happens. It doesn't happen *very often*, but it happens. But for every one who becomes a star, there are going to be 100 or 200 who sink beneath the waves without a trace.

The term "Grade D prospect" means that the indications about the player are *predominantly*, but not *overwhelmingly*, negative. The term Grade D prospect means that there is *something* here that you have to like.

If I could identify young players who had a 100 percent chance to be major league stars, that would be great. I can't. My guess is that a young player who is identified as a Grade A prospect, like Derek Jeter or Alex Rodriguez, has at least a 40 percent chance to be a major league star, a 65 percent chance to be a good, solid regular (or better), and an 85 percent chance to be a major league regular of some stripe, at least for a few years. Those are just estimates, and that's for position players only. A pitcher is a horse of a different color.

A Grade B prospect (non-pitcher) would have probably a 10 to 15 percent chance of becoming a major league star, a 40 to 50 percent chance of being a good player, and a 70 percent chance of being at least a marginal regular. Virtually all Grade A and Grade B prospects will at least play in the major leagues.

A Grade C prospect would have only a slight chance of being a major league star, and perhaps a 50-50 chance of even playing regularly for a couple of years.

For a Grade D prospect to turn things around and become a major league star has probably happened, but I'm not sure I could name one.

Those probabilities are for non-pitchers; for pitchers, everything is different. For a pitcher who is identified as a Grade A prospect, the probability that he will be a major league star, or superstar, or even a rotation starter, is less than 50 percent, primarily because of injuries. *Whereas there are only a few young position players who have everything going their way, and almost all of those will go on to have good careers, there are many young pitchers who look tremendous, most of whom will hurt their arms before they finish their second major league season.*

But on the other end, the Grade D prospects, the percentages for a pitcher are much *higher*. For a guy who can't hit to learn to hit is rare if the guy is 22, but it will happen. After age 25 it almost never happens. *A position player's level of ability very rarely takes a leap forward after the age of 25.*

But for a *pitcher* to make a great leap forward—that happens fairly regularly. I'm not talking about Alex Fernandez, who had great stuff all along and finally put it together. I'm talking about guys like Butch Henry and Marvin Freeman, who kicked around for years before finding themselves. In any given season, 30 percent of the best pitchers in baseball are guys who were left for dead at some point in their careers. Pitchers, for many reasons, are *vastly* less predictable than position players.

Another thing I need to explain is how the two scales tie together, the dollar scale and the prospect scale. A Grade A prospect is worth, in general, $20 to $40, depending on three things:

1. Whether he is a pitcher or a position player (a shortstop who is a Grade A prospect is worth more than a pitcher with an equally impressive record),
2. Gradations of quality within the range described by the class, and
3. Whether the player is ready to come to the major leagues right away.

A Grade B prospect is worth, in general, $10 to $25, depending on the same variables. A Grade C prospect is generally valued at anywhere up to $20, and a Grade D prospect is generally valued at $15 or less.

OK, end of the required elements. I have two more comments, before I shut up and get to the players. The two comments have to do with the Montreal Expos and the Kansas City Royals.

The most interesting thing I discovered, while working on this book, has to do with Felipe Alou's use of his bullpen. I focused on this, I suppose, because my next hardcover book will be about managers, so I've been thinking about subjects like the subtle differences between different managers, in how they use their bullpens.

Well, Felipe Alou's use of his bullpen is extremely unusual. STATS Inc. counts and publishes something called "Quick Hooks" and "Slow Hooks," which are based on definitions that I drew up 15 years ago.

A "quick hook" is when a starting pitcher is taken out of the game before he has pitched six innings, *and* before he has given up more than three runs.

A "slow hook" is any time a starting pitcher

1. Pitches more than nine innings,
2. Allows seven or more runs, or
3. Pitches until his combined innings and runs allowed are 13 or greater (seven innings, six runs, or eight innings, five runs, etc.).

In the major leagues as a whole there are about as many quick hooks as slow hooks, actually not quite as many (289 quick, 303 slow in 1994). There are about 50 percent more slow hooks in the American League, because of the DH rule, but about 50 percent more quick hooks in the National League.

Well, Felipe Alou is the quickest hook in the business, by far. Last year he had 22 quick hooks, only 3 slow hooks. The 22 quick hooks led the majors; the 3 slow hooks tied for the major league low. Alou had *no* games in which his starting pitcher threw more than 120 pitches.

Noticing this, I looked back at the 1993 data, and the same thing was true then. In 1993 Alou had 34 quick hooks, leading the National League (although not the majors), and had only 6 slow hooks.

From this point, I began to notice how far apart Alou stands from other managers, on this issue of how he uses the bullpen:

- The Expos have led the major leagues in saves each of the last two years.
- It's not just Wetteland. Wetteland has 68 saves over the two seasons, but Rojas has 26, and other pitchers have another 13.
- Although Alou is the quickest hook in the majors, he *doesn't* churn through a lot of relievers. The Expos used only 259 relief pitchers last year, well below the National League average.

If Alou is getting his starters out early and *isn't* using a high number of relievers, does this mean that he must be getting his closer(s) into the game earlier than anyone else?

That's exactly what it means. In 1993 the Expos had 30 saves in which the pitcher who got the save pitched more than one full inning. No one else in the National League had more than 14 such games. In 1994, again, the Expos had 26 long saves; no one else in the league had more than 12. The Expos have more saves than anyone else—and in more than *half* of their saves, the closer has pitched more than an inning.

Then I got to wondering . . . who's his lefty in the bullpen?

And guess what?

He doesn't have one.

His five relievers—Wetteland, Rojas, Scott, Shaw, and Heredia—are all right-handed.

Having noticed that on my own, it clicked in my head, and I remembered hearing announcers comment on it, talking about what a tremendous disadvantage this was to the Expos, not having a lefty in the bullpen. This "disadvantage" shows up in a measurable way. When the Expos brought in a relief pitcher, that reliever had the platoon advantage on the first batter only 46 percent of the time—by far the lowest percentage in the major leagues. The normal figure is about 60 percent.

So what we have here is a manager, Felipe Alou, who is handling his bullpen in a manner which is radically different from any other manager—and who is having great success while doing it. And that, in one sentence, is the engine that drives baseball. Baseball changes because strategy changes, and strategy changes because some manager decides to chuck the traditional way of doing things, and gets by with it. That's where platooning came from—George Stallings tried it, and it worked, and it's still with us, 80 years later.

I am certain that if you *asked* Felipe Alou about his lack of a lefty in the bullpen, he would tell you that he would like very much to have a lefty in the bullpen, but he doesn't have one, so he's not going to worry about it.

But the fact is, there are *many* managers around who don't have a good lefty in the bullpen, aren't there? What the other managers do, when they don't have a lefty, is go through eight guys in a season, trying to get somebody established in that role. Tony LaRussa, the quickest hook in the *American* League, always has two lefties in the bullpen, often three.

If you think about it, you can see obvious advantages to the way Alou is using his bullpen. Because he gets the starter out so early and so often, he is providing regular, scheduled work for his bullpen. If his starters have a couple of strong outings, his relievers don't sit around and rot. Because he uses his relievers *longer* than other managers, he doesn't have to warm them up and sit them down as often as another manager might.

He gets them in the game, and lets them pitch a little bit. And because he isn't using four relievers in two innings to go left, right, left, right, he has less chance of getting somebody in there who just has nothing going for him on this particular day.

Because his bullpen is relatively *small*, just five guys, he's got room on the roster for one or two extra pinch hitters or pinch runners.

And as to the announcers' claim that this is a tremendous disadvantage to the Expos, not to have a lefty in the bullpen . . . well, what's the evidence for that? They led the league in ERA and saves, and they had the best won-lost record in the majors. What did it cost them not to have a lefty in the pen?

Focusing on the stat I gave before—the Expos' relievers had the platoon advantage on the first batter only 46 percent of the time, lowest in the majors— what did that really cost them? One hit. They used 259 relievers, and the reliever had a first-batter edge 119 times, when he would probably have had a first-batter edge on another team about 155 times. Since that's a difference of 36 at bats with the platoon advantage, and since the platoon advantage is about 30 points (.030), there is an expected loss of one hit from *not* being in a position to get a lefty-on-lefty matchup.

Of course, there might be a second hit or a third hit later on down the line, but it still doesn't seem like a big deal to me. The advantages of it would seem, on the basis of what I can see, to easily outweigh the disadvantages.

The other thing I wanted to comment on was the Kansas City Royals. As a Royals fan, I am more excited about this organization now than I have been in a decade—and I'm not talking about the kids in A Ball. It's great to be reading that stuff, too, but that's an entirely separate issue. What I'm talking about is an organization that suddenly is doing all the little stuff right.

Royals Stadium, now called Kauffman Stadium, has always had the reputation of being the best of the cookie-cutter stadiums, the stadiums built 1966 to 1974, with the standard dimensions. Asked about this, what I have said for years is that it would be a pretty nice stadium if they'd get rid of that damned artificial turf, and put in some grass—and now they have.

There are numerous other little touches in the stadium that I also enjoy—a renovation of that miserable scoreboard, an entryway into the stadium so that you don't get into the "park" by passing though a chain-link fence in the middle of a huge asphalt parking lot.

Then there is the decision to move the Double-A franchise from Memphis, where it has been for about 10 years, to Wichita—that's wonderful news. You can drive from KC to Wichita in three hours; I'll buzz down there several times in '95, get acquainted with the kids on the way up. You might be amazed what an impact that will have on attendance, later on, the fact that you can follow these players as they develop.

And then, to cap it off, was the firing of Hal McRae. Now, I don't dislike Hal McRae, and he didn't do a *bad* job as manager—in fact, he was pretty good, and he was getting better. He still had to be fired, for one simple reason. He would not play the youngsters.

McRae liked to play veterans. As he explained it, he always preferred to play veterans because "you know what you're going to get with a veteran player." But what this meant in practice was that, whenever the Royals came up with a Jeff Conine or a Sean Berry or a Terry Shumpert or a Jon Lieber or a Danny Micelli, McRae would pressure them to get him a Stan Belinda or a Dave Henderson instead.

And you simply cannot build a championship team out of Dave Hendersons, Gary Gaettis, and Vince Colemans. It can't be done.

The sad thing is that the Royals could, by now, be well on the way toward having a championship team put together—not by doing anything terribly clever, but just simply by *not* making a series of stupid blunders, like protecting Bill Sampen and David Howard in the expansion draft, rather than Jeff Conine. The team they *should* have includes the catchers they have, MacFarlane and Mayne, Hamelin at first, Shumpert at second, Berry at third, Gagne at short, Conine and Brian McRae in the outfield with Felix Jose, Appier, Cone, and Lieber in the rotation, and Montgomery and Micelli in the bullpen. That may not be a championship team, but I'll take my chances with it. Instead, we're probably headed into a 90-loss season.

And I'm thrilled. I'm happy to have a 90-loss season, and I'm planning to see as many games as I can, because I've always believed in paying my dues. Watching the kids figure things out—that's part of the game. It makes the winning more fun. The *fear* of the 90-loss season had become the greatest obstacle to the organization's eventual success. Like a man who never finds love because he fears rejection, the Royals organization has lived in terror of those small moments of pain which are a presage to all joy.

Make a deal, guys. I'm ready to go.

THE PLAYERS

JIM ABBOTT / New York Yankees / Starting Pitcher $28

Sooner or later someone will make a movie of the Jim Abbott story, but it is becoming more and more clear that there isn't going to be a Cooperstown scene. He pitched well at times last year, but he ran out of gas. He was 6-2 with a 2.67 ERA on May 25. He pitched well for six innings. He didn't finish games, and he didn't finish his season.

YEAR	TEAM/LEVEL	G	IP	W-L	PCT	HITS	SO	BB	ERA
1992	California	29	211	7-15	.318	208	130	68	2.77
1993	New York	32	214	11-14	.440	221	95	73	4.37
1994	New York	24	160	9-8	.529	167	90	64	4.55

KURT ABBOTT / Florida Marlins / Shortstop $28

Had a solid year, improving steadily as the season went on, and will keep his job as the Marlins' shortstop. Arguably out of position at short—has more power than your typical shortstop, has a shortstop's arm, but doesn't have quick feet or exceptional agility. He will have some good years with the bat, and may eventually wind up at third base.

YEAR	TEAM/LEVEL	G	AB	R	H	2B	3B	HR	RBI	BB	SB	AVG	OBP	SLG
1993	Oakland	20	61	11	15	1	0	3	9	3	2	.246	.281	.410
1994	Florida	101	345	41	86	17	3	9	33	16	3	.249	.291	.394
1995	*Projected*	*138*	*487*	*56*	*125*	*22*	*4*	*11*	*51*	*29*	*10*	*.257*	*.290*	*.386*

KYLE ABBOTT / Philadelphia Phillies / Pitcher $10

He pitched in Japan last year, under some sort of agreement between the Phillies and the Kinetsu Buffaloes; he is supposed to return to Philadelphia this year. However, he pitched only 12 innings with Kinetsu, and I don't get Japanese ESPN, so I don't know what happened to him. I will be surprised if he wins a major league game in 1995.

YEAR	TEAM/LEVEL	G	IP	W-L	PCT	HITS	SO	BB	ERA
1991	California	5	20	1-2	.333	22	12	13	4.58
1992	Philadelphia	31	133	1-14	.067	147	88	45	5.13
1993	Scranton AAA	27	173	12-10	.545	163	109	62	3.95

MARK ACRE / Oakland Athletics / Right-handed Reliever $27

A 6-foot-8 right-hander, played basketball at New Mexico State. An undrafted free agent, signed on the off chance that he could develop, he throws in the low 90s, best pitch is a forkball. Intimidating to right-handed batters, who hit .159 against him last year. Grade B prospect; has a definite chance to become a closer.

YEAR	TEAM/LEVEL	G	IP	W-L	SAVES	HITS	SO	BB	ERA
1993	Huntsville AA	19	22	1-1	10	22	21	3	2.42
1994	Tacoma AAA	20	29	1-1	6	24	31	11	1.88
1994	Oakland	34	34	5-1	0	24	21	23	3.41

RICK AGUILERA / Minnesota Twins / Closer $44

After posting a 6.45 ERA through May 31, he pitched well the rest of the year (2.15), so his outlook for '95 is better than it might appear. The batting average against him was .306, which has got to give you some pause if you're counting on him to get the 27th out, but I suspect he'll have 35 saves again this year.

YEAR	TEAM/LEVEL	G	IP	W-L	SAVES	HITS	SO	BB	ERA
1992	Minnesota	64	67	2-6	41	60	52	17	2.84
1993	Minnesota	65	72	4-3	34	60	59	14	3.11
1994	Minnesota	44	45	1-4	23	57	46	10	3.63

MIKE ALDRETE / Oakland Athletics / First Base/Outfield $18

Used by Tony LaRussa at first base, in left field, and in right, but strictly as a platoon player. A player like this is hard to carry on the 40-man roster, but he has played well enough that he should catch on somewhere, even if the A's drop him. Pinch hitting has lowered his average, as it usually does. Was 3-for-25 as a pinch hitter last year.

YEAR	TEAM/LEVEL	G	AB	R	H	2B	3B	HR	RBI	BB	SB	AVG	OBP	SLG
1993	Oakland	95	255	40	68	13	1	10	33	34	1	.267	.353	.443
1994	Oakland	76	178	23	43	5	0	4	18	20	2	.242	.313	.337
1995	*Projected*	*70*	*184*	*21*	*44*	*9*	*0*	*3*	*20*	*22*	*1*	*.239*	*.320*	*.337*

LUIS ALICEA / St. Louis Cardinals / Second Base $25

Still engaged with Geronimo Pena in the longest-running job battle in the history of baseball. A switch hitter, he has become basically a left-handed platoon player, which doesn't help him, since over the last three years he's hit .325 right-handed, .250 left-handed. Runs well, and there's nothing much wrong with his defense. Above-average player.

YEAR	TEAM/LEVEL	G	AB	R	H	2B	3B	HR	RBI	BB	SB	AVG	OBP	SLG
1993	St. Louis	115	362	50	101	19	3	3	46	47	11	.279	.362	.373
1994	St. Louis	88	205	32	57	12	5	5	29	30	4	.278	.373	.459
1995	*Projected*	*133*	*381*	*48*	*98*	*18*	*6*	*5*	*45*	*52*	*8*	*.257*	*.346*	*.375*

ROBERTO ALOMAR / Toronto Blue Jays / Second Base $92

With the passage of Sandberg, his only rival for the mantle of baseball's best second baseman is Baerga, who is awfully good but probably not quite as good as Roberto. Already has 39 percent of his first three thousand hits . . . the number three candidate for the American League MVP Award, behind Frank Thomas and Ken Griffey. Overrated as a defensive player.

YEAR	TEAM/LEVEL	G	AB	R	H	2B	3B	HR	RBI	BB	SB	AVG	OBP	SLG
1993	Toronto	153	589	109	192	35	6	17	93	80	55	.326	.408	.492
1994	Toronto	107	392	78	120	25	4	8	38	51	19	.306	.386	.452
1995	*Projected*	*154*	*585*	*111*	*182*	*32*	*6*	*13*	*77*	*84*	*51*	*.311*	*.398*	*.453*

SANDY ALOMAR, JR. / Cleveland Indians / Catcher $36

Despite losing three weeks to a torn finger webbing (late April), he was having his best major league season. Had one of his better years against base stealers, catching 21 of 64. Usually a slow starter; hits 40 points better (career) after the All-Star break . . . the Alomar family now has 2,732 hits among the three of them, will get 3000 this summer.

YEAR	TEAM/LEVEL	G	AB	R	H	2B	3B	HR	RBI	BB	SB	AVG	OBP	SLG
1993	Cleveland	64	215	24	58	7	1	6	32	11	3	.270	.318	.395
1994	Cleveland	80	292	44	84	15	1	14	43	25	8	.288	.347	.490
1995	Projected	116	394	49	106	21	1	11	49	25	6	.269	.313	.411

MOISES ALOU / Montreal Expos / Left Field $70

When you're wrong about somebody it does almost no good to admit it, but boy, did I miss the boat on Moises. For the last three years he has come uncannily close to duplicating his father's stats when his father was the same age (1960-62). If he keeps this up he'll have a solid year in '95, struggle in '96, but have his best year in 1998.

YEAR	TEAM/LEVEL	G	AB	R	H	2B	3B	HR	RBI	BB	SB	AVG	OBP	SLG
1993	Montreal	136	482	70	138	29	6	18	85	38	17	.286	.340	.483
1994	Montreal	107	422	81	143	31	5	22	78	42	7	.339	.397	.592
1995	Projected	152	593	96	177	32	5	22	96	55	20	.298	.358	.481

WILSON ALVAREZ / Chicago White Sox / Starting Pitcher $51

He came to spring training ('94) carrying about 15 extra pounds, but worked it off and started the season 8-0. When he hits 30 that won't work so well, but he's just 25 now. He's the most pronounced cold-weather pitcher in baseball, with a three-year record of 20-1 in April, May, September, and October, but 12-18 in the hot months.

YEAR	TEAM/LEVEL	G	IP	W-L	PCT	HITS	SO	BB	ERA
1992	Chicago	34	100	5-3	.625	103	66	65	5.20
1993	Chicago	31	208	15-8	.652	168	155	122	2.95
1994	Chicago	24	162	12-8	.600	147	108	62	3.45

RICH AMARAL / Seattle Mariners / Infielder $19

The Mariners traded Bret Boone to play him at second base, but his glovework at second was frightening, and he played himself out of a job by mid-May. He has good leadoff-man type skills, and he hits left-handed pitching so well that he may be in the league until he's 40, even if he has to DH.

YEAR	TEAM/LEVEL	G	AB	R	H	2B	3B	HR	RBI	BB	SB	AVG	OBP	SLG
1993	Seattle	110	373	53	108	24	1	1	44	33	19	.290	.348	.367
1994	Seattle	77	228	37	60	10	0	4	18	24	5	.263	.333	.377
1995	Projected	100	304	42	81	20	1	2	23	29	17	.266	.330	.359

RUBEN AMARO / Cleveland Indians / Utility Outfielder $15

He has turned 30 without revealing himself to be a major league player, but after posting .500-plus slugging percentages the last two years, he may get 100 or so at bats this year to make people forget that .219 batting average of 1992. The Indians used him mostly to give Lofton a few innings off in center field.

YEAR	TEAM/LEVEL	G	AB	R	H	2B	3B	HR	RBI	BB	SB	AVG	OBP	SLG
1992	Philadelphia	126	374	43	82	15	6	7	34	37	11	.219	.303	.348
1993	Philadelphia	25	48	7	16	2	2	1	6	6	0	.333	.400	.521
1994	Cleveland	26	23	5	5	1	0	2	5	2	2	.217	.280	.522

LARRY ANDERSEN / Philadelphia Phillies / Relief Pitcher $14

Fighting for his professional life after an injury-plagued 1994 season. He had his knee scoped in the off-season, started the schedule on the roster but not 100 percent, then went out again in June with a sore rib cage. He'll be 42 in May, so you know he appreciated the strike, which probably cost him 30 percent of his remaining career. Can still pitch.

YEAR	TEAM/LEVEL	G	IP	W-L	SAVES	HITS	SO	BB	ERA
1992	San Diego	34	35	1-1	2	26	35	8	3.34
1993	Philadelphia	64	62	3-2	0	54	67	21	2.92
1994	Philadelphia	29	33	1-2	0	33	27	15	4.41

BRADY ANDERSON / Baltimore Orioles / Left Field $42

He was 31-for-32 as a base stealer, the highest percentage ever for a player with 30 or more attempts. Add in 42 extra-base hits and 57 walks, and he was on target to enter the free agent market with 110-120 runs scored. A natural left fielder, but played center while Devereaux was out, and looked good. A quality player.

YEAR	TEAM/LEVEL	G	AB	R	H	2B	3B	HR	RBI	BB	SB	AVG	OBP	SLG
1993	Baltimore	142	560	87	147	36	8	13	66	82	24	.263	.363	.425
1994	Baltimore	111	453	78	119	25	5	12	48	57	31	.263	.356	.419
1995	*Projected*	*152*	*602*	*89*	*149*	*24*	*4*	*14*	*61*	*87*	*40*	*.248*	*.346*	*.370*

BRIAN ANDERSON / California Angels / Starting Pitcher $27

The third player taken in the 1993 draft, he started the '94 season in the Angels' rotation, after a minor league career of 19 innings. He was 3-0 in April with a 2.61 ERA, but then broke his thumb, and didn't win again until mid-June. Left-hander, throws hard, excellent control. Intelligent, has command of four pitches. Should have a bright future.

YEAR	TEAM/LEVEL	G	IP	W-L	PCT	HITS	SO	BB	ERA
1993	Midland AA	2	11	0-1	.000	16	9	0	3.38
1993	California	4	11	0-0	.000	11	4	2	3.97
1994	California	18	102	7-5	.583	120	47	27	5.22

GARRET ANDERSON / California Angels / Outfielder $19

Drove in 102 runs at Vancouver, spent a week in the majors just before the strike. He offers neither power nor speed and he'll swing at anything, but the Angels need a left fielder, and of the four top possible solutions, Anderson is the only one who is truly an outfielder. Left-handed all the way, good athlete, only 23 years old.

YEAR	TEAM/LEVEL	G	AB	R	H	2B	3B	HR	RBI	BB	SB	AVG	OBP	SLG
1994	Vancouver AAA	123	505	75	162	42	6	12	102	28	3	.321	.356	.499
1994	MLE	123	477	56	134	33	3	9	77	20	2	.281	.310	.419
1995	*Projected*	*97*	*297*	*31*	*81*	*18*	*1*	*4*	*40*	*14*	*2*	*.273*	*.305*	*.380*

SHANE ANDREWS / Montreal Expos / Third Base $13

The Expos' first pick in the 1990 draft has taken a leisurely stroll through the system, one year per level, 558 minor league games so far. Has had problems with his weight and defense, and is not as good a player as Sean Berry at this point. His 1993 MLE was exactly like last year's, so we're pretty confident that that's what he would hit.

YEAR	TEAM/LEVEL	G	AB	R	H	2B	3B	HR	RBI	BB	SB	AVG	OBP	SLG
1993	MLE	124	427	62	100	27	0	13	56	44	7	.234	.306	.389
1994	Ottawa AAA	137	460	79	117	25	2	16	85	80	6	.254	.367	.422
1994	MLE	137	445	63	102	23	1	11	67	63	4	.229	.325	.360

ERIC ANTHONY / Seattle Mariners / Right Field $27

His chance of becoming a star, it appears, can be declared dead. Very strong, runs well, has a reputation for not working as hard as he should. The Mariners moved him to left field (he had played right for Houston), and he hit five home runs right away, but developed tendinitis in his knee and then went into a bigtime slump.

YEAR	TEAM/LEVEL	G	AB	R	H	2B	3B	HR	RBI	BB	SB	AVG	OBP	SLG
1993	Houston	145	486	70	121	19	4	15	66	49	3	.249	.319	.397
1994	Seattle	79	262	31	62	14	1	10	30	23	6	.237	.297	.412
1995	*Projected*	*131*	*416*	*51*	*102*	*19*	*2*	*15*	*59*	*41*	*5*	*.245*	*.315*	*.409*

KEVIN APPIER / Kansas City Royals / Starting Pitcher $68

His mechanics were messed up at the start of the '94 season, and he was hit hard through his first nine starts. (His career record in April is just 5-10.) He struck out 13 in five and two-thirds innings on May 25, and pitched at his usual level the rest of the season. His usual level is borderline phenomenal. One of the best pitchers in baseball.

YEAR	TEAM/LEVEL	G	IP	W-L	PCT	HITS	SO	BB	ERA
1992	Kansas City	30	208	15-8	.652	167	150	68	2.46
1993	Kansas City	34	239	18-8	.692	183	186	81	2.56
1994	Kansas City	23	155	7-6	.538	137	145	63	3.83

TONY AQUINO / Florida Marlins / Pitcher $25

My comment last year was that Aquino has been oddly consistent for a pitcher with no defined role. This is still true. Again last year, despite a broken toe which prevented him from pitching in June, he was effective the rest of the year, holding opponents to a .210 batting average. He has had ERAs under 3.75 in six of the last seven years.

YEAR	TEAM/LEVEL	G	IP	W-L	PCT	HITS	SO	BB	ERA
1992	Kansas City	15	68	3-6	.333	81	11	20	4.52
1993	Florida	38	111	6-8	.429	115	67	40	3.42
1994	Florida	29	51	2-1	.667	39	22	22	3.73

ALEX ARIAS / Florida Marlins / Infielder $24

My instinctive reading of Arias is that he is too good a player to be a backup infielder on an expansion team. He's not real quick and doesn't have any power, but he is a .270 hitter who will take a walk if it's offered, and he can play three positions adequately. There are worse players with better jobs.

YEAR	TEAM/LEVEL	G	AB	R	H	2B	3B	HR	RBI	BB	SB	AVG	OBP	SLG
1992	Chicago	32	99	14	29	6	0	0	7	11	0	.293	.375	.354
1993	Florida	96	249	27	67	5	1	2	20	27	1	.269	.344	.321
1994	Florida	59	113	4	27	5	0	0	15	9	0	.239	.298	.283

JACK ARMSTRONG / Texas Rangers / Starting Pitcher $10

Signed with the Rangers as a free agent, but after making two starts he missed the rest of the season with tendinitis in his shoulder. This probably didn't cost Tom Grieve his job, but it sure didn't help. Betting on a comeback is chancy but reasonable—but if he does come "back," his career record is 40-65.

YEAR	TEAM/LEVEL	G	IP	W-L	PCT	HITS	SO	BB	ERA
1992	Cleveland	35	167	6-15	.286	176	114	67	4.64
1993	Florida	36	196	9-17	.346	210	118	78	4.49
1994	Texas	2	10	0-1	.000	9	7	2	3.60

RENE AROCHA / St. Louis Cardinals / Pitcher $26

Opened 1994 in the rotation after a solid rookie season in 1993, but was hammered in five of seven starts. He was very effective out of the pen, posting a 2.36 ERA in 38 games, and earning 11 saves in 12 opportunities. He has *not* gained control of the closer job. Torre's plans for him, like Torre's plan for everybody, are unclear.

YEAR	TEAM/LEVEL	G	IP	W-L	SAVES	HITS	SO	BB	ERA
1992	Louisville AAA	25	167	12-7	0	145	128	67	2.70
1993	St. Louis	32	188	11-8	0	197	96	31	3.78
1994	St. Louis	45	83	4-4	11	94	62	21	4.01

ANDY ASHBY / San Diego Padres / Starting Pitcher $41

Despite the 6-11 record, he was the most improved pitcher in the major leagues last year. He's always had a good arm, but he became much more aggressive about throwing strikes early in the count . . . extreme ground-ball pitcher, with twice as many ground-outs as fly-outs. Twelve of his 43 walks were intentional, so he actually cut his walk rate in half.

YEAR	TEAM/LEVEL	G	IP	W-L	PCT	HITS	SO	BB	ERA
1992	Philadelphia	10	37	1-3	.250	42	24	21	7.54
1993	Two Teams	32	123	3-10	.231	168	77	56	6.80
1994	San Diego	24	164	6-11	.353	145	121	43	3.40

BILLY ASHLEY / Los Angeles Dodgers / Outfielder $28

Six-foot-seven right-hander, had Jeff Bagwell stats at Albuquerque. Albuquerque is a great place to hit, but Ashley has come a long way in two years. He's still going to strike out a lot, but he's a little more selective. I'm not betting on him to hit .280, but Ashley and Antonio Osuna are the Dodgers' top 1995 Rookie of the Year candidates.

YEAR	TEAM/LEVEL	G	AB	R	H	2B	3B	HR	RBI	BB	SB	AVG	OBP	SLG
1993	Albuquer. AAA	125	482	88	143	31	4	26	100	35	6	.297	.344	.539
1994	Albuquer. AAA	107	388	93	134	19	4	37	105	53	6	.345	.428	.701
1994	MLE	107	354	55	100	13	1	21	63	31	3	.282	.340	.503

PAUL ASSENMACHER / Chicago White Sox / Relief Pitcher $27

Struggled early, but gave up only two runs in his last 25 outings, winding up with another solid year in his tightly limited role. He's one of the few pitchers who is effective year-in and year-out in this role, as a left-handed middle reliever, gets a couple of guys out and then turns it over to the closer. Remains underrated.

YEAR	TEAM/LEVEL	G	IP	W-L	SAVES	HITS	SO	BB	ERA
1992	Chicago (N)	70	68	4-4	8	72	67	26	4.10
1993	Two Teams	72	56	4-3	0	54	45	22	3.38
1994	Chicago (A)	44	33	1-2	1	26	29	13	3.55

PEDRO ASTACIO / Los Angeles Dodgers / Starting Pitcher $29

Was utterly ineffective when away from Dodger Stadium, winning only two of 12 starts on the road, with a 6.31 ERA. Gave up 30 doubles, 18 homers in 563 at bats on the season. There are still many things about him to like, but his chance of becoming a star is half of what it was a year ago.

YEAR	TEAM/LEVEL	G	IP	W-L	PCT	HITS	SO	BB	ERA
1992	Los Angeles	11	82	5-5	.500	80	43	20	1.98
1993	Los Angeles	31	186	14-9	.609	165	122	68	3.57
1994	Los Angeles	23	149	6-8	.429	142	108	47	4.29

JOE AUSANIO / New York Yankees / Relief Pitcher $15

A 29-year-old right-hander, has always pitched well in the minors, but has made a habit of hurting himself just as he was about to break through. Career ERA, in the minors, is 2.23, 271 games, all in relief. Was in the Pirates system for years, then the Expos—should have gotten a better look than he did. Grade C prospect.

YEAR	TEAM/LEVEL	G	IP	W-L	SAVES	HITS	SO	BB	ERA
1993	Harrisburg AA	19	22	2-0	6	16	30	4	1.21
1994	Columbus AAA	44	60	3-3	13	45	69	16	2.39
1994	New York	13	16	2-1	0	16	15	6	5.17

BRAD AUSMUS / San Diego Padres / Catcher $25

Hit .308 with no one on base, but .235 with men on first base (only), and .143 with runners in scoring position. Good athlete, but below-average arm for a catcher. Has hit 12 homers in 487 major league at bats, which is surprising power for him, but that may disappear if they De-Juice the ball. Basically, he's an expansion player.

YEAR	TEAM/LEVEL	G	AB	R	H	2B	3B	HR	RBI	BB	SB	AVG	OBP	SLG
1993	San Diego	49	160	18	41	8	1	5	12	6	2	.256	.283	.412
1994	San Diego	101	327	45	82	12	1	7	24	30	5	.251	.314	.358
1995	*Projected*	*112*	*349*	*39*	*83*	*12*	*1*	*7*	*32*	*28*	*9*	*.238*	*.294*	*.338*

STEVE AVERY / Atlanta Braves / Starting Pitcher $62

Struggled with a tender arm in spring training, later was distracted by a family problem, and was just hitting his stride when the strike hit. In the last three starts before the strike he'd pitched 25 innings with 24 strike-outs and a 1.08 ERA. There's every reason to think he'll snap back strong in '95. Control was off, but strikeout rate was way up.

YEAR	TEAM/LEVEL	G	IP	W-L	PCT	HITS	SO	BB	ERA
1992	Atlanta	35	234	11-11	.500	216	129	71	3.20
1993	Atlanta	35	223	18-6	.750	216	125	43	2.94
1994	Atlanta	24	152	8-3	.727	127	122	55	4.04

BOBBY AYALA / Seattle Mariners / Closer $41

Struck out 12 men per nine innings, a stunning increase from his strikeout rate in previous seasons, when he was a starter. He pitched brilliantly through July 9, when his ERA was 1.64, but then struggled through the last month. This was also what he did in 1993—pitched great early, but faded in mid-summer. John Franco syndrome?

YEAR	TEAM/LEVEL	G	IP	W-L	SAVES	HITS	SO	BB	ERA
1992	Cincinnati	5	29	2-1	0	33	23	13	4.34
1993	Cincinnati	43	98	7-10	3	106	65	45	5.60
1994	Seattle	46	57	4-3	18	42	76	26	2.86

CARLOS BAERGA / Cleveland Indians / Second Base $84

An utterly amazing ballplayer, a 200-hit, 100-RBI machine who is also a fine second baseman and baserunner. Level swing, contact hitter but hits the ball hard. Hasn't been in a slump in several years. Makes a few errors at second base, but has above-average range, and turns the double play very well. Only 26 years old; could win the MVP Award.

YEAR	TEAM/LEVEL	G	AB	R	H	2B	3B	HR	RBI	BB	SB	AVG	OBP	SLG
1993	Cleveland	154	624	105	200	28	6	21	114	34	15	.321	.355	.486
1994	Cleveland	103	442	81	139	32	2	19	80	10	8	.314	.333	.525
1995	*Projected*	*155*	*637*	*103*	*203*	*32*	*3*	*24*	*109*	*29*	*12*	*.319*	*.348*	*.491*

JEFF BAGWELL / Houston Astros / First Base $94

Projected to 162 games: .368, 57 homers, 171 RBI. Basically the same numbers that Jimmie Foxx had in his best season, 1932, except with more doubles (47-33) and more stolen bases (22-3). Hit .457 against left-handers, with a slugging percentage of 1.095. I always thought I was Bagwell's biggest fan, but I never *dreamed* he would do that.

YEAR	TEAM/LEVEL	G	AB	R	H	2B	3B	HR	RBI	BB	SB	AVG	OBP	SLG
1993	Houston	142	535	76	171	37	4	20	88	62	13	.320	.388	.516
1994	Houston	110	400	104	147	32	2	39	116	65	15	.368	.451	.750
1995	*Projected*	*153*	*575*	*101*	*178*	*36*	*4*	*30*	*113*	*84*	*14*	*.310*	*.398*	*.543*

HAROLD BAINES / Baltimore Orioles / Designated Hitter $27

The things he *can* do are shrinking, and will soon disappear. He can't run. He doesn't play the field, at all, and doesn't hit against lefties (.176 against them in 51 at bats last year.) But he's a left-handed power hitter in a left-handed power hitter's park, and as long as he can hit .300, there's a job for him. . . . Hits best in midsummer.

YEAR	TEAM/LEVEL	G	AB	R	H	2B	3B	HR	RBI	BB	SB	AVG	OBP	SLG
1993	Baltimore	118	416	64	130	22	0	20	78	57	0	.313	.390	.510
1994	Baltimore	94	326	44	96	12	1	16	54	30	0	.294	.356	.485
1995	*Projected*	*116*	*392*	*51*	*105*	*20*	*2*	*13*	*62*	*46*	*1*	*.268*	*.345*	*.429*

SCOTT BANKHEAD / Boston Red Sox / Relief Pitcher $18

Groin injuries sent him to the DL twice during the '94 season. Small, very competitive, and knows how to pitch. Just 31 years old; if he'd been able to stay healthy he would have had a good career as a starter, but back and elbow problems pushed him to middle relief. He'd be a valuable reliever if he'd stop pulling his groin.

YEAR	TEAM/LEVEL	G	IP	W-L	SAVES	HITS	SO	BB	ERA
1992	Cincinnati	54	71	10-4	1	57	53	29	2.93
1993	Boston	40	64	2-1	0	59	47	29	3.50
1994	Boston	27	38	3-2	0	34	25	12	4.54

WILLIE BANKS / Chicago Cubs / Starting Pitcher $26

Traded from Minnesota for Matt Walbeck, he was diagnosed in spring training with a circulatory problem in his shoulder, which it was originally feared might cost him the season. Despite this, he was 8-6 with a good ERA at the end of June, then went into a terrible slump, which certainly looked to me as if he was trying to pitch through an injury.

YEAR	TEAM/LEVEL	G	IP	W-L	PCT	HITS	SO	BB	ERA
1992	Minnesota	16	71	4-4	.500	80	37	37	5.70
1993	Minnesota	31	171	11-12	.478	186	138	78	4.04
1994	Chicago	23	138	8-12	.400	139	91	56	5.40

BRET BARBERIE / Florida Marlins / Second Base $32

Started slowly, but hit .371 after the All-Star break, nosing his average over the .300 wire just before the strike. He's a good little second baseman, switch hitter, not the kind of player who wins pennants for you, but not the kind who loses them, either. Average defense at second base. Among the league leaders in getting hit with pitches.

YEAR	TEAM/LEVEL	G	AB	R	H	2B	3B	HR	RBI	BB	SB	AVG	OBP	SLG
1993	Florida	99	375	45	104	16	2	5	33	33	2	.277	.344	.371
1994	Florida	107	372	40	112	20	2	5	31	23	2	.301	.356	.406
1995	*Projected*	*155*	*550*	*57*	*153*	*22*	*2*	*8*	*53*	*54*	*7*	*.278*	*.343*	*.369*

KEVIN BASS / Houston Astros / Outfielder $19

Switch-hitting veteran, still runs fairly well, still more than adequate in right field. He wasn't expected to play much, but after the trade of Anthony some other guys didn't come up big, and Bass had a fine season, with an on-base percentage of almost .400. They'll try to give his job away again this year, but he'll get 200-300 at bats with somebody.

YEAR	TEAM/LEVEL	G	AB	R	H	2B	3B	HR	RBI	BB	SB	AVG	OBP	SLG
1993	Houston	111	229	31	65	18	0	3	37	26	7	.284	.359	.402
1994	Houston	82	203	37	63	15	1	6	35	28	2	.310	.393	.483
1995	*Projected*	*121*	*300*	*34*	*76*	*19*	*2*	*6*	*38*	*28*	*7*	*.253*	*.317*	*.390*

KIM BATISTE / Philadelphia Phillies / Fifth Infielder $16

A very odd player. In 209 at bats he grounded into 11 double plays (ouch), and drew *one* walk. (For those of you who like trivia, he was walked by John Smoltz on July 31 in Atlanta.) He can play third base or shortstop, but not very well (.919 fielding at third base last year), right-handed hitter but doesn't hit left-handers well.

YEAR	TEAM/LEVEL	G	AB	R	H	2B	3B	HR	RBI	BB	SB	AVG	OBP	SLG
1993	Philadelphia	79	156	14	44	7	1	5	29	3	0	.282	.298	.436
1994	Philadelphia	64	209	17	49	6	0	1	13	1	1	.234	.239	.278
1995	*Projected*	*63*	*168*	*15*	*42*	*7*	*1*	*2*	*18*	*3*	*1*	*.250*	*.263*	*.339*

DANNY BAUTISTA / Detroit Tigers / Outfield $21

In 48 major league games he has hit well enough (.262 with 24 RBI) to suggest that he should eventually hit major league pitching. Small, runs very well, has a right fielder's arm and good assists totals in the minors. He's still a baby, 22 years old, and he has a common failing: He doesn't respect the strike zone. Grade B prospect.

YEAR	TEAM/LEVEL	G	AB	R	H	2B	3B	HR	RBI	BB	SB	AVG	OBP	SLG
1993	Detroit	17	61	6	9	3	0	1	9	1	3	.311	.317	.410
1994	Detroit	31	99	12	23	4	1	4	15	3	1	.232	.255	.414
1995	*Projected*	*69*	*213*	*23*	*56*	*10*	*1*	*5*	*28*	*11*	*8*	*.263*	*.299*	*.390*

JOSE BAUTISTA / Chicago Cubs / Reliever/Starter $24

Had a terrific year in the Cubs' bullpen in 1993, but failed to sustain it last year, although he wasn't awful, either. I honestly believe that the Cubs might benefit from making him a starter, since he's durable and has good control, and they need starting pitchers. But Bautista was 6-15 as a starter in 1988, and may not get another chance.

YEAR	TEAM/LEVEL	G	IP	W-L	SAVES	HITS	SO	BB	ERA
1992	AA and AAA	41	114	3-10	2	131	67	30	4.88
1993	Chicago	58	112	10-3	2	105	63	27	2.82
1994	Chicago	58	69	4-5	1	75	45	17	3.89

BILLY BEAN / San Diego Padres / Outfielder $14

Used by the Padres at first base, in all three outfield spots, and as a pinch hitter. He went 12-for-33 (.364) as a pinch hitter, but 17-for-102 (.167) when playing the field. He's a left-handed line drive hitter, which is the basic description of a pinch hitter, plus he runs fairly well. This isn't enough to build a substantial career on.

YEAR	TEAM/LEVEL	G	AB	R	H	2B	3B	HR	RBI	BB	SB	AVG	OBP	SLG
1993	Las Vegas AAA	53	167	31	59	11	2	7	40	32	3	.353	.454	.569
1993	San Diego	88	177	19	46	9	0	5	32	6	2	.260	.284	.395
1994	San Diego	84	135	7	29	5	1	0	14	7	0	.215	.248	.267

ROD BECK / San Francisco Giants / Relief Pitcher $76

Jay Bell broke Beck's toe with a smash to the mound on the second day of the season, April 5. He was off his game when he returned, posting a 4.50 ERA in his next 25 games, but was very sharp the last six weeks before the strike . . . gives up more home runs than you would like, but remains among the top relievers in the game.

YEAR	TEAM/LEVEL	G	IP	W-L	SAVES	HITS	SO	BB	ERA
1992	San Francisco	65	92	3-3	17	62	87	15	1.76
1993	San Francisco	76	79	3-1	48	57	86	13	2.16
1994	San Francisco	48	49	2-4	28	49	39	13	2.77

RICHIE BECKER / Minnesota Twins / Center Fielder $26

A hot prospect, he has had two knee injuries, and will have more. He started last year in the majors, but had to have his knee scoped in April, and spent most of the summer at Salt Lake City, where he scored 64 runs in 71 games. Will be a good ballplayer. Should hit around .270 with some speed and some power, secondary average over .300.

YEAR	TEAM/LEVEL	G	AB	R	H	2B	3B	HR	RBI	BB	SB	AVG	OBP	SLG
1993	Nashville AA	138	516	93	148	25	7	15	66	94	29	.287	.398	.450
1993	MLE	138	504	75	136	26	7	12	53	66	20	.270	.354	.421
1994	Salt Lake AAA	71	282	64	89	21	3	2	38	40	7	.316	.401	.433

STEVE BEDROSIAN / Atlanta Braves / Relief Pitcher $20

A one-time Cy Young Award winner, his career was interrupted by a circulatory problem. Returning in 1993, he has been buried deep in the middle of a talented pitching staff, where he has worked in anonymity for most of the last two summers. He has pitched consistently well, but, at 37, is unlikely to get beyond that role.

YEAR	TEAM/LEVEL	G	IP	W-L	SAVES	HITS	SO	BB	ERA
1991	Minnesota	56	77	5-3	6	70	44	35	4.42
1993	Atlanta	49	50	5-2	0	34	33	14	1.63
1994	Atlanta	46	46	0-2	0	41	43	18	3.33

TIM BELCHER / Detroit Tigers / Starting Pitcher $17

At some point, there is a comeback left in Tim Belcher. It isn't going to happen with the Tigers. It will happen after he loses his starting role, goes to another team, and sorts through his equipment to see what works and what doesn't. For the moment, he is locked in a downward spiral which won't release him until he hits bottom.

YEAR	TEAM/LEVEL	G	IP	W-L	PCT	HITS	SO	BB	ERA
1992	Cincinnati	35	228	15-14	.517	201	149	80	3.91
1993	Two Teams	34	209	12-11	.523	198	135	74	4.44
1994	Detroit	25	162	7-15	.318	192	76	78	5.89

STAN BELINDA / Kansas City Royals / Relief Pitcher $23

The bright future which was once foreseen for him seems to be slipping away. He has experimented with a variety of off-speed pitches, a curve and a slider, and all of these look good at times, but he just isn't consistent with them. This leaves him with his fastball, which is a good fastball, but not *that* good. Has a 50/50 chance of a comeback.

YEAR	TEAM/LEVEL	G	IP	W-L	SAVES	HITS	SO	BB	ERA
1992	Pittsburgh	59	71	6-4	18	58	57	29	3.15
1993	Two Teams	63	70	4-2	19	65	55	17	3.88
1994	Kansas City	37	49	2-2	1	47	37	24	5.14

DAVID BELL / Cleveland Indians / Third Base | $26

A third-generation ballplayer, the grandson of David (Gus) and the son of David (Buddy). His skills are very much like his father's were at the same age, a slow .270-hitting third baseman with excellent defense and a little power. The Indians have a young third baseman (Thome) who is a better hitter than David will ever be, but no match for him with the glove.

YEAR	TEAM/LEVEL	G	AB	R	H	2B	3B	HR	RBI	BB	SB	AVG	OBP	SLG
1993	Canton AA	129	483	69	141	20	2	9	60	43	3	.292	.350	.398
1994	Charlotte AAA	134	481	66	141	17	4	18	88	41	2	.293	.355	.457
1994	MLE	134	469	57	129	16	2	16	76	35	1	.275	.325	.420

DEREK BELL / San Diego Padres / Center Field | $40

I've always been a Bell-booster, and after he has come on strong the last two years, obviously I still am. He's a .300 hitter with power *and* speed; if you're selling, I'll take three. His best years are way ahead of him. His command of the strike zone, though weak, is improving. As a center fielder, he's working on it.

YEAR	TEAM/LEVEL	G	AB	R	H	2B	3B	HR	RBI	BB	SB	AVG	OBP	SLG
1993	San Diego	150	542	73	142	19	1	21	72	23	26	.262	.303	.416
1994	San Diego	108	434	54	135	20	0	14	54	29	24	.311	.354	.454
1995	*Projected*	*149*	*531*	*69*	*148*	*19*	*4*	*16*	*65*	*33*	*26*	*.279*	*.321*	*.420*

JAY BELL / Pittsburgh Pirates / Shortstop | $68

A union leader, he will be one of the last players to come back if there is a scab league. The four best shortstops in baseball (Bell, Cordero, Ripken, and Larkin) all have their limitations; you can argue for any of the four. Bell's range is average/below average, and will decline—but he could move to second or third and play another seven years.

YEAR	TEAM/LEVEL	G	AB	R	H	2B	3B	HR	RBI	BB	SB	AVG	OBP	SLG
1993	Pittsburgh	154	604	102	187	32	9	9	51	77	16	.310	.392	.437
1994	Pittsburgh	110	424	68	117	35	4	9	45	49	2	.276	.353	.441
1995	*Projected*	*158*	*622*	*93*	*167*	*33*	*6*	*12*	*57*	*69*	*10*	*.268*	*.342*	*.399*

JUAN BELL / Montreal Expos / Infielder | $21

Started the '94 campaign in the minors, but played well and was called up May 13. He was used by Montreal as a backup second baseman, hitting left-handed 83 percent of the time (he's a switch hitter), and had a terrific year, with 15 walks giving him a handsome .372 on-base percentage. Also played very, very well at second base. No future as regular.

YEAR	TEAM/LEVEL	G	AB	R	H	2B	3B	HR	RBI	BB	SB	AVG	OBP	SLG
1992	Philadelphia	46	147	12	30	3	1	1	8	18	5	.204	.292	.259
1993	Two Teams	115	351	47	80	12	3	5	36	41	6	.228	.311	.322
1994	Montreal	38	97	12	27	4	0	2	10	15	4	.278	.372	.381

ALBERT BELLE / Cleveland Indians / Left Field/Designated Hitter $86

Hit better in Jacobs Field (.413 with 21 homers in 47 games) than on the road, as opposed to previous years, when he hit poorly in Cleveland. This, combined with the lively ball or whatever, caused his numbers to jump from "outstanding" to "can you believe this?!" . . . Concedes *nothing* with two strikes on him. Has hit 31 two-strike homers in last three years.

YEAR	TEAM/LEVEL	G	AB	R	H	2B	3B	HR	RBI	BB	SB	AVG	OBP	SLG
1993	Cleveland	159	594	93	172	36	3	38	129	76	23	.290	.370	.552
1994	Cleveland	106	412	90	147	35	2	36	101	58	9	.357	.438	.714
1995	*Projected*	*157*	*594*	*100*	*177*	*35*	*3*	*40*	*126*	*75*	*15*	*.298*	*.377*	*.569*

RAFAEL BELLIARD / Atlanta Braves / Infielder $14

If fielding percentages were as closely watched as batting averages, Rafael Belliard would be headed for Cooperstown. They're not, of course (and shouldn't be), but Belliard has gotten a 13-year career out of avoiding errors. I wouldn't bet on his making it 15, or even necessarily 14 . . . a slow .220 hitter with no power, but above average at both middle infield spots.

YEAR	TEAM/LEVEL	G	AB	R	H	2B	3B	HR	RBI	BB	SB	AVG	OBP	SLG
1992	Atlanta	144	285	20	60	6	1	0	14	14	0	.211	.255	.239
1993	Atlanta	91	79	6	18	5	0	0	6	4	0	.228	.291	.291
1994	Atlanta	46	120	9	29	7	1	0	9	2	0	.242	.264	.317

ESTEBAN BELTRE / Texas Rangers / Shortstop $17

I thought last year that he had improved as a hitter enough that he could probably stay in the majors. I didn't, and don't, think that he's a .280 hitter, but he filled in for Manny Lee during an injury, and played fairly well. If he keeps his average over .250, and he might, his playing time will continue to increase.

YEAR	TEAM/LEVEL	G	AB	R	H	2B	3B	HR	RBI	BB	SB	AVG	OBP	SLG
1993	Nashville AAA	134	489	67	143	24	4	8	52	33	18	.292	.337	.407
1993	MLE	134	470	52	124	20	2	6	41	26	12	.254	.302	.353
1994	Texas	48	131	12	37	5	0	0	12	16	2	.282	.358	.321

FREDDIE BENAVIDES / Montreal Expos / Utilityman $14

He hit a consistent .188: .188 with the bases empty, and .189 with men on base. The Expos got him as a security blanket at second base after they traded DeShields, but he didn't hit at all, and Juan Bell took over most of the backup job as the year went on. Benavides still has to prove there is any job he can do at a major league level.

YEAR	TEAM/LEVEL	G	AB	R	H	2B	3B	HR	RBI	BB	SB	AVG	OBP	SLG
1992	Cincinnati	74	173	14	40	10	1	1	17	10	0	.231	.277	.318
1993	Colorado	74	213	20	61	10	3	3	26	6	3	.286	.305	.404
1994	Montreal	47	85	8	16	5	1	0	6	3	0	.188	.222	.271

ALAN BENES / St. Louis Cardinals / Starting Pitcher $37

Is 23 years old, attended Creighton University. A right-handed pitcher, like his brother. Big, like his brother (6-5, 215). A first-round draft pick, like his brother. In 37 minor league starts he has gone 17-7 with every-thing you could want—2.48 ERA, 213 strikeouts, good control (66 walks). He'll be in the Cardinals' rotation, one suspects, by July.

YEAR	TEAM/LEVEL	G	IP	W-L	PCT	HITS	SO	BB	ERA
1994	St. Pete A	11	78	7-1	.875	55	69	18	1.61
1994	Arkansas AA	13	88	7-2	.778	58	75	26	2.98
1994	Louisville AAA	2	15	1-0	1.000	10	16	4	2.93

ANDY BENES / San Diego Padres / Starting Pitcher $68

He's one of the best starting pitchers in baseball, but the public will never know this as long as he's with the Padres. The schedule calls for him to be a free agent this winter (1994-95), but of course, this is up in the air. . . . Durable, smart, throws hard, has good control, knows what he's doing. A Cy Young candidate on the right team.

YEAR	TEAM/LEVEL	G	IP	W-L	PCT	HITS	SO	BB	ERA
1992	San Diego	34	231	13-14	.481	230	169	61	3.35
1993	San Diego	34	231	15-15	.500	200	179	86	3.78
1994	San Diego	25	172	6-14	.300	155	189	51	3.86

ARMANDO BENITEZ / Baltimore Orioles / Relief Pitcher $34

The American League's Rookie of the Year, if things go well. A Dominican right-hander, he is almost as big as Lee Smith (6-4, 220), and throws as hard as Smith once did. His ratios of strikeouts to hits allowed in the minors are phenomenal, as you can see, and his 10 innings in the majors don't discourage us from believing he is ready.

YEAR	TEAM/LEVEL	G	IP	W-L	SAVES	HITS	SO	BB	ERA
1993	Two Teams A	52	67	8-1	18	38	112	23	1.34
1994	Bowie AA	53	72	8-4	16	41	106	39	3.14
1994	Baltimore	3	10	0-0	0	8	14	4	0.90

MIKE BENJAMIN / San Francisco Giants / Shortstop $19

May have the largest platoon differential in baseball. Over the last three years he has hit .292 against left-handers, but .160 against right-handers . . . not a bad shortstop, and Clayton was having an off year, but Dusty Baker did something managers do sometimes. The more Clayton struggled, the more determined Baker was to show confidence in him by playing him every game.

YEAR	TEAM/LEVEL	G	AB	R	H	2B	3B	HR	RBI	BB	SB	AVG	OBP	SLG
1992	San Francisco	40	75	4	13	2	1	1	3	4	1	.173	.215	.267
1993	San Francisco	63	146	22	29	7	0	4	16	9	0	.199	.264	.329
1994	San Francisco	38	62	9	16	5	1	1	9	5	5	.258	.343	.419

TODD BENZINGER / San Francisco Giants / First Base $15

The defection of Clark and the failure to develop of J.R. Phillips led the Giants to dump the first base job on Todd Benzinger. Benzinger reminds me of a woman I knew, who was working her way through the men of the world one at a time. Benzinger is working his way through the 28 teams, demonstrating to each one that they *don't* want him as their first baseman.

YEAR	TEAM/LEVEL	G	AB	R	H	2B	3B	HR	RBI	BB	SB	AVG	OBP	SLG
1993	San Francisco	86	177	25	51	7	2	6	26	13	0	.288	.332	.452
1994	San Francisco	107	328	32	87	13	2	9	31	17	2	.265	.304	.399
1995	*Projected*	*103*	*243*	*25*	*59*	*14*	*1*	*5*	*25*	*15*	*1*	*.243*	*.287*	*.370*

JASON BERE / Chicago White Sox / Starting Pitcher $48

The Juan Guzman of the White Sox, has gone 24-7 in his career because a) he has a 94-MPH fastball, and b) the White Sox have scored six-plus runs a game for him. He walks too many and gives up too many home runs, and the six runs a game won't run forever, so he's got some work to do before he's Walter Johnson.

YEAR	TEAM/LEVEL	G	IP	W-L	PCT	HITS	SO	BB	ERA
1993	Nashville AAA	8	49	5-1	.833	36	52	25	2.37
1993	Chicago	24	143	12-5	.706	109	129	81	3.47
1994	Chicago	24	142	12-2	.857	119	127	80	3.81

SEAN BERGMAN / Detroit Tigers / Starting Pitcher $25

A right-handed pitcher with a hard, sinking fastball, he had a fine year at Toledo, and won two of three starts just before the strike. He is the best pitching prospect that the Tigers have had in several years, which is not high praise, and a ground-ball pitcher without a strong inner defense is like a lion tamer without a whip.

YEAR	TEAM/LEVEL	G	IP	W-L	PCT	HITS	SO	BB	ERA
1993	Detroit	9	40	1-4	.200	47	19	23	5.67
1994	Toledo AAA	25	155	11-8	.579	147	145	53	3.72
1994	Detroit	3	18	2-1	.667	22	12	7	5.60

GERONIMO BERROA / Oakland Athletics / Left Fielder $36

The best guess of what to expect from Berroa over the next few years is the performance of Mike Easler, 1982-86, after Easler finally overcame a reputation for being just a minor league hitter. Berroa, however, is a much better defensive player than Easler—in fact, he is a *good* left fielder, with excellent hustle. He's going to have a solid career now.

YEAR	TEAM/LEVEL	G	AB	R	H	2B	3B	HR	RBI	BB	SB	AVG	OBP	SLG
1993	MLE	90	306	42	86	27	2	12	44	25	0	.281	.335	.500
1994	Oakland	96	340	55	104	18	2	13	65	41	7	.306	.379	.485
1995	*Projected*	*145*	*537*	*74*	*152*	*26*	*2*	*17*	*80*	*49*	*8*	*.283*	*.343*	*.434*

SEAN BERRY / Montreal Expos / Third Base $29

Another player that Hal McRae just *knew* wasn't going to hit. Like a lot of hitters, he may have hit more than should be expected over the last two years, but he could shed a few points and stay in the league . . . not fast, but was 14-for-14 as a base stealer last year, and is 28-for-31 in his career. What does this tell you?

YEAR	TEAM/LEVEL	G	AB	R	H	2B	3B	HR	RBI	BB	SB	AVG	OBP	SLG
1993	Montreal	122	299	50	78	15	2	14	49	41	12	.261	.348	.465
1994	Montreal	103	320	43	89	19	2	11	41	32	14	.278	.347	.453
1995	*Projected*	*132*	*415*	*53*	*107*	*22*	*3*	*14*	*56*	*41*	*11*	*.258*	*.325*	*.427*

DAMON BERRYHILL / Boston Red Sox / Catcher $21

Bumped from Atlanta by the development of Javy Lopez, he caught on with the Red Sox, and wound up able to contribute significantly to getting Butch Hobson fired. His weaknesses are pretty significant: He's slow, even for a catcher, has a career on-base percentage way under .300, and doesn't throw particularly well. But, as a switch-hitting catcher, he'll be around for years.

YEAR	TEAM/LEVEL	G	AB	R	H	2B	3B	HR	RBI	BB	SB	AVG	OBP	SLG
1993	Atlanta	115	335	24	82	18	2	8	43	21	0	.245	.291	.382
1994	Boston	82	255	30	67	17	2	6	34	19	0	.263	.312	.416
1995	*Projected*	*99*	*264*	*22*	*62*	*13*	*1*	*6*	*32*	*17*	*0*	*.235*	*.291*	*.360*

DANTE BICHETTE / Colorado Rockies / Right Field $33

His batting stats are a kind of a joke on the ages, like those of Kenny Williams or Babe Herman—a set of immutable lines which are absurdly disproportionate to his true abilities, but which will stand through the years, convincing people that Bichette was something that he isn't. He's a fine defensive player with a strong arm, average hitter for a right fielder.

YEAR	TEAM/LEVEL	G	AB	R	H	2B	3B	HR	RBI	BB	SB	AVG	OBP	SLG
1993	Colorado	141	538	93	167	43	5	21	89	28	14	.310	.348	.526
1994	Colorado	116	484	74	147	33	2	27	95	19	21	.304	.334	.548
1995	*Projected*	*141*	*544*	*69*	*159*	*30*	*2*	*20*	*77*	*25*	*21*	*.281*	*.313*	*.454*

MIKE BIELECKI / Atlanta Braves / Starting Pitcher $14

The bottom man on the Braves pitching staff, worked four or five times a month in lost causes. Bielecki's a good pitcher; he just can't stay healthy, and has pitched 70 percent of his career trying to work himself back into peak shape. The Braves just give him a few innings, so he can't hurt himself. He's near the end.

YEAR	TEAM/LEVEL	G	IP	W-L	PCT	HITS	SO	BB	ERA
1992	Atlanta	19	81	2-4	.333	77	62	27	2.57
1993	Cleveland	13	69	4-5	.444	90	38	23	5.90
1994	Atlanta	19	27	2-0	1.000	28	18	12	4.00

CRAIG BIGGIO / Houston Astros / Second Base $67

No player since 1900 has made such a successful transition from catcher to middle infielder. This, among other things, speaks of a tremendous desire to succeed. Criticized for his declining base stealing, he was 39-for-43 in that department in '94, by far his best performance. With 44 doubles and 39 steals, he reached scoring position 94 times in 114 games.

YEAR	TEAM/LEVEL	G	AB	R	H	2B	3B	HR	RBI	BB	SB	AVG	OBP	SLG
1993	Houston	155	610	98	175	41	5	21	64	77	15	.287	.373	.474
1994	Houston	114	437	88	139	44	5	6	56	62	39	.318	.411	.483
1995	*Projected*	*160*	*619*	*102*	*174*	*35*	*4*	*12*	*58*	*92*	*38*	*.281*	*.374*	*.409*

BUD BLACK / San Francisco Giants / Starting Pitcher $19

The Giants designated him for reassignment at the end of the season. He is 37 and has been hurt for most of the last two years, but I wouldn't write him off, simply because he's still a good pitcher. No pitcher comes with a guarantee. A good pitcher who gets hurt is a better gamble than a bad pitcher who's always been healthy.

YEAR	TEAM/LEVEL	G	IP	W-L	PCT	HITS	SO	BB	ERA
1992	San Francisco	28	177	10-12	.455	178	82	59	3.97
1993	San Francisco	16	94	8-2	.800	89	45	33	3.56
1994	San Francisco	10	54	4-2	.667	50	28	16	4.47

WILLIE BLAIR / Colorado Rockies / Pitcher $15

On a real team, I wouldn't mind having him on my staff. His control used to be good, but pitching two years in one of the best hitting parks in baseball history has so undermined his confidence that his control has degenerated, and the results have turned pretty ugly. Now 29; career will end soon unless things start to break right for him.

YEAR	TEAM/LEVEL	G	IP	W-L	PCT	HITS	SO	BB	ERA
1992	Houston	29	79	5-7	.417	74	48	25	4.00
1993	Colorado	46	146	6-10	.375	184	84	42	4.75
1994	Colorado	47	78	0-5	.000	98	68	39	5.79

JEFF BLAUSER / Atlanta Braves / Shortstop $34

Did not play as well in any area last year as he did in his All-Star season, 1993. After struggling through April he went on the DL May 3 with a strained muscle in his side. On returning May 20 he played very well for six weeks, but then cooled down. Ratio of double plays to errors, 44 to 13, was poor. He has young players pushing him.

YEAR	TEAM/LEVEL	G	AB	R	H	2B	3B	HR	RBI	BB	SB	AVG	OBP	SLG
1993	Atlanta	161	597	110	182	29	2	15	73	85	16	.305	.401	.436
1994	Atlanta	96	380	56	98	21	4	6	45	38	1	.258	.329	.382
1995	*Projected*	*150*	*529*	*88*	*144*	*26*	*3*	*13*	*63*	*70*	*9*	*.272*	*.357*	*.406*

GREG BLOSSER / Boston Red Sox / Outfielder $18

A number-one draft pick who has been touted as the top prospect in the Red Sox system. I had him tagged a year ago as a Grade D prospect. He played a little better last year, and I would upgrade him to Grade C. He could hit .250 with a little power and a little speed, but will strike out far too much to be projected as a star.

YEAR	TEAM/LEVEL	G	AB	R	H	2B	3B	HR	RBI	BB	SB	AVG	OBP	SLG
1993	MLE	130	467	50	85	22	1	16	50	44	1	.210	.278	.364
1993	Boston	17	28	1	2	1	0	0	1	2	0	.071	.133	.107
1994	MLE	97	346	43	87	22	0	13	45	37	7	.251	.324	.428

MIKE BLOWERS / Seattle Mariners / Third Base $25

The return of Edgar Martinez took his job away, but he played a little first, a little third, and a few games in the outfield, and hit well enough, driving in runs at a 100-RBI pace, to solidify his claim to being a quality platoon player, at least with the bat. His .951 fielding percentage in 1993 wasn't considered good. Last year it was .939.

YEAR	TEAM/LEVEL	G	AB	R	H	2B	3B	HR	RBI	BB	SB	AVG	OBP	SLG
1993	Seattle	127	379	55	106	23	3	15	57	44	1	.280	.357	.475
1994	Seattle	85	270	37	78	13	0	9	49	25	2	.289	.348	.437
1995	*Projected*	*126*	*374*	*50*	*99*	*23*	*2*	*10*	*52*	*42*	*2*	*.265*	*.339*	*.417*

JOE BOEVER / Detroit Tigers / Relief Pitcher $22

Despite bouncing around from team to team (Atlanta to Philadelphia to Houston to Oakland to Detroit), he has been healthy and has kept his ERA under four for six straight seasons . . . mixes up changeups and palmballs to make his fastball look better, but if his location is off the batter has a holiday. Allowed 21 of 37 inherited runners to score, which is awful.

YEAR	TEAM/LEVEL	G	IP	W-L	SAVES	HITS	SO	BB	ERA
1992	Houston	81	111	3-6	2	103	67	45	2.51
1993	Two Teams	61	102	6-3	3	101	63	44	3.61
1994	Detroit	46	81	9-2	3	80	49	37	3.98

TIM BOGAR / New York Mets / Shortstop $15

The acquisition of Jose Vizcaino left him without a position. Although I am not personally convinced that Vizcaino is a better player than Bogar, this is argumentative, and not particularly helpful. Bogar has no position, and will have to play better off the bench than he did in '94 if he's going to stay in the majors.

YEAR	TEAM/LEVEL	G	AB	R	H	2B	3B	HR	RBI	BB	SB	AVG	OBP	SLG
1992	MLE	129	462	41	115	27	0	3	29	10	5	.249	.265	.327
1993	New York	78	205	19	50	13	0	3	25	14	0	.244	.300	.351
1994	New York	50	52	5	8	0	0	2	5	4	1	.154	.211	.269

WADE BOGGS / New York Yankees / Third Base $33

Where does he rank, among all the third basemen ever? I have him among the top 20, but probably not among the top 10 . . . had 200-plus hits and scored 100-plus runs every year from 1983 to 1989, but hasn't met either standard in the 90s, and wasn't on target to do so last year, despite hitting .342 with more power . . . very slow, but defense remains solid.

YEAR	TEAM/LEVEL	G	AB	R	H	2B	3B	HR	RBI	BB	SB	AVG	OBP	SLG
1993	New York	143	560	83	169	26	1	2	59	74	0	.302	.378	.363
1994	New York	97	366	61	125	19	1	11	55	61	2	.342	.433	.489
1995	Projected	136	513	81	161	33	2	8	65	75	1	.314	.401	.433

BRIAN BOHANON / Texas Rangers / Relief Pitcher $12

Continues to get chances, but now more out of desperation than hope. He was determined to throw more strikes last year, and he did, and the batters hit the hell out of them. There aren't many pitchers who can't win with a good K/W ratio, but Bohanon may be one. A left-hander, but from 1992 to 1994 left-handers have hit .329 against him.

YEAR	TEAM/LEVEL	G	IP	W-L	PCT	HITS	SO	BB	ERA
1993	Texas	36	93	4-4	.500	107	45	46	4.76
1994	Ok. City AAA	15	98	5-10	.333	106	88	33	4.12
1994	Texas	11	37	2-2	.500	51	26	8	7.23

BARRY BONDS / San Francisco Giants / Left Field $100

Another year, another set of astonishing numbers. If it wasn't for the strike, he'd have gone 40/40 last year, the goal that narrowly eluded his father. Actually, he'd have made 50/40 . . . Henry Aaron had .600 slugging percentages six times in his career, but never twice in a row. Bonds has done it three straight times. He is still the best player in baseball.

YEAR	TEAM/LEVEL	G	AB	R	H	2B	3B	HR	RBI	BB	SB	AVG	OBP	SLG
1993	San Francisco	159	539	129	181	38	4	46	123	126	29	.336	.458	.677
1994	San Francisco	112	391	89	122	18	1	37	81	74	29	.312	.426	.647
1995	Projected	160	551	125	162	35	4	38	106	132	38	.294	.430	.579

RICKY BONES / Milwaukee Brewers / Starting Pitcher $26

In his three years in Milwaukee he has a 2.54 ERA in April, but is over 4.00 in all of the other months—4.85 in May, 4.37 in June, 4.74 in July, 4.09 in August, 4.66 in September, 10.80 in October. I remain immensely skeptical about his ability to continue to pitch .500 ball. You can't win 10 games a year with 60 strikeouts a year.

YEAR	TEAM/LEVEL	G	IP	W-L	PCT	HITS	SO	BB	ERA
1992	Milwaukee	31	163	9-10	.474	169	65	48	4.57
1993	Milwaukee	32	204	11-11	.500	222	63	63	4.86
1994	Milwaukee	24	171	10-9	.526	166	57	45	3.43

BOBBY BONILLA / New York Mets / Right Field/Third Base $50

Explain to me again: Why was this man the highest-paid player in baseball? . . . Settled in at third base, and battled it to a draw, making 18 errors but at least that many nice plays. Surrounded by good players, he'd look like a great player. Surrounded by New York Mets, he looks like a good New York Met. . . . Has hit 10 home runs off of Tom Browning.

YEAR	TEAM/LEVEL	G	AB	R	H	2B	3B	HR	RBI	BB	SB	AVG	OBP	SLG
1993	New York	139	502	81	133	21	3	34	87	72	3	.265	.352	.522
1994	New York	108	403	60	117	24	1	20	67	55	1	.290	.374	.504
1995	*Projected*	*141*	*505*	*73*	*129*	*29*	*3*	*22*	*79*	*74*	*3*	*.255*	*.351*	*.455*

BRET BOONE / Cincinnati Reds / Second Base $44

Criticized in Seattle for swinging from the heels, he hit only five homers through the All-Star break, then added seven in the last month. He might hit seven a month from now on. It is hard to imagine what the Mariners didn't like, but there is precedent: They didn't like Danny Tartabull, either. Bad teams tend to focus their frustrations on their best players.

YEAR	TEAM/LEVEL	G	AB	R	H	2B	3B	HR	RBI	BB	SB	AVG	OBP	SLG
1993	Seattle	76	271	31	68	12	2	12	38	17	2	.251	.301	.443
1994	Cincinnati	108	381	59	122	25	2	12	68	24	3	.320	.368	.491
1995	*Projected*	*155*	*550*	*69*	*154*	*26*	*2*	*18*	*80*	*40*	*7*	*.280*	*.329*	*.433*

PEDRO BORBON, JR. / Atlanta Braves / Relief Pitcher $13

Now 27 years old, has been consistently good in the minor leagues for years, but can't get a foothold on a major league staff. The Braves are going to run out of options on him, so he should be in the majors somewhere in 1995. He never shows up on hot prospect lists, but his numbers look like a pitcher.

YEAR	TEAM/LEVEL	G	IP	W-L	SAVES	HITS	SO	BB	ERA
1992	Greenville AA	39	94	8-2	3	73	79	42	3.06
1993	Richmond AAA	52	77	5-5	1	71	95	42	4.23
1994	Richmond AAA	59	81	3-4	4	66	82	41	2.79

PAT BORDERS / Toronto Blue Jays / Catcher $27

Granting that his skill is in an area which is difficult to evaluate (handling the pitching staff), his tangible contributions to the team are so meager that it is becoming increasingly difficult to justify his playing time. Slow, extremely low on-base percentage, arm just fair. It's easy to make excuses for him when you're winning, but Toronto didn't win last year.

YEAR	TEAM/LEVEL	G	AB	R	H	2B	3B	HR	RBI	BB	SB	AVG	OBP	SLG
1992	Toronto	138	480	47	116	26	2	13	53	33	1	.242	.290	.385
1993	Toronto	138	488	38	124	30	0	9	55	20	2	.254	.285	.371
1994	Toronto	85	295	24	73	13	1	3	26	15	1	.247	.284	.329

MIKE BORDICK / Oakland Athletics / Shortstop $45

He's not quite Ozzie Smith, but there's some Ozzie here—a very durable shortstop who can really play the position, and doesn't drag the team down too much on the other end. Draws enough walks to score 60 runs a year, runs fairly well. His average loses a few points because he plays in Oakland . . . rates with Guillen and Gagne among the better shortstops.

YEAR	TEAM/LEVEL	G	AB	R	H	2B	3B	HR	RBI	BB	SB	AVG	OBP	SLG
1993	Oakland	159	546	60	136	21	2	3	48	60	10	.249	.332	.311
1994	Oakland	114	391	38	99	18	4	2	37	38	7	.253	.320	.335
1995	*Projected*	*155*	*523*	*55*	*131*	*18*	*2*	*3*	*44*	*50*	*10*	*.250*	*.316*	*.310*

TOBY BORLAND / Philadelphia Phillies / Relief Pitcher $19

Minor league veteran, tall and thin. A 27th-round pick in 1987, he throws sidearm and has pretty good stuff, but fought his control until last year, when he switched from closer to middle relief. The Phillies are not predicting great things for him, and I won't either, but if I was desperate for a closer, I'd think about him.

YEAR	TEAM/LEVEL	G	IP	W-L	SAVES	HITS	SO	BB	ERA
1993	AA & AAA	70	84	4-6	14	67	100	40	3.67
1994	Scranton AAA	27	54	4-1	4	36	61	21	1.68
1994	Philadelphia	24	34	1-0	1	31	26	14	2.36

CHRIS BOSIO / Seattle Mariners / Starting Pitcher $28

He didn't pitch as bad last year as the 4-10 record would indicate, which isn't going to be much comfort if his career continues to roll off a cliff. He's going through a career transition now, but he's not going to emerge on the other side of it unless he gets serious about conditioning. Chance of a comeback probably 20-25 percent.

YEAR	TEAM/LEVEL	G	IP	W-L	PCT	HITS	SO	BB	ERA
1992	Milwaukee	33	231	16-6	.727	223	120	44	3.62
1993	Seattle	29	164	9-9	.500	138	119	59	3.45
1994	Seattle	19	125	4-10	.286	137	67	40	4.32

SHAWN BOSKIE / Seattle Mariners / Starter/Reliever $14

Ended the season on the DL with a strained lower back. Before that he bounced from Chicago to Philadelphia to Seattle, all of whom could have saved themselves the experience of finding out he wasn't a starting pitcher if they had just checked his record. His control is OK and his hits ratio is fair, but he just gives up too many homers.

YEAR	TEAM/LEVEL	G	IP	W-L	PCT	HITS	SO	BB	ERA
1992	Chicago	23	92	5-11	.313	96	39	36	5.01
1993	Chicago	39	66	5-3	.625	63	39	21	3.43
1994	Three Teams	22	91	4-7	.364	92	61	30	5.06

DARYL BOSTON / New York Yankees / Outfielder $16

The Yankees signed him as a free agent, but didn't give him enough playing time to stay sharp. He hit a couple of pinch-hit home runs, but went 5-for-25 as a pinch hitter, played a few innings in center field. He's a real good left-handed extra outfielder, and, at 32, he should have a couple of years left.

YEAR	TEAM/LEVEL	G	AB	R	H	2B	3B	HR	RBI	BB	SB	AVG	OBP	SLG
1992	New York (N)	130	289	37	72	14	2	11	35	38	12	.249	.338	.426
1993	Colorado	124	291	46	76	15	1	14	40	26	1	.261	.325	.464
1994	New York (A)	52	77	11	14	2	0	4	14	6	0	.182	.250	.364

KENT BOTTENFIELD / San Francisco / Starting Pitcher $13

Colorado tried to send him out in June. He refused the assignment, signed with the Giants, pitched with Phoenix for six weeks, then was called up just before the strike. He doesn't throw real hard, doesn't get everything over the plate, and took forever to work his way through the Expos system, but he does have an outside chance to be a pitcher.

YEAR	TEAM/LEVEL	G	IP	W-L	PCT	HITS	SO	BB	ERA
1992	Indianapolis AAA	25	152	12-8	.600	139	111	58	3.43
1993	Two Teams	37	160	5-10	.333	179	63	71	5.07
1994	Colorado/San F.	16	26	3-1	.750	33	15	10	6.15

RAFAEL BOURNIGAL / Los Angeles Dodgers / Shortstop $15

A 28-year-old middle infielder, was hitting .332 in the desert when Lasorda's exasperation with Offerman finally reached the boiling point, and the Dodgers rotated them—Offerman to Triple-A, Bournigal as the Dodgers' starting shortstop. He kept the job until the strike, not playing well enough to claim the position or poorly enough to blow it. Limited future, probably.

YEAR	TEAM/LEVEL	G	AB	R	H	2B	3B	HR	RBI	BB	SB	AVG	OBP	SLG
1993	MLE	134	433	44	97	17	0	2	32	17	1	.224	.253	.277
1994	Albuquerque	61	208	29	69	8	0	1	22	9	2	.332	.358	.385
1994	Los Angeles	40	116	2	26	3	1	0	11	9	0	.224	.291	.267

RYAN BOWEN / Florida Marlins / Starting Pitcher $15

His 1993 season was ended early by knee surgery; his 1994 season ended in May due to a strained rib cage muscle. Adding to his problems, he can't really pitch; he's 15-28 in his career, and it's not all the fault of his cleanup hitters. He's a great athlete and he throws real hard . . . 15 percent chance of turning into a good pitcher.

YEAR	TEAM/LEVEL	G	IP	W-L	PCT	HITS	SO	BB	ERA
1992	Houston	11	34	0-7	.000	48	22	30	10.96
1993	Florida	27	157	8-12	.400	156	98	87	4.42
1994	Florida	8	47	1-5	.167	50	32	19	4.94

DARREN BRAGG / Seattle Mariners / Outfielder/Catcher $22

Left-handed hitter, a 22nd-round pick in 1990, in line for an extended major league trial after hitting .350 at Calgary. Short (5-9), solid, runs well but doesn't have a position. Drew a lot of walks at lower levels, career OBP of .408 in the minors. If Buhner leaves there will be an opening for him, but, as much as the Mariners need a catcher . . .

YEAR	TEAM/LEVEL	G	AB	R	H	2B	3B	HR	RBI	BB	SB	AVG	OBP	SLG
1993	MLE	131	436	59	104	24	2	9	37	55	12	.239	.324	.365
1994	Calgary	126	500	112	175	33	6	17	85	68	28	.350	.430	.542
1994	MLE	126	462	71	137	29	3	11	54	44	18	.297	.358	.444

JEFF BRANSON / Cincinnati Reds / Middle Infielder $21

The acquisition of Bret Boone and Tony Fernandez and the unusually good health of Barry Larkin took most of his playing time, but he filled in a few innings here and there, and made the most of his chances with a .505 slugging percentage. Won't be a regular, but he hit well as a backup in '92, and hit well the first half of '93.

YEAR	TEAM/LEVEL	G	AB	R	H	2B	3B	HR	RBI	BB	SB	AVG	OBP	SLG
1993	Cincinnati	125	381	40	92	15	1	3	22	19	4	.241	.275	.310
1994	Cincinnati	58	109	18	31	4	1	6	16	5	0	.284	.316	.505
1995	*Projected*	*108*	*258*	*29*	*65*	*12*	*1*	*4*	*23*	*13*	*2*	*.252*	*.288*	*.353*

JEFF BRANTLEY / Cincinnati Reds / Relief Pitcher $32

Beaten out of the closer job in San Francisco by Rod Beck, he tried to work as a starter. That failing, he was traded to Cincinnati, where he pitched fairly well as the Reds' ace, saving 15 games in 21 tries. He is supposed to be a free agent, although of course that is in chaos. Should remain effective within his role.

YEAR	TEAM/LEVEL	G	IP	W-L	SAVES	HITS	SO	BB	ERA
1992	San Francisco	56	92	7-7	7	67	86	45	2.95
1993	San Francisco	53	114	5-6	0	112	76	46	4.28
1994	Cincinnati	50	65	6-6	15	46	63	28	2.48

SID BREAM / Houston Astros / First Base $18

Has backed up the two best first basemen in the National League, McGriff in 1993, Bagwell last year. He missed playing time in '94 with a back injury and a problem with his left foot, plus of course how much time is he going to take away from Jeff Bagwell, but went 13-for-32 as a pinch hitter (.406). Good defensive first baseman.

YEAR	TEAM/LEVEL	G	AB	R	H	2B	3B	HR	RBI	BB	SB	AVG	OBP	SLG
1993	Atlanta	117	277	33	72	14	1	9	35	31	4	.260	.332	.415
1994	Houston	46	61	7	21	5	0	0	7	9	0	.344	.429	.426
1995	*Projected*	*83*	*131*	*13*	*33*	*7*	*0*	*3*	*17*	*16*	*2*	*.252*	*.333*	*.374*

BILLY BREWER / Kansas City Royals / Left-handed Spot Reliever $23

May miss Hal McRae as much as any of the Royals. McRae spotted him well, bringing him in to face lefties, and moving on to the next guy after he got a couple of outs. He was effective in that role, although inclined to hang one once in a while. Whether he can handle a slightly larger assignment is an open question.

YEAR	TEAM/LEVEL	G	IP	W-L	SAVES	HITS	SO	BB	ERA
1992	Harrisburg AA	20	23	2-0	0	25	18	18	5.01
1993	Kansas City	46	39	2-2	0	31	28	20	3.46
1994	Kansas City	50	39	4-1	3	28	25	16	2.56

BRAD BRINK / San Francisco Giants / Starting Pitcher $15

A 30-year-old right-hander who was a first-round draft pick of the Phillies, sometime in the Reagan administration. He battled shoulder injuries throughout the George Bush years, but has been healthy for two years and has pitched fairly well at Triple-A, getting a few innings in the majors. Good control, could probably help the Giants.

YEAR	TEAM/LEVEL	G	IP	W-L	PCT	HITS	SO	BB	ERA
1992	Philadelphia	8	41	0-4	.000	53	16	13	4.14
1993	Scranton AAA	18	107	7-7	.500	104	89	27	4.22
1994	Phoenix AAA	23	128	7-5	.583	140	79	41	4.15

JOHN BRISCOE / Oakland Athletics / Right-handed Reliever $14

In the tradition of Ryne Duren, Bobby Witt, and Brad Pennington, a hard thrower who has not demonstrated that he can distinguish between the strike zone and a map of Rwanda. He has progressed in his craft to the point at which he can blow away minor league hitters at an impressive rate, but has yet to show much in the majors. Grade C prospect.

YEAR	TEAM/LEVEL	G	IP	W-L	SAVES	HITS	SO	BB	ERA
1993	Huntsville AA	30	39	4-0	16	28	62	16	3.03
1993	Oakland	17	25	1-0	0	26	24	26	8.03
1994	Oakland	37	49	4-2	1	31	45	39	4.01

DOUG BROCAIL / San Diego Padres / Starting Pitcher $14

Had elbow surgery in spring training, and spent the first couple of months on a rehab. He returned in late June, and was just rounding into form when the strike hit. He's not the worst pitcher in the league, and I wouldn't be surprised if he eventually won a few games. But Andy Benes can't win with this team, and he's no Andy Benes.

YEAR	TEAM/LEVEL	G	IP	W-L	PCT	HITS	SO	BB	ERA
1993	Las Vegas AAA	10	51	4-2	.667	51	32	14	3.68
1993	San Diego	24	128	4-13	.235	143	70	42	4.56
1994	San Diego	12	17	0-0	.000	21	11	5	5.82

RICO BROGNA / New York Mets / First Base $23

After 760 minor league games he got a chance to impress the Mets, and he didn't waste it. He's not really a .351 hitter, nor even a .301 hitter, nor a .281 hitter. He's Sid Bream, a .250 hitter with a little power and good defense. His hot streak will give him a full shot at a 600-at-bat season, and he'll be around for years.

YEAR	TEAM/LEVEL	G	AB	R	H	2B	3B	HR	RBI	BB	SB	AVG	OBP	SLG
1994	MLE	67	252	29	58	12	3	10	32	13	0	.226	.264	.417
1994	New York (N)	39	131	16	46	11	2	7	20	6	1	.351	.380	.626
1995	*Projected*	*115*	*351*	*36*	*87*	*16*	*2*	*11*	*43*	*21*	*2*	*.248*	*.290*	*.399*

JEFF BRONKEY / Milwaukee Brewers / Relief Pitcher $11

His season ended in late May, due to bone chips in his elbow. There was very little evidence, anywhere in his career, that he was going to be a successful pitcher, even if he was healthy. His career minor league record is 19-35, with a 4.34 ERA and a poor K/W ratio. So I really don't know why he was in the majors, anyway.

YEAR	TEAM/LEVEL	G	IP	W-L	SAVES	HITS	SO	BB	ERA
1993	Ok. City AAA	29	37	2-2	14	29	19	7	2.65
1993	Texas	21	36	1-1	1	39	18	11	4.00
1994	Milwaukee	16	21	1-1	1	20	13	12	4.35

JERRY BROOKS / Los Angeles Dodgers / Outfielder $13

A 28-year-old minor league free agent. He's not the worst player in the world, a .260-to-.280 hitter with a little power, but slow and with no peripheral skills to call attention to him. If there *isn't* a scab league, he'll probably be a pinch hitter/extra outfielder somewhere. If there is, he could play.

YEAR	TEAM/LEVEL	G	AB	R	H	2B	3B	HR	RBI	BB	SB	AVG	OBP	SLG
1993	MLE	116	384	40	108	19	1	6	42	12	1	.281	.303	.383
1994	Albuquer. AAA	115	390	76	125	23	1	16	79	31	4	.321	.375	.508
1994	MLE	115	358	45	93	16	0	9	47	18	2	.260	.295	.380

SCOTT BROSIUS / Oakland Athletics / Third Base $26

Took advantage of an opportunity, and has a career going for him. He played center field for the A's over the last few weeks of 1993, and played well enough that LaRussa wanted to keep him in the lineup after the A's added Javier to play center. Craig Paquette had failed at third base, so Brosius got that job, and was . . . well, better than Paquette.

YEAR	TEAM/LEVEL	G	AB	R	H	2B	3B	HR	RBI	BB	SB	AVG	OBP	SLG
1993	Oakland	70	213	26	53	10	1	6	25	14	6	.249	.296	.390
1994	Oakland	96	324	31	77	14	1	14	49	24	2	.238	.289	.417
1995	*Projected*	*123*	*399*	*46*	*94*	*21*	*1*	*13*	*50*	*28*	*8*	*.236*	*.286*	*.391*

SCOTT BROW / Toronto Blue Jays / Right-handed Starting Pitcher $13

Brow went 14-2 at Dunedin in 1992, but has yet to do anything at Double-A or above. The Blue Jays have given him 24 major league games, for reasons that I absolutely can't figure out. He is *not* progressing; he seems to be going backward. He needs to go back to a level that he can handle, and experience some success.

YEAR	TEAM/LEVEL	G	IP	W-L	PCT	HITS	SO	BB	ERA
1993	Syracuse AAA	20	121	6-8	.429	119	64	37	4.38
1994	Syracuse	14	79	5-3	.625	77	30	38	4.31
1994	Toronto	18	29	0-3	.000	34	15	19	5.90

KEVIN BROWN / Texas Rangers / Starting Pitcher $29

I'm not saying he won't come back, but his problems are fairly serious. First, there are very, very few right-handed ground-ball pitchers who are consistently successful (Brown is an *extreme* ground-ball pitcher). Second, he has established a pattern of decline. Third, left-handed hitters hit .332 against him last year. Throws hard, throws strikes; may need to develop another pitch.

YEAR	TEAM/LEVEL	G	IP	W-L	PCT	HITS	SO	BB	ERA
1992	Texas	35	266	21-11	.656	262	173	76	3.32
1993	Texas	34	233	15-12	.555	228	142	74	3.59
1994	Texas	26	170	7-9	.438	218	123	50	4.82

JERRY BROWNE / Florida Marlins / Third Base/Utility $23

Had an impressive comeback season in Florida, playing wherever Gary Sheffield didn't want to play. He had a .392 on-base percentage, built of both hits and walks, and would have batted 500 times if not for the strike. At third base, where he played most often, he was obviously out of position. He's not a bad outfielder . . . will continue to bounce up and down.

YEAR	TEAM/LEVEL	G	AB	R	H	2B	3B	HR	RBI	BB	SB	AVG	OBP	SLG
1993	Oakland	76	260	27	65	13	0	2	19	22	4	.250	.306	.323
1994	Florida	101	329	42	97	17	4	3	30	52	3	.295	.392	.398
1995	*Projected*	*91*	*276*	*37*	*76*	*12*	*2*	*3*	*26*	*36*	*3*	*.275*	*.359*	*.366*

TOM BROWNING / Cincinnati Reds / Starting Pitcher $13

Was pitching fairly well when he broke his left arm delivering a pitch May 10, a freak injury. There is no way of knowing when or if he will come back, or whether he will be 100 percent if he does. He is 35 now, and hasn't pitched more than 114 innings in a season since 1991. Career record is now 123-88.

YEAR	TEAM/LEVEL	G	IP	W-L	PCT	HITS	SO	BB	ERA
1992	Cincinnati	16	87	6-5	.545	108	33	28	5.07
1993	Cincinnati	21	114	7-7	.500	159	53	20	4.74
1994	Cincinnati	7	41	3-1	.750	34	22	13	4.20

JACOB BRUMFIELD / Cincinnati Reds / Outfielder | $23

Continues to play well, filling in for injured Cincinnati outfielders. He'll be 30 in May, so it's unlikely that he'll be able to play his way into an everyday job, but you have to be impressed by what he has done as a major league hitter—.271 average in 424 at bats, 10 homers, 32 stolen bases. Right-handed hitter, above-average defensive center fielder.

YEAR	TEAM/LEVEL	G	AB	R	H	2B	3B	HR	RBI	BB	SB	AVG	OBP	SLG
1993	Cincinnati	103	272	40	73	17	3	6	23	21	20	.268	.321	.419
1994	Cincinnati	68	122	36	38	10	2	4	11	15	6	.311	.381	.525
1995	*Projected*	*113*	*285*	*49*	*78*	*17*	*2*	*6*	*26*	*28*	*22*	*.274*	*.339*	*.411*

TOM BRUNANSKY / Boston Red Sox / Right Field | $12

He is immortal. In the year 2525, if man is still alive, they'll still be asking "Can Brunansky come back?" He hasn't played *well* for more than two weeks at a time since 1987, but has kept his career going with a series of well-timed one-week hot streaks. His .449 slugging percentage last year was his best since he left Minnesota.

YEAR	TEAM/LEVEL	G	AB	R	H	2B	3B	HR	RBI	BB	SB	AVG	OBP	SLG
1993	Milwaukee	80	224	20	41	7	3	6	29	25	3	.183	.265	.321
1994	Mil/Boston	64	205	24	48	12	1	10	34	24	0	.234	.309	.449
1995	*Projected*	*79*	*242*	*24*	*53*	*11*	*1*	*8*	*33*	*33*	*2*	*.213*	*.305*	*.391*

GARY BUCKELS / St. Louis Cardinals / Relief Pitcher | $12

Released by the California system, he was out of baseball in 1992, but caught on with Louisville in 1993. He was pitching the best ball of his long Triple-A career last July when the Cardinals needed bullpen help, so he got three weeks in the majors. Is 29 years old, throws a sinking fastball and a knuckle curve. Grade D prospect.

YEAR	TEAM/LEVEL	G	IP	W-L	SAVES	HITS	SO	BB	ERA
1993	Louisville AAA	40	88	4-2	1	116	64	25	5.42
1994	Louisville AAA	48	77	7-2	2	69	69	21	3.26
1994	St. Louis	10	12	0-1	0	8	9	7	2.25

STEVE BUECHELE / Chicago Cubs / Third Base | $28

The Cubs need a new manager every few months, and it may not be long before one of those new managers decides to look for a new third baseman. Buechele is not the defensive wizard he once was, and a .242 batting average, in Wrigley Field in a hitter's year, isn't good. He did hit .325 with men on base, as opposed to .168 with the bases empty.

YEAR	TEAM/LEVEL	G	AB	R	H	2B	3B	HR	RBI	BB	SB	AVG	OBP	SLG
1993	Chicago	133	460	53	125	27	2	15	65	48	1	.272	.345	.437
1994	Chicago	104	339	33	82	11	1	14	52	39	1	.242	.325	.404
1995	*Projected*	*140*	*494*	*48*	*116*	*19*	*1*	*13*	*60*	*61*	*2*	*.240*	*.312*	*.364*

DAMON BUFORD / Baltimore Orioles / Outfielder $16

He has made some progress in the last couple of years, and, with a new manager coming in and Mike Devereaux probably leaving, he may be in line for a shot at some serious playing time. I remain skeptical about whether he will hit enough to be an everyday outfielder, but he should be a useful platoon player/pinch runner/defensive sub.

YEAR	TEAM/LEVEL	G	AB	R	H	2B	3B	HR	RBI	BB	SB	AVG	OBP	SLG
1993	Baltimore	53	79	18	18	5	0	2	9	9	2	.228	.315	.367
1994	Rochester	111	452	89	122	21	4	16	66	35	31	.270	.329	.440
1994	MLE	111	435	70	105	17	2	13	52	27	21	.241	.286	.379

JAY BUHNER / Seattle Mariners / Right Field $73

He was expected to be a free agent this winter (1994-95), and was looking forward to carrying his impressive resume into the market. He has power, is a fine outfielder, gets on base very well, and runs well (although he is the worst pecentage base stealer in the majors—6 for 26 in his career). In tremendous physical condition, and just entering his thirties.

YEAR	TEAM/LEVEL	G	AB	R	H	2B	3B	HR	RBI	BB	SB	AVG	OBP	SLG
1993	Seattle	158	563	91	153	28	3	27	98	100	2	.272	.379	.476
1994	Seattle	101	358	74	100	23	4	21	68	66	0	.279	.394	.542
1995	*Projected*	*155*	*557*	*89*	*145*	*26*	*3*	*28*	*91*	*93*	*2*	*.260*	*.366*	*.469*

JIM BULLINGER / Chicago Cubs / Relief Pitcher $22

A shortstop who converted to the mound and vaulted to the majors too quickly for his own good, Bullinger has made tremendous strides in the last two years, and might now be ready to contribute. He shuttled back and forth between the bullpen and a starting job last year, and pitched well in both roles. No longer afraid to throw his fastball over the plate.

YEAR	TEAM/LEVEL	G	IP	W-L	SAVES	HITS	SO	BB	ERA
1992	Chicago	39	85	2-8	7	72	36	54	4.66
1993	Chicago	15	17	1-0	1	18	10	9	4.32
1994	Chicago	33	100	6-2	2	87	72	34	3.60

DAVE BURBA / San Francisco Giants / Starter/Reliever $20

Pitching 20 fewer innings in 1994 than he had in '93, he nonetheless walked eight more men, a 56 percent increase in walks per inning. A right-handed pitcher, he had been vulnerable to left-handed batters before last year. In '94 he held lefties to a .178 batting average—but unfortunately, he accomplished this by simply walking all the tough left-handed hitters.

YEAR	TEAM/LEVEL	G	IP	W-L	SAVES	HITS	SO	BB	ERA
1992	San Francisco	23	71	2-7	0	80	47	31	4.97
1993	San Francisco	54	95	10-3	0	95	88	37	4.25
1994	San Francisco	57	74	3-6	0	59	84	45	4.38

JOHN BURKETT / San Francisco Giants / Starting Pitcher $35

When was the last time you saw a pitcher go from 22-7 to 6-8—and *improve* his ERA? His real abilities are about halfway in between there; he's a 14-11 type of pitcher.

With his exceptional control, an assortment of five pitches, and the ability to work 200 innings a year, he should be a valuable pitcher for several more seasons.

YEAR	TEAM/LEVEL	G	IP	W-L	PCT	HITS	SO	BB	ERA
1992	San Francisco	32	190	13-9	.591	194	107	45	3.84
1993	San Francisco	34	232	22-7	.759	224	145	40	3.65
1994	San Francisco	25	159	6-8	.429	176	85	36	3.62

ELLIS BURKS / Colorado Rockies / Center Field $33

The hottest hitter in baseball the first three weeks of 1994, Burks hurt his wrist while checking a swing (Hey, check out *that* swing), and was gone for *10 weeks*. I don't know how this is possible, but anyway, Burks is a fine player when he's healthy, which isn't too often . . . has lost his speed, and probably should move out of center field.

YEAR	TEAM/LEVEL	G	AB	R	H	2B	3B	HR	RBI	BB	SB	AVG	OBP	SLG
1993	Chicago	146	499	75	137	24	4	17	74	60	6	.275	.352	.441
1994	Colorado	42	149	33	48	8	3	13	24	16	3	.322	.388	.678
1995	*Projected*	*126*	*410*	*67*	*109*	*23*	*4*	*15*	*57*	*50*	*7*	*.268*	*.346*	*.451*

JEROMY BURNITZ / New York Mets / Right Field $23

If Burnitz gets ahead in the count, he's really a very good hitter—a .342 hitter in his career. *Behind* in the count, he's hopeless (.128). Hits right-handers OK, but can't handle a lefty. He's probably not going to hit .270 in the majors, so he's probably not going to be a regular, but should have a good career as a platoon player.

YEAR	TEAM/LEVEL	G	AB	R	H	2B	3B	HR	RBI	BB	SB	AVG	OBP	SLG
1993	New York	86	263	49	64	10	6	13	38	38	3	.243	.339	.475
1994	New York	45	143	26	34	4	0	3	15	23	1	.238	.347	.329
1995	*Projected*	*88*	*295*	*43*	*67*	*12*	*3*	*10*	*36*	*36*	*10*	*.227*	*.311*	*.390*

MIKE BUTCHER / California Angels / Relief Pitcher $12

Butcher was pitching well a year ago, but went out with bone chips in his elbow, and has been unable to get back where he was. This is not surprising, because Butcher a) doesn't throw strikes, and b) has no history of success to fall back on, even in the minor leagues. The surprise was that he did pitch well, for a few weeks there.

YEAR	TEAM/LEVEL	G	IP	W-L	SAVES	HITS	SO	BB	ERA
1992	California	19	28	2-2	0	29	24	13	3.25
1993	California	23	28	1-0	8	21	24	15	2.86
1994	California	33	30	2-1	1	31	19	23	6.67

BRETT BUTLER / Los Angeles Dodgers / Center Field $44

A union activist; unlikely to return quickly, even if holding out means he won't get 3000 hits. Butler will be 38 in June, but in tremendous shape and playing his best. His stolen base percentage in 1994 (77 percent) was a career best; his on-base percentage missed his career high by just two points. He'll play into the next century, if he wants to.

YEAR	TEAM/LEVEL	G	AB	R	H	2B	3B	HR	RBI	BB	SB	AVG	OBP	SLG
1993	Los Angeles	156	607	80	181	21	10	1	42	86	39	.298	.387	.371
1994	Los Angeles	111	417	79	131	13	9	8	33	68	27	.314	.411	.446
1995	*Projected*	*153*	*581*	*81*	*162*	*18*	*6*	*4*	*34*	*92*	*37*	*.278*	*.377*	*.351*

ROB BUTLER / Toronto Blue Jays / Outfielder $13

A Toronto native, Butler wears his socks up around his knees, like a '50s player, and isn't afraid to get his uniform dirty. His attempts to be a Brett Butler–type player have been undermined by his poor command of the strike zone, but he's working on that, and doing a little better. Left-handed hitter, runs well; future is probably as a fourth outfielder.

YEAR	TEAM/LEVEL	G	AB	R	H	2B	3B	HR	RBI	BB	SB	AVG	OBP	SLG
1993	Syracuse AAA	55	208	30	59	11	2	1	14	15	7	.284	.338	.370
1993	Toronto	17	48	8	13	4	0	0	2	7	2	.271	.375	.354
1994	Toronto	41	74	13	13	0	1	0	5	7	0	.176	.250	.203

FRANCISCO CABRERA / Orix Blue Wave / First Base/Catcher/Pinch Hitter $13

Frustrated by his inability to get playing time commensurate with his abilities, he spent the 1994 season in Japan. His plan was to get free of the system, then come back and find a job, but he didn't hit well in Japan. Whether he would come back to play in a scab league, I don't know. The big sucker can hit, I know that.

YEAR	TEAM/LEVEL	G	AB	R	H	2B	3B	HR	RBI	BB	SB	AVG	OBP	SLG
1992	Atlanta	12	10	2	3	0	0	2	3	1	0	.300	.364	.900
1993	Atlanta	70	83	8	20	3	0	4	11	8	0	.241	.308	.422
1994	Orix JPN	—	296	35	69	—	—	11	41	—	—	.233	—	—

GREG CADARET / Detroit Tigers / Left-handed Pitcher $17

Major league managers are always looking for a left-hander, and they're going to start looking somewhere else any minute now. Cadaret's ERAs over the last four years: 3.62, 4.25, 4.31, and 4.72. His walk rates have accelerated to 7.42 walks per nine innings. Even his address book shows you he's on the way out: New York, Cincinnati, KC, Detroit . . .

YEAR	TEAM/LEVEL	G	IP	W-L	SAVES	HITS	SO	BB	ERA
1992	New York	46	104	4-8	1	104	73	74	4.25
1993	Two Teams	47	48	3-2	1	54	25	30	4.31
1994	Detroit	38	40	1-1	2	41	29	33	4.72

KEN CAMINITI / Houston Astros / Third Base $44

Despite the strike he established a career high in home runs, 18, and missed his career high in RBI by only five. Normally plays very well in May and June, but tends to fade a little in the hot months. This is fairly normal for a player playing 95 percent of his team's games in a hot weather city . . . excellent defensive third baseman with powerful arm.

YEAR	TEAM/LEVEL	G	AB	R	H	2B	3B	HR	RBI	BB	SB	AVG	OBP	SLG
1993	Houston	143	543	75	142	31	0	13	75	49	8	.262	.321	.390
1994	Houston	111	406	63	115	28	2	18	75	43	4	.283	.352	.495
1995	*Projected*	*145*	*545*	*71*	*143*	*28*	*1*	*13*	*69*	*51*	*8*	*.262*	*.326*	*.399*

KEVIN CAMPBELL / Minnesota Twins / Relief Pitcher $17

A 30-year-old sinker/slider pitcher, was in the Dodger system for years, then failed three trials with Oakland, largely because his control, his strongest asset in the minors, deserted him when he came to The Show. He got his fourth chance last June with Minnesota, and this time remembered to pack his control. I like him, and Kelly is good with relievers.

YEAR	TEAM/LEVEL	G	IP	W-L	SAVES	HITS	SO	BB	ERA
1993	Tacoma AAA	40	56	3-5	12	42	46	19	2.75
1994	Salt Lake AAA	29	40	3-2	7	39	35	14	3.60
1994	Minnesota	14	25	1-0	0	20	15	5	2.92

TOM CANDIOTTI / Los Angeles Dodgers / Starting Pitcher $34

His contract ends with the 1995 season, so he should be motivated to perform well, if the world is normal. I wouldn't be afraid of him, as a free agent. He's 37 (38 in August), but in good shape, and he won't forget how to throw a knuckleball. I suspect he's got four-five more good years left, and will be around even beyond then.

YEAR	TEAM/LEVEL	G	IP	W-L	PCT	HITS	SO	BB	ERA
1992	Los Angeles	32	204	11-15	.423	177	152	63	3.00
1993	Los Angeles	33	214	8-10	.444	192	155	71	3.12
1994	Los Angeles	23	153	7-7	.500	149	102	54	4.12

JOSE CANSECO / Texas Rangers / Designated Hitter $64

Was headed toward his best season since 1991; it would have been the third time he's hit 40 homers, and the sixth time he's driven in 100. Needs at least three more big years to be a Hall of Fame candidate. Even if he stays healthy, that's a 40/60 shot at best, before time runs out on him . . . established a career high in GIDP (20).

YEAR	TEAM/LEVEL	G	AB	R	H	2B	3B	HR	RBI	BB	SB	AVG	OBP	SLG
1993	Texas	60	231	30	59	14	1	10	46	16	6	.255	.308	.455
1994	Texas	111	429	88	121	19	2	31	90	69	15	.282	.386	.552
1995	*Projected*	*135*	*513*	*91*	*133*	*24*	*1*	*30*	*96*	*71*	*12*	*.259*	*.349*	*.485*

MATTIAS CARILLO / Florida Marlins / Right Field $14

A left-handed line drive hitter who spent his twenties in the Mexican League, he had a couple of trials with major league systems in the '80s, but didn't stick. He wasn't impressive last year with Florida, either—a .250 hitter with no power who can't play the field—but might stick around if he can make the .250 into .275.

YEAR	TEAM/LEVEL	G	AB	R	H	2B	3B	HR	RBI	BB	SB	AVG	OBP	SLG
1991	Denver AAA	120	421	56	116	18	5	8	56	32	11	.276	.325	.399
1993	Florida	24	55	4	14	6	0	0	3	1	0	.255	.281	.364
1994	Florida	80	136	13	34	7	0	0	9	9	3	.250	.295	.301

CRIS CARPENTER / Texas Rangers / Relief Pitcher $19

Started and ended the year pitching well, but got pasted several times in June and early July. Throws his fastball in the strike zone and takes his chances . . . very effective against right-handed batters, but lefties hit .363 against him last year, which means you can't ever let him face a left-hander with the game on the line, which limits his value.

YEAR	TEAM/LEVEL	G	IP	W-L	SAVES	HITS	SO	BB	ERA
1992	St. Louis	73	88	5-4	1	69	46	27	2.97
1993	Two Teams	56	69	4-2	1	64	53	25	3.50
1994	Texas	47	59	2-5	2	69	39	20	5.03

CHUCK CARR / Florida Marlins / Outfielder $26

He didn't play quite as well last year as he did in '93, plus he faces serious job competition from Carl Everett, who had a good year at Edmonton. It's hard to play a leadoff man with a .305 on-base percentage. Still, as a .260 hitter, base stealer, and good defensive center fielder, we would have to expect him to stay in the lineup.

YEAR	TEAM/LEVEL	G	AB	R	H	2B	3B	HR	RBI	BB	SB	AVG	OBP	SLG
1993	Florida	142	551	75	147	19	2	4	41	49	58	.267	.327	.330
1994	Florida	106	433	61	114	19	2	2	30	22	32	.263	.305	.330
1995	*Projected*	*141*	*528*	*72*	*137*	*19*	*4*	*4*	*39*	*39*	*50*	*.259*	*.310*	*.333*

HECTOR CARRASCO / Cincinnati Reds / Right-handed Reliever $29

A hard thrower, he was dumped by the Mets, Astros, and Marlins, none of whom could get him above A Ball. The Reds skipped the intermediate stages, and brought him straight to the majors, where Jose Rijo took him under his wing, and he pitched fairly well, not as well as the ERA would suggest. You can't count on him, but he has upside potential.

YEAR	TEAM/LEVEL	G	IP	W-L	SAVES	HITS	SO	BB	ERA
1992	Asheville A	49	78	5-5	8	66	67	47	2.99
1993	Kane County A	28	149	6-12	0	153	127	76	4.11
1994	Cincinnati	45	65	5-5	6	56	41	30	2.24

MARK CARREON / San Francisco Giants / Outfielder $21

The Benny Ayala of the 1990s. It is a tough job, to bat 150 times a year and stay sharp, and we should respect the men who can do it. At any moment, there are fewer good pinch hitters than good players at any other position. In large part this is an allocation-of-resources decision, but it is also in part because it's a hard job.

YEAR	TEAM/LEVEL	G	AB	R	H	2B	3B	HR	RBI	BB	SB	AVG	OBP	SLG
1993	San Francisco	78	150	22	49	9	1	7	33	13	1	.327	.373	.540
1994	San Francisco	51	100	8	27	4	0	3	20	7	0	.270	.324	.400
1995	*Projected*	*74*	*165*	*18*	*43*	*7*	*0*	*6*	*25*	*12*	*1*	*.261*	*.311*	*.394*

ANDY CARTER / Philadelphia Phillies / Left-handed Pitcher $13

A big lefty, 6-5, 200, Carter has been in the minors since 1987. His best attribute has been an ability to stay healthy. He's lost more than he's won, but he got a chance with the big club after the Phillies pitching staff was killed in a plane crash, or contracted food poisoning, or whatever happened to them all. Grade D prospect.

YEAR	TEAM/LEVEL	G	IP	W-L	SAVES	HITS	SO	BB	ERA
1993	Scranton AAA	30	109	7-7	1	104	68	35	4.54
1994	Scranton AAA	25	31	1-0	2	22	27	13	2.61
1994	Philadelphia	20	34	0-2	0	34	18	12	4.46

JOE CARTER / Toronto Blue Jays / Right Field $70

Among the countless records which were spared by the strike: Carter was closing in on the season record for sacrifice flies. He had 13; the AL record is 17, by Roy White. Now has nine straight seasons of 98 or more RBI . . . with his 11 stolen bases in '94 (in 11 attempts) he now has 200 stolen bases in his career, to go with 302 home runs.

YEAR	TEAM/LEVEL	G	AB	R	H	2B	3B	HR	RBI	BB	SB	AVG	OBP	SLG
1993	Toronto	155	603	92	153	33	5	33	121	47	8	.254	.312	.489
1994	Toronto	111	435	70	118	25	2	27	103	33	11	.271	.317	.524
1995	*Projected*	*156*	*608*	*88*	*153*	*31*	*3*	*28*	*112*	*44*	*10*	*.252*	*.302*	*.451*

LARRY CASIAN / Cleveland Indians / Left-handed Relief Pitcher $12

Man, was that *ugly*. The American League hit .358 against Casian in 1994, with a .613 slugging percentage. That means, more or less, that the *typical* American League hitter was transformed into Frank Thomas. What would Frank Thomas hit against Larry Casian? I wouldn't bet on Frank Thomas to be average next year, and I wouldn't bet on Larry Casian to be average, either.

YEAR	TEAM/LEVEL	G	IP	W-L	SAVES	HITS	SO	BB	ERA
1992	Minnesota	6	7	1-0	0	7	2	1	2.70
1993	Minnesota	54	57	5-3	1	59	31	14	3.02
1994	Two Teams	40	49	1-5	1	73	20	16	7.35

VINNY CASTILLA / Colorado Rockies / Shortstop $25

In '93 he won the shortstop job, but couldn't hold it. The Rockies got Walt Weiss, and sent Castilla out. After hitting .244 at Colorado Springs, Vinny was recalled by the Rockies last June, and was very, very good the rest of the year. He'll never be Jay Bell, but he'll be around for several years, and will play well at times.

YEAR	TEAM/LEVEL	G	AB	R	H	2B	3B	HR	RBI	BB	SB	AVG	OBP	SLG
1993	Colorado	105	337	36	86	9	7	9	30	13	2	.255	.283	.404
1994	Colorado	52	130	16	43	11	1	3	18	7	2	.331	.357	.500
1994	*Projected*	*106*	*332*	*35*	*88*	*19*	*3*	*7*	*34*	*16*	*2*	*.265*	*.299*	*.404*

FRANK CASTILLO / Chicago Cubs / Starting Pitcher $23

Drifting for several years, he tore a tendon in his finger last April, and had to go back to Daytona Beach to start over. He made it to Iowa in late May, where he pitched extremely well, and back to Chicago in late July. I've always liked him and always recommended him, but up to now, I've always been wrong. I still like him.

YEAR	TEAM/LEVEL	G	IP	W-L	PCT	HITS	SO	BB	ERA
1992	Chicago	33	205	10-11	.476	179	135	63	3.46
1993	Chicago	29	141	5-8	.385	162	84	39	4.84
1994	Chicago	4	23	2-1	.667	25	19	5	4.30

JUAN CASTILLO / New York Mets / Right-handed Pitcher $13

A native Venezuelan, he had pitched winter ball until last winter (1993-94), when the Mets leaned on him to stop doing that. He agreed and got off to a hot start at Binghamton, so, although he's never been regarded as a terrific prospect, the Mets called him up for a week in late July. Right-hander, grade D prospect.

YEAR	TEAM/LEVEL	G	IP	W-L	PCT	HITS	SO	BB	ERA
1994	Binghamton AA	18	111	11-2	.846	98	80	44	2.59
1994	Norfolk AAA	6	29	1-5	.167	35	9	15	7.22
1994	New York	2	12	0-0	.000	17	1	5	6.94

TONY CASTILLO / Toronto Blue Jays / Left-handed Relief Pitcher $20

Did an excellent job as the Blue Jays' top left-handed reliever. Opposing hitters hit .287 against him with no one on, but .225 with men on base, .176 with runners in scoring position, and .135 (5-for-37) with men in scoring position and two out. He's been around for years, failed trials with several other teams. These guys are all year-to-year.

YEAR	TEAM/LEVEL	G	IP	W-L	SAVES	HITS	SO	BB	ERA
1992	Toledo AAA	12	45	2-3	2	48	24	14	3.63
1993	Toronto	51	51	3-2	0	44	28	22	3.38
1994	Toronto	41	68	5-2	1	66	43	28	2.51

ANDUJAR CEDENO   /   Houston Astros   /   Shortstop | $36 |

His batting averages over the last four years look just like Honus Wagner, only backward (.342, .371, .382, .362). His batting average always *ends* with a 3 . . . average/above average hitter for a shortstop, probably below average on defense. He fields about .950 and has below-average range. He's still young enough to move up a notch.

YEAR	TEAM/LEVEL	G	AB	R	H	2B	3B	HR	RBI	BB	SB	AVG	OBP	SLG
1993	Houston	149	505	69	143	24	4	11	56	48	9	.283	.346	.412
1994	Houston	98	342	38	90	26	0	9	49	29	1	.263	.334	.418
1994	*Projected*	*147*	*498*	*53*	*127*	*27*	*4*	*12*	*62*	*39*	*6*	*.255*	*.309*	*.398*

DOMINGO CEDENO   /   Toronto Blue Jays   /   Infielder | $14 |

It is a general rule that if you don't break the Mendoza line, they're going to look at somebody else. Cedeno, 26 years old, hit .235 in his minor league career, but has yet to hit with such authority in the major leagues. He is supposed to be a defensive wizard at short, but played mostly at second base last year, during Alomar's little injury.

YEAR	TEAM/LEVEL	G	AB	R	H	2B	3B	HR	RBI	BB	SB	AVG	OBP	SLG
1993	MLE	103	374	50	96	15	9	2	24	28	11	.257	.308	.361
1993	Toronto	15	46	5	8	0	0	0	7	1	1	.174	.188	.174
1994	Toronto	47	97	14	19	2	3	0	10	10	1	.196	.261	.278

ROGER CEDENO   /   Los Angeles Dodgers   /   Center Fielder | $22 |

A wonderful athlete—6-2, 190 pounds, fast, strong, and can throw. A native of Venezuela, he hit .321 last year at Albuquerque (Triple-A), and didn't turn 20 until August. Not a wild swinger; has career on-base percentage of .385 in the minors. His power has not yet developed, and he probably needs another year at Albuquerque, but he's unquestionably a **Grade A prospect.**

YEAR	TEAM/LEVEL	G	AB	R	H	2B	3B	HR	RBI	BB	SB	AVG	OBP	SLG
1993	San Antonio	122	465	70	134	13	8	4	30	45	28	.288	.352	.376
1994	Albuquer. AAA	104	383	84	123	18	5	4	43	51	30	.321	.395	.426
1994	MLE	104	352	50	92	11	1	2	29	30	18	.261	.319	.315

WES CHAMBERLAIN   /   Boston Red Sox   /   Right Field | $27 |

In 1993 he platooned with Jim Eisenreich, and was very effective. He tore the cartilage in his knee in spring training, returned in late April, but was traded to the Red Sox in May. He's a natural platoon player—kills left-handers (.304 over the last three years), but doesn't hit right-handers well (.243). Has improved dramatically as an outfielder.

YEAR	TEAM/LEVEL	G	AB	R	H	2B	3B	HR	RBI	BB	SB	AVG	OBP	SLG
1993	Philadelphia	96	284	34	80	20	2	12	45	17	2	.282	.320	.493
1994	Two Teams	75	233	20	61	14	1	6	26	15	0	.262	.306	.408
1995	*Projected*	*110*	*351*	*35*	*90*	*21*	*2*	*10*	*48*	*19*	*3*	*.258*	*.295*	*.413*

ARCHI CIANFROCCO / San Diego Padres / First/Third Base $18

He's one of my favorite players, but let's face it: he's kind of a fluke. The Expos pulled him out of Double-A, for reasons that no one has ever really understood. He doesn't do anything well enough that you can keep him around to do it. He's an awkward third baseman, a .230 hitter, doesn't walk, hits right-handed, and has just a little power.

YEAR	TEAM/LEVEL	G	AB	R	H	2B	3B	HR	RBI	BB	SB	AVG	OBP	SLG
1993	San Diego	96	296	30	72	11	2	12	48	17	2	.243	.287	.416
1994	San Diego	59	146	9	32	8	0	4	13	3	2	.219	.252	.356
1995	*Projected*	*82*	*233*	*23*	*57*	*11*	*1*	*6*	*30*	*11*	*2*	*.245*	*.279*	*.378*

FRANK CIMORELLI / St. Louis Cardinals / Right-handed Reliever $12

A 37th-round draft pick in 1989, was a starter in the minors until 1991, losing more than he won. He switched to the bullpen at Springfield in 1992, with better results, reaching the majors last July 21. Has been durable. Doesn't throw hard, has never been dominant. Control good, but not sensational. Grade D prospect; will have to battle for a job.

YEAR	TEAM/LEVEL	G	IP	W-L	SAVES	HITS	SO	BB	ERA
1993	AA & AAA	64	100	3-2	3	78	60	48	2.70
1994	Louisville AAA	48	61	5-3	4	64	46	20	4.01
1994	St. Louis	11	13	0-0	1	20	1	10	8.77

JEFF CIRILLO / Milwaukee Brewers / Third Base $34

I love this kid. A .280 hitter, and a Gold Glove candidate at third base. He was a DH/pitcher at Southern Cal, and wasn't taken in the 1990 draft, when he was a junior. He switched to infield as a senior, and was picked in the 11th round. He has hit .317 in the minors, making steady progress, but has received almost *no* press attention.

YEAR	TEAM/LEVEL	G	AB	R	H	2B	3B	HR	RBI	BB	SB	AVG	OBP	SLG
1993	MLE	125	442	66	126	25	2	9	58	39	2	.285	.343	.412
1994	Milwaukee	39	126	17	30	9	0	3	12	11	0	.238	.309	.381
1995	*Projected*	*121*	*394*	*59*	*109*	*25*	*1*	*10*	*54*	*37*	*2*	*.277*	*.339*	*.421*

DAVE CLARK / Pittsburgh Pirates / Outfielder/Pinch Hitter $25

One of the best platoon players in the majors. Jim Leyland deserves all the credit in the world for taking a player regarded by the rest of baseball as a failure, because he's not a great outfielder and not Frank Thomas, and assigning him a role which would enable him to help his team. He should be able to do that for several years.

YEAR	TEAM/LEVEL	G	AB	R	H	2B	3B	HR	RBI	BB	SB	AVG	OBP	SLG
1993	Pittsburgh	110	277	43	75	11	2	11	46	38	1	.271	.358	.444
1994	Pittsburgh	86	223	37	66	11	1	10	46	22	2	.296	.355	.489
1995	*Projected*	*111*	*319*	*48*	*86*	*15*	*1*	*12*	*55*	*39*	*3*	*.270*	*.349*	*.436*

MARK CLARK / Cleveland Indians / Starting Pitcher · $35

His season was ended by a line drive from Gary Redus, July 20, which broke his wrist. He was on the fringes of the Cy Young derby up to then, and may well be again. Throws a good sinking fastball, mixes it up with three other pitches, and works ahead in the count. With a good team behind him, which he has, he can win 15 to 20.

YEAR	TEAM/LEVEL	G	IP	W-L	PCT	HITS	SO	BB	ERA
1992	St. Louis	20	113	3-10	.231	117	44	36	4.45
1993	Cleveland	26	109	7-5	.583	119	57	25	4.28
1994	Cleveland	20	127	11-3	.786	133	60	40	3.82

PHIL CLARK / San Diego Padres / Utility Player · $21

A talented right-handed hitter who doesn't have a defensive position, he started the season slowly with the bat, and his playing time all but disappeared. He was hitting .186 through the end of June, rallied late. He's a good hitter, like Dave Clark (last page) and sooner or later somebody is going to find a way to use him successfully.

YEAR	TEAM/LEVEL	G	AB	R	H	2B	3B	HR	RBI	BB	SB	AVG	OBP	SLG
1993	Detroit	23	54	3	22	4	0	1	5	6	1	.407	.467	.537
1993	San Diego	102	240	33	75	17	0	9	33	8	2	.313	.345	.496
1994	San Diego	61	149	14	32	6	0	5	20	5	1	.215	.250	.356

WILL CLARK / Texas Rangers / First Base · $53

The four players whose Hall of Fame chances were most damaged by the strike are Will Clark, Jimmy Key, David Cone, and Gregg Jefferies. Those four players a) figure to have, or may have, *marginal* Hall of Fame credentials, and b) were having perhaps the best seasons of their careers. Otherwise, the significance of Clark's season is that it reverses a pattern of decline.

YEAR	TEAM/LEVEL	G	AB	R	H	2B	3B	HR	RBI	BB	SB	AVG	OBP	SLG
1993	San Francisco	132	491	82	139	27	2	14	73	63	2	.283	.367	.432
1994	Texas	110	389	73	128	24	2	13	80	71	5	.329	.431	.501
1995	*Projected*	*146*	*529*	*84*	*157*	*31*	*3*	*19*	*85*	*79*	*6*	*.297*	*.388*	*.474*

ROYCE CLAYTON / San Francisco Giants / Shortstop · $32

As his 1993 season was *less* impressive under scrutiny than it was at a glance, his 1994 season was *more* impressive. A poor percentage base stealer before 1994, he went 23-for-26 last year. He improved his fielding percentage and increased his walk rate. Although he bats right, a .176 batting average against left-handed pitching undermined his average.

YEAR	TEAM/LEVEL	G	AB	R	H	2B	3B	HR	RBI	BB	SB	AVG	OBP	SLG
1993	San Francisco	153	549	54	155	21	5	6	70	38	11	.282	.331	.372
1994	San Francisco	108	385	38	91	14	6	3	30	30	23	.236	.295	.327
1995	*Projected*	*153*	*548*	*56*	*138*	*20*	*6*	*6*	*53*	*42*	*18*	*.252*	*.305*	*.343*

ROGER CLEMENS / Boston Red Sox / Starting Pitcher $75

He didn't get credit for pitching great, because a) the Red Sox didn't give him the won-lost record he deserved, and b) people still have impossible expectations for him. He pitched great. The battle for the distinction of being the greatest pitcher of the generation, which used to be Clemens, Gooden, and Saberhagen, is now just pretty much Roger Clemens.

YEAR	TEAM/LEVEL	G	IP	W-L	PCT	HITS	SO	BB	ERA
1992	Boston	32	247	18-11	.621	203	208	62	2.41
1993	Boston	29	192	11-14	.440	175	160	67	4.46
1994	Boston	24	171	9-7	.563	124	168	71	2.85

GREG COLBRUNN / Florida Marlins / First Base $26

The failure of Orestes Destrade opened up a job, and Colbrunn was among those who attempted to move into the breach. He played well and hit well, despite missing two weeks with a pulled muscle, and was more or less in possession of the job at season's end. He's 25, still the age of a rookie, and may hold the job for a good number of years.

YEAR	TEAM/LEVEL	G	AB	R	H	2B	3B	HR	RBI	BB	SB	AVG	OBP	SLG
1993	Montreal	70	153	15	39	9	0	4	23	6	4	.255	.282	.392
1994	Florida	47	155	17	47	10	0	6	31	9	1	.303	.345	.484
1995	*Projected*	*128*	*419*	*43*	*117*	*25*	*0*	*12*	*62*	*16*	*4*	*.279*	*.306*	*.425*

ALEX COLE / Minnesota Twins / Center Field $24

He was released a year ago by Colorado. The Twins signed him to a minor league contract and, when Shane Mack couldn't open in center field, gave him most of that job, sitting him down against lefties. This was good judgment as, over a three-year period, he has a 95-point platoon differential (.281 to .186). Poor center fielder, but outstanding leadoff man.

YEAR	TEAM/LEVEL	G	AB	R	H	2B	3B	HR	RBI	BB	SB	AVG	OBP	SLG
1993	Colorado	126	348	50	89	9	4	0	24	43	30	.256	.339	.305
1994	Minnesota	105	345	68	102	15	5	4	23	44	29	.296	.375	.403
1995	*Projected*	*103*	*257*	*42*	*69*	*7*	*3*	*1*	*18*	*30*	*21*	*.268*	*.345*	*.331*

VINCE COLEMAN / Kansas City Royals / Left Field $25

Had a one-year contract with the Royals, and may or may not be invited to return. The Royals are probably going to play Michael Tucker in left field, and would probably prefer some other anonymous kid to Coleman. Also, the Royals are taking out the turf. Coleman hits far better on turf than on grass. . . . Will probably be looking for work.

YEAR	TEAM/LEVEL	G	AB	R	H	2B	3B	HR	RBI	BB	SB	AVG	OBP	SLG
1993	New York (N)	92	373	64	104	14	8	2	25	21	38	.279	.316	.375
1994	Kansas City	104	438	61	105	14	12	2	33	29	50	.240	.285	.340
1995	*Projected*	*104*	*374*	*54*	*94*	*11*	*4*	*2*	*25*	*28*	*40*	*.251*	*.303*	*.318*

DARNELL COLES / Toronto Blue Jays / Outfielder/Third Baseman | $15

Hit three homers at Minnesota on July 5—among the most improbable three-homer games ever. He filled in for Toronto at four positions, left field being the preferred spot (24 games, 21 starts). He didn't hit much and the team didn't play well, so he's in the free agent market as of this writing. I'd guess he'll catch on somewhere.

YEAR	TEAM/LEVEL	G	AB	R	H	2B	3B	HR	RBI	BB	SB	AVG	OBP	SLG
1992	Cincinnati	55	141	16	44	11	2	3	18	3	1	.312	.322	.482
1993	Toronto	64	194	26	49	9	1	4	26	16	1	.253	.319	.371
1994	Toronto	48	143	15	30	6	1	4	15	10	0	.210	.263	.350

DAVID CONE / Kansas City Royals / Starting Pitcher | $78

He made a decision last winter (1993-94) to get batters out with fewer pitches, conserving his arm. This worked out very well. Rather than trying to make unhittable pitches, he poured the first pitch over, and worked ahead in the count 58 percent of the time (50 percent in previous years) . . . see comment on Will Clark. He deserved the Cy Young Award, which he won.

YEAR	TEAM/LEVEL	G	IP	W-L	PCT	HITS	SO	BB	ERA
1992	Two Teams	35	250	17-10	.630	201	261	111	2.81
1993	Kansas City	34	254	11-14	.440	205	191	114	3.33
1994	Kansas City	23	172	16-5	.762	130	132	54	2.94

JEFF CONINE / Florida Marlins / Outfielder/First Base | $57

Well, I can certainly see why the Royals wouldn't want *him*. I mean, who needs a .300 hitter with power? The Royals, who also gave up the best player taken in the last expansion draft (Ruppert Jones), protected Bill Sampen and David Howard, but let Conine go . . . hit .283 in Miami, .357 on the road. . . . Has played in every game in Marlins history.

YEAR	TEAM/LEVEL	G	AB	R	H	2B	3B	HR	RBI	BB	SB	AVG	OBP	SLG
1993	Florida	162	595	75	174	24	3	12	79	52	2	.292	.351	.403
1994	Florida	115	451	60	144	27	6	18	82	40	1	.319	.373	.525
1995	*Projected*	*162*	*600*	*74*	*172*	*32*	*4*	*18*	*86*	*54*	*3*	*.287*	*.346*	*.443*

JIM CONVERSE / Seattle Mariners / Starting Pitcher | $12

He throws 90, keeps the ball down, and has thrown strikes in the minor leagues. It would be the understatement of the book to say that this has not translated, so far, into major league success. In two trials, major league hitters have hit .337 against him, with walks lifting the on-base percentage to .439 . . . probably several years away from major league success.

YEAR	TEAM/LEVEL	G	IP	W-L	PCT	HITS	SO	BB	ERA
1993	Seattle	4	20	1-3	.250	23	10	14	5.31
1994	Calgary AAA	14	74	5-3	.625	105	53	21	5.11
1994	Seattle	13	49	0-5	.000	73	39	40	8.69

DENNIS COOK / Cleveland Indians / Relief Pitcher | $18

A big left-hander who has also worked for San Francisco, Philadelphia, Los Angeles, and Chicago. He's a little odd . . . he works *up* in the strike zone without outstanding stuff, but gets by with timing and location.

Tricky move to first; impossible to run on, but sometimes balks. Excellent hitter. Has had some success as a starter, but that's probably in the past.

YEAR	TEAM/LEVEL	G	IP	W-L	PCT	HITS	SO	BB	ERA
1992	Cleveland	32	158	5-7	.417	156	96	50	3.82
1993	Cleveland	25	54	5-5	.500	62	34	16	5.67
1994	Chicago	38	33	3-1	.750	29	26	14	3.55

STEVE COOKE / Pittsburgh Pirates / Starting Pitcher | $31

He didn't pitch as bad as his 4-11 record, but he didn't pitch as well as he's capable of pitching. He gave up 21 homers in 134 innings. His problem in a nutshell: His

first pitch wasn't effective. He gave up seven first-pitch homers, and despite his good control record, he worked behind in the count more than half the time.

YEAR	TEAM/LEVEL	G	IP	W-L	PCT	HITS	SO	BB	ERA
1992	Pittsburgh	11	23	2-0	1.000	22	10	4	3.52
1993	Pittsburgh	32	211	10-10	.500	207	132	59	3.89
1994	Pittsburgh	25	134	4-11	.267	157	74	46	5.02

SCOTT COOPER / Boston Red Sox / Third Base | $34

His season ended a few days early due to surgery on his right shoulder. If it affects his arm, that's serious, because that's his best asset . . . comparable to Caminiti, except he bats left—a .280 hitter with some power, a

cannon arm. Is very vulnerable to left-handed pitchers (.194 last year, .318 vs. right-handers). Hard-nosed player, like his ex-manager.

YEAR	TEAM/LEVEL	G	AB	R	H	2B	3B	HR	RBI	BB	SB	AVG	OBP	SLG
1993	Boston	156	526	67	147	29	3	9	63	58	5	.279	.355	.397
1994	Boston	104	369	49	104	16	4	13	53	30	0	.282	.333	.453
1995	*Projected*	*146*	*501*	*61*	*139*	*26*	*2*	*12*	*60*	*53*	*3*	*.277*	*.347*	*.409*

JOEY CORA / Chicago White Sox / Second Base | $36

His '94 season was interrupted by a strained rib cage, but he played as well as he had in 1993, which is very well. Runs well, quick at second, has .350 on-base percentage, exceptional bunter, switch hitter. He's not

Ryne Sandberg, but he may be the best second baseman the White Sox have had since Nellie Fox. Will face job competition from Ray Durham.

YEAR	TEAM/LEVEL	G	AB	R	H	2B	3B	HR	RBI	BB	SB	AVG	OBP	SLG
1992	Chicago	68	122	27	30	7	1	0	9	22	10	.246	.371	.320
1993	Chicago	153	579	95	155	15	13	2	51	67	20	.268	.351	.349
1994	Chicago	90	312	55	86	13	4	2	30	38	8	.276	.353	.362

WILFREDO CORDERO / Montreal Expos / Shortstop $70

By the end of this season, he might be universally recognized as the best shortstop in baseball. He was probably the best last year, but you can't really proclaim him that based on one good year, particularly when it's not even a full year. But he's very young, and *very* good . . . with any luck, there's an MVP Award in his future.

YEAR	TEAM/LEVEL	G	AB	R	H	2B	3B	HR	RBI	BB	SB	AVG	OBP	SLG
1993	Montreal	138	475	56	118	32	2	10	58	34	12	.248	.308	.387
1994	Montreal	110	415	65	122	30	3	15	63	41	16	.294	.363	.489
1995	*Projected*	*154*	*597*	*82*	*168*	*33*	*3*	*16*	*77*	*50*	*17*	*.281*	*.337*	*.427*

RHEAL CORMIER / St. Louis Cardinals / Starting Pitcher $22

Zane Smith, Jr. As I wrote about him last year, a ground-ball pitcher with a 3-1 strikeout/walk ratio has *got* to win more than he loses. If he doesn't get beat by walks, and he doesn't get beat by homers, there's no way you're going to beat him with singles. But he's got to stop having a major injury every 45 innings.

YEAR	TEAM/LEVEL	G	IP	W-L	PCT	HITS	SO	BB	ERA
1992	St. Louis	31	186	10-10	.500	194	117	33	3.68
1993	St. Louis	38	145	7-6	.538	163	75	27	4.33
1994	St. Louis	7	40	3-2	.600	40	26	7	5.45

BRAD CORNETT / Toronto Blue Jays / Right-handed Pitcher $13

Another example of the Blue Jays' puzzling incompetence with young pitchers. Cornett pitched well at Hagerstown (A Ball) in 1993, so the Blue Jays just decided to skip the rest of his education, and put him to work in the factory. He was awful—just like the other half-dozen pitchers the Blue Jays have done this with, like Willie Blair and Denis Boucher.

YEAR	TEAM/LEVEL	G	IP	W-L	PCT	HITS	SO	BB	ERA
1993	Hagerstown A	31	172	10-8	.556	164	161	31	2.40
1994	AA and AAA	10	56	3-5	.375	52	38	15	2.08
1994	Toronto	9	31	1-3	.250	40	22	11	6.68

ROD CORREIA / California Angels / Infielder $15

He was sent out last spring, which was somewhat surprising in view of his reasonably good performance over the second half of the '93 season. He is 27, and not to be confused with a future All-Star, but has hit around .270 in the minors, runs well, and can play second base or shortstop passably enough.

YEAR	TEAM/LEVEL	G	AB	R	H	2B	3B	HR	RBI	BB	SB	AVG	OBP	SLG
1992	MLE	123	445	43	103	16	0	3	33	13	10	.231	.253	.288
1993	California	64	128	12	34	5	0	0	9	6	2	.266	.319	.305
1994	MLE	106	359	40	86	9	1	4	36	18	5	.240	.276	.304

DANNY COX / Toronto Blue Jays / Relief Pitcher $25

Had shoulder surgery in the off-season (before 1994), and was building himself back up until early July. His performance in the last month was quite impressive, as he limited hitters to a .113 batting average, and he is counted on to help restore the Toronto bullpen in '95. Injuries will plague him the rest of his career.

YEAR	TEAM/LEVEL	G	IP	W-L	SAVES	HITS	SO	BB	ERA
1992	Two Teams	25	63	5-3	3	66	48	27	4.60
1993	Toronto	44	84	7-6	2	73	84	29	3.12
1994	Toronto	10	19	1-1	3	7	14	7	1.45

CHUCK CRIM / Chicago Cubs / Relief Pitcher $15

Released by the Angels in May 1993, he signed a minor league contract with the Cubs, and was back in majors by April 12. He pitched very well through his first 21 outings, posting a 1.42 ERA, but was hit hard by Montreal on June 2, and was never really effective the rest of the year. Limited future; might get another chance.

YEAR	TEAM/LEVEL	G	IP	W-L	SAVES	HITS	SO	BB	ERA
1992	California	57	87	7-6	1	100	30	29	5.17
1993	California	11	15	2-2	0	17	10	5	5.87
1994	Chicago	49	64	5-4	2	69	43	24	4.48

TRIPP CROMER / St. Louis Cardinals / Shortstop $13

He's not a bad option, as the Cardinals wonder who will play shortstop after Ozzie. He's always been regarded as a defensive standout who couldn't hit, but he has hit much better the last two years at Louisville and, at 27, probably could play shortstop every day without hurting the team. No star potential; most likely will be a bench player.

YEAR	TEAM/LEVEL	G	AB	R	H	2B	3B	HR	RBI	BB	SB	AVG	OBP	SLG
1993	MLE	86	297	30	73	7	2	8	25	11	0	.246	.273	.364
1994	Louisville AAA	124	419	53	115	23	9	9	50	33	5	.274	.330	.437
1994	MLE	124	406	44	102	21	6	7	41	27	3	.251	.298	.384

FAUSTO CRUZ / Oakland Athletics / Shortstop $14

A 23-year-old Dominican, looks like Alvaro Espinoza. He hit .319 at Reno in '92, .335 at Huntsville in '93, .321 at Tacoma last year, and thus earned a major league look although the A's already have a quality shortstop. He is probably *not* that extraordinary young talent who can take a job away from somebody like Bordick, but he looks like he can play.

YEAR	TEAM/LEVEL	G	AB	R	H	2B	3B	HR	RBI	BB	SB	AVG	OBP	SLG
1993	MLE	84	307	45	84	13	1	2	29	16	3	.274	.310	.342
1994	MLE	65	205	20	57	15	0	0	13	13	1	.278	.321	.351
1994	Oakland	17	28	2	3	0	0	0	0	4	0	.107	.219	.107

JOHN CUMMINGS / Seattle Mariners / Starting Pitcher $12

A 6-foot-3 left-hander, reportedly a direct descendant of Candy Cummings, who invented the curveball. He went 16-6 at Peninsula in 1992, on the basis of which he has started the last two seasons in the major leagues.

With no history of success to fall back on, with no organization surrounding him to bring him along, he faces an uphill battle.

YEAR	TEAM/LEVEL	G	IP	W-L	PCT	HITS	SO	BB	ERA
1993	Calgary AAA	11	65	3-4	.429	69	42	21	4.13
1993	Seattle	10	46	0-6	.000	59	19	16	6.02
1994	Seattle	17	64	2-4	.333	66	33	37	5.63

MIDRE CUMMINGS / Pittsburgh Pirates / Outfielder $22

His minor league apprenticeship is probably over; it is a good guess that he is in the majors to stay, if he starts hitting just a little. He's a left-handed hitter, runs well, throws well, and has hit .305 in 438 minor league games. He is only 23. But with limited power and few walks, he will have to develop to truly help his team.

YEAR	TEAM/LEVEL	G	AB	R	H	2B	3B	HR	RBI	BB	SB	AVG	OBP	SLG
1993	MLE	123	448	53	113	25	1	10	37	25	6	.252	.292	.379
1994	Pittsburgh	24	86	11	21	4	0	1	12	4	0	.244	.283	.326
1995	*Projected*	*127*	*423*	*53*	*117*	*24*	*2*	*9*	*49*	*26*	*5*	*.277*	*.318*	*.407*

CHAD CURTIS / California Angels / Center Field $32

Has given California three years of solid play, and will give them (or somebody) many more. He hasn't, to this point, gotten any better. He has no natural offensive role, being neither a leadoff nor a middle-of-the-order type. But Curtis has played better for the Angels than their previous center fielder, who was Devon White. His best years may be just ahead.

YEAR	TEAM/LEVEL	G	AB	R	H	2B	3B	HR	RBI	BB	SB	AVG	OBP	SLG
1993	California	152	583	94	166	25	3	6	59	70	48	.285	.361	.369
1994	California	114	453	67	116	23	4	11	50	37	25	.256	.317	.397
1995	*Projected*	*153*	*550*	*84*	*150*	*25*	*4*	*10*	*61*	*61*	*45*	*.273*	*.345*	*.387*

MILT CUYLER / Detroit Tigers / Center Field $23

After two years of Cuyler's struggles the Tigers began to look at other center fielders (Davis, Bautista, Felix). Cuyler hit a little better off the bench, despite a trip to the DL with a dislocated finger, and the other guys didn't take control, so Sparky gave the center field job back to Cuyler, about 10 days before the strike. He needs to start hitting.

YEAR	TEAM/LEVEL	G	AB	R	H	2B	3B	HR	RBI	BB	SB	AVG	OBP	SLG
1993	Detroit	82	249	46	53	11	7	0	19	19	13	.213	.276	.313
1994	Detroit	48	116	20	28	3	1	1	11	13	5	.241	.318	.310
1995	*Projected*	*106*	*321*	*50*	*82*	*10*	*5*	*2*	*31*	*22*	*14*	*.255*	*.303*	*.338*

JIM CZAJKOWSKI / Colorado Rockies / Relief Pitcher $14

A 31-year-old right-hander who has been in numerous other organizations, but got his first major league innings with Colorado just before the strike. Years ago he was seen as a potential relief ace (he has 99 career saves in the minors), but now he just throws strikes and tries to survive. If he throws strikes, he'll survive.

YEAR	TEAM/LEVEL	G	IP	W-L	SAVES	HITS	SO	BB	ERA
1993	Iowa AAA	42	70	7-5	0	64	43	32	3.84
1994	Colo. Sp. AAA	44	63	5-4	8	53	36	16	2.71
1994	Colorado	5	9	0-0	0	9	2	6	4.15

OMAR DAAL / Los Angeles Dodgers / Left-handed Relief Pitcher $19

As the ratios of games to innings continue to flatten out, Daal may become the first pitcher in history to pitch 100 games in a season, but 50 innings. In his two-year "career" he has held left-handed hitters to a .218 average, but has been hit hard by right-handers (.333), so he's got to get in and out quickly. Native Venezuelan.

YEAR	TEAM/LEVEL	G	IP	W-L	SAVES	HITS	SO	BB	ERA
1992	San Antonio AA	35	57	2-6	5	60	52	33	5.02
1993	Los Angeles	47	35	2-3	0	36	19	21	5.09
1994	Los Angeles	24	14	0-0	0	12	9	5	3.29

MARK DALESANDRO / California Angels / Catcher $13

An 18th-round 1990 draft from the University of Illinois, he played the outfield, first base, and third before settling in at catcher in 1993. Right-handed line drive hitter, not much power, slow, doesn't walk or strike out much. Raw behind the plate, but has a strong arm. Grade D prospect; will not be a regular unless he can hit .280.

YEAR	TEAM/LEVEL	G	AB	R	H	2B	3B	HR	RBI	BB	SB	AVG	OBP	SLG
1993	MLE	83	326	37	85	13	0	2	39	9	0	.261	.281	.319
1994	Vancouver	51	199	29	63	9	1	1	31	7	1	.317	.340	.387
1994	California	19	25	5	5	1	0	1	2	2	0	.200	.259	.360

RON DARLING / Oakland Athletics / Starting Pitcher $28

He was, believe it or not, the big winner on the A's staff; he also led the team in innings and ERA. A hot July (5-0, 2.95 ERA) redeemed an otherwise ugly record, but he's always been streaky. He has a contract for 1995 and the A's need pitching, so I suppose he should be in the rotation again this year.

YEAR	TEAM/LEVEL	G	IP	W-L	PCT	HITS	SO	BB	ERA
1992	Oakland	33	206	15-10	.600	198	99	72	3.66
1993	Oakland	31	178	5-9	.357	198	95	72	5.16
1994	Oakland	25	160	10-11	.476	162	108	59	4.50

DANNY DARWIN / Boston Red Sox / Starting Pitcher | $19

The Red Sox scored eight-plus runs a game for him, which gave him a winning record despite allowing a .317 batting average. He was 7-2 on May 21, including some good games and some lucky ones, but then his back began to bother him, and ended his season in early June. His contract is up; will have offers if he's healthy.

YEAR	TEAM/LEVEL	G	IP	W-L	PCT	HITS	SO	BB	ERA
1992	Boston	51	161	9-9	.500	159	124	53	3.96
1993	Boston	34	229	15-11	.577	196	130	49	3.26
1994	Boston	13	76	7-5	.583	101	54	24	6.30

DARREN DAULTON / Philadelphia Phillies / Catcher | $52

A foul tip slammed into his shoulder and broke his collarbone (June 28), and he missed the rest of the season. Up to that point, he was an MVP candidate, as he had been the previous two years. He is 34, will be 35 in July (remember all those years before he got good), but he's a conditioning fanatic, and should continue to thrive.

YEAR	TEAM/LEVEL	G	AB	R	H	2B	3B	HR	RBI	BB	SB	AVG	OBP	SLG
1992	Philadelphia	145	485	80	131	32	5	27	109	88	11	.270	.385	.524
1993	Philadelphia	147	510	90	131	35	4	24	105	117	5	.257	.392	.482
1994	Philadelphia	69	257	43	77	17	1	15	56	33	4	.300	.380	.549

CHILI DAVIS / California Angels / Designated Hitter | $35

He's had two careers, really, one before he lost his speed, one after. The "after" is more impressive. He has 250 home runs now, and his first hit of 1995 will be his 1800th. These aren't Hall of Fame numbers, but they're in the next group down, the guys you don't really appreciate until they're gone, because you thought they might have been better.

YEAR	TEAM/LEVEL	G	AB	R	H	2B	3B	HR	RBI	BB	SB	AVG	OBP	SLG
1993	California	153	573	74	139	32	0	27	112	71	4	.243	.327	.440
1994	California	108	392	72	122	18	1	26	84	69	3	.311	.410	.561
1995	*Projected*	*142*	*504*	*70*	*128*	*24*	*1*	*18*	*83*	*77*	*3*	*.254*	*.353*	*.413*

ERIC DAVIS / Detroit Tigers / Center Field | $29

Remember all the pundits who wrote last spring that Sparky would be able to keep Davis in the lineup? Doesn't it occur to anybody but me that this is insulting to Eric? It assumes that his injuries aren't *real*; he only needs to be "handled" better. Of course, his injuries are *real*, and they won't go away because his manager smiles at him.

YEAR	TEAM/LEVEL	G	AB	R	H	2B	3B	HR	RBI	BB	SB	AVG	OBP	SLG
1993	Two Teams	131	451	71	107	18	1	20	68	55	35	.237	.319	.415
1994	Detroit	37	120	19	22	4	0	3	13	18	5	.183	.290	.292
1995	*Projected*	*81*	*273*	*37*	*65*	*10*	*1*	*11*	*40*	*36*	*19*	*.238*	*.327*	*.403*

RUSS DAVIS / New York Yankees / Third Base $25

He has paid his dues, with interest. Davis, who by the most conservative estimate is better than 30 percent of the third basemen in the majors, had the misfortune of being drafted by the Yankees, who had no intention of letting him play. He's played 805 minor league games, but should be in the majors this year. Defense OK, power will get him a job.

YEAR	TEAM/LEVEL	G	AB	R	H	2B	3B	HR	RBI	BB	SB	AVG	OBP	SLG
1992	MLE	132	473	63	122	20	2	17	58	34	2	.258	.308	.416
1993	MLE	113	410	52	94	21	0	21	68	33	0	.229	.287	.434
1994	MLE	117	404	66	103	27	1	21	60	53	2	.255	.341	.483

STORM DAVIS / Detroit Tigers / Relief Pitcher $19

There are numerous puzzles in his statistical profile, mostly related to his walk rate. He limited *left*-handers to a .116 batting average (8-69), but walked 20 percent of the left-handed hitters that he faced. He worked *ahead* of the majority of hitters (56 percent), but issued 34 walks in 48 innings . . . 3.56 ERA will certainly keep him in the league.

YEAR	TEAM/LEVEL	G	IP	W-L	SAVES	HITS	SO	BB	ERA
1992	Baltimore	48	89	7-3	4	79	53	36	3.43
1993	Two Teams	43	98	2-8	4	93	73	48	5.05
1994	Detroit	35	48	2-4	0	36	38	34	3.56

TIM DAVIS / Seattle Mariners / Left-handed Reliever $21

Short lefty, doesn't throw hard. The Mariners' sixth-round pick in the 1992 draft, from Florida State. The Mariners have rushed several minor league pitchers to the majors since Piniella took over the club, and Davis has been the only one to handle it so far, which speaks well of him (if not the Mariners). There is little evidence that he *can't* pitch.

YEAR	TEAM/LEVEL	G	IP	W-L	SAVES	HITS	SO	BB	ERA
1992	Florida St. Un.	25	114	9-4	9	79	142	40	2.60
1993	Two Teams A	34	108	13-2	9	68	145	42	1.83
1994	Seattle	42	49	2-2	2	57	28	25	4.01

ANDRE DAWSON / Boston Red Sox / Designated Hitter/Right Field $20

His knee problems have made it almost impossible to continue; at season's end he was still vacillating about whether to retire. Playing 75 games last year, he wasn't half bad; certainly he was more effective than the other players the Red Sox had at those positions. If he plays this year, it will be his last one—and he's not going to play 140 games.

YEAR	TEAM/LEVEL	G	AB	R	H	2B	3B	HR	RBI	BB	SB	AVG	OBP	SLG
1992	Chicago	143	542	60	150	27	2	22	90	30	6	.277	.316	.456
1993	Boston	121	461	44	126	29	1	13	67	17	2	.273	.313	.425
1994	Boston	75	292	34	70	18	0	16	48	9	2	.240	.271	.466

STEVE DECKER / Florida Marlins / Catcher $22

In 1993 he opened the season 0-for-15, and was unable to report to the minors because of a back injury. His career appeared to be over. Last year, he not only reported to Edmonton, he went Ape Woolies with the bat, hitting .390. Whether he'll be able to carry through in the majors, I don't know—but he has major league ability.

YEAR	TEAM/LEVEL	G	AB	R	H	2B	3B	HR	RBI	BB	SB	AVG	OBP	SLG
1993	Florida	8	15	0	0	0	0	0	1	3	0	.000	.158	.000
1994	Edmonton	73	259	38	101	23	0	11	48	27	0	.390	.447	.606
1994	MLE	73	238	24	80	18	0	7	31	18	0	.336	.383	.500

JOSE DEJESUS / Kansas City Royals / Starting Pitcher $14

He was working relief at Omaha when the Royals decided they needed another arm at the major league level. They gave him a couple of quick starts and called him up. He didn't pitch very well, but the Royals at the time were winning every game . . . tremendous movement on his fastball will continue to make it difficult for him to hit the strike zone.

YEAR	TEAM/LEVEL	G	IP	W-L	PCT	HITS	SO	BB	ERA
1993	Clearwater A	11	55	3-6	.333	65	33	19	4.07
1994	Omaha AAA	30	58	4-4	.500	51	54	37	4.03
1994	Kansas City	5	27	3-1	.750	27	12	13	4.73

JOSE DELEON / Chicago White Sox / Long Reliever/Spot Starter $22

Has moved to the anonymity of middle relief, and has had two consecutive good seasons. He's tough to hit, limiting batters to a .200 average last year, not too much better in '93. He still walks too many, but gives his team a couple of good innings when the starter leaves early, and forces the opposition to get the left-handed hitters in the game.

YEAR	TEAM/LEVEL	G	IP	W-L	PCT	HITS	SO	BB	ERA
1992	Two Teams	32	117	2-8	.200	111	79	48	4.37
1993	Two Teams	35	57	3-0	1.000	44	40	30	2.98
1994	Chicago	42	67	3-2	.600	48	67	31	3.36

CARLOS DELGADO / Toronto Blue Jays / Catcher $36

If he'd been a veteran, no one would have thought anything of his slump. His average went down to .215; it would have come back. If the Blue Jays had been winning, no one would have paid any attention to him . . . he'll be back, and he'll be great. I have *no* doubt that Delgado is going to be an MVP candidate in the year 2000.

YEAR	TEAM/LEVEL	G	AB	R	H	2B	3B	HR	RBI	BB	SB	AVG	OBP	SLG
1994	MLE	85	300	45	91	10	0	18	50	36	0	.303	.378	.517
1994	Toronto	43	130	17	28	2	0	9	24	25	1	.215	.352	.438
1995	*Projected*	*137*	*473*	*75*	*137*	*20*	*0*	*29*	*84*	*73*	*3*	*.290*	*.385*	*.516*

RICH DELUCIA / Cincinnati Reds / Reliever/Starter $15

What I said last year is that he "will eventually have some excellent seasons in middle relief." This, now, is obviously where we are headed. Healthy for the first time since 1991, he struck out 52 men in 43 innings at Indianapolis, plus 15 in 11 innings in the majors. He has no fastball, so will always have difficultly making a team believe in him.

YEAR	TEAM/LEVEL	G	IP	W-L	SAVES	HITS	SO	BB	ERA
1993	Seattle	30	43	3-6	0	46	48	23	4.64
1994	Indianapolis AAA	36	43	5-1	19	22	54	24	2.30
1994	Cincinnati	8	11	0-0	0	9	15	5	4.22

JIM DESHAIES / Minnesota Twins / Batting Practice Machine $12

He posted ERAs of 7.44 in April, 5.88 in May, 6.21 in June, 8.49 in July, and 12.46 in August. He gave up 30 homers and 109 runs in 130 innings. Despite this, he was still in the rotation when the strike arrived, mercifully in his case. This was his fifth consecutive losing season . . . I'm not sure what Kelly is waiting for.

YEAR	TEAM/LEVEL	G	IP	W-L	PCT	HITS	SO	BB	ERA
1992	San Diego	15	96	4-7	.364	92	46	33	3.28
1993	Two Teams	32	184	13-15	.464	183	85	57	4.39
1994	Minnesota	25	130	6-12	.333	170	78	54	7.39

DELINO DESHIELDS / Los Angeles Dodgers / Second Base $57

His batting average dropped 40 points and he missed three weeks with a sprained finger, but he remains impressive. His walks and stolen bases insure that he will score runs, even if he hits .250. At second base he has outstanding range, and constantly escalating fielding percentages. The only big difference between Delino and Roberto is that DeShields doesn't play 155 games a year.

YEAR	TEAM/LEVEL	G	AB	R	H	2B	3B	HR	RBI	BB	SB	AVG	OBP	SLG
1993	Montreal	123	481	75	142	17	7	2	29	72	43	.295	.389	.372
1994	Los Angeles	89	320	51	80	11	3	2	33	54	27	.250	.357	.322
1995	*Projected*	*135*	*517*	*85*	*150*	*20*	*6*	*6*	*52*	*73*	*48*	*.290*	*.378*	*.387*

JOHN DETTMER / Texas Rangers / Right-handed Starter $20

Eleventh-round 1992 draft from the University of Missouri; set a Big Eight record for career strikeouts. Throws slurve, changeup, sinking fastball. Good mechanics, outstanding minor league record, is said to be quite bright and coachable. His favorite pitcher is Bob Tewksbury. Like Tewksbury he will face an uphill battle because he doesn't throw hard, but will probably make it eventually.

YEAR	TEAM/LEVEL	G	IP	W-L	PCT	HITS	SO	BB	ERA
1993	Charlotte A	27	163	16-3	.842	132	128	33	2.15
1994	AA and AAA	18	121	9-3	.750	116	94	23	3.64
1994	Texas	11	54	0-6	.000	63	27	20	4.33

MIKE DEVEREAUX / Baltimore Orioles / Center Field $23

1994 was his free agent option year, so there goes that theory. He was OK in the field, but miserable at bat, and, since his career got a late start, is now 32 years old. The Orioles don't want him back, and the demand for his services elsewhere will be light . . . Once appeared in an episode of *The Young and the Restless*.

YEAR	TEAM/LEVEL	G	AB	R	H	2B	3B	HR	RBI	BB	SB	AVG	OBP	SLG
1993	Baltimore	131	527	72	132	31	3	14	75	43	3	.250	.306	.400
1994	Baltimore	85	301	35	61	8	2	9	33	22	1	.203	.256	.332
1995	*Projected*	*120*	*461*	*52*	*112*	*19*	*3*	*13*	*62*	*33*	*5*	*.243*	*.294*	*.384*

MARK DEWEY / Pittsburgh Pirates / Relief Pitcher $17

Was designated for reassignment at the end of the season, and may be somewhere else by next spring. Dewey pitched brilliantly through his first 18 appearances of 1995, posting a 1.00 ERA, but went on the DL May 12 with a muscle strain in his left side, and was not sharp when he returned. I've always liked him, and expect his stock to recover.

YEAR	TEAM/LEVEL	G	IP	W-L	SAVES	HITS	SO	BB	ERA
1992	New York	20	33	1-0	0	37	24	10	4.32
1993	Pittsburgh	21	27	1-2	7	14	14	10	2.36
1994	Pittsburgh	45	51	2-1	1	61	30	19	3.68

ALEX DIAZ / Seattle Mariners / Pinch Runner/Outfield $18

Came to the majors as a pinch runner/defensive sub in the outfield, but has hit surprisingly well so far. He was taken by the Mariners on waivers, after the '94 season. Started 35 games in center last year, nine in right. Switch hitter, stole 40 bases a year in the minors. . . . I don't *expect* him to be good, but he might surprise.

YEAR	TEAM/LEVEL	G	AB	R	H	2B	3B	HR	RBI	BB	SB	AVG	OBP	SLG
1992	Milwaukee	22	9	5	1	0	0	0	1	0	3	.111	.111	.111
1993	Milwaukee	32	69	9	22	2	0	0	1	0	5	.319	.319	.348
1994	Milwaukee	79	187	17	47	5	7	1	17	10	5	.251	.285	.369

MARIO DIAZ / Florida Marlins / Utility Infielder $15

Released by the Rangers, he signed a minor league contract with the Marlins, was cut by them in spring training, then signed with them again in May. He's not a Gold Glove candidate at any spot, but you'd think managers would like to have a utility infielder around who could be used as a pinch hitter. Apparently they don't.

YEAR	TEAM/LEVEL	G	AB	R	H	2B	3B	HR	RBI	BB	SB	AVG	OBP	SLG
1993	Texas	71	205	24	56	10	1	2	24	8	1	.273	.297	.361
1994	Florida	32	77	10	25	4	2	0	11	6	0	.325	.376	.429
1995	*Projected*	*75*	*204*	*19*	*57*	*9*	*0*	*2*	*19*	*6*	*1*	*.279*	*.300*	*.353*

ROB DIBBLE / Cincinnati Reds / Relief Pitcher/Head Case $14

He missed the 1994 season after surgery on his rotator cuff. If he comes back at all, we would have to assume that it will be a year or so before he's back to 100 percent. He never was what we could call a shrewd pitcher; his theory was more like "Hit *this*, sucker." I would be surprised if he was able to come back strong.

YEAR	TEAM/LEVEL	G	IP	W-L	SAVES	HITS	SO	BB	ERA
1992	Cincinnati	63	70	3-5	25	48	110	31	3.07
1993	Cincinnati	45	42	1-4	19	34	49	42	6.48
1994	Cincinnati				(Did Not Pitch)				

JERRY DIPOTO / Cleveland Indians / Relief Pitcher $18

Won the Indians' closer job in the final weeks of the 1993 season, but had surgery March 22, 1994, to remove a cancerous thyroid gland. Unable to pitch until June, and didn't get back to the majors until late July. The Indians sent him down during the strike, and he pitched well enough to give hope that he'll be at full strength in '95.

YEAR	TEAM/LEVEL	G	IP	W-L	SAVES	HITS	SO	BB	ERA
1993	Charlotte AAA	34	47	6-3	12	34	44	13	1.93
1993	Cleveland	46	56	4-4	11	57	41	30	2.40
1994	Cleveland	7	16	0-0	0	26	9	10	8.04

GARY DISARCINA / California Angels / Shortstop $30

Had his best year with the bat in '94, and really, it wasn't much to brag about—an on-base percentage under .300, a slugging percentage of .329, and a 3-for-10 performance as a base stealer. He bats ninth and should stay there, but his game is defense, and he was very, very good on defense, probably deserving of the AL Gold Glove, which went to Vizquel.

YEAR	TEAM/LEVEL	G	AB	R	H	2B	3B	HR	RBI	BB	SB	AVG	OBP	SLG
1993	California	126	416	44	99	20	1	3	45	15	5	.238	.273	.313
1994	California	112	389	53	101	14	2	3	33	18	3	.260	.294	.329
1995	*Projected*	*152*	*550*	*60*	*135*	*19*	*2*	*5*	*47*	*25*	*7*	*.245*	*.278*	*.315*

JOHN DOHERTY / Detroit Tigers / Starting Pitcher $20

Season ended July 10 due to a sore back. Doherty had a streak in May when he pitched well (5-1, 3.88 ERA), but was ineffective the rest of the year. He gets most of his outs on ground balls, and his control is excellent. In theory there *should* be many such pitchers who are consistently effective—but in fact there are almost none.

YEAR	TEAM/LEVEL	G	IP	W-L	PCT	HITS	SO	BB	ERA
1992	Detroit	47	116	7-4	.636	131	37	25	3.88
1993	Detroit	32	185	14-11	.560	205	63	48	4.44
1994	Detroit	18	101	6-7	.462	139	28	26	6.48

CHRIS DONNELS / Houston Astros / Infielder/Pinch Hitter $19

With his .267 average and .364 on-base percentage of 1994, we might say that he is finally on top of the curve, finally able to actually do in the majors what his minor league record showed that he ought to. With Caminiti and Bagwell both having great years he wasn't in much demand apart from pinch hitting, but he had a nice season.

YEAR	TEAM/LEVEL	G	AB	R	H	2B	3B	HR	RBI	BB	SB	AVG	OBP	SLG
1993	Houston	88	179	18	46	14	2	2	24	19	2	.257	.327	.391
1994	Houston	54	86	12	23	5	0	3	5	13	1	.267	.364	.430
1995	*Projected*	*101*	*227*	*24*	*58*	*15*	*1*	*3*	*29*	*35*	*4*	*.256*	*.355*	*.370*

JOHN DOPSON / California Angels (Released) / Starting Pitcher $14

Opened the '94 season in the Angels' rotation, but posted a 6.00 ERA through five starts, and was sent to the bullpen. He wasn't any better there, went on the DL in June with an inflamed shoulder, and was released in October. Hasn't had a winning record since 1989, and may have to go to the minors if he wants to continue his career.

YEAR	TEAM/LEVEL	G	IP	W-L	PCT	HITS	SO	BB	ERA
1992	Boston	25	141	7-11	.389	159	55	38	4.08
1993	Boston	34	156	7-11	.389	170	89	59	4.97
1994	California	21	59	1-4	.200	67	33	26	6.14

BRIAN DORSETT / Cincinnati Reds / Catcher $21

A 34-year-old catcher who reached the majors with Cleveland in 1987 and had played for California, the Yankees, and San Diego, but had more at bats last year than in all of his previous seasons combined. He wasn't great, and his position is not secure, particularly if Joe Oliver is able to return. Dorsett is a better hitter than Oliver.

YEAR	TEAM/LEVEL	G	AB	R	H	2B	3B	HR	RBI	BB	SB	AVG	OBP	SLG
1993	MLE	77	266	30	71	24	0	13	45	22	1	.267	.323	.504
1993	Cincinnati	25	63	7	16	4	0	2	12	3	0	.254	.288	.413
1994	Cincinnati	76	216	21	53	8	0	5	26	21	0	.245	.313	.352

DOUG DRABEK / Houston Astros / Starting Pitcher $70

His fine comeback season gave him six winning records in the last seven years, and a career record of 120-94. He is 32, hardly an old man, and in view of his excellent health record, his self-discipline in conditioning, and his still *improving* strikeout/walk ratios, I would not be surprised if the better part of his career is still ahead of him.

YEAR	TEAM/LEVEL	G	IP	W-L	PCT	HITS	SO	BB	ERA
1992	Pittsburgh	34	257	15-11	.577	218	177	54	2.77
1993	Houston	34	238	9-18	.333	242	157	60	3.79
1994	Houston	23	165	12-6	.667	132	121	45	2.84

BRIAN DRAHMAN / Florida Marlins / Relief Pitcher $16

He throws fairly hard, has piled up 133 minor league saves, and has pitched well during his four brief trials in the major leagues, but has been unable to convince anybody to give him a steady job. His ERA, in 57 major league games, is 3.16, although his other numbers (strikeouts, walks, and hits allowed) are not impressive. He carries a little extra weight.

YEAR	TEAM/LEVEL	G	IP	W-L	SAVES	HITS	SO	BB	ERA
1993	Nashville AAA	54	56	9-4	20	59	49	19	2.91
1993	Chicago	5	5	0-0	1	7	3	2	0.00
1994	Florida	19	25	0-0	1	28	11	10	3.91

DARREN DREIFORT / Los Angeles Dodgers / Right-handed Pitcher $26

The second player taken in the 1993 draft, Dreifort made the big team and was closing some games in April and May. He throws in the mid-90s with a hard slider, but the league hit .357 against him, and he was sent out. At San Antonio he was used as a *starting* pitcher, so that may still be an option . . . an outstanding hitter.

YEAR	TEAM/LEVEL	G	IP	W-L	SAVES	HITS	SO	BB	ERA
1993	Wichita State	30	102	11-1	4	67	120	34	2.48
1994	Los Angeles	27	29	0-5	6	45	22	15	6.21
1994	San Antonio AA	8	35	3-1	0	36	32	13	2.80

STEVE DREYER / Texas Rangers / Starting Pitcher $14

Considered one of the top pitching prospects in the Rangers' system, he lost his 1994 season after bone chips were discovered living in his elbow. He had them evicted, and hopes to be ready to start the 1995 season in the majors. He's never been a real hard thrower, and can't afford to come out of this with his fastball shortened up any.

YEAR	TEAM/LEVEL	G	IP	W-L	PCT	HITS	SO	BB	ERA
1993	AA and AAA	21	138	6-8	.429	134	86	39	3.19
1993	Texas	10	41	3-3	.500	48	23	20	5.71
1994	Texas	5	17	1-1	.500	19	11	8	5.71

MARIANO DUNCAN / Philadelphia Phillies / Infielder $27

Started games for the Phillies at all four infield positions—three games at first, 34 at second, 28 at third, 19 at short. His best position is second base, but his real *value* is that he's not terrible no matter where you put him, plus he runs well and can hit a little. He's 32, and I wouldn't expect him to be around at 35.

YEAR	TEAM/LEVEL	G	AB	R	H	2B	3B	HR	RBI	BB	SB	AVG	OBP	SLG
1993	Philadelphia	124	496	68	140	26	4	11	73	12	6	.282	.304	.417
1994	Philadelphia	88	347	49	93	22	1	8	48	17	10	.268	.306	.406
1995	*Projected*	*132*	*525*	*61*	*133*	*23*	*3*	*10*	*58*	*17*	*13*	*.253*	*.277*	*.366*

STEVE DUNN / Minnesota Twins / First Base $17

Left-handed power hitter with a vicious swing, has been in the minors since 1988, but had injuries early on. A good athlete, good first baseman. With Hrbek retiring, the obvious candidates to replace him are Mc-Carty and Dunn. They are pretty much even as hitters, so Tom Kelly will have to make that decision in his mystical and borderline divine manner.

YEAR	TEAM/LEVEL	G	AB	R	H	2B	3B	HR	RBI	BB	SB	AVG	OBP	SLG
1993	MLE	97	358	38	88	19	1	11	48	24	0	.246	.293	.397
1994	MLE	90	313	41	85	18	1	10	49	16	0	.272	.307	.431
1994	Minnesota	14	35	2	8	5	0	0	4	1	0	.229	.250	.371

SHAWON DUNSTON / Chicago Cubs / Shortstop $31

As Roseanne Roseannadanna said, it's always something; either you have back surgery, or they call a strike and wipe out half the season on you. Dunston's .278 average matched his career high (1989), and his slugging percentage was a career high, so he doesn't appear to have lost anything at bat. He has lost a step on the bases and in the field.

YEAR	TEAM/LEVEL	G	AB	R	H	2B	3B	HR	RBI	BB	SB	AVG	OBP	SLG
1993	Chicago	7	10	3	4	2	0	0	2	0	0	.400	.400	.600
1994	Chicago	88	331	38	92	19	0	11	35	16	3	.278	.313	.435
1995	*Projected*	*128*	*403*	*46*	*101*	*19*	*3*	*10*	*41*	*20*	*5*	*.251*	*.286*	*.387*

RAY DURHAM / Chicago White Sox / Second Base $32

The White Sox have two good second basemen anyway, but Durham may force his way onto the roster. He's an impressive athlete—very fast, an outstanding football player in high school. The Sox tested the vertical leap of all their minor leaguers last year, and Michael Jordan finished second. He's a switch hitter, and coming on strong with the bat. **Grade A prospect.**

YEAR	TEAM/LEVEL	G	AB	R	H	2B	3B	HR	RBI	BB	SB	AVG	OBP	SLG
1993	MLE	137	511	67	126	18	6	2	29	28	26	.247	.286	.317
1994	Nashville AAA	133	527	89	156	33	12	16	66	46	34	.296	.364	.495
1994	MLE	133	509	74	138	28	7	13	55	37	24	.271	.321	.430

MIKE DYER / Pittsburgh Pirates / Right-handed Pitcher $13

After pitching for Minnesota in 1989, Dyer came down with "Thoracic Outlet Compression Syndrome," the same condition which caused J. R. Richard's stroke. An operation relieved the problem, but it took him years to get back into playing condition. After a hot start as the closer at Buffalo, he was called up to Pittsburgh. Throws hard, but shows the effects of the missed time.

YEAR	TEAM/LEVEL	G	IP	W-L	SAVES	HITS	SO	BB	ERA
1989	Minnesota	16	71	4-7	0	74	37	37	4.82
1994	Buffalo AAA	29	35	3-3	12	33	26	16	2.34
1994	Pittsburgh	14	15	1-1	4	15	13	12	5.87

LENNY DYKSTRA / Philadelphia Phillies / Center Field $49

Played better in May '94 than he did in any month of his amazing 1993 season, hitting .392 with 15 doubles, 26 runs scored in May. He started having health problems then, and went on the DL following an emergency appendectomy June 22. The Phillies have a long tradition of outstanding center fielders who were also lead-off men, dating back to Billy Hamilton (1890-95).

YEAR	TEAM/LEVEL	G	AB	R	H	2B	3B	HR	RBI	BB	SB	AVG	OBP	SLG
1993	Philadelphia	161	637	143	194	44	6	19	66	129	37	.305	.420	.482
1994	Philadelphia	84	315	68	86	26	5	5	24	68	15	.273	.404	.435
1995	*Projected*	*131*	*507*	*94*	*142*	*30*	*3*	*10*	*45*	*93*	*34*	*.280*	*.392*	*.410*

DAMION EASLEY / California Angels / Infielder $25

At one time he was the Angels' regular second baseman. He lost that job in June 1993 to shin splints, then to Harold Reynolds. Last year he opened up as the regular *third* baseman, but lost that to a sore right shoulder, and returned, when healthy, to second base. He may turn out to be a good second baseman, but we haven't seen it yet.

YEAR	TEAM/LEVEL	G	AB	R	H	2B	3B	HR	RBI	BB	SB	AVG	OBP	SLG
1993	California	73	230	33	72	13	2	2	22	28	6	.313	.392	.413
1994	California	88	316	41	68	16	1	6	30	29	4	.215	.288	.329
1995	*Projected*	*126*	*402*	*49*	*103*	*17*	*1*	*5*	*37*	*33*	*14*	*.256*	*.313*	*.341*

DENNIS ECKERSLEY / Oakland Athletics / Closer $31

Oakland passed on his option, making him a free agent. Eckersley comes from third base, and, as I pointed out last year, developed a weakness common to pitchers who do that: left-handers. They hit .323 against him in 1993, and .322 last year. This suggests that he has been unable to fix the problem, and therefore that he is through as baseball's best reliever.

YEAR	TEAM/LEVEL	G	IP	W-L	SAVES	HITS	SO	BB	ERA
1992	Oakland	69	80	7-1	51	62	93	11	1.91
1993	Oakland	64	67	2-4	36	67	80	13	4.16
1994	Oakland	45	44	5-4	19	49	47	13	4.26

TOM EDENS / Philadelphia Phillies / Relief Pitcher $21

Spent most of the year in Houston, and was traded to Philadelphia in late July. He's been around the block a few times—started in the Kansas City system (1983) and has belonged to the Mets, Phillies (1989), Milwaukee, Minnesota, Florida, Houston, now back to Philadelphia. He's 33, but has pitched fairly well for three straight years.

YEAR	TEAM/LEVEL	G	IP	W-L	SAVES	HITS	SO	BB	ERA
1992	Minnesota	52	76	6-3	3	65	57	36	2.83
1993	Houston	38	49	1-1	0	47	21	19	3.12
1994	Two Teams	42	54	5-1	1	59	39	18	4.33

JIM EDMONDS / California Angels / Left Field $21

"Left Field" for short; actually, he played left, right, first base, and center. Since he has no power or speed and had almost as many strikeouts as hits, that .273 average is more like .240 in terms of the runs it produces, but he is still young, and could develop into a good platoon player. Faces competition from Garret Anderson and Orlando Palmeiro.

YEAR	TEAM/LEVEL	G	AB	R	H	2B	3B	HR	RBI	BB	SB	AVG	OBP	SLG
1993	California	18	61	5	15	4	1	0	4	2	0	.246	.270	.344
1994	California	94	289	35	79	13	1	5	37	30	4	.273	.343	.377
1995	*Projected*	*104*	*345*	*45*	*97*	*19*	*2*	*8*	*47*	*31*	*4*	*.281*	*.340*	*.417*

ROBERT EENHOORN / New York Yankees / Shortstop $14

Eenhoorn played in the Oolyympics in 1988, for the Netherlands, then came to college in the U.S., and was drafted in 1990. He's a glove man, good range, sure hands, strong arm, weak bat. His .239 average at Columbus does not encourage us to believe that he can hit well enough to stay in the majors, but he has had better years.

YEAR	TEAM/LEVEL	G	AB	R	H	2B	3B	HR	RBI	BB	SB	AVG	OBP	SLG
1993	MLE	82	302	38	76	21	1	4	37	14	2	.252	.285	.368
1994	Columbus AAA	99	343	38	82	10	2	5	39	14	2	.239	.270	.324
1994	MLE	99	334	33	73	9	1	4	34	12	1	.219	.246	.287

MARK EICHORN / Baltimore Orioles / Relief Pitcher $28

Is this a fluke stat, or is there some story here? Eichorn, always known as weak against left-handed hitters, limited lefties to a .177 batting average last year, no power (.219 slugging), no inordinate number of walks. This, among other things, contributed to his highly effective season. But then, he's had *lots* of effective seasons, as witness his career ERA of 2.93.

YEAR	TEAM/LEVEL	G	IP	W-L	SAVES	HITS	SO	BB	ERA
1992	Two Teams	65	88	4-4	2	86	61	25	3.08
1993	Toronto	54	73	3-1	0	76	47	22	2.72
1994	Baltimore	43	71	6-5	1	62	35	19	2.15

JIM EISENREICH / Philadelphia Phillies / Right Field $23

An exceptional defensive outfielder, and has hit .293 or better in four of the last six seasons (the other averages being .280 and .269). A good percentage base stealer (except in 1990, when he kept running into pitchouts), walks as much as the league average. It is unusual for a platoon player to be this consistent, or to contribute in so many different ways.

YEAR	TEAM/LEVEL	G	AB	R	H	2B	3B	HR	RBI	BB	SB	AVG	OBP	SLG
1993	Philadelphia	153	362	51	115	17	4	7	54	26	5	.318	.363	.445
1994	Philadelphia	104	290	42	87	15	4	4	43	33	6	.300	.371	.421
1995	*Projected*	*134*	*373*	*44*	*104*	*21*	*3*	*4*	*45*	*32*	*7*	*.279*	*.336*	*.383*

CAL ELDRED / Milwaukee Brewers / Starting Pitcher $31

Continues to trace the career of Jim Nash. Nash went 12-1 in his first half-season, and was 37-31 after three years; Eldred started out 11-2 and is now 38-29. . . . A good pitcher, but the degeneration in Eldred's strike-out/walk ratio, combined with his weak finish (6.36 ERA over last six weeks), suggests that you avoid him in '95.

YEAR	TEAM/LEVEL	G	IP	W-L	PCT	HITS	SO	BB	ERA
1992	Milwaukee	14	100	11-2	.846	76	62	23	1.79
1993	Milwaukee	36	258	16-16	.500	232	180	91	4.01
1994	Milwaukee	25	179	11-11	.500	158	98	84	4.68

DONNIE ELLIOT / San Diego Padres / Right-handed Reliever $13

Product of the Phillies system, traded to the Braves and then to the Padres, in the McGriff deal. He's big (6-5, 200), and has pitched well in the minors, when he has been healthy. The Padres gave him a shot in the bullpen and he was OK, but ended the season on the DL due to a "sprained rotator cuff." I wouldn't expect too much.

YEAR	TEAM/LEVEL	G	IP	W-L	PCT	HITS	SO	BB	ERA
1993	Two Teams AAA	26	144	10-10	.500	156	143	63	5.19
1994	Las Vegas AAA	6	13	2-0	1.000	13	12	11	5.40
1994	San Diego	30	33	0-1	.000	31	24	21	3.27

SCOTT ERICKSON / Minnesota Twins / Starting Pitcher $22

Has requested a trade, prompting Andy McPhail to publicly wonder why anyone would want him. The radar says he looks the same, his slider still looks good, his strikeout rates have actually increased, and he does have occasional good starts. Erickson himself blames scouting reports, bad luck, and bad teammates for his troubles. That should tell us something about where his problems lie.

YEAR	TEAM/LEVEL	G	IP	W-L	PCT	HITS	SO	BB	ERA
1992	Minnesota	32	212	13-12	.520	197	101	83	3.40
1993	Minnesota	34	219	8-19	.296	266	116	71	5.19
1994	Minnesota	23	144	8-11	.421	173	104	59	5.44

ALVARO ESPINOZA / Cleveland Indians / Third Base/Shortstop $18

He wound up playing more than expected, because a) Vizquel was hurt, and b) Thome has hands of stone. He's a very good defensive shortstop, arguably better than Vizquel, but doesn't generate enough offense to play every day, although he has hit .313 over the last three years against left-handed pitchers . . . knee injuries have taken his speed, and a little bit of his range.

YEAR	TEAM/LEVEL	G	AB	R	H	2B	3B	HR	RBI	BB	SB	AVG	OBP	SLG
1993	Cleveland	129	263	34	73	15	0	4	27	8	2	.278	.298	.380
1994	Cleveland	90	231	27	55	13	0	1	19	6	1	.238	.258	.307
1995	*Projected*	*82*	*209*	*21*	*52*	*11*	*0*	*2*	*21*	*6*	*1*	*.249*	*.270*	*.330*

TONY EUSEBIO / Houston Astros / Catcher | $24

Tony Pena–, Manny Sanguillen–type catcher, best cast in a platoon role. He runs well, throws well, should hit .270 or better, not much power. Like many Dominicans, he likes to swing the bat. Injuries slowed his rise through the minors, so he's 28. I would expect him to have a 10-year major league career, mostly as a platoon player or backup.

YEAR	TEAM/LEVEL	G	AB	R	H	2B	3B	HR	RBI	BB	SB	AVG	OBP	SLG
1993	MLE	78	260	24	70	15	0	0	27	13	0	.269	.304	.327
1994	Houston	55	159	18	47	9	1	5	30	8	0	.296	.320	.459
1995	*Projected*	*97*	*319*	*31*	*89*	*14*	*1*	*4*	*40*	*17*	*0*	*.279*	*.315*	*.367*

CARL EVERETT / Florida Marlins / Center Field | $25

Will be in the majors in '95, one way or another. Perhaps the best long-range prospect taken by the Marlins in the expansion draft, he has come on strong, and may shove Carr aside and take center field, or could play right field, moving Sheffield to left and Conine to first. Runs well, strong enough to develop power, must conquer the strike zone.

YEAR	TEAM/LEVEL	G	AB	R	H	2B	3B	HR	RBI	BB	SB	AVG	OBP	SLG
1994	Edmonton AAA	78	321	63	108	17	2	11	47	19	16	.336	.380	.505
1994	MLE	78	299	41	86	13	1	7	30	13	10	.288	.317	.408
1994	Florida	16	51	7	11	1	0	2	6	3	4	.216	.259	.353

BRYAN EVERSGERD / St. Louis Cardinals / Left-handed Reliever | $15

Signed out of a tryout camp in 1989, he worked his way up as a left-handed one-out specialist, and was effective in that role until he reached the majors last year. His strikeout/walk data was good, but he allowed an average of .295, and will have to do better to keep his job . . . only major leaguer who attended Kaskaskia College.

YEAR	TEAM/LEVEL	G	IP	W-L	SAVES	HITS	SO	BB	ERA
1993	Arkansas AA	62	66	4-4	0	60	68	19	2.18
1994	Louisville AAA	9	12	1-1	0	11	8	8	4.50
1994	St. Louis	40	68	2-3	0	75	47	20	4.52

JORGE FABREGAS / California Angels / Catcher | $23

He looks distinctly better than the other young catchers whom the Angels have put forward in recent years—Orton, Turner, Dalesandro, Gonzales, etc. He's 25, a left-handed hitter, probably not a .280 hitter, but over .250. According to Buck Rodgers, he was the best defensive catcher in the Angels' camp last year . . . a Miami native, a first-round pick in 1991.

YEAR	TEAM/LEVEL	G	AB	R	H	2B	3B	HR	RBI	BB	SB	AVG	OBP	SLG
1994	MLE	66	203	12	39	4	0	0	18	8	0	.192	.223	.212
1994	California	43	127	12	36	3	0	0	16	7	2	.283	.321	.307
1995	*Projected*	*122*	*337*	*36*	*84*	*13*	*0*	*3*	*37*	*17*	*1*	*.249*	*.285*	*.316*

HECTOR FAJARDO / Texas Rangers / Pitcher $16

A big right-hander with a great arm, who until 1994 had never pitched more than 61 innings for a team anywhere because of an absurd number of injuries. Despite the lack of any proper education, Kevin Kennedy put him in his rotation, and he occasionally pitched well. He was good at Oklahoma City after being sent down, and could improve substantially in his second season.

YEAR	TEAM/LEVEL	G	IP	W-L	SAVES	HITS	SO	BB	ERA
1993	Rangers R	6	30	3-1	0	21	27	5	1.80
1993	Charlotte A	2	5	0-0	0	5	3	1	1.80
1994	Texas	18	83	5-7	0	95	45	26	6.91

RIKKERT FANEYTE / San Francisco Giants / Outfield $15

The Netherlands' answer to Henry Cotto, a right-handed-hitting outfielder who can run and throw and hit enough singles to get periodic playing time, but not produce big numbers of runs. He will probably be on the Giants' roster in '95, and could play quite a bit if Strawberry isn't back. The Giants have cut Willie McGee.

YEAR	TEAM/LEVEL	G	AB	R	H	2B	3B	HR	RBI	BB	SB	AVG	OBP	SLG
1994	Phoenix AAA	94	365	62	122	17	6	6	57	30	15	.334	.392	.463
1994	MLE	94	339	42	96	13	3	4	39	20	9	.283	.323	.375
1994	San Francisco	19	26	1	3	3	0	0	4	3	0	.115	.207	.231

STEVE FARR / Boston Red Sox / Reliever $10

Started the '94 season as the Indians' closer, but lost that with a few off games in early May. He went on the DL in June with a tight elbow, was traded to Boston before he returned, and was cut by Boston after the year. His ability to come back, after two straight off seasons and at 38 years old, is highly suspect.

YEAR	TEAM/LEVEL	G	IP	W-L	SAVES	HITS	SO	BB	ERA
1992	New York	50	52	2-2	30	34	37	19	1.56
1993	New York	49	47	2-2	25	44	39	28	4.21
1994	Two Teams	30	28	2-1	4	41	20	18	5.72

JEFF FASSERO / Montreal Expos / Left-handed Pitcher $46

Every season is a revelation, every success a shock. Given up on by three organizations, he signed with Montreal as a minor league free agent, and has been nothing but brilliant for three years, first as a reliever, then as a starter. The only question left is whether his arm will hold up to 35 starts, 200 innings . . . throws fastball, slider, and forkball.

YEAR	TEAM/LEVEL	G	IP	W-L	PCT	HITS	SO	BB	ERA
1992	Montreal	70	86	8-7	.533	81	63	34	2.84
1993	Montreal	56	150	12-5	.706	119	140	54	2.29
1994	Montreal	21	139	8-6	.571	119	119	40	2.99

MIKE FELDER / Houston Astros / Outfield | $15

The Felder jinx: Whoever acquires him immediately loses two outfielders to injury, and has to wind up playing Mike Felder. Felder, who is a good fifth outfielder, has had numerous chances to take over a job, including last year, when the Astros had to use him in right field, although he doesn't have a right fielder's arm. Good speed, switch hitter.

YEAR	TEAM/LEVEL	G	AB	R	H	2B	3B	HR	RBI	BB	SB	AVG	OBP	SLG
1993	Seattle	109	342	31	72	7	5	1	20	22	15	.211	.262	.269
1994	Houston	58	117	10	28	2	2	0	13	4	3	.239	.264	.291
1995	*Projected*	*50*	*95*	*10*	*23*	*3*	*1*	*1*	*7*	*6*	*4*	*.242*	*.287*	*.326*

JUNIOR FELIX / Detroit Tigers / Center Field | $29

A stunning comeback from a player whom many had written off. He hit .300 for the first time, increased his on-base percentage by almost 100 points and his slugging percentage by more than 100. You can't *count* on him, but this season has always been within his reach. . . . Once a speed merchant, he was 1-for-7 stealing bases last year.

YEAR	TEAM/LEVEL	G	AB	R	H	2B	3B	HR	RBI	BB	SB	AVG	OBP	SLG
1993	Florida	57	214	25	51	11	1	7	22	10	2	.238	.276	.397
1994	Detroit	86	301	54	92	25	1	13	49	26	1	.306	.372	.525
1995	*Projected*	*114*	*402*	*56*	*106*	*20*	*4*	*11*	*54*	*28*	*5*	*.264*	*.312*	*.415*

FELIX FERMIN / Seattle Mariners / Shortstop | $22

He hit .400 against left-handed pitchers, which drove his average over .300 for the first time in professional ball (he once hit .280 in the minors). He would be high on my list of players to avoid in '95, because a) he's not really a .300 hitter, b) he's past 30, and c) even if he hits .300, he doesn't help you.

YEAR	TEAM/LEVEL	G	AB	R	H	2B	3B	HR	RBI	BB	SB	AVG	OBP	SLG
1993	Cleveland	140	480	48	126	16	2	2	45	24	4	.263	.303	.317
1994	Seattle	101	379	52	120	21	0	1	35	11	4	.317	.338	.380
1995	*Projected*	*129*	*444*	*45*	*115*	*13*	*1*	*2*	*34*	*21*	*3*	*.259*	*.292*	*.306*

ALEX FERNANDEZ / Chicago White Sox / Starting Pitcher | $68

He's constantly compared to Tom Seaver, but in a way he is more comparable to the Catfish Hunter/Ferguson Jenkins/Robin Roberts type of pitcher, who gives up bases-empty homers but survives to win. Those guys are always durable and consistent, so I'd be very optimistic about Fernandez continuing to win. It will help him if they de-juice the baseballs.

YEAR	TEAM/LEVEL	G	IP	W-L	PCT	HITS	SO	BB	ERA
1992	Chicago	29	188	8-11	.421	199	95	50	4.27
1993	Chicago	34	247	18-9	.667	221	169	67	3.13
1994	Chicago	24	170	11-7	.611	163	122	50	3.86

SID FERNANDEZ / Baltimore Orioles / Starting Pitcher $27

Joe Carter batted 435 times last year and hit 27 homers and 25 doubles. Sid Fernandez *faced* 439 hitters, and gave up 27 homers and 25 doubles. So the typical hitter, facing Sid Fernandez, was Joe Carter . . . he's a better pitcher than that. He's not as good as his 2.80 ERAs in Shea Stadium, but he's better than the 5.15 mark last year.

YEAR	TEAM/LEVEL	G	IP	W-L	PCT	HITS	SO	BB	ERA
1992	New York	32	215	14-11	.560	162	193	67	2.73
1993	New York	18	120	5-6	.455	82	81	36	2.93
1994	Baltimore	19	115	6-6	.500	109	95	46	5.15

TONY FERNANDEZ / Cincinnati Reds / Third Base $32

If you can count on any 32-year-old player, you can count on him. He hasn't missed more than a few games with an injury in 10 years. 1994 was the fifth consecutive season he has hit between .272 and .279, which must be some sort of record. His on-base and slugging percentages were up a little last year, as most everybody's were.

YEAR	TEAM/LEVEL	G	AB	R	H	2B	3B	HR	RBI	BB	SB	AVG	OBP	SLG
1993	Two Teams	142	526	65	147	23	11	5	64	56	21	.279	.348	.394
1994	Cincinnati	104	366	50	102	18	6	8	50	44	12	.279	.361	.426
1995	*Projected*	*143*	*543*	*68*	*146*	*26*	*5*	*6*	*52*	*55*	*18*	*.269*	*.336*	*.368*

MIKE FETTERS / Milwaukee Brewers / Relief Pitcher $37

Fetters did not give up a home run in 1994, facing more than 200 batters. He's a ground-ball pitcher (2.7-to-1 ground ball/fly ball ratio), a good fielder, throws fairly hard, controls the running game, and has now pitched well for three years in a row. With the shortage of reliable closers right now, he's near the top of the list.

YEAR	TEAM/LEVEL	G	IP	W-L	SAVES	HITS	SO	BB	ERA
1992	Milwaukee	50	63	5-1	2	38	43	24	1.87
1993	Milwaukee	45	59	3-3	0	59	23	22	3.34
1994	Milwaukee	42	46	1-4	17	41	31	27	2.54

CECIL FIELDER / Detroit Tigers / First Base $44

Career ratio of GIDP to stolen bases: 102 to nothing. The average ratio is about 1 to 1 . . . I know I'm in a minority, but I wouldn't put him among the five top first basemen in the American League. Thomas, obviously, is in another league, but I'd rather have Olerud, Clark, Palmeiro, or Vaughn. I'm not sure about Mattingly or Hamelin.

YEAR	TEAM/LEVEL	G	AB	R	H	2B	3B	HR	RBI	BB	SB	AVG	OBP	SLG
1993	Detroit	154	573	80	153	23	0	30	117	90	0	.267	.368	.464
1994	Detroit	109	425	67	110	16	2	28	90	50	0	.259	.337	.504
1995	*Projected*	*154*	*584*	*82*	*147*	*20*	*1*	*34*	*118*	*78*	*0*	*.252*	*.340*	*.464*

CHUCK FINLEY / California Angels / Starting Pitcher $53

Started slowly, but finished strong. His first win of 1995 will be the 100th of his career, and my guess is that he has another hundred in front of him. He's 32 but in excellent shape, still throws hard, and knows how to get batters out without wasting his arm. I also believe that, on the right team, he could have a big season.

YEAR	TEAM/LEVEL	G	IP	W-L	PCT	HITS	SO	BB	ERA
1992	California	31	204	7-12	.368	212	124	98	3.96
1993	California	35	251	16-14	.533	243	187	82	3.15
1994	California	25	183	10-10	.500	178	148	71	4.32

STEVE FINLEY / Houston Astros / Center Field $52

His season was the opposite of '93. In '93 he started slowly but saved his season with a strong second half. Last year he hit .323 with 7 homers, 16 RBI in April, but struggled in May and broke his hand in June. He's not an All-Star, but he's a valuable player, an above-average defensive center fielder who chips in on the offense.

YEAR	TEAM/LEVEL	G	AB	R	H	2B	3B	HR	RBI	BB	SB	AVG	OBP	SLG
1993	Houston	142	545	69	145	15	13	8	44	28	19	.266	.304	.385
1994	Houston	94	373	64	103	16	5	11	33	28	13	.276	.329	.434
1995	*Projected*	*146*	*560*	*75*	*152*	*21*	*8*	*9*	*50*	*43*	*28*	*.271*	*.323*	*.380*

GAR FINNVOLD / Boston Red Sox / Starting Pitcher $15

Finnvold does not fit the profile of a young pitcher who is going to be outstanding. He doesn't throw exceptionally hard, doesn't have knockout K/W ratios, hasn't won 60 percent of his games in the minors. Despite this, I like him, and predict modest success. If he can get 150 innings in and stay in the league, his intelligence and solid mechanics will take over.

YEAR	TEAM/LEVEL	G	IP	W-L	PCT	HITS	SO	BB	ERA
1993	Pawtucket AAA	24	136	5-9	.357	128	123	51	3.77
1994	Pawtucket AAA	7	42	5-1	.833	32	32	15	3.61
1994	Boston	8	36	0-4	.000	45	17	15	5.94

JOHN FLAHERTY / Boston Red Sox / Catcher $12

Obviously he's not a *good* hitter. I don't believe he's a .150 hitter, either, but a marginal prospect can't afford to start slowly, or the next manager will look at another marginal prospect. Flaherty now goes into the pile of Grade D prospects who had a shot and didn't do anything with it. It is usually difficult to get out of that pile.

YEAR	TEAM/LEVEL	G	AB	R	H	2B	3B	HR	RBI	BB	SB	AVG	OBP	SLG
1993	Pawtucket AAA	105	365	29	99	22	0	6	35	26	0	.271	.327	.381
1993	MLE	105	354	22	88	22	0	4	26	19	0	.249	.287	.345
1994	Detroit	34	40	2	6	1	0	0	4	1	0	.150	.167	.175

DAVE FLEMING / Seattle Mariners / Starting Pitcher $24

The lesson here is the same as the lesson of Scott Erickson, Randy Tomlin, and a hundred others: It is almost impossible to sustain success on 4.5 strikeouts per game. It seems clear that Fleming *won't* be a pitcher you can count on for 14-17 wins. He might occasionally have a good season, but I doubt that 1995 will be one of them.

YEAR	TEAM/LEVEL	G	IP	W-L	PCT	HITS	SO	BB	ERA
1992	Seattle	33	228	17-10	.630	225	112	60	3.39
1993	Seattle	26	167	12-5	.706	189	75	67	4.36
1994	Seattle	23	117	7-11	.389	152	65	65	6.46

DARRIN FLETCHER / Montreal Expos / Catcher $31

As in '93, had the poorest percentage of runners caught stealing of any NL catcher (16 percent). Now ask Felipe Alou if he cares. Fletcher has a so-so arm, but works well with the pitchers, and hits . . . the anomaly in his record is that he has an exceptional RBI rate, but has actually hit *poorly* with runners in scoring position, both in '93 and '94.

YEAR	TEAM/LEVEL	G	AB	R	H	2B	3B	HR	RBI	BB	SB	AVG	OBP	SLG
1993	Montreal	133	396	33	101	20	1	9	60	34	0	.255	.320	.379
1994	Montreal	94	285	28	74	18	1	10	57	25	0	.260	.314	.435
1995	*Projected*	*135*	*393*	*32*	*97*	*21*	*1*	*9*	*59*	*33*	*1*	*.247*	*.305*	*.374*

SCOTT FLETCHER / Boston Red Sox / Second Base $16

Refused assignment to the minor leagues after the season, and declared free agency. His career will probably be over by the end of spring training, barring one more comeback. He's 36, and not the kind of player who can ordinarily survive an off season in his mid-30s . . . excellent defensive second baseman, 24-for-28 as a base stealer over the last two years.

YEAR	TEAM/LEVEL	G	AB	R	H	2B	3B	HR	RBI	BB	SB	AVG	OBP	SLG
1992	Milwaukee	123	386	53	106	18	3	3	51	30	17	.275	.335	.360
1993	Boston	121	480	81	137	31	5	5	45	37	16	.285	.341	.402
1994	Boston	63	185	31	42	9	1	3	11	16	8	.227	.296	.335

BRYCE FLORIE / San Diego Padres / Right-handed Pitcher $14

A fifth-round pick in 1988, he has made slow progress due to poor control, but vaulted forward the last two years because the Padres have few pitching prospects. After going 11-8 with a 3.96 ERA at Wichita in '93, he was named the organization's Pitcher of the Year. Made the majors last year despite mediocre performance at Las Vegas. Grade C prospect.

YEAR	TEAM/LEVEL	G	IP	W-L	PCT	HITS	SO	BB	ERA
1993	Wichita AA	27	155	11-8	.579	128	133	100	3.96
1994	Las Vegas AAA	50	72	2-5	.286	76	67	47	5.15
1994	San Diego	9	9	0-0	.000	8	8	3	0.96

CLIFF FLOYD / Montreal Expos / First Base/Outfield $46

As you can see below, his performance essentially matched what we should have expected based on his minor league numbers, except that most of the home runs we would have expected him to hit became doubles instead. He hit well against left-handers (.319) in limited action. There is, as there was last year, every reason to expect that he will be an outstanding player.

YEAR	TEAM/LEVEL	G	AB	R	H	2B	3B	HR	RBI	BB	SB	AVG	OBP	SLG
1993	MLE	133	482	75	132	17	3	20	94	49	23	.274	.341	.446
1994	Montreal	100	334	43	94	19	4	4	41	24	10	.281	.332	.398
1995	*Projected*	*141*	*503*	*76*	*145*	*23*	*4*	*17*	*82*	*47*	*17*	*.288*	*.349*	*.451*

TOM FOLEY / Pittsburgh Pirates / Infielder $15

Was used by Leyland at all four infield spots, but most often at second base (17 games, 13 starts). He also pinch hit 17 times, almost always hitting for the pitcher. He's a very good second baseman, possibly better than Garcia, although Garcia is quite good. At 35, his career is obviously a month-to-month proposition.

YEAR	TEAM/LEVEL	G	AB	R	H	2B	3B	HR	RBI	BB	SB	AVG	OBP	SLG
1992	Montreal	72	115	7	20	3	1	0	5	8	3	.174	.230	.217
1993	Pittsburgh	86	194	18	49	11	1	3	22	11	0	.253	.287	.366
1994	Pittsburgh	59	123	13	29	7	0	3	15	13	0	.236	.307	.366

BROOK FORDYCE / New York Mets / Catcher $13

He's had a bad year. Fordyce, considered the Mets' possible catcher of the future, has been bumped out of line by Kelly Stinnett, and also, Todd Hundley improved with the bat, which diminishes Fordyce's place in the Mets' plans. Fordyce is 25, a year younger than Hundley, a good receiver, and will probably hit at least enough to hang around the majors.

YEAR	TEAM/LEVEL	G	AB	R	H	2B	3B	HR	RBI	BB	SB	AVG	OBP	SLG
1992	MLE	118	412	49	105	26	0	8	51	26	0	.255	.299	.376
1993	MLE	116	397	27	94	18	1	1	33	21	1	.237	.275	.295
1994	MLE	66	223	22	54	11	2	2	28	16	0	.242	.293	.336

TONY FOSSAS / Boston Red Sox / Relief Pitcher $13

Limited left-handed hitters to a sub-.200 batting average, as he has done for years, but gave up a .320 average to right-handers, with a .500-plus slugging percentage, as he has done for years. So for him to be effective, as he was in 1992, he really has to pitch about one-half of an inning per outing.

YEAR	TEAM/LEVEL	G	IP	W-L	SAVES	HITS	SO	BB	ERA
1992	Boston	60	30	1-2	2	31	19	14	2.43
1993	Boston	71	40	1-1	0	38	39	15	5.18
1994	Boston	44	34	2-0	1	35	31	15	4.76

KEVIN FOSTER / Chicago Cubs / Relief Pitcher | $34

Has been traded from Montreal to Seattle to Philadelphia to Chicago, and I am damned if I know why. Originally drafted (in the 31st round, 1987) as a third baseman, he moved to the mound in 1990, and has done nothing but win since then. At Double-A in '93 he threw a one-hitter with 16 strikeouts. Good arm, shows good mound savvy.

YEAR	TEAM/LEVEL	G	IP	W-L	PCT	HITS	SO	BB	ERA
1993	Philadelphia	2	7	0-1	.000	13	6	7	14.85
1994	AA and AAA	10	59	4-1	.800	43	59	17	3.38
1994	Chicago	13	81	3-4	.429	70	75	35	2.89

ERIC FOX / Oakland Athletics / Outfield | $12

Called up June 3, he appeared in almost every game for six weeks, collecting a total of nine hits. Sometimes he played center field, sometimes right, sometimes starting, sometimes playing late-inning defense. LaRussa was desperate for outfielders. A 31-year-old switch hitter, runs well, good defense, but out of chances after hitting .170 the last two years.

YEAR	TEAM/LEVEL	G	AB	R	H	2B	3B	HR	RBI	BB	SB	AVG	OBP	SLG
1992	Oakland	51	143	24	34	5	2	3	13	13	3	.238	.299	.364
1993	Oakland	29	56	5	8	1	0	1	5	2	0	.143	.172	.214
1994	Oakland	26	44	7	9	2	0	1	1	3	2	.205	.255	.318

JOHN FRANCO / New York Mets / Relief Pitcher | $37

Reversed three years of decline with a league-leading 30 saves. His tendency to start well and degenerate as the schedule wears on is not a calumny; it is a very well-established fact. That he is an exceptional pitcher is also a well-established fact. Whether any manager can nurse him along and get a full season's work is yet to be seen.

YEAR	TEAM/LEVEL	G	IP	W-L	SAVES	HITS	SO	BB	ERA
1992	New York	31	33	6-2	15	24	20	11	1.64
1993	New York	35	36	4-3	10	46	29	19	5.20
1994	New York	47	50	1-4	30	47	42	19	2.70

JULIO FRANCO / Chicago White Sox / Designated Hitter | $40

A tremendous hitter; a perennial over-achiever who doesn't get credit for getting better and better because he's Latin and doesn't suck up to the press. In good shape despite some knee injuries, he runs better than the typical DH . . . a career .300 hitter with 1900-plus hits, could get 3000. But if he lasts that long, he'll establish a career record for GIDP.

YEAR	TEAM/LEVEL	G	AB	R	H	2B	3B	HR	RBI	BB	SB	AVG	OBP	SLG
1993	Texas	144	532	85	154	31	3	14	84	62	9	.289	.360	.438
1994	Chicago	112	433	72	138	19	2	20	98	62	8	.319	.406	.510
1995	*Projected*	*140*	*501*	*71*	*142*	*23*	*2*	*12*	*81*	*63*	*7*	*.283*	*.363*	*.409*

MICAH FRANKLIN / Pittsburgh Pirates / Outfielder | $15

A third-round draft pick of the Mets in '90, he was released by them in 1992 after two years as a discipline problem. He explains his problems by saying that, as the child of a mixed-race marriage, he grew up fighting. Given a second chance by the Reds, he behaved better, and has finally started to hit. Powerfully built, runs fairly well.

YEAR	TEAM/LEVEL	G	AB	R	H	2B	3B	HR	RBI	BB	SB	AVG	OBP	SLG
1993	Two Teams A	122	412	66	106	15	5	20	74	53	8	.257	.342	.464
1994	Winston A	42	150	44	45	7	0	21	44	27	7	.300	.424	.767
1994	Chattanooga AA	79	279	46	77	17	0	10	40	33	2	.276	.375	.444

LOU FRAZIER / Montreal Expos / Outfield/Pinch Hitter | $19

Felipe Alou's secret weapon, a 30-year-old switch hitter with outstanding speed, didn't hit anything in the minors, but began wearing glasses in 1992, and has hit better since then. He's always drawn a lot of walks. Basically a left fielder, has played a few innings at second base . . . won't be a regular, good bench player as long as he keeps hitting.

YEAR	TEAM/LEVEL	G	AB	R	H	2B	3B	HR	RBI	BB	SB	AVG	OBP	SLG
1992	MLE	129	464	76	107	12	2	0	30	73	42	.231	.335	.265
1993	Montreal	112	189	27	54	7	1	1	16	16	17	.286	.340	.349
1994	Montreal	76	140	25	38	3	1	0	14	18	20	.271	.358	.307

MARVIN FREEMAN / Colorado Rockies / Relief Pitcher | $39

Is there an award for the Surprise Player of the Year? I wrote last year that I "suspect he has good years ahead, if not great ones." This is not to imply that I am not shocked by his 1994 performance. Released by Atlanta, he took the Rockies his usual intimidating equipment, and stopped walking *anybody*. As long as he stays healthy, he should win.

YEAR	TEAM/LEVEL	G	IP	W-L	PCT	HITS	SO	BB	ERA
1992	Atlanta	58	64	7-5	.583	61	41	29	3.22
1993	Atlanta	21	24	2-0	1.000	24	25	10	6.08
1994	Colorado	19	113	10-2	.833	113	67	23	2.80

STEVE FREY / San Francisco Giants / Relief Pitcher | $15

He saved 13 games and posted a 2.98 ERA for California in 1993, after which the Angels decided not to tender him a contract. Returning to his role as a left-handed one-out guy last year, he wasn't effective, allowing a .322 batting average, and walking four-plus men per nine innings. There are always left-handed one-out guys looking for jobs.

YEAR	TEAM/LEVEL	G	IP	W-L	SAVES	HITS	SO	BB	ERA
1992	California	51	45	4-2	4	39	24	22	3.57
1993	California	55	48	2-3	13	41	22	26	2.98
1994	San Francisco	44	31	1-0	0	37	20	15	4.94

TODD FROHWIRTH / Boston Red Sox / Relief Pitcher $12

Bounced up and down in 1994, pitching well at Pawtucket (55 strikeouts in 52 innings) but getting the bejeebers beat out of him in Boston. I don't know what has gone wrong in his career, and suspect that, like Mark Eichorn, he might get it figured out, come back, and pitch well for several years. Don't draft him until you see some evidence of it.

YEAR	TEAM/LEVEL	G	IP	W-L	SAVES	HITS	SO	BB	ERA
1992	Baltimore	65	106	4-3	4	97	58	41	2.46
1993	Baltimore	70	96	6-7	3	91	50	44	3.83
1994	Boston	22	27	0-3	1	40	13	17	10.80

JEFF FRYE / Texas Rangers / Second Base $35

The Rangers have been looking for a leadoff hitter, and this is the man. After playing well the second half of 1992, he missed all of 1993 with a knee injury, and started 1994 at Oklahoma City. Called up in late April, he hit .327 with a .408 on-base percentage the rest of the year, missing three weeks in June with a pulled hamstring.

YEAR	TEAM/LEVEL	G	AB	R	H	2B	3B	HR	RBI	BB	SB	AVG	OBP	SLG
1993	Texas				(On Disabled List)									
1994	Texas	57	205	37	67	20	3	0	18	29	6	.327	.408	.454
1995	*Projected*	*116*	*395*	*60*	*111*	*28*	*4*	*2*	*37*	*50*	*9*	*.281*	*.362*	*.387*

TRAVIS FRYMAN / Detroit Tigers / Third Base $67

For a young superstar, he sure isn't doing much. His power was up a little last year, but then, so was everybody else's. His batting average, .263, just missed being the poorest of his career, and he struck out 128 times in 114 games, matching his total in 151 games in 1993. He wasn't adequate at shortstop, and he isn't anything special at third base.

YEAR	TEAM/LEVEL	G	AB	R	H	2B	3B	HR	RBI	BB	SB	AVG	OBP	SLG
1993	Detroit	151	607	98	182	37	5	22	97	77	9	.300	.379	.486
1994	Detroit	114	464	66	122	34	5	18	85	45	2	.263	.326	.474
1995	*Projected*	*158*	*641*	*96*	*181*	*39*	*4*	*25*	*103*	*65*	*7*	*.282*	*.348*	*.479*

GARY GAETTI / Kansas City Royals / Third Base $21

Has played amazingly well since joining the Royals in mid-1993, to my surprise; in fact, if I were to choose an all-guys-I-was-wrong-about All-Star team, I don't know if I'd put him or Tim Wallach at third base. He is 36, extremely slow, and he doesn't get on base. But as long as he drives in runs, he'll play.

YEAR	TEAM/LEVEL	G	AB	R	H	2B	3B	HR	RBI	BB	SB	AVG	OBP	SLG
1993	Two Teams	102	331	40	81	20	1	14	50	21	1	.245	.300	.438
1994	Kansas City	90	327	53	94	15	3	12	57	19	0	.287	.328	.462
1995	*Projected*	*119*	*405*	*41*	*92*	*20*	*1*	*11*	*52*	*24*	*1*	*.227*	*.270*	*.363*

GREG GAGNE / Kansas City Royals / Shortstop $34

He went 10-for-27 as a base stealer, the third straight year he has been under 50 percent. Most of these were busted hit-and-run plays . . . would have established a career high in walks, were it not for the strike. Heck, he might have had 40 . . . a fine player, and will probably keep his job despite KC's youth movement and new manager.

YEAR	TEAM/LEVEL	G	AB	R	H	2B	3B	HR	RBI	BB	SB	AVG	OBP	SLG
1993	Kansas City	159	540	66	151	32	3	10	57	33	10	.280	.319	.406
1994	Kansas City	107	375	39	97	23	3	7	51	27	10	.259	.314	.392
1995	*Projected*	*149*	*493*	*53*	*121*	*25*	*3*	*9*	*52*	*30*	*9*	*.245*	*.289*	*.363*

ANDRES GALARRAGA / Colorado Rockies / First Base $44

Andres is now in his mid-30s, and I still don't know what to make of him. His value has bounced up and down so much that I still don't really know how good he is. . . . He is the first player in history to hit 30 homers with 20 or fewer walks. And the trend line is down; in 1988, when he hit 29 homers, he drew 39 walks.

YEAR	TEAM/LEVEL	G	AB	R	H	2B	3B	HR	RBI	BB	SB	AVG	OBP	SLG
1993	Colorado	120	470	71	174	35	4	22	98	24	2	.370	.403	.602
1994	Colorado	103	417	77	133	21	0	31	85	19	8	.319	.356	.592
1995	*Projected*	*141*	*533*	*72*	*154*	*29*	*2*	*22*	*84*	*24*	*6*	*.289*	*.320*	*.475*

DAVE GALLAGHER / Atlanta Braves / Utility Outfielder $13

Most of his work last year was as a defensive replacement in left field, as the Braves were using a rookie first baseman in left field. Gallagher was released by the Mets a year ago after he hit .274 with a .443 slugging percentage, so his chance of finding a job after hitting .224 with a sub-.300 slugging percentage is not good.

YEAR	TEAM/LEVEL	G	AB	R	H	2B	3B	HR	RBI	BB	SB	AVG	OBP	SLG
1993	New York (N)	99	201	34	55	12	2	6	28	20	1	.274	.338	.443
1994	Atlanta	89	152	27	34	5	0	2	14	22	0	.224	.326	.296
1995	*Projected*	*64*	*99*	*15*	*25*	*7*	*1*	*1*	*12*	*11*	*1*	*.253*	*.327*	*.374*

MIKE GALLEGO / New York Yankees / Shortstop $27

He was more-or-less the Yankees shortstop last year, after a year at second base (1991), an injury year (1992), and a year playing all around the infield (1993). It is obviously risky to predict where he will be, with Derek Jeter coming in, but since he played well at short and the Yankees had a good year, I'd guess he will play somewhere.

YEAR	TEAM/LEVEL	G	AB	R	H	2B	3B	HR	RBI	BB	SB	AVG	OBP	SLG
1992	New York	53	173	24	44	7	1	3	14	20	0	.254	.343	.358
1993	New York	119	403	63	114	20	1	10	54	50	3	.283	.364	.412
1994	New York	89	306	39	73	17	1	6	41	38	0	.239	.327	.359

RON GANT / Cincinnati Reds / Left Field $41

He missed the year with a broken leg. The Reds, no longer satisfied with acquiring outfielders who immediately injure themselves, decided to save a step by signing one who was already injured. He will be useful, because he can play any of the three outfield positions, which will enable him to fill in for Kevin Mitchell or whichever Sanders is unavailable at the moment.

YEAR	TEAM/LEVEL	G	AB	R	H	2B	3B	HR	RBI	BB	SB	AVG	OBP	SLG
1992	Atlanta	153	544	74	141	22	6	17	80	45	32	.259	.321	.415
1993	Atlanta	157	606	113	166	27	4	36	117	67	26	.274	.345	.510
1994	Cincinnati						(Injured—Broken Leg)								

KEITH GARAGOZZO / New York Yankees / Left-handed Pitcher $12

A ninth-round 1991 pick out of the University of Delaware. The Twins took him in the Rule 5 draft, and he made the team with a solid spring training, but was returned to the Yankees in May. His best pitch is a forkball. The Yankees have better prospects, and it may take him two or three years to re-emerge, if he does.

YEAR	TEAM/LEVEL	G	IP	W-L	PCT	HITS	SO	BB	ERA
1993	Albany AA	17	86	4-6	.400	88	71	24	4.48
1994	Minnesota	7	9	0-0	.000	9	3	13	9.64
1994	AA and AAA	20	58	2-1	.667	57	39	38	4.63

CARLOS GARCIA / Pittsburgh Pirates / Second Base $37

He didn't hit quite as well in his second season as he did in his first, plus he made more errors in 98 games than he had made as a rookie in 140. Nobody's complaining; he's one of the better second basemen in the league, and headed up. Despite the error total, he played second more aggressively, and showed substantial improvement on the double play.

YEAR	TEAM/LEVEL	G	AB	R	H	2B	3B	HR	RBI	BB	SB	AVG	OBP	SLG
1993	Pittsburgh	141	546	77	147	25	5	12	47	31	18	.269	.316	.399
1994	Pittsburgh	98	412	49	114	15	2	6	28	16	18	.277	.309	.367
1995	*Projected*	*147*	*561*	*74*	*150*	*24*	*4*	*10*	*55*	*27*	*20*	*.267*	*.301*	*.379*

MIKE GARDINER / Detroit Tigers / Relief Pitcher $16

His ERA, 4.14, was the best of his five-year career, and his won-lost record was even for the first time. He held opponents to a .233 batting average. This may not keep him in the league. He had no defined role on a sorry staff, and his ERAs, by months, were 2.13, 2.79, 4.11, 5.40, and 7.50.

YEAR	TEAM/LEVEL	G	IP	W-L	PCT	HITS	SO	BB	ERA
1992	Boston	28	131	4-10	.286	126	79	58	4.75
1993	Two Teams	34	49	2-3	.400	52	25	26	4.93
1994	Detroit	38	59	2-2	.500	53	31	23	4.14

MARK GARDNER / Florida Marlins / Starting Pitcher $17

A 33-year-old right-hander, doesn't throw hard but gets strikeouts with good curve and a high, slow leg kick that destroys the hitter's timing. Allows very high average to left-handed hitters, but more power to right-handers. I don't understand this, but it must have something to do with his pitch selection . . . serviceable pitcher, nothing big in store for him.

YEAR	TEAM/LEVEL	G	IP	W-L	PCT	HITS	SO	BB	ERA
1992	Montreal	33	180	12-10	.545	179	132	60	4.36
1993	Kansas City	17	92	4-6	.400	92	54	36	6.19
1994	Florida	20	92	4-4	.500	97	57	30	4.87

BRENT GATES / Oakland Athletics / Second Base $34

Visited the disabled list twice in '94, once with a sprained thumb, and once with a sprained knee. In every generation of players there are several young second basemen who look like they will be great players, but who never get beyond where they were when they entered the league, because of injuries. Gates is a tremendous player if he is healthy.

YEAR	TEAM/LEVEL	G	AB	R	H	2B	3B	HR	RBI	BB	SB	AVG	OBP	SLG
1993	Oakland	139	535	64	155	29	2	7	69	56	7	.290	.357	.391
1994	Oakland	64	223	29	66	11	1	2	24	21	3	.283	.337	.365
1995	*Projected*	*142*	*523*	*66*	*155*	*30*	*2*	*7*	*67*	*54*	*6*	*.296*	*.362*	*.402*

KIRK GIBSON / Detroit Tigers / Outfield/Designated Hitter $24

At age 37, he had his best year since 1988, when he was the National League MVP. He hit .358 with runners in scoring position, which, combined with his power, gave him almost as many RBI in 330 at bats (72) as he had in 542 at bats in his MVP year (76) . . . obviously, we should not expect the same level of performance in '95.

YEAR	TEAM/LEVEL	G	AB	R	H	2B	3B	HR	RBI	BB	SB	AVG	OBP	SLG
1993	Detroit	116	403	62	105	18	6	13	62	44	15	.261	.337	.433
1994	Detroit	98	330	71	91	17	2	23	72	42	4	.276	.358	.548
1995	*Projected*	*99*	*314*	*50*	*78*	*13*	*2*	*12*	*48*	*37*	*9*	*.248*	*.328*	*.417*

PAUL GIBSON / New York Yankees / Relief Pitcher $19

He pitched well most of the year, but lost his ERA with a few bad outings in June, and didn't pitch enough innings to get it back . . . a left-handed short reliever, but actually is no more effective against left-handers than he is against right-handers, in part because he has no fastball, and therefore no intimidation effect.

YEAR	TEAM/LEVEL	G	IP	W-L	SAVES	HITS	SO	BB	ERA
1992	New York (N)	43	62	0-1	0	70	49	25	5.23
1993	Two Teams	28	44	3-1	0	45	37	11	3.47
1994	New York (A)	30	29	1-1	0	26	21	17	4.97

BERNARD GILKEY / St. Louis Cardinals / Left Field | $31

Continued to hit .300 on the road (.310), but hit only .189 with no home runs in St. Louis. In his career, only 34 percent of his home runs have been hit in St. Louis.

The Cardinals have four outfielders, so they may move one. If they do, Gilkey might be the man to leave—and another park might be the best thing for him.

YEAR	TEAM/LEVEL	G	AB	R	H	2B	3B	HR	RBI	BB	SB	AVG	OBP	SLG
1993	St. Louis	137	557	99	170	40	5	16	70	56	15	.305	.370	.481
1994	St. Louis	105	380	52	96	22	1	6	45	39	15	.253	.336	.363
1995	*Projected*	*130*	*457*	*67*	*124*	*25*	*3*	*9*	*52*	*49*	*17*	*.271*	*.342*	*.398*

JOE GIRARDI / Colorado Rockies / Catcher | $24

Well, we can say this much for him: He's consistent. He had a good year throwing out runners, catching 30 of 91, third-best percentage among NL catchers. Girardi hits the ball on the ground 68 percent of the time, and thus probably won't be hurt by moving out of Mile High Stadium. He's an OK platoon player, stretched to be a regular.

YEAR	TEAM/LEVEL	G	AB	R	H	2B	3B	HR	RBI	BB	SB	AVG	OBP	SLG
1993	Colorado	86	310	35	90	14	5	3	31	24	6	.290	.346	.397
1994	Colorado	93	330	47	91	9	4	4	34	21	3	.276	.321	.364
1995	*Projected*	*129*	*434*	*46*	*119*	*16*	*3*	*3*	*37*	*32*	*4*	*.274*	*.324*	*.346*

TOM GLAVINE / Atlanta Braves / Starting Pitcher | $78

Has given up only three homers in the last three years to left-handed hitters. . . . His strikeout rate went *up* dramatically last year, as he struck out more men in 165 innings than he had struck out the previous two years in 230. The previous two years he was working *behind* most the hitters. Last year he was getting ahead of the hitters.

YEAR	TEAM/LEVEL	G	IP	W-L	PCT	HITS	SO	BB	ERA
1992	Atlanta	33	225	20-8	.714	197	129	70	2.76
1993	Atlanta	36	239	22-6	.786	236	120	90	3.20
1994	Atlanta	25	165	13-9	.591	173	140	70	3.97

GEORGE GLINATSIS / Seattle Mariners / Right-handed Starter | $13

A 32nd-round draft pick from the University of Cincinnati, big, smart, changes speeds well and has good location. The Mariners could solve 80 percent of their long-range pitching problems if they would adopt a simple, hard-and-fast rule: 300 innings at Double- and Triple-A. For *everybody*. Instead, anybody pitches two good games in AA Ball, and he's in the rotation.

YEAR	TEAM/LEVEL	G	IP	W-L	PCT	HITS	SO	BB	ERA
1994	Riverside A	14	89	7-3	.700	84	80	17	2.94
1994	Jacksonville AA	9	54	5-2	.714	44	44	16	2.32
1994	Seattle	2	5	0-1	.000	9	1	6	13.50

JERRY GOFF / Pittsburgh Pirates / Catcher $11

A left-handed hitter, hit .297 in a late-season callup in 1993, which earned him a shot at the Pirates' roster last spring. He struck out 11 times in 25 at bats, which sent him back to Buffalo. He's hit 100 homers in the minor leagues, about 14 a year. He's not likely to get another clean shot at a job, except possibly during a strike.

YEAR	TEAM/LEVEL	G	AB	R	H	2B	3B	HR	RBI	BB	SB	AVG	OBP	SLG
1993	Pittsburgh	14	37	5	11	2	0	2	6	8	0	.297	.422	.514
1994	MLE	79	269	23	62	17	0	3	27	27	0	.230	.301	.327
1994	Pittsburgh	8	25	0	2	0	0	0	1	0	0	.080	.080	.080

GREG GOHR / Detroit Tigers / Starting Pitcher $18

The Tigers first-round pick in 1989, Gohr has been regarded as the best pitching prospect in the organization, based on nothing except an outstanding arm. He finally began to pitch well last year at Toledo, and was called up in June. He was very impressive at first, but faded in July, and went on the DL with an inflamed shoulder. Grade B prospect.

YEAR	TEAM/LEVEL	G	IP	W-L	PCT	HITS	SO	BB	ERA
1993	Detroit	16	23	0-0	.000	26	23	14	5.96
1994	Toledo AAA	12	73	6-4	.600	75	58	18	3.56
1994	Detroit	8	34	2-2	.500	36	21	21	4.50

CHRIS GOMEZ / Detroit Tigers / Shortstop/Second Base $26

Split time between short and second, resting Tinker or Evers. He hit better than expected in view of the fact that he hit .274 at Long Beach State, but I would be surprised if he continued to hit at this level. He participated in the league-wide slugfest in May (.346 with 5 homers, 26 RBI), but slipped steadily backward as the season wore on.

YEAR	TEAM/LEVEL	G	AB	R	H	2B	3B	HR	RBI	BB	SB	AVG	OBP	SLG
1993	MLE	87	271	27	62	10	1	0	19	22	4	.229	.287	.273
1993	Detroit	46	128	11	32	7	1	0	11	9	2	.250	.304	.320
1994	Detroit	84	296	32	76	19	0	8	53	33	5	.257	.336	.402

LEO GOMEZ / Baltimore Orioles / Third Base $29

After losing his 1993 season to tendinitis and a cyst on his wrist, Gomez lost his job when the Orioles signed Sabo to play third base. Sabo's injury gave Gomez a second chance, and he had an early-season hot streak. Right-handed power hitter, very slow, should be in his prime. I'd rather have him than Sabo, but we'll see what Phil Regan thinks.

YEAR	TEAM/LEVEL	G	AB	R	H	2B	3B	HR	RBI	BB	SB	AVG	OBP	SLG
1993	Baltimore	71	244	30	48	7	0	10	25	32	0	.197	.295	.348
1994	Baltimore	84	285	46	78	20	0	15	56	41	0	.274	.366	.502
1995	*Projected*	*119*	*399*	*56*	*96*	*19*	*1*	*17*	*57*	*57*	*2*	*.241*	*.336*	*.421*

PAT GOMEZ / San Francisco Giants / Relief Pitcher $15

A 27-year-old left-hander who was just wandering around the Atlanta system until he had a hot streak at Greenville in '92, going 7-0 with a 1.13 ERA. For most of his career he has had trouble throwing strikes, in- cluding last year, when he held left-handed hitters to an .061 batting average (2-for-33), but issued 20 walks in 33 innings.

YEAR	TEAM/LEVEL	G	IP	W-L	SAVES	HITS	SO	BB	ERA
1992	Richmond AAA	23	71	3-5	0	79	48	42	5.45
1993	San Diego	27	32	1-2	0	35	26	19	5.12
1994	San Francisco	26	33	0-1	0	23	14	20	3.78

RENE GONZALES / California Angels / Infield $13

Turned loose by California after two good years with the bat, Gonzales signed with Baltimore, was cut by them in spring training, and signed with Cleveland. He got a month in the majors, played all around the infield (mostly third base), and didn't discourage us from be- lieving that he can hit. Not a regular, but should be a useful sixth infielder.

YEAR	TEAM/LEVEL	G	AB	R	H	2B	3B	HR	RBI	BB	SB	AVG	OBP	SLG
1992	California	104	329	47	91	17	1	7	38	41	7	.277	.363	.398
1993	California	118	335	34	84	17	0	2	31	49	5	.251	.346	.319
1994	Cleveland	22	23	6	8	1	1	1	5	5	2	.348	.448	.609

ALEX GONZALEZ / Toronto Blue Jays / Shortstop $35

Was the hottest of hot prospects after playing well at Knoxville in '93, and opened the season as the Toronto shortstop. Six errors and 17 strikeouts in 15 games ended that, but he played as well at Syracuse as he had at Knoxville, or maybe better, and a second chance is unquestionably going to come, and soon. My guess is, he'll be an All-Star.

YEAR	TEAM/LEVEL	G	AB	R	H	2B	3B	HR	RBI	BB	SB	AVG	OBP	SLG
1993	MLE	142	544	75	145	27	5	14	55	26	27	.267	.300	.412
1994	Toronto	15	53	7	8	1	0	1	3	4	3	.151	.224	.245
1994	MLE	110	428	60	115	21	3	11	50	46	18	.269	.340	.409

JUAN GONZALEZ / Texas Rangers / Left Field $80

He was slowed by the new park in Texas, where it is 388 feet to left-center, and, apparently, by a degener- ating marriage. Despite this, he was on target to drive in 125 runs before the strike hit. His strikeout/walk ratio was the best of his career, and he established career highs in triples and stolen bases. There is no limit to his future.

YEAR	TEAM/LEVEL	G	AB	R	H	2B	3B	HR	RBI	BB	SB	AVG	OBP	SLG
1993	Texas	140	536	105	166	33	1	46	118	37	4	.310	.368	.632
1994	Texas	107	422	57	116	18	4	19	85	30	6	.275	.330	.472
1995	*Projected*	*152*	*582*	*92*	*165*	*30*	*3*	*38*	*112*	*41*	*4*	*.284*	*.331*	*.541*

LUIS GONZALEZ / Houston Astros / Left Field | $35

The pitching pattern changed to him after he hit .300 for the first time in '93—a lot more breaking pitches early in the count, a lot less willingness to give in to him—and Gonzalez struggled to adjust to it. He did adjust, by late June, and hit .350 over the last six weeks to finish at .273. A solid regular, not a star.

YEAR	TEAM/LEVEL	G	AB	R	H	2B	3B	HR	RBI	BB	SB	AVG	OBP	SLG
1993	Houston	154	540	82	162	34	3	15	72	47	20	.300	.361	.457
1994	Houston	112	392	57	107	29	4	8	67	49	15	.273	.353	.429
1995	*Projected*	*159*	*559*	*80*	*156*	*34*	*5*	*16*	*83*	*57*	*18*	*.279*	*.346*	*.444*

DWIGHT GOODEN / New York Mets / Starting Pitcher | $23

Missed five weeks early in the season with an injury to his toe, and went out in June when he failed a drug test. After three straight losing years, after 10 years of decline, he's hit bottom now; the question now is how far can he come back. He still has the equipment to be a good pitcher, if he can get his life together.

YEAR	TEAM/LEVEL	G	IP	W-L	PCT	HITS	SO	BB	ERA
1992	New York	31	206	10-13	.435	197	145	70	3.67
1993	New York	29	209	12-15	.444	188	149	61	3.45
1994	New York	7	41	3-4	.429	46	40	15	6.31

TOM GORDON / Kansas City Royals / Relief Pitcher | $44

Hal McRae deserves high marks for getting Gordon's career headed back north. He's had two winning years now, and from late July to late July he went 18-10 in a calendar year. His curveball is back, and there's never been anything wrong with his arm . . . gave up 40 stolen bases in '94, the most of any major league pitcher.

YEAR	TEAM/LEVEL	G	IP	W-L	PCT	HITS	SO	BB	ERA
1992	Kansas City	40	118	6-10	.375	116	98	55	4.59
1993	Kansas City	48	156	12-6	.667	125	143	77	3.58
1994	Kansas City	24	155	11-7	.611	136	126	87	4.35

GOOSE GOSSAGE / Seattle Mariners / Relief Pitcher | $16

A free agent at this writing, he will be looking for his 10th major league team (White Sox, Pittsburgh, Yankees, Padres, Cubs, Giants, Rangers, A's, and Mariners). He pitched reasonably well for the Mariners, and became the third major league pitcher to pitch in 1000 games. Keep pitchin', Goose; you're going to be retired a long time.

YEAR	TEAM/LEVEL	G	IP	W-L	SAVES	HITS	SO	BB	ERA
1992	Oakland	30	38	0-2	0	32	26	19	2.84
1993	Oakland	39	48	4-5	1	49	40	26	4.53
1994	Seattle	36	47	3-0	1	44	29	15	4.18

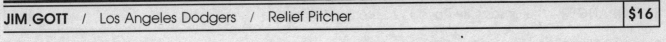

JIM GOTT / Los Angeles Dodgers / Relief Pitcher $16

Refused assignment to the minors and became a free agent in early October. His dismal season ended a string of five straight years with ERAs under 3.00, and was the first time he has really pitched badly since 1986. I suspect he'll come back somewhere else and pitch well, although probably not as a closer. He's 35.

YEAR	TEAM/LEVEL	G	IP	W-L	SAVES	HITS	SO	BB	ERA
1992	Los Angeles	68	88	3-3	6	72	75	41	2.45
1993	Los Angeles	62	78	4-8	25	71	67	17	2.32
1994	Los Angeles	37	36	5-3	2	46	29	20	5.94

MAURO GOZZO / New York Mets / Starting Pitcher $15

He's pitched 1100 innings in the minors, but apparently isn't quite ready yet. No, I'd like to see Gozzo succeed, because you always have to root for somebody who has paid his dues, but the league hit .304 against him, and he probably won't get another year to prove himself. Control good, durability excellent, fair stuff, needs major league innings, which he won't get.

YEAR	TEAM/LEVEL	G	IP	W-L	PCT	HITS	SO	BB	ERA
1993	New York	10	14	0-1	.000	11	6	5	2.57
1994	Norfolk AAA	4	29	2-2	.500	22	12	4	1.86
1994	New York	23	69	3-5	.375	86	33	28	4.83

MARK GRACE / Chicago Cubs / First Base $35

A revealing stat (about the Cubs): In the last three years, playing 419 games and batting 3-4-5, Grace has batted only 12 times with the bases loaded. A more typical figure would be 30 . . . as a left-handed hitter with a .370 on-base percentage, he'd be an excellent number-two hitter. There is no reason I can think of to hit him third.

YEAR	TEAM/LEVEL	G	AB	R	H	2B	3B	HR	RBI	BB	SB	AVG	OBP	SLG
1993	Chicago	155	594	86	193	39	4	14	98	71	8	.325	.393	.475
1994	Chicago	106	403	55	120	23	3	6	44	48	0	.298	.370	.414
1995	*Projected*	*154*	*589*	*76*	*176*	*32*	*3*	*11*	*75*	*69*	*5*	*.299*	*.372*	*.419*

JOE GRAHE / California Angels / Reliever $21

His season is a smorgasbord of unsightly numbers: a .362 opposition batting average (.405 by left-handed hitters), an ERA of 11.32 after July 1, and 65 percent of his inherited runners crossed the plate (13 of 20). He backed into the closer job here with no real credentials, just because the Angels were desperate, and has held onto it by timely hot streaks.

YEAR	TEAM/LEVEL	G	IP	W-L	SAVES	HITS	SO	BB	ERA
1992	California	46	95	5-6	21	85	39	39	3.52
1993	California	45	57	4-1	11	54	31	25	2.86
1994	California	40	43	2-5	13	68	26	18	6.65

JEFF GRANGER / Kansas City Royals / Starting Pitcher $22

A quarterback at Texas A&M, he was the Royals' first-round draft pick in 1993. Throws hard, looks good on the mound, does well in the post-game interviews. He hasn't shown much yet as a pitcher, doesn't have a major league breaking ball, and doesn't change speeds well. There is no obvious reason he can't learn these things, but it's early.

YEAR	TEAM/LEVEL	G	IP	W-L	PCT	HITS	SO	BB	ERA
1993	Kansas City	1	1	0-0	.000	3	1	2	27.00
1994	Memphis AA	25	140	7-7	.500	155	112	61	3.87
1994	Kansas City	2	9	0-1	.000	13	3	6	6.75

CRAIG GREBECK / Chicago White Sox / Shortstop/Second Base $23

Had a good year when he got to play. He backs up three good and durable players (Cora, Ventura, and Guillen), and also missed more than a month with a torn deltoid ligament. 1995 may, or may not, be his free agent year, depending on how the service time issue is resolved. Grebeck deserves a chance to play regularly, which may come in '96.

YEAR	TEAM/LEVEL	G	AB	R	H	2B	3B	HR	RBI	BB	SB	AVG	OBP	SLG
1993	Chicago	72	190	25	43	5	0	1	12	26	1	.226	.319	.268
1994	Chicago	35	97	17	30	5	0	0	5	12	0	.309	.391	.361
1995	*Projected*	*85*	*236*	*27*	*61*	*11*	*1*	*2*	*22*	*30*	*1*	*.258*	*.342*	*.339*

SHAWN GREEN / Toronto Blue Jays / Outfielder $34

The Blue Jays' first-round draft pick in 1991, he showed tremendous improvement in his first season at Triple-A. He is, like Ted Williams, a tall, skinny left-handed batter from California. A year ago I wasn't impressed by him, but he is very young, and his '93 batting stats may have been misleading because of a broken thumb. **Grade A prospect.**

YEAR	TEAM/LEVEL	G	AB	R	H	2B	3B	HR	RBI	BB	SB	AVG	OBP	SLG
1993	MLE	99	348	32	90	13	1	3	27	17	2	.259	.293	.328
1994	MLE	109	423	71	139	26	2	12	53	35	14	.329	.380	.485
1994	Toronto	14	33	1	3	1	0	0	1	1	1	.091	.118	.121

TYLER GREEN / Philadelphia Phillies / Starting Pitcher $13

Freckle-faced six-foot-five-inch right-hander, who apparently can be added to the long list of hard-throwing youngsters who threw their arms out before they reached the majors. A dominating pitcher at Wichita State, he pitched well in the low minors, but had several injuries, which the Phillies announced were very minor. The results of these minor injuries can be seen below.

YEAR	TEAM/LEVEL	G	IP	W-L	PCT	HITS	SO	BB	ERA
1993	Scranton AAA	28	118	6-10	.375	102	87	43	3.95
1993	Philadelphia	3	7	0-0	.000	16	7	5	7.36
1994	Scranton AAA	27	162	7-16	.304	179	95	77	5.56

TOMMY GREENE / Philadelphia Phillies / Starting Pitcher $20

A tremendous pitcher, but it now seems obvious that he's not going to stay healthy. His 1994 season was ended in May by surgery on his rotator cuff, his second major injury in three years. His career record is 38-19 . . . has career batting average over .200, and has hit four major league home runs.

YEAR	TEAM/LEVEL	G	IP	W-L	PCT	HITS	SO	BB	ERA
1992	Philadelphia	13	64	3-3	.500	75	39	34	5.32
1993	Philadelphia	31	200	16-4	.800	175	167	62	3.42
1994	Philadelphia	7	36	2-0	1.000	37	28	22	4.54

WILLIE GREENE / Cincinnati Reds / Third Base $32

If they ever let him play, he's going to hit 20 or 30 home runs. Greene, who is only 23, has been a visible prospect for about four years now, and hit very well in a 29-game trial in 1992. Since then the Reds have lain awake at night, figuring out ways to keep him from playing. The 1994 innovation was to sign Tony Fernandez.

YEAR	TEAM/LEVEL	G	AB	R	H	2B	3B	HR	RBI	BB	SB	AVG	OBP	SLG
1992	MLE	96	340	38	88	17	1	15	54	34	5	.259	.326	.447
1993	MLE	98	332	49	82	17	0	20	46	42	1	.247	.332	.479
1994	MLE	114	423	64	112	22	0	21	67	49	6	.265	.341	.466

MIKE GREENWELL / Boston Red Sox / Left Field $34

Had exactly the same number of doubles, homers, and RBI as Marquis Grissom—but had a better on-base percentage and a better slugging percentage than Grissom did. His season ended a few days early (August 4) due to arthroscopic surgery on his left shoulder. He's a career .300 hitter (.304), and has more extra-base hits every year than strikeouts (last year, 37-26).

YEAR	TEAM/LEVEL	G	AB	R	H	2B	3B	HR	RBI	BB	SB	AVG	OBP	SLG
1993	Boston	146	540	77	170	38	6	13	72	54	5	.315	.379	.480
1994	Boston	95	327	60	88	25	1	11	45	38	2	.269	.348	.453
1995	*Projected*	*142*	*526*	*76*	*152*	*31*	*3*	*14*	*68*	*56*	*5*	*.289*	*.357*	*.439*

RUSTY GREER / Texas Rangers / Right Field $35

A 26-year-old left-handed hitter, basically a first baseman but was forced to play the outfield because the Rangers don't need a first baseman. If it turns out that he's really a .314 hitter I'll be surprised, but should hit .270-.280 with some walks and some power. He's a better hitter than Dan Peltier, whose roster spot he took, or David Hulse.

YEAR	TEAM/LEVEL	G	AB	R	H	2B	3B	HR	RBI	BB	SB	AVG	OBP	SLG
1993	MLE	137	483	65	126	23	4	12	50	40	7	.261	.317	.400
1994	Texas	80	277	36	87	16	1	10	46	46	0	.314	.410	.487
1995	*Projected*	*147*	*503*	*69*	*140*	*29*	*3*	*12*	*60*	*62*	*3*	*.278*	*.358*	*.419*

KEN GRIFFEY, JR. / Seattle Mariners / Center Field — $99

With 174 career home runs he leads Henry Aaron at the same age, 174-140. He has played 113 more games than Aaron had (845-732), but has also homered more often per game or at bat. . . . Has already been intentionally walked 100 times in his career . . . in my own humble opinion, he is *not* extremely fast, and not a Gold Glove outfielder.

YEAR	TEAM/LEVEL	G	AB	R	H	2B	3B	HR	RBI	BB	SB	AVG	OBP	SLG
1993	Seattle	156	582	113	180	38	3	45	109	96	17	.309	.408	.617
1994	Seattle	111	433	94	140	24	4	40	90	56	11	.323	.402	.674
1995	*Projected*	*159*	*613*	*114*	*196*	*37*	*4*	*41*	*116*	*82*	*10*	*.320*	*.400*	*.594*

JASON GRIMSLEY / Cleveland Indians / Starting Pitcher — $28

Started the season at Charlotte, but started 7-0, earning a callup. He just hit his stride before the strike, going 4-1 after the All-Star game. He is no longer the immature pitcher who came up with Philadelphia in '89, and I believe he is now ready to be a winning pitcher. I expect him to win 14 to 17 games this year.

YEAR	TEAM/LEVEL	G	IP	W-L	PCT	HITS	SO	BB	ERA
1993	Charlotte AAA	28	135	6-6	.500	138	102	49	3.39
1993	Cleveland	10	42	3-4	.429	52	27	20	5.31
1994	Cleveland	14	83	5-2	.714	91	59	34	4.57

MARQUIS GRISSOM / Montreal Expos / Center Field — $77

Until last year, his batting average and slugging percentage had gone up every year. They didn't go *up* in '94, but they didn't go down much, either . . . alternates between hitting first and third for Montreal, often dropping to third against lefties (although, over three years, his average is actually better against right-handers) . . . a tremendous player, at bat and in the field.

YEAR	TEAM/LEVEL	G	AB	R	H	2B	3B	HR	RBI	BB	SB	AVG	OBP	SLG
1993	Montreal	157	630	104	188	27	2	19	95	52	53	.298	.351	.438
1994	Montreal	110	475	96	137	25	4	11	45	41	36	.288	.344	.427
1995	*Projected*	*157*	*650*	*108*	*183*	*30*	*5*	*15*	*73*	*52*	*62*	*.282*	*.335*	*.412*

BUDDY GROOM / Detroit Tigers / Starting Pitcher — $20

He is 28 years old and has yet to win a game in the major leagues (he is 0-8), but I still believe he will eventually be a decent major league pitcher. His combination of ground balls, good control, good mechanics, and a good health record—it's got to pay off sooner or later. Pitched well in a very limited role in '94.

YEAR	TEAM/LEVEL	G	IP	W-L	SAVES	HITS	SO	BB	ERA
1992	Detroit	12	39	0-5	1	48	15	22	5.82
1993	Detroit	19	37	0-2	0	48	15	13	6.14
1994	Detroit	40	32	0-1	1	31	27	13	3.94

KEVIN GROSS / Los Angeles Dodgers / Starting Pitcher | $31

Posted a winning record for the first time since 1985, when he was 15-13 for Philadelphia. What's amazing is that he managed to stay in the rotation almost without fail for all those years, starting 30 or more times in '86, '87, '88, '89, '92 and '93. He's reached 120 wins—and he's a better pitcher now than he's ever been.

YEAR	TEAM/LEVEL	G	IP	W-L	PCT	HITS	SO	BB	ERA
1992	Los Angeles	34	205	8-13	.381	182	158	77	3.17
1993	Los Angeles	33	202	13-13	.500	224	150	74	4.14
1994	Los Angeles	25	157	9-7	.563	162	124	43	3.60

EDDIE GUARDADO / Minnesota Twins / Starting Pitcher | $18

Guardado made 16 starts for the Twins in 1993, occasionally getting someone out. He's a short, heavy left-hander who usually throws his fastball above the belt and his curveball below. Back at Salt Lake City this year, he pitched fairly well (remember, ERAs in the PCL are inflated), but was again ineffective in a major league trial. Grade B prospect.

YEAR	TEAM/LEVEL	G	IP	W-L	PCT	HITS	SO	BB	ERA
1993	Minnesota	19	95	3-8	.273	123	46	36	6.18
1994	Salt Lake AAA	24	151	12-7	.632	171	87	51	4.83
1994	Minnesota	4	17	0-2	.000	26	8	4	8.47

MARK GUBICZA / Kansas City Royals / Reliever/Starter | $20

Every year he becomes more of a ground-ball pitcher, last year getting 255 ground-ball outs, as opposed to 106 flies and popups. The league hit .301 against him, which offset all the good things he was doing—not walking anybody, not giving up home runs, cutting off the running game. Will have to prove to Bob Boone that he can still pitch.

YEAR	TEAM/LEVEL	G	IP	W-L	PCT	HITS	SO	BB	ERA
1992	Kansas City	18	111	7-6	.538	110	81	36	3.72
1993	Kansas City	49	104	5-8	.385	128	80	43	4.66
1994	Kansas City	22	130	7-9	.438	158	59	26	4.50

OZZIE GUILLEN / Chicago White Sox / Shortstop | $32

He doesn't run as well as he did before his collision with Tim Raines in April 1992, but otherwise he's just the same, maybe a little bit better as a hitter. His on-base percentage last year, .311, is a) lousy, but b) just one point short of his career high. His .288 average was a career high. He'll play another 10 years.

YEAR	TEAM/LEVEL	G	AB	R	H	2B	3B	HR	RBI	BB	SB	AVG	OBP	SLG
1993	Chicago	134	457	44	128	23	4	4	50	10	5	.280	.292	.374
1994	Chicago	100	365	46	105	9	5	1	39	14	5	.288	.311	.348
1995	Projected	138	457	48	120	17	3	2	47	13	5	.263	.283	.326

BILL GULLICKSON / Detroit Tigers / Starting Pitcher $22

Opponents hit .322 against him, with 24 homers in 484 at bats. His 1994 season was awful, but I wouldn't rule out another comeback. He's always been a put-the-ball-in-play-and-let-your-defense-work kind of pitcher, and may have been hampered by a) the super-lively ball, and b) the fact that he had no defense behind him.

YEAR	TEAM/LEVEL	G	IP	W-L	PCT	HITS	SO	BB	ERA
1992	Detroit	34	222	14-13	.519	228	64	50	4.34
1993	Detroit	28	159	13-9	.591	186	70	44	5.37
1994	Detroit	21	115	4-5	.444	156	65	25	5.93

MARK GUTHRIE / Minnesota Twins / Relief Pitcher $22

A highly effective reliever in '92, he lost most of the '93 season to a blood clot in his shoulder. Beginning 1994 as a starting pitcher, he was bounced from the rotation after two dismal starts, and gave up 24 earned runs in his first 24 innings. After that, he pitched pretty well. A gamble for '95, but a good gamble.

YEAR	TEAM/LEVEL	G	IP	W-L	SAVES	HITS	SO	BB	ERA
1992	Minnesota	54	75	2-3	5	59	76	23	2.88
1993	Minnesota	22	21	2-1	0	20	15	16	4.71
1994	Minnesota	50	51	4-2	1	65	38	18	6.14

RICKY GUTIERREZ / San Diego Padres / Shortstop $23

Gutierrez has had two years to show what he could do at shortstop, but he hasn't shown much. His .250 batting average is OK and the walks help, but he strikes out a lot and has no power. He's fast, but 6-for-15 as a base stealer. At short he was fair in '93, but very poor in '94. Holbert or Lopez will probably take his job away.

YEAR	TEAM/LEVEL	G	AB	R	H	2B	3B	HR	RBI	BB	SB	AVG	OBP	SLG
1992	Rochester AAA	125	431	54	109	9	3	0	41	53	14	.253	.331	.288
1993	San Diego	133	438	76	110	10	5	5	26	50	4	.251	.334	.331
1994	San Diego	90	275	27	66	11	2	1	28	32	2	.240	.321	.305

JOSE GUZMAN / Chicago Cubs / Starting Pitcher $15

Guzman lost two years out of his career earlier (1989-90) with a back injury and a partially torn rotator cuff. Last year it was his shoulder. His shoulder bothered him from opening day, and he had arthroscopic surgery in late May, missing the rest of the season. I don't know how to estimate the odds on a second comeback, but I wouldn't be wildly optimistic.

YEAR	TEAM/LEVEL	G	IP	W-L	PCT	HITS	SO	BB	ERA
1992	Texas	33	224	16-11	.593	229	179	73	3.66
1993	Chicago	30	191	12-10	.545	188	163	74	4.34
1994	Chicago	4	20	2-2	.500	22	11	13	9.15

JUAN GUZMAN / Toronto Blue Jays / Starting Pitcher $37

He had a winning record, and his career winning percentage dropped almost a hundred points, from .784 to .693. Because of his inability to get his curve in the strike zone consistently, I've never thought that Guz-man was an outstanding pitcher—but he's healthy, he pitched well in July and early August, and his outlook is as good now as it has ever been.

YEAR	TEAM/LEVEL	G	IP	W-L	PCT	HITS	SO	BB	ERA
1992	Toronto	28	181	16-5	.762	135	165	72	2.64
1993	Toronto	33	221	14-3	.824	211	194	110	3.99
1994	Toronto	25	147	12-11	.522	165	124	76	5.68

CHRIS GWYNN / Los Angeles Dodgers / Left Field $18

He was cut by the Royals in spring training, despite a .300 average in '93, and returned to the Dodgers. Lasorda used him mainly as a pinch hitter, and he was good in that role (11-for-35, .314, with two homers). He also started nine games in left field. He's well cast as a pinch hitter, and could continue to thrive.

YEAR	TEAM/LEVEL	G	AB	R	H	2B	3B	HR	RBI	BB	SB	AVG	OBP	SLG
1992	Kansas City	34	84	10	24	3	2	1	7	3	0	.286	.303	.405
1993	Kansas City	103	287	36	86	14	4	1	25	24	0	.300	.354	.387
1994	Los Angeles	58	71	9	19	0	0	3	13	7	0	.268	.333	.394

TONY GWYNN / San Diego Padres / Right Field $70

If there was any doubt about Tony being a Hall of Famer, I would think that fifth batting title with a .394 average should just about do it. His career batting av-erage is now .3335. He could now go 0-for-738 and he would still be a lifetime .300 hitter . . . grounded into 19 double plays, one per 22 at bats. Ouch.

YEAR	TEAM/LEVEL	G	AB	R	H	2B	3B	HR	RBI	BB	SB	AVG	OBP	SLG
1993	San Diego	122	489	70	175	41	3	7	59	36	14	.358	.398	.497
1994	San Diego	110	419	79	165	35	1	12	64	48	5	.394	.454	.568
1995	*Projected*	*133*	*527*	*73*	*171*	*28*	*4*	*7*	*55*	*50*	*7*	*.324*	*.383*	*.433*

JOHN HABYAN / St. Louis Cardinals / Middle Relief $22

Hadn't given up a run in six weeks when the strike hit. Of course, he'd been on the DL with a pulled rib cage muscle for three of those weeks, but still had a scoreless streak of about a dozen outings . . . a competent and consistent middle reliever, a sinker/slider pitcher with very good control. As safe a player as there is in his category.

YEAR	TEAM/LEVEL	G	IP	W-L	SAVES	HITS	SO	BB	ERA
1992	New York	56	73	5-6	7	84	44	21	3.84
1993	Two Teams	48	56	2-1	1	59	39	20	4.15
1994	St. Louis	52	47	1-0	1	50	46	20	3.23

CHIP HALE / Minnesota Twins / Infielder $17

Once a prospect, he has finally settled into the role of backup infielder, and done well there for two years. He started 24 games last year, 18 of them at third base, and played a little bit of defense all around the infield. Thirty years old, as good a player as some of the guys who play every day.

YEAR	TEAM/LEVEL	G	AB	R	H	2B	3B	HR	RBI	BB	SB	AVG	OBP	SLG
1992	MLE	132	463	61	124	23	7	0	42	59	3	.268	.351	.348
1993	Minnesota	69	186	25	62	6	1	3	27	18	2	.333	.408	.425
1994	Minnesota	67	118	13	31	9	0	1	11	16	0	.263	.350	.364

DARREN HALL / Toronto Blue Jays / Right-handed Reliever $23

After spending nine seasons in the minors, Hall got a shot in the Blue Jay bullpen with Duane Ward's injury, and made the best of it, getting 17 saves in 20 opportunities. He has a good arm, but his future is probably very limited. He's 30, had rotator cuff surgery in 1990, and has never pitched consistently well at any level.

YEAR	TEAM/LEVEL	G	IP	W-L	SAVES	HITS	SO	BB	ERA
1992	Syracuse AAA	55	69	4-6	5	62	49	35	4.30
1993	Syracuse AAA	60	79	6-7	13	75	68	31	5.33
1994	Toronto	30	32	2-3	17	26	28	14	3.41

JOE HALL / Chicago White Sox / Outfield $16

After six years on the farm, Hall hit .290 at Nashville in 1993, and appeared to have a shot at the major league roster. He gets to spring training, and there's Michael Jordan—wanting the same job. Hall out-hit Michael in spring training by 400 points, won the job, and was on the opening-day roster . . . best asset is his throwing arm.

YEAR	TEAM/LEVEL	G	AB	R	H	2B	3B	HR	RBI	BB	SB	AVG	OBP	SLG
1993	Nashville	116	424	66	123	33	5	10	59	52	10	.290	.371	.462
1993	MLE	116	407	52	106	28	3	8	45	41	7	.260	.328	.403
1994	Chicago	17	28	8	11	3	0	1	5	2	0	.393	.452	.607

BOB HAMELIN / Kansas City Royals / Designated Hitter $37

An enormous man, officially listed at 235 pounds. Comparable to Kent Hrbek in terms of what he can produce, but his stroke is very different—a long, flat stroke with a lot of arm movement, unlike Hrbek's quick wrist action. He has an unusual ability to adjust his swing while his bat is moving at a high speed, find the ball, and still hit hard.

YEAR	TEAM/LEVEL	G	AB	R	H	2B	3B	HR	RBI	BB	SB	AVG	OBP	SLG
1993	Kansas City	16	49	2	11	3	0	2	5	6	0	.224	.309	.408
1994	Kansas City	101	312	64	88	25	1	24	65	56	4	.282	.388	.599
1995	*Projected*	*155*	*550*	*78*	*136*	*23*	*1*	*27*	*92*	*80*	*5*	*.247*	*.343*	*.440*

DARYL HAMILTON / Milwaukee Brewers / Center Field $31

His season was truncated by elbow surgery in early June; the elbow had been bothering him most of the year, so he didn't get much done. A career .295 hitter with good speed, bats left. I see no reason why he would not recover, and rank among the better center fielders in the American League.

YEAR	TEAM/LEVEL	G	AB	R	H	2B	3B	HR	RBI	BB	SB	AVG	OBP	SLG
1993	Milwaukee	135	520	74	161	21	1	9	48	45	21	.310	.367	.406
1994	Milwaukee	36	141	23	37	10	1	1	13	15	3	.262	.331	.369
1995	*Projected*	*133*	*449*	*64*	*129*	*18*	*3*	*5*	*48*	*44*	*26*	*.287*	*.351*	*.374*

JOEY HAMILTON / San Diego Padres / Starting Pitcher $38

The Padres' first-round draft pick in 1991, he was generally unimpressive in the minor leagues (20-21 career record), but awfully impressive once he got to the majors. Called up May 23, he pitched well almost every time he took the mound . . . good size, good mechanics, throws hard. Will be the ace of the San Diego staff when Andy Benes moves on.

YEAR	TEAM/LEVEL	G	IP	W-L	PCT	HITS	SO	BB	ERA
1993	Las Vegas AAA	8	47	3-2	.600	49	33	22	4.40
1994	Las Vegas AAA	9	59	3-5	.375	69	32	22	2.73
1994	San Diego	16	109	9-6	.600	98	61	29	2.98

ATLEE HAMMAKER / Chicago White Sox / Relief Pitcher $17

A 36 years old (turned 37 in January), he had been out of baseball for two years before deciding to launch a comeback. He started at Birmingham, pitched well there, moved up to Nashville, pitched well there, and made it back to the majors a few days before the strike. He's always been a good pitcher; if his workload doesn't exceed his limits, he'll be effective.

YEAR	TEAM/LEVEL	G	IP	W-L	SAVES	HITS	SO	BB	ERA
1994	Birmingham AA	13	18	1-0	0	13	17	10	2.00
1994	Nashville AAA	21	29	2-1	3	24	29	11	2.79
1994	Chicago	2	1	0-0	0	1	1	0	0.00

CHRIS HAMMOND / Florida Marlins / Starting Pitcher $23

Hammond has 29 wins in his career—26 before the All-Star break, and 3 after. His losses are almost evenly distributed (18 before the break, 17 after). He went out in June last year with a strained back . . . a good pitcher when healthy, better than his records show. He needs to work on four days' rest; with longer rest his control goes.

YEAR	TEAM/LEVEL	G	IP	W-L	PCT	HITS	SO	BB	ERA
1992	Cincinnati	28	147	7-10	.412	149	79	55	4.21
1993	Florida	32	191	11-12	.478	207	108	66	4.66
1994	Florida	13	73	4-4	.500	79	40	23	3.07

JEFF HAMMONDS / Baltimore Orioles / Outfielder $20

Had major surgery in October to repair a degenerated ligament in his left knee. He is expected to be out until at least June, and may miss the 1995 season. Highly touted last year. I was skeptical because reports were that he would swing at anything, and I figured pitchers would take advantage of this. That turned out to be not such a big problem.

YEAR	TEAM/LEVEL	G	AB	R	H	2B	3B	HR	RBI	BB	SB	AVG	OBP	SLG
1993	MLE	60	232	29	62	9	0	6	26	9	6	.267	.295	.384
1993	Baltimore	33	105	10	32	8	0	3	19	2	4	.305	.312	.467
1994	Baltimore	68	250	45	74	18	2	8	31	17	5	.295	.339	.480

MIKE HAMPTON / Houston Astros / Starting Pitcher $23

A starter in the minor leagues, with Seattle, he was converted to the bullpen because the Astros' rotation is solid, or perhaps because Terry Collins was following Earl Weaver's rule that the best place for a rookie pitcher is long relief. In any case, I like him. Small left-hander, above-average fastball, changes speeds well, slider is coming around. Could have a good career.

YEAR	TEAM/LEVEL	G	IP	W-L	PCT	HITS	SO	BB	ERA
1993	Jacksonville AA	15	87	6-4	.600	71	84	33	3.71
1993	Seattle	13	17	1-3	.250	28	8	17	9.53
1994	Houston	44	41	2-1	.667	46	24	16	3.70

CHRIS HANEY / Kansas City Royals / Starting Pitcher $22

He's a weird pitcher. He pitches very, very well 20 percent of the time. Five to 10 starts a year, he paints the black, works in and out, and has everybody off stride. The rest of the time he just throws the ball up there. His new manager, Bob Boone, may be able to do something with him that McRae never was.

YEAR	TEAM/LEVEL	G	IP	W-L	PCT	HITS	SO	BB	ERA
1992	Two Teams	16	80	4-6	.400	75	54	26	4.61
1993	Kansas City	23	124	9-9	.500	141	65	53	6.02
1994	Kansas City	6	28	2-2	.500	36	18	11	7.31

TODD HANEY / Chicago Cubs / Infielder $15

Primarily a second baseman, 29 years old, right-handed hitter, designated for reassignment at the end of the season. I'd compare him to Doug Strange or Chip Hale—a knockaround player who doesn't have any skill which demands immediate playing time, but who is nonetheless probably as good a player as Jody Reed or Mickey Morandini or Chico Lind, if a chance came his way.

YEAR	TEAM/LEVEL	G	AB	R	H	2B	3B	HR	RBI	BB	SB	AVG	OBP	SLG
1993	MLE	136	484	53	125	27	2	2	35	27	8	.258	.297	.335
1994	MLE	83	293	37	77	19	0	2	27	21	6	.263	.312	.348
1994	Chicago	17	37	6	6	0	0	1	2	3	2	.162	.238	.243

DAVE HANSEN / Los Angeles Dodgers / Third Base $21

Hansen failed his shot at being the Dodgers' third baseman in '92, hit rockets off the bench in '93, and opened '94 hoping to get back in the lineup. A strained abdominal muscle and Tim Wallach's stunning comeback prevented that from happening, but he continued to hit rockets. He is 26, so time is on his side—but only if he keeps hitting.

YEAR	TEAM/LEVEL	G	AB	R	H	2B	3B	HR	RBI	BB	SB	AVG	OBP	SLG
1992	Los Angeles	132	341	30	73	11	0	6	22	34	0	.214	.286	.299
1993	Los Angeles	84	105	13	38	3	0	4	30	21	0	.362	.465	.505
1994	Los Angeles	40	44	3	15	3	0	0	5	5	0	.341	.408	.409

ERIK HANSON / Cincinnati Reds / Starting Pitcher $22

His strikeout-to-walk ratio is so impressive that one keeps expecting the rest of his record to follow along, and eventually it will, if he can get healthy. His '94 season was ended by a torn anterior cruciate ligament, a serious injury, but no followup information has appeared. He's frustrating, but I still believe that sooner or later he will have a big year.

YEAR	TEAM/LEVEL	G	IP	W-L	PCT	HITS	SO	BB	ERA
1992	Seattle	31	187	8-17	.320	209	112	57	4.82
1993	Seattle	31	215	11-12	.478	215	163	60	3.47
1994	Cincinnati	22	123	5-5	.500	137	101	23	4.11

MIKE HARKEY / Colorado Rockies / Starting Pitcher $19

At this point, his chance to be good is almost gone. The problem isn't simply that he's had shoulder injuries. The problem is that he's had so many shoulder injuries for so long that it's disrupted the learning curve. He's 28. He doesn't have the fastball he had when he was 22, and he hasn't had the opportunity to develop anything else.

YEAR	TEAM/LEVEL	G	IP	W-L	PCT	HITS	SO	BB	ERA
1992	Chicago	7	38	4-0	1.000	38	21	15	1.89
1993	Chicago	28	157	10-10	.500	187	67	43	5.26
1994	Colorado	24	92	1-6	.143	125	39	35	5.79

PETE HARNISCH / Houston Astros / Starting Pitcher $51

Started badly, carrying a 7.15 ERA into late May. An examination discovered a slight tear of a tendon in his shoulder, and he went to the DL. After he returned he was 6-1 with a 3.81 ERA, so I would say the outlook for 1995 was not reduced any by his high ERA last year. He's among the better pitchers in the league.

YEAR	TEAM/LEVEL	G	IP	W-L	PCT	HITS	SO	BB	ERA
1992	Houston	34	207	9-10	.474	182	164	64	3.70
1993	Houston	33	218	16-9	.640	171	185	79	2.98
1994	Houston	17	95	8-5	.615	100	62	39	5.40

BRIAN HARPER / Milwaukee Brewers / Catcher/Designated Hitter $34

Started 24 games at catcher for the Brewers, a few games in the outfield, mostly worked as DH. His season ended June 26 due to a broken wrist. He's 35, terribly slow, no defense. Never forget this, in evaluting talent:

For *nine years*, major league executives were unanimously convinced that Harper couldn't play. But he has now played 999 major league games, hitting .296.

YEAR	TEAM/LEVEL	G	AB	R	H	2B	3B	HR	RBI	BB	SB	AVG	OBP	SLG
1993	Minnesota	147	530	52	161	26	1	12	73	29	1	.304	.347	.425
1994	Milwaukee	64	251	23	73	15	0	4	32	9	0	.291	.318	.398
1995	*Projected*	*95*	*331*	*32*	*95*	*17*	*0*	*6*	*44*	*17*	*1*	*.287*	*.322*	*.393*

GENE HARRIS / Detroit Tigers / Relief Pitcher $14

Started the '94 season as San Diego's closer, but blew his first three save chances, and had an 8.03 ERA through 13 games. He was traded to the Tigers, but wasn't much better there, and also took a turn on the DL with a sprained elbow. He doesn't have closer stuff, and he doesn't have any record of consistent success.

YEAR	TEAM/LEVEL	G	IP	W-L	SAVES	HITS	SO	BB	ERA
1992	Two Teams	22	30	0-2	0	23	25	15	4.15
1993	San Diego	59	59	6-6	23	57	39	37	3.03
1994	Two Teams	24	24	1-1	1	34	19	12	7.61

GREG HARRIS / Released / Relief Pitcher $14

He's pushing 40, and it's probably time to see how he can do left-handed. Harris was released by Boston July 2, signed with the Yankees, cut by them. It is certainly possible that his career is over, but I will not be surprised if he comes back and pitches well. He's in good shape, knows what he is doing, and has unusual determination.

YEAR	TEAM/LEVEL	G	IP	W-L	SAVES	HITS	SO	BB	ERA
1992	Boston	70	108	4-9	4	82	73	60	2.51
1993	Boston	80	112	6-7	8	95	103	60	3.77
1994	Two Teams	38	51	3-5	2	64	48	26	7.99

GREG W. HARRIS / Colorado Rockies / Starting Pitcher $19

Allowing 99 runs in 130 innings, he led the league in runs allowed for the second consecutive year. He dropped from the rotation in June, worked out of the bullpen for a month, wasn't any more effective, returned to the rotation in late July. He's probably not as bad as his record, but he's not likely to overcome the Rockies and win 20, either.

YEAR	TEAM/LEVEL	G	IP	W-L	PCT	HITS	SO	BB	ERA
1992	San Diego	20	118	4-8	.333	113	66	35	4.12
1993	Two Teams	35	225	11-17	.393	239	123	69	4.59
1994	Colorado	29	130	3-12	.200	154	82	52	6.65

LENNY HARRIS / Cincinnati Reds / Utilityman $21

For the fourth time in five years, he hit well—.304 in '90, .287 in '91, .271 in '92, .310 last year . . . 45 of his 100 at bats were as a pinch hitter. He's a left-handed hitter, a 75 percent base stealer, not a bad second baseman. That doesn't make him Carlos Baerga, or even Bret Boone, but it's a long way from Craig Shipley.

YEAR	TEAM/LEVEL	G	AB	R	H	2B	3B	HR	RBI	BB	SB	AVG	OBP	SLG
1993	Los Angeles	107	160	20	38	6	1	2	11	15	3	.238	.303	.325
1994	Cincinnati	66	100	13	31	3	1	0	14	5	7	.310	.340	.360
1995	*Projected*	*110*	*207*	*22*	*56*	*9*	*1*	*1*	*20*	*15*	*9*	*.271*	*.320*	*.338*

BRYAN HARVEY / Florida Marlins / Closer $36

Various injuries to his elbow and abdomen took his 1994 season away, the second lost season for him in three years. The other year was wonderful. If he's healthy, he is possibly the best reliever in the game. Over the last five years, the batting average against him is .196, plus he never walks anybody. He is tougher on left-handers than on right-handers.

YEAR	TEAM/LEVEL	G	IP	W-L	SAVES	HITS	SO	BB	ERA
1992	California	25	29	0-4	13	22	34	11	2.83
1993	Florida	59	69	1-5	45	45	73	13	1.70
1994	Florida	12	10	0-0	6	12	10	4	5.23

BILL HASELMAN / Seattle Mariners / Catcher $14

Was sent to the minors in July. The way he played last year, there wasn't much choice. He's not a defensive catcher. He was sharing the catching job with another right-handed hitter, and he didn't hit anything. Back at Calgary he hit .331 with 15 homers, 46 RBI in 44 games, so he might return. He can hit a little; he just didn't.

YEAR	TEAM/LEVEL	G	AB	R	H	2B	3B	HR	RBI	BB	SB	AVG	OBP	SLG
1992	MLE	105	340	36	71	15	1	12	40	35	1	.209	.283	.365
1993	Seattle	58	137	21	35	8	0	5	16	12	2	.255	.316	.423
1994	Seattle	38	83	11	16	7	1	1	8	3	1	.193	.230	.337

BILLY HATCHER / Philadelphia Phillies / Center Field $15

Now 34 years old, Hatcher never really had any business being a regular center fielder. He has the skills of a decent platoon outfielder, a fifth outfielder/pinch runner, but he was always in the right place at the right time, and he saved his career several times by well-timed hot streaks. Dave Gallagher is a better player.

YEAR	TEAM/LEVEL	G	AB	R	H	2B	3B	HR	RBI	BB	SB	AVG	OBP	SLG
1993	Boston	136	508	71	146	24	3	9	57	28	14	.287	.336	.400
1994	Two Teams	87	298	39	73	14	2	3	31	17	8	.245	.283	.336
1995	*Projected*	*96*	*316*	*40*	*81*	*15*	*2*	*4*	*31*	*17*	*7*	*.256*	*.294*	*.354*

LATROY HAWKINS / Minnesota Twins / Starting Pitcher $21

A hot prospect, a 6-5 stringbean from Gary, Indiana, compared to Satchel Paige. Fastball in upper 80s with good movement, good slider, inconsistent curve, pretty good control. A friend of basketball star Glenn Robin-son, also wears the number 13. Lack of consistent curve makes him Grade B prospect. He may be a good pitcher, but probably not before 1997.

YEAR	TEAM/LEVEL	G	IP	W-L	PCT	HITS	SO	BB	ERA
1993	Fort Wayne A	26	157	15-5	.750	110	179	41	2.06
1994	Fort Myers A	5	34	3-0	1.000	30	29	5	2.67
1994	AA and AAA	23	155	14-6	.700	142	90	59	3.25

CHARLIE HAYES / Colorado Rockies / Third Base $43

His batting average started out in the .230s, and was driving toward .300 when the strike halted it . . . .288, I'll believe. He had a career year in '93, plus he has shown steady, consistent progress over the years, but he's not Ken Boyer, and I wouldn't really expect him to drive in 98 runs again. Badly overrated defensive third baseman, doesn't go to his left well.

YEAR	TEAM/LEVEL	G	AB	R	H	2B	3B	HR	RBI	BB	SB	AVG	OBP	SLG
1993	Colorado	157	573	89	175	45	2	25	98	43	11	.305	.355	.522
1994	Colorado	113	423	46	122	23	4	10	50	36	3	.288	.348	.433
1995	*Projected*	*158*	*581*	*68*	*155*	*28*	*2*	*18*	*72*	*44*	*7*	*.267*	*.318*	*.415*

HEATH HAYNES / Montreal Expos / Right-handed Reliever $19

A right-handed Kirk Reuter, to quote the Expos—an undrafted free agent who has showy numbers in the minor leagues because a) minor leaguers can't deal with a guy who changes speeds well, or b) his fastball is under-rated, depending on who you believe. Any-way, he's 29-9 in the minors, 2.26 ERA, 330 strikeouts, 68 walks in 271 innings.

YEAR	TEAM/LEVEL	G	IP	W-L	SAVES	HITS	SO	BB	ERA
1993	Harrisburg AA	57	66	8-0	5	46	78	19	2.59
1994	Ottawa AAA	56	87	6-7	4	72	75	15	2.38
1994	Montreal	4	4	0-0	0	3	1	3	0.00

JIMMY HAYNES / Baltimore Orioles / Starting Pitcher $29

A big easy-going Georgia boy with an explosive fast-ball, has come along more rapidly than the Orioles an-ticipated, and may be in the majors by mid-season. He's 22 and built like a teen-ager, but has been durable. Throws fastball for strike one, curveball for strike two, a different curve for strike three, uses the change if something misses. **Grade A prospect.**

YEAR	TEAM/LEVEL	G	IP	W-L	PCT	HITS	SO	BB	ERA
1993	Frederick A	27	172	12-8	.600	139	174	61	3.03
1994	Bowie AA	25	174	13-8	.619	154	177	46	2.90
1994	Rochester AAA	3	13	1-0	1.000	20	14	6	6.75

RICKEY HELLING / Texas Rangers / Starting Pitcher $21

Struck out 205 in 188 innings in the minors in '93, and began the '94 season in the Rangers rotation. He gave up 14 homers in nine starts, and was sent back to Oklahoma City. He didn't pitch well there, but I suspect he was probably working on a breaking pitch or something, and may be back in the majors this year. I like him.

YEAR	TEAM/LEVEL	G	IP	W-L	PCT	HITS	SO	BB	ERA
1993	Tulsa AA	26	177	12-8	.600	150	188	46	3.60
1994	Texas	9	52	3-2	.600	62	25	18	5.88
1994	Ok. City AAA	20	132	4-12	.250	153	85	43	5.78

SCOTT HEMOND / Oakland Athletics / Catcher/Second Baseman $17

Your basic catcher/second baseman, started 24 games at catcher, 25 at second base, six at third base, four at first. Runs unusually well for a catcher, stole 45 bases one year in the minors, 14 in the majors. Went to the same college as Tony LaRussa, University of South Florida. Not outstanding defensively at any position, won't hit enough to be a regular.

YEAR	TEAM/LEVEL	G	AB	R	H	2B	3B	HR	RBI	BB	SB	AVG	OBP	SLG
1993	Oakland	91	215	31	55	16	0	6	26	32	14	.256	.353	.414
1994	Oakland	91	198	23	44	11	0	3	20	16	7	.222	.280	.323
1995	*Projected*	*111*	*258*	*33*	*58*	*15*	*0*	*5*	*26*	*32*	*11*	*.225*	*.310*	*.341*

DAVE HENDERSON / Kansas City Royals (Released) / Outfield/Designated Hitter $15

Over the last five years has hit .304 with a .558 slugging percentage against left-handed pitchers, but .230 with a .382 percentage against right-handers. His 1994 data was about the same—but Hal McRae didn't platoon him, giving him 58 percent of his at bats against right-handers. Now 36; can still help a team in a limited role.

YEAR	TEAM/LEVEL	G	AB	R	H	2B	3B	HR	RBI	BB	SB	AVG	OBP	SLG
1992	Oakland	20	63	1	9	1	0	0	2	2	0	.143	.169	.159
1993	Oakland	107	382	37	84	19	0	20	53	32	0	.220	.275	.427
1994	Kansas City	56	198	27	49	14	1	5	31	16	2	.247	.304	.404

RICKEY HENDERSON / Oakland Athletics / Left Field $40

Wasn't running well early in the season because of a swollen knee. By May 10 he was hitting .228 and was 3-for-8 as a base stealer, so he went on the DL to get the knee worked on. After he returned, he was a devastating player, as he always has been. He had a .411 on-base percentage, and he still scores runs.

YEAR	TEAM/LEVEL	G	AB	R	H	2B	3B	HR	RBI	BB	SB	AVG	OBP	SLG
1993	Two Teams	134	481	114	139	22	2	21	59	120	53	.289	.432	.474
1994	Oakland	87	296	66	77	13	0	6	20	72	22	.260	.411	.365
1995	*Projected*	*129*	*437*	*87*	*115*	*20*	*2*	*12*	*42*	*110*	*43*	*.263*	*.411*	*.400*

ROD HENDERSON / Montreal Expos / Right-handed Starter $16

A big right-hander, a four-pitch pitcher a year ago, but after a year of working with Rich Gale at Ottawa he's probably trying to throw about 20 pitches. He went 17-7 in the minors in '93, won his first two starts last year and was called up to be the Expos' fifth starter during an injury. This lasted two starts. Grade B prospect.

YEAR	TEAM/LEVEL	G	IP	W-L	PCT	HITS	SO	BB	ERA
1994	Harrisburg AA	2	12	2-0	1.000	5	16	4	1.50
1994	Montreal	3	7	0-1	.000	9	3	7	9.45
1994	Ottawa AAA	23	123	6-9	.400	123	100	67	4.62

TOM HENKE / Texas Rangers / Closer $39

Was slowed in '94 by a sore lower back, and didn't hit his stride until June. One could hardly say that a pitcher is washed up after he strikes out 39 in 38 innings, walks only 12 and gives up a batting average of .232, but on the other hand, you'd have to worry about a 37-year-old pitcher with a back problem.

YEAR	TEAM/LEVEL	G	IP	W-L	SAVES	HITS	SO	BB	ERA
1992	Toronto	57	56	3-2	34	40	46	22	2.26
1993	Texas	66	74	5-5	40	55	79	27	2.91
1994	Texas	37	38	3-6	15	33	39	12	3.79

MIKE HENNEMAN / Detroit Tigers / Closer $19

He has been ineffective since early August 1993 due to shoulder problems, and at one point last summer he was seriously considering retirement . . . in the last five years has pitched 72 times on zero days' rest, with an ERA of 1.55. Pitching 83 times with three days' rest or more, his ERA is 5.04 . . . good chance of a comeback.

YEAR	TEAM/LEVEL	G	IP	W-L	SAVES	HITS	SO	BB	ERA
1992	Detroit	60	77	2-6	24	75	58	20	3.96
1993	Detroit	63	72	5-3	24	69	58	32	2.64
1994	Detroit	30	35	1-3	8	43	27	17	5.19

BUTCH HENRY / Montreal Expos / Starting Pitcher $30

The best evidence yet that Felipe Alou is a genius . . . began the year in the Montreal bullpen. He was effective there, and moved to the rotation as injuries thinned the ranks of Montreal starters. Throws curve, slider, sinking fastball, has exceptional control. Ineffective after throwing about 70 pitches . . . I'm skeptical about his future, but I'm certainly impressed by his season.

YEAR	TEAM/LEVEL	G	IP	W-L	PCT	HITS	SO	BB	ERA
1992	Houston	28	165	6-9	.400	185	96	41	4.02
1993	Two Teams	30	103	3-9	.250	135	47	28	6.12
1994	Montreal	24	107	8-3	.727	97	70	20	2.43

DOUG HENRY / Milwaukee Brewers / Relief Pitcher $14

Was troubled by tendinitis early in the season, aggravated by the fact that he's really not a very good pitcher. He posted a 1.00 ERA in 32 games when he first came to the majors (1991), which made him the Brewers' closer, but his career since then has been one sustained decline . . . intense, throws fairly hard, throws forkball and slider. Has *no* platoon differential.

YEAR	TEAM/LEVEL	G	IP	W-L	SAVES	HITS	SO	BB	ERA
1992	Milwaukee	60	77	2-6	24	75	58	20	3.96
1993	Milwaukee	54	55	4-4	17	67	38	25	5.56
1994	Milwaukee	25	31	2-3	0	32	20	23	4.60

PAT HENTGEN / Toronto Blue Jays / Starting Pitcher $45

My guess a year ago was that Hentgen was a one-year wonder, about which it now appears I was completely wrong. His strikeout rate in '94 improved by 49 percent. Strikeouts often increase in a starting pitcher's second season, but very rarely by that margin. His control did not suffer. He was consistent, he stayed healthy, and he got better as the season wore on.

YEAR	TEAM/LEVEL	G	IP	W-L	PCT	HITS	SO	BB	ERA
1992	Toronto	28	50	5-2	.714	49	39	32	5.36
1993	Toronto	34	216	19-9	.679	215	122	74	3.87
1994	Toronto	24	175	13-8	.619	158	147	59	3.40

GIL HEREDIA / Montreal Expos / Right-handed Pitcher $25

The Expos collect large numbers of pitching prospects, and sort through them patiently. Heredia has pitched well for two years, and his shot at the rotation arrived just before the strike. In three starts he was 2-0 with a 1.45 ERA. I like Heredia, and think that he will be a highly successful pitcher, although his elbow problems may well return.

YEAR	TEAM/LEVEL	G	IP	W-L	PCT	HITS	SO	BB	ERA
1992	Two ML Teams	20	44	2-3	.400	44	22	20	4.23
1993	Montreal	20	57	4-2	.667	66	40	14	3.92
1994	Montreal	39	75	6-3	.667	85	62	13	3.46

CARLOS HERNANDEZ / Los Angeles Dodgers / Catcher $22

Starved for playing time behind Piazza, and because of that his skills are retreating, rather than advancing. I suspect that if someone can pry him loose in a trade, his pent-up desire to play could break out, in either an All-Star season (he has that ability) or a spectacular wipeout. As long as he stays with the Dodgers, there's nothing he can do.

YEAR	TEAM/LEVEL	G	AB	R	H	2B	3B	HR	RBI	BB	SB	AVG	OBP	SLG
1993	Los Angeles	50	99	6	25	5	0	2	7	2	0	.253	.267	.364
1994	Los Angeles	32	64	6	14	2	0	2	6	1	0	.219	.231	.344
1995	*Projected*	*77*	*162*	*12*	*42*	*7*	*0*	*3*	*18*	*7*	*0*	*.259*	*.290*	*.358*

JEREMY HERNANDEZ / Florida Marlins / Relief Pitcher $22

He was with San Diego and then Cleveland, traded to the Marlins at the end of spring training. When Harvey went down Hernandez moved into the closer's spot, and was among the league leaders in saves by mid- May. He began having neck problems, eventually requiring surgery on a herniated disc in his neck, and didn't pitch after May. I anticipate a solid return.

YEAR	TEAM/LEVEL	G	IP	W-L	SAVES	HITS	SO	BB	ERA
1992	San Diego	26	36	1-4	1	39	25	11	4.17
1993	Two Teams	70	112	6-7	8	116	70	34	3.63
1994	Florida	21	23	3-3	9	16	13	14	2.70

ROBERTO HERNANDEZ / Chicago White Sox / Relief Pitcher $54

For most of the year, he was an effective pitcher, despite the 4.91 ERA. He went through a sinking spell, beginning about May 10, when he lost his release point, and got his mechanics fouled up. For five weeks he couldn't get anybody out, and his ERA skyrocketed. It was late June before he was back in the closer role. Outlook is solid.

YEAR	TEAM/LEVEL	G	IP	W-L	SAVES	HITS	SO	BB	ERA
1992	Chicago	43	71	7-3	12	45	68	20	1.65
1993	Chicago	70	79	3-4	38	66	71	20	2.29
1994	Chicago	45	48	4-4	14	44	50	19	4.91

XAVIER HERNANDEZ / New York Yankees / Relief Pitcher $19

After two good years in Houston the Yankees traded Andy Stankiewicz and Domingo Jean to acquire him, but then didn't give him enough work to stay sharp. Like many relievers, he is much more effective when he works a lot. In Houston, 74 percent of his innings were with two days' rest or less. In New York, 63 percent of his innings were with long rest.

YEAR	TEAM/LEVEL	G	IP	W-L	SAVES	HITS	SO	BB	ERA
1992	Houston	77	111	9-1	7	81	96	42	2.11
1993	Houston	72	97	4-5	9	75	101	28	2.61
1994	New York	31	40	4-4	6	48	37	21	5.85

OREL HERSHISER / Los Angeles Dodgers / Starting Pitcher $32

A union leader; will be one of the last players to return if there is a scab league. He had a sinking spell in June, probably trying to pitch through a minor injury, but came out of it and was his usual efficient self after July 1. For some unknown reason, had extreme difficulty getting out the leadoff man in '94.

YEAR	TEAM/LEVEL	G	IP	W-L	PCT	HITS	SO	BB	ERA
1992	Los Angeles	33	211	10-15	.400	209	130	69	3.67
1993	Los Angeles	33	216	12-14	.462	201	141	72	3.59
1994	Los Angeles	21	135	6-6	.500	146	72	42	3.79

JOE HESKETH / Boston Red Sox / Left-handed Pitcher $25

Viola's injury gave him an opening, and he took advantage of it. At the time of the strike he was pitching the best ball he has pitched since 1991. In his last seven starts he was 4-1 with a 3.05 ERA. He's always been a good pitcher; he just can't stay healthy. . . . Has always pitched very well in Fenway Park.

YEAR	TEAM/LEVEL	G	IP	W-L	PCT	HITS	SO	BB	ERA
1992	Boston	30	149	8-9	.471	162	104	58	4.36
1993	Boston	28	53	3-4	.429	62	34	29	5.06
1994	Boston	25	114	8-5	.615	117	83	46	4.26

PHIL HIATT / Kansas City Royals / Third Base $17

Hiatt was a spring-training surprise in '93, opened that season as the Royals third baseman, and hit well for a month before degenerating. He has come along substantially since that time, and would play better if given another chance, which may happen if the Royals' youth movement flushes out Gaetti. Slow, excellent arm, low on-base percentage but has real power.

YEAR	TEAM/LEVEL	G	AB	R	H	2B	3B	HR	RBI	BB	SB	AVG	OBP	SLG
1993	Kansas City	81	238	30	52	12	1	7	36	16	6	.218	.285	.366
1994	AA and AAA	114	422	59	124	27	4	18	68	40	12	.294	.374	.505
1994	MLE	114	409	47	111	25	3	11	54	27	8	.271	.317	.428

GREG HIBBARD / Seattle Mariners / Starting Pitcher $12

Boy, the Mariners are lucky with pitchers, aren't they? Hibbard, with 10 to 15 wins in each of the previous four seasons (overall, 50-38) signed with the Mariners last winter, and won one game before going on the 60-day disabled list with a "strained shoulder." I don't know if he'll be back—but vague, indistinct descriptions of injuries are almost always bad news.

YEAR	TEAM/LEVEL	G	IP	W-L	PCT	HITS	SO	BB	ERA
1992	Chicago (A)	31	176	10-7	.588	187	69	57	4.40
1993	Chicago (N)	31	191	15-11	.577	209	82	47	3.96
1994	Seattle	15	81	1-5	.167	115	39	31	6.69

BRYAN HICKERSON / San Francisco Giants / Left-handed Pitcher $19

Opponents hit .301 against him, and he gave up 20 home runs in 98 innings. This ended a string of three years in which he had pitched better than anyone had expected. He's a lefty, relies on changing speeds and locating the ball well, jams left-handed hitters very well most of the time. His natural role is as a left-handed one-out guy.

YEAR	TEAM/LEVEL	G	IP	W-L	SAVES	HITS	SO	BB	ERA
1992	San Francisco	61	87	5-3	0	74	68	21	3.09
1993	San Francisco	47	120	7-5	0	137	69	39	4.26
1994	San Francisco	28	98	4-8	1	118	59	38	5.40

TED HIGUERA / Milwaukee Brewers / Starting Pitcher $10

He's been trying to rebuild his career since 1991, and the next sign of progress (in his stats) will be the first one. He was throwing well in spring training last year, and reporters were talking about a comeback, but it didn't happen, and apparently won't. . . . He has two sons, named Teo Jr. and Teo de Jesus.

YEAR	TEAM/LEVEL	G	IP	W-L	PCT	HITS	SO	BB	ERA
1992	Milwaukee			(On Major League Disabled List)					
1993	Milwaukee	8	30	1-3	.250	43	27	16	7.20
1994	Milwaukee	17	59	1-5	.167	74	35	36	7.06

GLENALLEN HILL / Chicago Cubs / Outfielder $27

An interesting split in his records: Over the last five years he has hit .316 against ground-ball pitchers, but .197 against fly-ball pitchers. . . . A player with outstanding skills, a "scouts" player who came along slowly until joining the Cubs in August 1993. Since then he has hit .309 with 20 homers in 356 at bats. He's 30, but his best years should be coming up.

YEAR	TEAM/LEVEL	G	AB	R	H	2B	3B	HR	RBI	BB	SB	AVG	OBP	SLG
1993	Two Teams	97	261	33	69	14	2	15	47	17	8	.264	.307	.506
1994	Chicago	89	269	48	80	12	1	10	38	29	19	.297	.365	.461
1995	*Projected*	*129*	*410*	*52*	*104*	*17*	*2*	*17*	*57*	*31*	*17*	*.254*	*.306*	*.429*

KEN HILL / Montreal Expos / Starting Pitcher $74

Was on target for 22 wins until the strike hit, although a) he wasn't pitching great at the time, and b) in the past he has tended to bog down in August and September. He has had four straight winning seasons, and is probably as safe a bet as you could find this side of Greg Maddux to make it five straight.

YEAR	TEAM/LEVEL	G	IP	W-L	PCT	HITS	SO	BB	ERA
1992	Montreal	33	218	16-9	.640	187	150	75	2.68
1993	Montreal	28	184	9-7	.563	163	90	74	3.23
1994	Montreal	23	155	16-5	.762	145	85	44	3.32

MILT HILL / Seattle Mariners / Relief Pitcher $14

He is getting to be well acquainted with the waiver process, having been cut or cleared waivers/sent to the minors by three teams in 10 months. He's a right-handed pitcher, listed at six foot but looks shorter, doesn't throw hard, but had pitched well in the minors before 1993. No star potential; might sneak in a good year sometime.

YEAR	TEAM/LEVEL	G	IP	W-L	SAVES	HITS	SO	BB	ERA
1992	Cincinnati	14	20	0-0	1	15	10	5	3.15
1993	Cincinnati	19	29	3-0	0	34	23	9	5.65
1994	Atlanta & Seattle	23	35	1-0	0	48	26	17	6.94

ERIC HILLMAN / New York Mets / Left-handed Pitcher $13

A 6-foot-10 lefty, has excellent control but doesn't throw hard. Sent to Norfolk in June, he was 10-1 with a 2.89 ERA there, which will earn him another opportunity. In his previous three trials, the batting average against him has been so high (.306 in his career) that it would be difficult to imagine him having any great success.

YEAR	TEAM/LEVEL	G	IP	W-L	PCT	HITS	SO	BB	ERA
1992	New York	11	52	2-2	.500	67	16	10	5.33
1993	New York	27	145	2-9	.182	173	60	24	3.97
1994	New York	11	35	0-3	.000	45	20	11	7.79

STERLING HITCHCOCK / New York Yankees / Starting Pitcher $20

Has a chance to be a very fine pitcher. He's a lefty, average size, good fastball, has been reasonably healthy (although he did have a shoulder problem in '93). His comment about the Yankees: "As long as I remember, it's been give a guy six, seven starts, and if he doesn't do anything, then get him out of there and bring in Dave LaPoint."

YEAR	TEAM/LEVEL	G	IP	W-L	PCT	HITS	SO	BB	ERA
1993	Columbus AAA	16	77	3-5	.375	80	85	28	4.81
1993	New York	6	31	1-2	.333	32	26	14	4.65
1994	New York	23	49	4-1	.800	48	37	29	4.20

DENNY HOCKING / Minnesota Twins / Shortstop $14

Converted catcher, among a half-dozen players scrambling for the Twins' shortstop job. He was called up in mid-summer for two weeks, hit .323 and made no errors at shortstop, but got sent back down anyway. Would be a .240-.250 hitter in the majors, no power, no walks, a little speed. Grade D prospect; I don't expect him to win a regular job.

YEAR	TEAM/LEVEL	G	AB	R	H	2B	3B	HR	RBI	BB	SB	AVG	OBP	SLG
1993	MLE	107	399	43	99	9	4	6	40	24	11	.248	.291	.336
1994	MLE	112	376	41	92	13	5	3	38	19	9	.245	.281	.330
1994	Minnesota	11	31	3	10	3	0	0	2	2	2	.323	.323	.419

TREVOR HOFFMAN / San Diego Padres / Relief Pitcher $55

If you're wondering who the Dennis Eckersley of the late '90s will be, Trevor Hoffman is as good a guess as you can make. He throws very hard, and his mechanics look good. The fact that he started as an infielder is a major plus, as it prevented his arm from being abused in his formative years. Throws a good hard slider also.

YEAR	TEAM/LEVEL	G	IP	W-L	SAVES	HITS	SO	BB	ERA
1992	Nashville AAA	42	65	4-6	6	57	63	32	4.27
1993	Two Teams	67	90	4-6	5	80	79	39	3.90
1994	San Diego	47	56	4-4	20	39	68	20	2.57

CHRIS HOILES / Baltimore Orioles / Catcher $66

Who is the best catcher in Orioles history? Triandos? Etchebarren? Dempsey? It might be that "Chris Hoiles" is already the answer. His arm is just OK, and his other defensive skills aren't anything special, but his power

and .380 on-base percentages set him apart from most of the other catchers . . . Orioles had 4.24 ERA with Hoiles catching, 4.70 without him.

YEAR	TEAM/LEVEL	G	AB	R	H	2B	3B	HR	RBI	BB	SB	AVG	OBP	SLG
1993	Baltimore	126	419	80	130	28	0	29	82	69	1	.310	.416	.585
1994	Baltimore	99	332	45	82	10	0	19	53	63	2	.247	.371	.449
1995	*Projected*	*144*	*477*	*79*	*134*	*22*	*0*	*27*	*74*	*88*	*2*	*.281*	*.393*	*.497*

RAY HOLBERT / San Diego Padres / Shortstop $21

He is breathing down Gutierrez' neck, and could take his job if Gutierrez doesn't develop. The two men are the same age, the same size, both right-handed hitters, and have similar skills. Holbert is a little faster, and

might hit with a little more punch. He has soft hands and a strong arm. He doesn't improve the Padres, but he gives them an option.

YEAR	TEAM/LEVEL	G	AB	R	H	2B	3B	HR	RBI	BB	SB	AVG	OBP	SLG
1993	MLE	112	375	45	88	10	3	4	38	37	20	.235	.303	.309
1994	MLE	118	398	43	100	15	2	6	33	32	17	.251	.307	.344
1994	San Diego	5	5	1	1	0	0	0	0	0	0	.200	.200	.200

DAVE HOLLINS / Philadelphia Phillies / Third Base $31

He broke bones in both hands during the '94 season, which gives him three broken hands in two years, and clearly disproves the old suspicion that his hands are made of stone. No speed, awful defense. Switch hitter,

only 29, has good years ahead of him. He's a terrific hitter, but he probably should go to the American League and be a DH.

YEAR	TEAM/LEVEL	G	AB	R	H	2B	3B	HR	RBI	BB	SB	AVG	OBP	SLG
1993	Philadelphia	143	543	104	148	30	4	18	93	85	2	.273	.372	.442
1994	Philadelphia	44	162	28	36	7	1	4	26	23	1	.222	.328	.352
1995	*Projected*	*140*	*516*	*95*	*132*	*25*	*4*	*18*	*80*	*78*	*5*	*.256*	*.354*	*.424*

DARREN HOLMES / Colorado Rockies / Relief Pitcher $20

His season was ruined by elbow problems described as a "sore elbow" or an "inflamed right elbow." As I said about Greg Hibbard, vague descriptions of arm injuries scare the hell out of me. A broken bone heals; an "in-

flamed elbow" is probably going to recur at least until you figure out why it is acting up . . . throws hard, outstanding pitcher if healthy.

YEAR	TEAM/LEVEL	G	IP	W-L	SAVES	HITS	SO	BB	ERA
1992	Milwaukee	41	42	4-4	6	35	31	11	2.55
1993	Colorado	62	67	3-3	25	56	60	20	4.05
1994	Colorado	29	28	0-3	3	35	33	24	6.35

RICK HONEYCUTT / Texas Rangers / Left-handed Reliever $13

He is in the game to get out left-handed hitters, and they hit .412 against him (21-for-51), so this doesn't help his career. He will be 41 years old in June, and he was on the DL last year with a "strained elbow," al-though he hadn't pitched enough to strain his imagination. He has been a fine pitcher, but his future is murky.

YEAR	TEAM/LEVEL	G	IP	W-L	SAVES	HITS	SO	BB	ERA
1992	Oakland	54	39	1-4	3	41	32	10	3.69
1993	Oakland	52	42	1-4	1	30	21	20	2.81
1994	Texas	42	25	1-2	1	37	18	9	7.20

JOHN HOPE / Pittsburgh Pirates / Right-handed Pitcher $15

A big control pitcher; I wrote last year that he gets a strikeout about as often as a pig gets caviar. An article about him says he throws 90, but I doubt it. Has a pudgy face, suggesting that he may be inclined to put on weight as he ages. His control is exceptional, and his minor league record is generally good; Grade C prospect.

YEAR	TEAM/LEVEL	G	IP	W-L	PCT	HITS	SO	BB	ERA
1993	Pittsburgh	7	38	0-2	.000	47	8	8	4.03
1994	Buffalo	18	100	4-9	.308	98	54	23	3.87
1994	Pittsburgh	9	14	0-0	.000	19	6	4	5.79

VINCE HORSMAN / Oakland Athletics / Relief Pitcher $16

LaRussa shuttles pitchers in and out, keeping two or three left-handers on his staff, each of whom pitches very few innings. Horsman pitches so few innings in a year that his numbers in any year aren't very meaningful, but looking at his career as a whole, he's fairly impressive. The slugging percentage of left-handed hitters against Horsman, career, is .285.

YEAR	TEAM/LEVEL	G	IP	W-L	SAVES	HITS	SO	BB	ERA
1992	Oakland	58	43	2-1	1	39	18	21	2.49
1993	Oakland	40	25	2-0	0	25	17	15	5.40
1994	Oakland	33	29	0-1	0	29	20	11	4.91

DWAYNE HOSEY / Kansas City Royals / Outfielder $19

This guy has been given up on by four other organizations (Milwaukee, San Diego, Oakland, and the White Sox) and doesn't have a single major league at bat, but he *isn't* a bad player; he can play, if he gets a chance. He's a small switch hitter with some speed and some power, and a reasonably disciplined hitter. He will have a career.

YEAR	TEAM/LEVEL	G	AB	R	H	2B	3B	HR	RBI	BB	SB	AVG	OBP	SLG
1993	MLE	118	418	55	106	17	2	19	56	24	13	.254	.294	.440
1994	Omaha AAA	112	406	95	135	23	8	27	80	61	27	.333	.425	.628
1994	MLE	112	387	70	116	22	8	14	59	44	18	.300	.371	.506

STEVE HOSEY / California Angels / Outfielder $13

A first-round draft pick in 1989. He's big and strong and he can run, but he's been at Triple-A since 1992, and it's becoming apparent that he's not destined for the All-Star team. He doesn't control the strike zone, for a common reason: He doesn't recognize a curve until it breaks. He could be a major league platoon player.

YEAR	TEAM/LEVEL	G	AB	R	H	2B	3B	HR	RBI	BB	SB	AVG	OBP	SLG
1992	MLE	125	433	42	103	22	3	6	42	24	9	.238	.278	.344
1993	MLE	129	428	48	106	32	2	11	58	44	10	.248	.318	.409
1994	MLE	112	358	50	81	17	1	13	45	34	5	.226	.293	.388

CHRIS HOWARD / Seattle Mariners / Catcher $12

He's the same player as Dan Wilson, except that Wilson somehow acquired the reputation of being a hot prospect, and Howard never did. He's a slow right-handed-hitting catcher who is very good defensively, but can't hit enough to hold a job. A few guys like this will catch a break and hang around the majors for 10 years. Most never do.

YEAR	TEAM/LEVEL	G	AB	R	H	2B	3B	HR	RBI	BB	SB	AVG	OBP	SLG
1993	MLE	94	309	26	84	19	0	3	37	15	0	.272	.306	.362
1994	MLE	75	251	26	52	8	0	6	28	17	0	.207	.257	.311
1994	Seattle	9	25	2	5	1	0	0	2	1	0	.200	.250	.240

CHRIS HOWARD / Boston Red Sox / Pitcher $20

Good pitcher, ended an eight-year battle for a job by pitching well as a left-handed middle reliever. An undrafted free agent, he signed with the Yankees in 1986, pitched well for four years and made it to Albany, where the Yankees released him anyway. Signed by the White Sox, he pitched well in their system for three years, and was cut by them.

YEAR	TEAM/LEVEL	G	IP	W-L	SAVES	HITS	SO	BB	ERA
1993	Nashville AAA	43	67	4-3	3	55	53	16	3.38
1993	Chicago	3	2	1-0	0	2	1	3	0.00
1994	Boston	37	40	1-0	1	35	22	12	3.63

DAVID HOWARD / Kansas City Royals / Infield $15

A decent backup infielder, was used by the Royals primarily at third base, starting 12 games there and playing the late innings in 13 other games; also started 11 games at short. Switch hitter, good bunter, good base-runner, a better shortstop than some guys who play the position every day. He walks enough to keep his on-base percentage over .300.

YEAR	TEAM/LEVEL	G	AB	R	H	2B	3B	HR	RBI	BB	SB	AVG	OBP	SLG
1992	Kansas City	74	219	19	49	6	2	1	18	15	3	.224	.271	.283
1993	Kansas City	15	24	5	8	0	1	0	2	2	1	.333	.370	.417
1994	Kansas City	46	83	9	19	4	0	1	13	11	3	.229	.309	.313

THOMAS HOWARD / Cincinnati Reds / Left Field/Center Field $19

Switch-hitting outfielder who can run, can play center if needed, average arm, doesn't hit enough to be a regular. Much better left-handed batter than right. Almost indistinguishable from Mike Felder, has a little more power. Both Howard and Felder hit over .400 when they hit the first pitch—but both usually hit behind in the count because they chase the first pitch.

YEAR	TEAM/LEVEL	G	AB	R	H	2B	3B	HR	RBI	BB	SB	AVG	OBP	SLG
1993	Two Teams	112	319	48	81	15	3	7	36	24	10	.254	.302	.386
1994	Cincinnati	83	178	24	47	11	0	5	24	10	4	.264	.302	.410
1995	*Projected*	*121*	*308*	*40*	*81*	*16*	*2*	*6*	*34*	*19*	*10*	*.263*	*.306*	*.377*

STEVE HOWE / New York Yankees / Relief Pitcher $34

Doesn't throw as hard as he did before his problems. Still, he is the Yankees' closer, he did have a 1.80 ERA, and he held opponents to a .194 average. Limited leadoff men to an .037 batting average (1-for-27). Like many relievers, he is dramatically more effective when he pitches on short rest than when he has a couple of days off.

YEAR	TEAM/LEVEL	G	IP	W-L	SAVES	HITS	SO	BB	ERA
1992	New York	20	22	3-0	6	9	12	3	2.45
1993	New York	51	51	3-5	4	58	19	10	4.97
1994	New York	40	40	3-0	15	28	18	7	1.80

JAY HOWELL / Texas Rangers / Relief Pitcher $15

Is 39 years old, bouncing from team to team. His stats last year look like he is washed up, and it is extremely likely that the new management in Texas will want to place somebody else in his role. I would caution, however, that when a pitcher faces only 189 batters in a year, it is treacherous to read very much into his statistics.

YEAR	TEAM/LEVEL	G	IP	W-L	SAVES	HITS	SO	BB	ERA
1992	Los Angeles	41	47	1-3	4	41	36	18	1.54
1993	Atlanta	54	58	3-3	0	48	37	16	2.31
1994	Texas	40	43	4-1	2	44	22	16	5.44

DANN HOWITT / Chicago White Sox / Outfielder $12

Spent most of 1994 at Nashville, but got a month on the White Sox roster, playing occasionally. He didn't do much at Nashville (.255 with 8 homers, 36 RBI). A big, strong guy, runs all right, bats left, has a little power. He's 31 years old, so there is no chance that he will develop, but could continue to collect a few at bats a year.

YEAR	TEAM/LEVEL	G	AB	R	H	2B	3B	HR	RBI	BB	SB	AVG	OBP	SLG
1992	Two AL Teams	35	85	7	16	4	1	2	10	8	1	.188	.250	.329
1993	Seattle	32	76	6	16	3	1	2	8	4	0	.211	.250	.355
1994	Chicago	10	14	4	5	3	0	0	0	1	0	.357	.400	.571

TRENT HUBBARD / Colorado Rockies / Outfield/Pinch Runner $14

Short, fast, right-handed hitter, was in the Houston system for many years. He'll be 29 in May, and until last year his MLEs suggested that he was a .260 hitter, albeit with enough speed to make him interesting. Last year he hit .363 at Colorado Springs, either because he figured something out, was highly motivated, or got lucky. No potential; might make the roster.

YEAR	TEAM/LEVEL	G	AB	R	H	2B	3B	HR	RBI	BB	SB	AVG	OBP	SLG
1993	MLE	117	404	49	103	18	4	3	33	28	21	.255	.303	.342
1994	MLE	79	307	54	103	19	3	6	26	32	18	.336	.398	.476
1994	Colorado	18	25	3	7	1	1	1	3	3	0	.280	.357	.520

JOHN HUDEK / Houston Astros / Closer $37

Was second in the NL Rookie of the Year voting. He throws hard, but never did anything in the White Sox system (1988-92) or the Tigers' (1993). The Astros claimed him on waivers, sent him to Winter Ball, where he developed a breaking pitch, improved his control, and emerged as the Astros' closer. He was great last year; I doubt that he'll be consistent.

YEAR	TEAM/LEVEL	G	IP	W-L	SAVES	HITS	SO	BB	ERA
1993	Toledo AAA	16	39	1-3	0	44	32	22	5.82
1993	Tucson AAA	13	19	3-1	0	17	18	11	3.79
1994	Houston	42	39	0-2	16	24	39	18	2.97

REX HUDLER / California Angels / Utility Player $21

A hustling, aggressive player and an exceptional athlete as well, he could probably have had a good career had he been able to get a fair shot at a regular job before he was 30. That's behind him now, but he's a fine bench player. The Angels used him mostly at second base and in left field, also a little at first and third.

YEAR	TEAM/LEVEL	G	AB	R	H	2B	3B	HR	RBI	BB	SB	AVG	OBP	SLG
1992	St. Louis	61	98	17	24	4	0	3	5	2	2	.245	.265	.378
1993	Yakult Japan	120	410	48	123	26	3	14	64	32	1	.300	.356	.480
1994	California	56	124	17	37	8	0	8	20	6	2	.298	.326	.556

MIKE HUFF / Toronto Blue Jays / Left Field $23

I'm not suggesting that Huff is a legitimate .300 hitter, but he's a good fourth outfielder. He has leadoff skills—hits for an OK average, walks, runs—and there are teams that don't have anybody with those skills. He was close to establishing himself as a regular in 1992, but broke his shoulder at the wrong moment. He's 31 years old, right-handed hitter, weak arm.

YEAR	TEAM/LEVEL	G	AB	R	H	2B	3B	HR	RBI	BB	SB	AVG	OBP	SLG
1993	Chicago (A)	43	44	4	8	2	0	1	6	9	1	.182	.321	.295
1994	Toronto	80	207	31	63	15	3	3	25	27	2	.304	.392	.449
1995	*Projected*	*93*	*230*	*32*	*60*	*12*	*2*	*3*	*21*	*31*	*5*	*.261*	*.349*	*.370*

TIM HULETT / Baltimore Orioles / Utilityman $17

Popular backup infielder, used mostly at third base in 1993, when Gomez was off his form, and mostly at second last year. I wouldn't have him on my roster. His batting averages are usually OK, but a backup infielder who doesn't run, doesn't have any power, and can't play a passable shortstop is a luxury that I just don't think a championship team can afford.

YEAR	TEAM/LEVEL	G	AB	R	H	2B	3B	HR	RBI	BB	SB	AVG	OBP	SLG
1992	Baltimore	57	142	11	41	7	2	2	21	10	0	.289	.340	.408
1993	Baltimore	85	260	40	78	15	0	2	23	23	1	.300	.361	.381
1994	Baltimore	36	92	11	21	2	1	2	15	12	0	.228	.314	.337

DAVID HULSE / Texas Rangers / Center Field $24

In 76 outfield games he had *no* assists. He hit .326 in April, .241 in May, .238 in June, .174 in July, and Oklahoma City in mid-July, as Kevin Kennedy's patience ran out. He has two positives: He is fast, and he could, possibly, hit .300. Everything else is a negative. He has no power, can't throw, will swing at anything, is injury-prone.

YEAR	TEAM/LEVEL	G	AB	R	H	2B	3B	HR	RBI	BB	SB	AVG	OBP	SLG
1993	Texas	114	407	71	118	9	10	1	29	26	29	.290	.333	.369
1994	Texas	77	310	58	79	8	4	1	19	21	18	.255	.305	.316
1995	*Projected*	*106*	*384*	*58*	*106*	*11*	*5*	*2*	*26*	*22*	*21*	*.276*	*.315*	*.346*

TODD HUNDLEY / New York Mets / Catcher $34

Changed his approach, swinging at the first pitch much less often, and swinging for downtown when he was ahead in the count. He saw four-plus pitches per at bat last year, as opposed to 3.4 in previous years. He threw out 33 percent of opposing base stealers, fourth-best in the league. He's not Mike Piazza, but he was among the better catchers.

YEAR	TEAM/LEVEL	G	AB	R	H	2B	3B	HR	RBI	BB	SB	AVG	OBP	SLG
1993	New York	130	417	40	95	17	2	11	53	23	1	.228	.269	.357
1994	New York	91	291	45	69	10	1	16	42	25	2	.237	.303	.443
1995	*Projected*	*136*	*417*	*48*	*96*	*18*	*2*	*12*	*49*	*27*	*2*	*.230*	*.277*	*.369*

BRIAN HUNTER / Cincinnati Reds / First Base $18

He can't find a job, but is developing a convincing argument that his power is such that he should play, despite his weaknesses. He's slow, not a good first baseman, and his on-base percentage is awful. But over the last three years, batting 574 times, he has hit 32 doubles, 29 homers, and driven in 106 runs. Good platoon player, at least.

YEAR	TEAM/LEVEL	G	AB	R	H	2B	3B	HR	RBI	BB	SB	AVG	OBP	SLG
1993	Atlanta	37	80	4	11	3	1	0	8	2	0	.138	.153	.200
1994	Two Teams	85	256	34	60	16	1	15	57	17	0	.234	.277	.480
1995	*Projected*	*92*	*228*	*28*	*51*	*12*	*1*	*11*	*39*	*16*	*1*	*.224*	*.275*	*.430*

BRIAN HUNTER / Houston Astros / Center Field $26

Is 24 years old, a hot prospect after 688 minor league games. He spent a week in the majors, while Finley was out, and the rest of the year at Tucson, where he hit .372. Tall and thin, very fast—in fact, the Astros claim he is faster than Kenny Lofton. Grade B prospect; has as good a chance as anyone to be 1995 Rookie of the Year.

YEAR	TEAM/LEVEL	G	AB	R	H	2B	3B	HR	RBI	BB	SB	AVG	OBP	SLG
1993	MLE	133	502	68	133	19	3	7	42	23	27	.265	.297	.357
1994	Tucson AAA	128	513	113	191	28	9	10	51	52	49	.372	.432	.520
1994	MLE	128	470	72	148	22	4	5	32	33	32	.315	.360	.411

JAMES HURST / Texas Rangers / Left-handed Pitcher $13

Left-handed pitcher with an average/above average fastball, good control. He was released by the Indians in 1991, out of baseball for a couple of months, signed with the Rangers, and made the 40-man roster last year after he pitched well in Venezuela. Throws fastball and curve, last year junked the split-fingered fastball in favor of a change. Grade C prospect.

YEAR	TEAM/LEVEL	G	IP	W-L	PCT	HITS	SO	BB	ERA
1993	AA and AAA	27	141	6-9	.400	147	104	41	4.09
1994	AA and AAA	28	106	5-8	.385	124	73	43	5.94
1994	Texas	8	11	0-0	.000	17	5	8	10.13

JON (SKEETER) HURST / New York Mets / Right-handed Reliever $15

A 6-3, 190-pound right-hander, has labored in the vineyards for the Rangers, Expos, and Dodgers. A starting pitcher until last year, he spent a long, long time getting out of A Ball. The Mets signed him as a minor league free agent, and moved him to the bullpen. Grade C prospect, good control. I don't see any reason he shouldn't have a career.

YEAR	TEAM/LEVEL	G	IP	W-L	PCT	HITS	SO	BB	ERA
1993	Albuquerque AAA	18	87	7-2	.778	101	62	29	4.15
1994	Norfolk AAA	41	67	5-4	.556	63	48	27	3.78
1994	New York	7	10	0-1	.000	15	10	12	12.60

MARK HUTTON / New York Yankees / Starting Pitcher $18

An Australian giant who was a hot prospect a year ago, he sustains the Yankees record for failing to develop their pitchers. After going 10-4 at Columbus in '93, he opened '94 back at Columbus, spent two weeks in May in the majors, went back to Columbus and didn't pitch much the rest of the year due to pulled groin muscles.

YEAR	TEAM/LEVEL	G	IP	W-L	PCT	HITS	SO	BB	ERA
1993	New York	7	22	1-1	.500	24	12	17	5.73
1994	Columbus AAA	22	35	2-5	.286	31	27	12	3.63
1994	New York	2	4	0-0	.000	4	1	0	4.91

TIM HYERS / San Diego Padres / First Base $15

A singles-hitting first baseman with an on-base percentage in the low threes, real useful. It is impossible to imagine why, with Plantier, Clark, Gwynn, Staton, and Cianfrocco clogging the left end of the defensive spectrum anyway, Riggleman would bring some guy like this out of Double-A. Good defense, could be .300 hitter. Should have Todd Benzinger/Gerald Perry type career.

YEAR	TEAM/LEVEL	G	AB	R	H	2B	3B	HR	RBI	BB	SB	AVG	OBP	SLG
1993	Knoxville AA	140	487	72	149	26	3	3	61	53	12	.306	.375	.390
1993	MLE	140	470	58	132	24	2	2	49	36	8	.281	.332	.353
1994	San Diego	52	118	13	30	3	0	0	7	9	3	.254	.307	.280

MIKE IGNASIAK / Milwaukee Brewers / Pitcher $20

A highly effective reliever in the minors in '92 and '93. The Brewers, in their unique and wonderful way, brought him up in May and attempted to convert him, at the major league level, to a starting pitcher. He had a 5.56 ERA through five starts, moved back to the pen, went on the DL, and posted a 1.98 ERA after returning. I like him.

YEAR	TEAM/LEVEL	G	IP	W-L	SAVES	HITS	SO	BB	ERA
1993	New Orleans AAA	35	58	6-0	9	26	61	20	1.09
1993	Milwaukee	27	37	1-1	0	32	28	21	3.65
1994	Milwaukee	23	48	3-1	0	51	24	13	4.53

BLAISE ILSLEY / Chicago Cubs (Released) / Left-handed Pitcher $12

A 31-year-old lefty, cut in October, has minor league record of 90-55. Baseball men believe that pitchers like this, who throw strikes and change speeds, but don't throw hard, are effective in the minors but don't follow through in the majors. There is evidence that this is true, but I still feel Ilsley should be given an opportunity, because you just never know.

YEAR	TEAM/LEVEL	G	IP	W-L	SAVES	HITS	SO	BB	ERA
1993	Iowa AAA	48	135	12-7	4	147	78	32	3.94
1994	Iowa AAA	22	116	10-4	0	120	51	21	4.42
1994	Chicago	10	15	0-0	0	25	9	9	7.80

PETE INCAVIGLIA / Philadelphia Phillies / Left Field $21

Is 31 years old, hasn't played regularly since 1990. We think of him as a platoon player, but actually he had 58 percent of his at bats against right-handed pitchers last year, and 56 percent in '93. Had a tremendous year in '93, relapsed into Pete Incaviglia last year. Over the last five years he's hit .190 in the late innings of close games (65-for-342).

YEAR	TEAM/LEVEL	G	AB	R	H	2B	3B	HR	RBI	BB	SB	AVG	OBP	SLG
1993	Philadelphia	116	368	60	101	16	3	24	89	21	1	.274	.318	.530
1994	Philadelphia	80	244	28	56	10	1	13	32	16	1	.230	.278	.439
1995	*Projected*	*115*	*338*	*41*	*85*	*18*	*1*	*16*	*57*	*22*	*1*	*.251*	*.297*	*.453*

GAREY INGRAM / Los Angeles Dodgers / Infielder $15

He spent a month in the majors, during DeShields's injury, and hit better in the majors than he has in the minors, also fielded extremely well. A 44th-round draft pick in 1989, he has some things you have to like—a good glove, speed, and he works the pitcher. He has often hit well in April and May, but faded late in the season.

YEAR	TEAM/LEVEL	G	AB	R	H	2B	3B	HR	RBI	BB	SB	AVG	OBP	SLG
1994	San Antonio AA	99	345	68	89	24	3	8	28	43	19	.258	.355	.414
1994	MLE	101	341	58	79	20	1	6	23	30	13	.232	.294	.349
1994	Los Angeles	26	78	10	22	1	0	3	8	7	0	.282	.341	.410

RICCARDO INGRAM / Detroit Tigers / Center Field $14

A defensive back at Georgia Tech, he was ACC Player of the Year in 1987, but chose baseball. He has good tools, enormously strong, with the speed and arm to play center, but it took him several years to start to hit. Minor league records (1992-94) are much better than they look; Toledo's a tough place to hit. At 28, he's ready to play.

YEAR	TEAM/LEVEL	G	AB	R	H	2B	3B	HR	RBI	BB	SB	AVG	OBP	SLG
1994	Toledo AAA	90	314	39	90	16	4	9	56	23	11	.287	.344	.449
1994	MLE	90	309	38	85	14	3	9	55	24	9	.275	.327	.427
1994	Detroit	12	23	3	5	0	0	0	2	1	0	.217	.240	.217

JASON ISRINGHAUSEN / New York Mets / Right-handed Starting Pitcher $26

Another 44th-round draft pick (like Ingram), his fastball developed late, and he throws in the low 90s. Has a good curve and control, and the Mets say that he will be given a chance to make their rotation in '95, although he has only 14 starts above A Ball. Had bone spurs shaved from his elbow in '92; that will recur. Grade B prospect.

YEAR	TEAM/LEVEL	G	IP	W-L	PCT	HITS	SO	BB	ERA
1993	Pittsfield R	15	90	7-4	.636	68	104	28	3.29
1994	St. Lucie A	14	101	6-4	.600	76	59	27	2.23
1994	Binghamton AA	14	92	5-4	.556	78	69	23	3.02

BO JACKSON / California Angels / Left Field/Designated Hitter $22

Started 41 games in left field, also DH'd a little. Since returning from hip replacement surgery he has batted 485 times and hit 29 homers, driven in 88. Without speed, he's basically the same as Pete Incaviglia—a slow right-handed power hitter who strikes out more than once a game. He is still good enough to play in the majors.

YEAR	TEAM/LEVEL	G	AB	R	H	2B	3B	HR	RBI	BB	SB	AVG	OBP	SLG
1993	Chicago	85	284	32	66	9	0	16	45	23	0	.232	.289	.433
1994	California	75	201	23	56	7	0	13	43	20	1	.279	.344	.507
1995	*Projected*	*115*	*349*	*40*	*95*	*14*	*2*	*18*	*59*	*29*	*1*	*.244*	*.302*	*.450*

DANNY JACKSON / Philadelphia Phillies / Starting Pitcher $43

Coming off two consecutive winning seasons for the first time in his career—in fact, before 1993 he had had only two winning seasons. 1994 strikeout/walk ratio was dramatically better than any previous season. The Phillies scored 6.6 runs per game for him, most in the NL, and he also benefited from the lively ball, since he has always surrendered very few home runs.

YEAR	TEAM/LEVEL	G	IP	W-L	PCT	HITS	SO	BB	ERA
1992	Two Teams	34	201	8-13	.381	211	97	77	3.84
1993	Philadelphia	32	210	12-11	.522	214	120	80	3.77
1994	Philadelphia	25	179	14-6	.700	183	129	46	3.26

DARRIN JACKSON / Chicago White Sox / Right Field $29

Disabled much of '93 by a hyperthyroid condition, he was en route to his best season in '94. I've never cared for him, because of his low on-base percentages (under .300 in his career, even now). If he can keep his OBP where it was last year, .362, that's different . . . runs well, has power, doesn't have the arm you'd want in right field.

YEAR	TEAM/LEVEL	G	AB	R	H	2B	3B	HR	RBI	BB	SB	AVG	OBP	SLG
1993	Two Teams	77	263	19	55	9	0	6	26	10	0	.209	.237	.312
1994	Chicago	104	369	43	115	17	3	10	51	27	7	.312	.362	.455
1995	*Projected*	*134*	*481*	*49*	*121*	*16*	*2*	*14*	*57*	*28*	*7*	*.252*	*.293*	*.380*

MIKE JACKSON / San Francisco Giants / Relief Pitcher $35

Was having the best season of his career, and the best season of any major league pitcher in his role, until stopped by tendinitis in early June. A two-pitch pitcher, throws a 90-plus fastball and a hard slider, has excellent control and works ahead of the hitters. Until last year he had worked 60-plus games for six straight years, 55 the year before that.

YEAR	TEAM/LEVEL	G	IP	W-L	SAVES	HITS	SO	BB	ERA
1992	San Francisco	67	82	6-6	2	76	80	33	3.73
1993	San Francisco	81	77	6-6	1	58	70	24	3.03
1994	San Francisco	36	42	3-2	4	23	51	11	1.49

JASON JACOME / New York Mets / Left-handed Starter $29

A low-round draft selection, like Isringhausen, who has come on strong. An Arizona native, he went to junior college, and was a 12th-round pick coming out. He was very thin, but bulked up last winter (1993-94), adding 25 pounds. Best pitches are a curve and change, also throws a slider, spots the fastball. Could be Bruce Hurst/Charlie Leibrandt type.

YEAR	TEAM/LEVEL	G	IP	W-L	PCT	HITS	SO	BB	ERA
1993	Binghamton AA	14	87	8-4	.667	85	56	38	3.21
1994	Norfolk AAA	19	127	8-6	.571	138	80	42	2.84
1994	New York	8	54	4-3	.571	54	30	17	2.67

JOHN JAHA / Milwaukee Brewers / First Base $25

A 14th-round draft pick with no flashy skills, he got out of the minors by battering pitchers at three levels. This took him eight years, so time is not on his side. The Milwaukee park has hurt him; he has homered only half as often in Milwaukee as he has on the road. Good first baseman, OK baserunner, needs to hit better, and might.

YEAR	TEAM/LEVEL	G	AB	R	H	2B	3B	HR	RBI	BB	SB	AVG	OBP	SLG
1993	Milwaukee	153	515	78	136	21	0	19	70	51	13	.264	.337	.416
1994	Milwaukee	84	291	45	70	14	0	12	39	32	3	.241	.332	.412
1995	*Projected*	*141*	*471*	*75*	*124*	*25*	*1*	*19*	*70*	*55*	*10*	*.263*	*.340*	*.442*

CHRIS JAMES / Texas Rangers / Right Field $26

Nineteen of his 34 hits were for extra bases, and he averaged more than two bases per hit, giving him a .500-plus slugging percentage for the second consecutive year. His secondary average last year was .433. . . . The Rangers used him almost entirely in right field, occasionally as a pinch hitter. Good platoon player; obviously will keep his job, in Texas or somewhere else.

YEAR	TEAM/LEVEL	G	AB	R	H	2B	3B	HR	RBI	BB	SB	AVG	OBP	SLG
1992	San Francisco	111	248	25	60	10	4	5	32	14	2	.242	.285	.375
1993	Two Teams	73	160	24	44	11	1	9	26	18	2	.275	.348	.525
1994	Texas	52	133	28	34	8	4	7	19	20	0	.256	.361	.534

KEVIN JARVIS / Cincinnati Reds / Right-handed Starter $22

Moved through the minor league levels rapidly despite being a 21st-round draft pick, and will receive an extended trial as a major league pitcher this year. His control is outstanding, and according to reports (I haven't seen him) he changes speeds well and has an excellent curve. Velocity is major league average. Grade B prospect; he's got nothing left to prove in the minors.

YEAR	TEAM/LEVEL	G	IP	W-L	PCT	HITS	SO	BB	ERA
1993	Winston-Salem A	21	145	8-7	.533	133	101	48	3.41
1994	Indianapolis AAA	21	132	10-2	.833	136	90	34	3.54
1994	Cincinnati	6	18	1-1	.500	22	10	5	7.13

STAN JAVIER / Oakland Athletics / Center Fielder $31

After eight years as a reserve outfielder, he finally got a chance to play regularly in '94, and he wasn't bad. He batted second for the A's (first when Henderson was out), and would have scored 100 runs had the season run to its conclusion. A switch hitter, average defensive center fielder, arm OK, excellent base runner. There's no reason he *shouldn't* be a regular.

YEAR	TEAM/LEVEL	G	AB	R	H	2B	3B	HR	RBI	BB	SB	AVG	OBP	SLG
1993	California	92	237	33	69	10	4	3	28	27	12	.291	.362	.405
1994	Oakland	109	419	75	114	23	0	10	44	49	24	.272	.349	.399
1995	*Projected*	*132*	*406*	*55*	*103*	*14*	*2*	*5*	*38*	*47*	*22*	*.254*	*.331*	*.335*

MIKE JEFFCOAT / Florida Marlins / Future Pitching Coach $10

Also known as the pitcher who would not die. Jeffcoat has pitched professional baseball since 1980, appearing in the majors with Cleveland, San Francisco, Texas, and now Florida. He's what he's always been . . . a savvy, soft-tossing lefty just a few bad outings away from Triple-A or an outright release. His control has gone from very good to exceptional.

YEAR	TEAM/LEVEL	G	IP	W-L	PCT	HITS	SO	BB	ERA
1993	Edmonton AAA	33	54	0-3	.000	58	32	6	4.14
1994	Edmonton AAA	23	35	4-0	1.000	31	26	8	2.04
1994	Florida	4	3	0-0	.000	4	1	0	10.13

GREGG JEFFERIES / St. Louis Cardinals / First Base $66

He is supposed to be a free agent; Lord knows whether he will return to St. Louis. With the exception of Tony Gwynn, he is the best two-strike hitter in baseball today . . . a California native, he is very much a hot-weather hitter, hitting 70 points better in June and July than he does in April and October. Defense OK at first base.

YEAR	TEAM/LEVEL	G	AB	R	H	2B	3B	HR	RBI	BB	SB	AVG	OBP	SLG
1993	St. Louis	142	544	89	186	24	3	16	83	62	46	.342	.408	.485
1994	St. Louis	103	397	52	129	27	1	12	55	45	12	.325	.391	.489
1995	*Projected*	*152*	*589*	*80*	*183*	*32*	*3*	*16*	*93*	*60*	*31*	*.311*	*.374*	*.457*

REGGIE JEFFERSON / Seattle Mariners / First Base/Designated Hitter $26

A switch hitter, but was used by Piniella strictly as a left-handed platoon player. He didn't have a hit against a left-handed pitcher. Looking backward, he had always hit much better left-handed than right-handed, a hundred points better, so he might continue to thrive as a platoon player . . . 70 percent of his playing time was as a DH.

YEAR	TEAM/LEVEL	G	AB	R	H	2B	3B	HR	RBI	BB	SB	AVG	OBP	SLG
1993	Cleveland	113	366	35	91	11	2	10	34	28	1	.249	.310	.372
1994	Seattle	63	162	24	53	11	0	8	32	17	0	.327	.392	.543
1995	*Projected*	*122*	*398*	*53*	*114*	*22*	*2*	*13*	*50*	*34*	*1*	*.286*	*.343*	*.450*

DEREK JETER / New York Yankees / Shortstop $40

Baseball America's 1994 Minor League Player of the Year, he hit .329 at Tampa (A Ball), .377 at Albany (Double-A), and .349 at Columbus (Triple-A). Altogether he stole 50 bases, and the Major League Equivalent of his Double-A and Triple-A work is a .342 average. A 20-year-old right-handed hitter, has every skill except power, and may develop that.

YEAR	TEAM/LEVEL	G	AB	R	H	2B	3B	HR	RBI	BB	SB	AVG	OBP	SLG
1993	Greensboro A	128	515	85	152	14	11	5	71	58	18	.295	.376	.394
1994	Tampa A	69	292	61	96	13	8	0	39	23	28	.329	.380	.428
1994	AA and AAA	69	248	42	90	14	3	5	29	35	22	.362	.447	.504

MIGUEL JIMINEZ / Oakland Athletics / Starting Pitcher | $12

The Achilles' heel of many great men is arrogance. Jiminez spent several weeks on the A's roster, although it could not possibly be more obvious that he is not ready to pitch in the major leagues. He has a great arm, and LaRussa and Duncan figure they can teach him what he needs to know. They can, too, but it will take several years.

YEAR	TEAM/LEVEL	G	IP	W-L	PCT	HITS	SO	BB	ERA
1993	Oakland	5	27	1-0	1.000	27	13	16	4.00
1994	Tacoma AAA	23	74	3-9	.250	82	64	79	9.12
1994	Oakland	8	34	1-4	.200	38	22	32	7.41

BRIAN JOHNSON / San Diego Padres / Catcher | $17

The starting quarterback at Stanford in '88 and '89, he was a 16th-round draft pick of the Yankees, taken by San Diego in the Rule 5 draft, and hit .339 at Las Vegas in '93. A 27-year-old right-handed hitter, he is not any worse a player than Brad Ausmus, and might be better. He threw out 35 percent of opposing base stealers.

YEAR	TEAM/LEVEL	G	AB	R	H	2B	3B	HR	RBI	BB	SB	AVG	OBP	SLG
1992	MLE	75	230	19	56	15	0	2	17	12	1	.243	.281	.335
1993	MLE	115	385	37	110	26	2	7	46	26	0	.286	.331	.418
1994	San Diego	36	93	7	23	4	1	3	16	5	0	.247	.283	.409

CHARLES JOHNSON / Florida Marlins / Catcher | $34

A Florida native, was the Marlins' first-ever first-round draft pick, in 1992. Since signing he has dominated the Midwest League (1993), hit 28 homers in the Eastern League, and gone 5-for-11 in the majors. He has an outstanding arm. The Marlins are expected to get rid of Benito Santiago, and Johnson is among the top candidates for Rookie of the Year.

YEAR	TEAM/LEVEL	G	AB	R	H	2B	3B	HR	RBI	BB	SB	AVG	OBP	SLG
1993	Kane County A	135	488	74	134	29	5	19	94	62	9	.275	.356	.471
1994	Portland AA	132	443	64	117	29	1	28	80	74	4	.264	.371	.524
1994	MLE	132	425	47	99	25	0	20	58	47	2	.233	.309	.433

DANE JOHNSON / Chicago White Sox / Right-handed Relief Pitcher | $14

A big right-hander who was in the Toronto system, 1984-89, and since has a) pitched two years in Taiwan, and b) spent two years as an assistant coach at Lamar University. He got a tryout with the Brewers in '93, and has pitched well in the minors since then. Is 32 years old, throws heavy sinking fastball, hard slider. He can pitch a little.

YEAR	TEAM/LEVEL	G	IP	W-L	SAVES	HITS	SO	BB	ERA
1993	AA and AAA	28	40	2-2	7	34	36	14	3.35
1994	Nashville AAA	39	44	1-5	24	40	40	18	2.25
1994	Chicago	15	12	2-1	0	16	7	11	6.57

HOWARD JOHNSON / Colorado Rockies / Left Field $22

Did a great job as a pinch hitter, 10-for-33 with four home runs, but hit under .200 when he was in the lineup. After *two* off years, 1992 and 1993, I didn't see any reason why he shouldn't come back strong. After *three* off years, it's a long shot. Tim Wallach came back after three off years, but it's very rare.

YEAR	TEAM/LEVEL	G	AB	R	H	2B	3B	HR	RBI	BB	SB	AVG	OBP	SLG
1992	New York (N)	100	350	48	78	19	0	7	43	55	22	.223	.329	.337
1993	New York (N)	72	235	32	56	8	2	7	26	43	6	.238	.354	.379
1994	Colorado	93	227	30	48	10	2	10	40	39	11	.211	.323	.405

LANCE JOHNSON / Chicago White Sox / Center Field $35

Are we sure that this is a real player, and not just some guy generating numbers with an APBA card? How can anybody be this consistent? Has led the American League in triples for four straight years, making him the first player in major league history to do that . . . exceptional center fielder, good base stealer. The White Sox are smart not to lead him off.

YEAR	TEAM/LEVEL	G	AB	R	H	2B	3B	HR	RBI	BB	SB	AVG	OBP	SLG
1993	Chicago	147	540	75	168	18	14	0	47	36	35	.311	.354	.396
1994	Chicago	106	412	56	114	11	14	3	54	26	26	.277	.321	.393
1995	*Projected*	*152*	*562*	*69*	*156*	*16*	*9*	*2*	*50*	*35*	*39*	*.278*	*.320*	*.349*

RANDY JOHNSON / Seattle Mariners / Starting Pitcher $83

You need to appreciate this man, if you're a baseball fan, because you're never going to see another one like him, no matter how long you live. He's now 31, and missed a couple of starts with a tired arm, but I expect him to be an effective pitcher for another 10 years. He needs to win 20 to be a Hall of Fame candidate.

YEAR	TEAM/LEVEL	G	IP	W-L	PCT	HITS	SO	BB	ERA
1992	Seattle	31	210	12-14	.462	154	241	144	3.77
1993	Seattle	35	255	19-8	.704	185	308	99	3.24
1994	Seattle	23	172	13-6	.684	132	204	72	3.19

JOHN JOHNSTONE / Florida Marlins / Pitcher $15

He's posted an ERA of 5.91 twice in a row, so I suppose we must say that he's consistent. Taken from the Mets in the expansion draft, he is a true expansion player, just getting a chance to play because he's all the team has. Has a good arm, good control, impressive strikeout/walk ratio at Edmonton (43-9 in 42 innings).

YEAR	TEAM/LEVEL	G	IP	W-L	PCT	HITS	SO	BB	ERA
1993	Florida	7	11	0-2	.000	16	5	7	5.91
1994	Edmonton AAA	29	42	5-3	.625	46	43	9	4.46
1994	Florida	17	21	1-2	.333	23	23	16	5.91

BOBBY J. JONES / New York Mets / Starting Pitcher $35

Pitched poorly in Shea Stadium (4-6, 4.25 ERA) but was great almost every time out on the road (8-1, 1.77). The most important thing in his career is that his strike-

outs increase significantly this year. If they do, he'll probably have a long career. If they don't, he'll drop out of the rotation in two or three years.

YEAR	TEAM/LEVEL	G	IP	W-L	PCT	HITS	SO	BB	ERA
1993	Norfolk AAA	24	166	12-10	.545	149	126	32	3.63
1993	New York	9	62	2-4	.333	61	35	22	3.65
1994	New York	24	160	12-7	.632	157	80	56	3.15

CHIPPER JONES / Atlanta Braves / Shortstop $31

Missed the 1994 season with a torn anterior cruciate ligament suffered in spring training. Considered among the top prospects in baseball for three years, he is now 23, and has three more things going for him—off sea-

sons by Blauser and Pendleton, and the Braves' failure to finish first. My guess is that he'll be in Atlanta's lineup in '95.

YEAR	TEAM/LEVEL	G	AB	R	H	2B	3B	HR	RBI	BB	SB	AVG	OBP	SLG
1992	MLE	67	258	35	84	15	5	9	35	7	9	.326	.343	.527
1993	MLE	139	512	71	150	26	5	11	65	40	14	.293	.344	.428
1994	Atlanta						(On Disabled List)							

CHRIS JONES / Colorado Rockies / Center Field $15

A 29-year-old right-handed outfielder from the Reds system; the Rockies are working hard to insure that he knows his place. He hit .273 for them in '93, and they made him sign a minor league contract for '94. They

called him up for a month, he hit .300, they sent him back down. He's a lousy center fielder, and has ugly strikeout/walk ratios.

YEAR	TEAM/LEVEL	G	AB	R	H	2B	3B	HR	RBI	BB	SB	AVG	OBP	SLG
1993	Colorado	86	209	29	57	11	4	6	31	10	9	.273	.305	.450
1994	MLE	98	372	54	110	19	2	16	52	25	8	.296	.340	.487
1994	Colorado	21	40	6	12	2	1	0	2	2	0	.300	.333	.400

DOUG JONES / Philadelphia Phillies / Closer $41

The Orioles had a guy like this in the early '60s, Stu Miller. He raised deception to an art form, changing speeds among slow, slower, and slowest, hitting corners, changing arm speeds. He threw so softly you al-

ways thought the ball would drop to the ground before it reached home plate, and sometimes it did . . . the exact opposite of Mitch Williams.

YEAR	TEAM/LEVEL	G	IP	W-L	SAVES	HITS	SO	BB	ERA
1992	Houston	80	112	11-8	36	96	93	17	1.85
1993	Houston	71	85	4-10	26	102	66	21	4.54
1994	Philadelphia	47	54	2-4	27	55	38	6	2.17

TODD JONES / Houston Astros / Relief Pitcher $26

Hard-throwing right-hander who has been troubled most of his career by control lapses, but apparently has put that in the past. He wants to be the Astros' closer, and had a shot at that job last spring, but didn't pitch well, and was beaten out by Hudek. He pitched great the rest of the year, and will have more chances.

YEAR	TEAM/LEVEL	G	IP	W-L	SAVES	HITS	SO	BB	ERA
1993	Tucson AAA	41	49	4-2	12	49	45	31	4.44
1993	Houston	27	37	1-2	2	28	25	15	3.13
1994	Houston	48	73	5-2	5	52	63	26	2.72

BRIAN JORDAN / St. Louis Cardinals / Outfielder $29

Season was ended in early July by broken ribs. He now has 594 major league at bats—about one season's worth. He's hit 27 doubles, 12 triples, 20 homers, driven in 81 runs, stolen 17 bases, averaged .261. This is a lot more impressive if you do it in one year, rather than three, but still, we have to conclude that he can play.

YEAR	TEAM/LEVEL	G	AB	R	H	2B	3B	HR	RBI	BB	SB	AVG	OBP	SLG
1992	St. Louis	55	193	17	40	9	4	5	22	10	7	.207	.250	.373
1993	St. Louis	67	223	33	69	10	6	10	44	12	6	.309	.351	.510
1994	St. Louis	53	178	14	46	8	2	5	15	16	4	.258	.320	.410

RICKY JORDAN / Philadelphia Phillies / First Base $22

Perhaps the only player in baseball who can bat 200 times a year and hit .280 every year. For the last four years he has hit .272 or better each year, with slugging percentages always in the .400s. His .282 average last year was exactly his career average . . . hits left-handers very well, .300-plus. Never walks, has no speed, can't throw.

YEAR	TEAM/LEVEL	G	AB	R	H	2B	3B	HR	RBI	BB	SB	AVG	OBP	SLG
1993	Philadelphia	90	159	21	46	4	1	5	18	8	0	.289	.324	.421
1994	Philadelphia	72	220	29	62	14	2	8	37	6	0	.282	.303	.473
1995	*Projected*	*98*	*243*	*28*	*65*	*16*	*1*	*5*	*31*	*7*	*1*	*.267*	*.288*	*.403*

FELIX JOSE / Kansas City Royals / Right Field $31

I swear this man makes more baserunning mistakes than anyone I have ever seen. Two or three times every week, you see him wandering around the basepaths like a squirrel on the highway, with no regard to where the baseball is. He's the same in the outfield; his manager can never be sure what in the hell he is doing out there. Good hitter.

YEAR	TEAM/LEVEL	G	AB	R	H	2B	3B	HR	RBI	BB	SB	AVG	OBP	SLG
1993	Kansas City	149	499	64	126	24	3	6	43	36	31	.253	.303	.349
1994	Kansas City	99	366	56	111	28	1	11	55	35	10	.303	.362	.475
1995	*Projected*	*149*	*540*	*71*	*147*	*30*	*3*	*11*	*65*	*46*	*27*	*.272*	*.328*	*.400*

WALLY JOYNER / Kansas City Royals / First Base $32

His three-year contract, signed as a free agent, is up now, and the Royals have other guys who could play first—Hamelin, Vitiello, Glenn Davis. Still, I would expect him to remain as the KC first baseman . . . good defense, .300 hitter, good on-base percentages. Is 32 years old with a back problem, so he probably won't last more than two or three more years.

YEAR	TEAM/LEVEL	G	AB	R	H	2B	3B	HR	RBI	BB	SB	AVG	OBP	SLG
1992	Kansas City	149	572	66	154	36	2	9	66	55	11	.269	.336	.386
1993	Kansas City	141	497	83	145	36	3	15	65	66	5	.292	.375	.467
1994	Kansas City	97	363	52	113	20	3	8	57	47	3	.311	.386	.449

JEFF JUDEN / Philadelphia Phillies / Starting Pitcher $14

Was once a hot prospect in the Astros system, traded to Philadelphia a year ago. With Houston he had a reputation for putting on weight. He was in great shape last spring, but ineffective and apparently hurt, since he pitched only six times in the minors after being sent down May 19 . . . listed at 6-8, but I think he's more like 6-5½.

YEAR	TEAM/LEVEL	G	IP	W-L	PCT	HITS	SO	BB	ERA
1992	Tucson AAA	26	147	9-10	.474	149	120	71	4.04
1993	Tucson AAA	27	169	11-6	.647	174	156	76	4.63
1994	Philadelphia	6	28	1-4	.200	29	22	12	6.18

DAVE JUSTICE / Atlanta Braves / Right Field $43

I commented last year that Justice' 1993 stats paralleled those of Jeff Burroughs in '77. He was on target last year to match Burroughs in '78, too. He'd better hope this doesn't continue. Burroughs' bat died in '79 . . . a poor outfielder, poor baserunner, but has grounded into only 25 double plays in his entire career, an amazingly low total for a player who doesn't bunt.

YEAR	TEAM/LEVEL	G	AB	R	H	2B	3B	HR	RBI	BB	SB	AVG	OBP	SLG
1993	Atlanta	157	585	90	158	15	4	40	120	78	3	.270	.357	.515
1994	Atlanta	104	352	61	110	16	2	19	59	69	2	.313	.427	.531
1995	*Projected*	*145*	*507*	*86*	*144*	*23*	*3*	*29*	*91*	*85*	*3*	*.284*	*.387*	*.513*

SCOTT KAMIENIECKI / New York Yankees / Starting Pitcher $26

Perpetual fourth/fifth starter, 31 years old and still trying to solidify his position. Throws 90 but doesn't have a strikeout pitch. His control was good a couple of years ago, but has gone backward. Good fielder, gets 60 percent ground balls. He's capable of winning 15 if he stays in the rotation, but more likely to go 7-12 and drop out of it.

YEAR	TEAM/LEVEL	G	IP	W-L	PCT	HITS	SO	BB	ERA
1992	New York	28	188	6-14	.300	193	88	74	4.36
1993	New York	30	154	10-7	.588	163	72	59	4.08
1994	New York	22	117	8-6	.571	115	71	59	3.76

RON KARKOVICE / Chicago White Sox / Catcher $28

Generally regarded as the best defensive catcher in the American League, if not the best in baseball, and a better hitter than his low averages would suggest. He averaged two bases per hit last year, had a secondary average of .386, and grounded into *no* double plays . . . 70 percent of his career home runs have been hit on the road, only 30 percent in Chicago.

YEAR	TEAM/LEVEL	G	AB	R	H	2B	3B	HR	RBI	BB	SB	AVG	OBP	SLG
1993	Chicago	128	403	60	92	17	1	20	54	29	2	.228	.287	.424
1994	Chicago	77	207	33	44	9	1	11	29	36	0	.213	.325	.425
1995	*Projected*	*124*	*355*	*46*	*79*	*15*	*1*	*13*	*45*	*36*	*5*	*.223*	*.294*	*.380*

ERIC KARROS / Los Angeles Dodgers / First Base $30

The National League's answer to John Jaha. He established career highs last year in batting average (.266) and on-base percentage (.310), and matched his career high in slugging percentage (.426). These are not impressive numbers. Geronimo Pena is a better hitter. Sean Berry is a better hitter. Karros could hit 25-30 homers.

YEAR	TEAM/LEVEL	G	AB	R	H	2B	3B	HR	RBI	BB	SB	AVG	OBP	SLG
1993	Los Angeles	158	619	74	153	27	2	23	80	34	0	.247	.287	.409
1994	Los Angeles	111	406	51	108	21	1	14	46	29	2	.266	.310	.426
1995	*Projected*	*156*	*590*	*73*	*157*	*32*	*2*	*22*	*83*	*38*	*2*	*.266*	*.311*	*.439*

STEVE KARSAY / Oakland Athletics / Starting Pitcher $26

Oakland's compensation for loaning Rickey Henderson to Toronto, Karsay pitched well in September 1993 and opened '94 in the A's rotation. After four starts he went on the DL with a sore elbow, and never came off. If healthy, Karsay is an excellent pitcher: a good arm, great feel for pitching. It doesn't matter how good he looks if he can't stay on the mound.

YEAR	TEAM/LEVEL	G	IP	W-L	PCT	HITS	SO	BB	ERA
1993	Two Teams AA	21	118	8-4	.667	111	122	35	3.58
1993	Oakland	8	49	3-3	.500	49	33	16	4.04
1994	Oakland	4	28	1-1	.500	26	15	8	2.57

MIKE KELLY / Atlanta Braves / Outfield $18

The first three picks in the 1991 draft, Brien Taylor, Mike Kelly, and Dave McCarty, may all be busts. Kelly has speed and power and can field, but strikes out and hasn't suggested that he will hit for average. He may well turn out to be a decent player, but his star potential is nil unless he learns to hit the curve. Grade C prospect.

YEAR	TEAM/LEVEL	G	AB	R	H	2B	3B	HR	RBI	BB	SB	AVG	OBP	SLG
1993	MLE	123	411	46	90	11	0	15	42	26	7	.219	.265	.355
1994	MLE	82	302	34	71	12	2	11	34	23	5	.235	.289	.397
1994	Atlanta	30	77	14	21	10	1	2	9	2	0	.273	.300	.506

PAT KELLY / New York Yankees / Second Base $36

Despite missing a couple of weeks with a jammed thumb, he established career highs in batting, slugging, and on-base percentage, putting him among the better-hitting second basemen, as well as among the better fielders. Excellent bunter. Only question about his future is the development of Jeter, which could push Gallego into a contest for the second base job.

YEAR	TEAM/LEVEL	G	AB	R	H	2B	3B	HR	RBI	BB	SB	AVG	OBP	SLG
1993	New York	127	406	49	111	24	1	7	51	24	14	.273	.317	.389
1994	New York	93	286	35	80	21	2	3	41	19	6	.280	.330	.399
1995	*Projected*	*147*	*525*	*65*	*138*	*31*	*3*	*10*	*62*	*36*	*14*	*.263*	*.310*	*.390*

ROBERTO KELLY / Atlanta Braves / Center Field $43

Hit .286 after joining Atlanta, which is exactly his career average—.286 with 40 walks a year, 30 stolen bases, 15 homers, adequate defense in center. He would have scored almost 100 runs last year, given a full schedule . . . hit .347 last year with men in scoring position, .377 in the late innings of close games. Has tended to hit best early in the season.

YEAR	TEAM/LEVEL	G	AB	R	H	2B	3B	HR	RBI	BB	SB	AVG	OBP	SLG
1993	Cincinnati	78	320	44	102	17	3	9	35	17	21	.319	.354	.475
1994	Two Teams	110	434	73	127	23	3	9	45	35	19	.293	.347	.422
1995	*Projected*	*137*	*539*	*79*	*156*	*25*	*3*	*14*	*61*	*36*	*27*	*.289*	*.334*	*.425*

JEFF KENT / New York Mets / Second Base $45

Improved his fielding percentage at second base, his double play rate, his range, his batting average, his on-base percentage, his slugging percentage . . . he was having a good year. He hit .373 against left-handed pitchers. Who's the best second baseman the Mets have had? Ron Hunt? Felix Millan? Doug Flynn? We're getting ahead of ourselves, but it *should* be Jeff Kent.

YEAR	TEAM/LEVEL	G	AB	R	H	2B	3B	HR	RBI	BB	SB	AVG	OBP	SLG
1993	New York	140	496	65	134	24	0	21	80	30	4	.270	.320	.446
1994	New York	107	415	53	121	24	5	14	68	23	1	.292	.341	.475
1995	*Projected*	*153*	*589*	*79*	*157*	*31*	*2*	*22*	*88*	*38*	*4*	*.267*	*.311*	*.438*

JIMMY KEY / New York Yankees / Starting Pitcher $65

See comment on Will Clark. . . . Underwent arthroscopic surgery on his left shoulder, October 19, but should be ready for spring training, or whenever they decide to play baseball again. His 17-4 record was greatly abetted by his offense, which scored 7.4 runs per game for him (the most for any major league pitcher), but he's also a terrific pitcher.

YEAR	TEAM/LEVEL	G	IP	W-L	PCT	HITS	SO	BB	ERA
1992	Toronto	33	217	13-13	.500	205	117	59	3.53
1993	New York	34	237	18-6	.750	219	173	43	3.00
1994	New York	25	168	17-4	.810	177	97	52	3.27

MARK KIEFER / Milwaukee Brewers / Pitcher | $15

A 26-year-old right-hander, started the '94 season in the majors after allowing no runs in six games in September 1993. He was sent to New Orleans in late April, where he had his best Triple-A season. There's nothing impressive about him, and he has had elbow problems, but there's also no obvious reason that he *couldn't* survive a year in the rotation.

YEAR	TEAM/LEVEL	G	IP	W-L	PCT	HITS	SO	BB	ERA
1993	AA and AAA	16	80	6-6	.500	76	67	36	4.39
1994	New Orleans AAA	21	125	9-7	.563	111	116	48	3.90
1994	Milwaukee	7	11	1-0	1.000	15	8	8	8.44

BROOKS KIESCHNICK / Chicago Cubs / Left Field | $20

A left-handed-hitting outfielder who is regarded as the top prospect in the Cubs' system. The Cubs took him in the first round in 1993, and were criticized at the time for drafting a DH in the first round, but he's worked hard to prove he could play the outfield. Extremely competitive, has the best bat speed in the Cubs' organization, including major leaguers.

YEAR	TEAM/LEVEL	G	AB	R	H	2B	3B	HR	RBI	BB	SB	AVG	OBP	SLG
1993	Orlando AA	25	91	12	31	8	0	2	10	7	1	.341	.388	.495
1994	Orlando AA	126	468	57	132	25	3	14	55	33	3	.282	.332	.438
1994	MLE	126	459	49	123	23	2	12	47	24	2	.268	.304	.405

DARRYL KILE / Houston Astros / Starting Pitcher | $30

His control is wobbly, to put it as nicely as we can. With 82 walks, 10 wild pitches, 9 hit batsmen, and 13 homers allowed in 148 innings, he was damned lucky to escape with a 9-6 record. He was doing better just before the strike, walking *no one* in his last two starts, so he may be able to continue to win.

YEAR	TEAM/LEVEL	G	IP	W-L	PCT	HITS	SO	BB	ERA
1992	Houston	22	125	5-10	.333	124	90	63	3.95
1993	Houston	32	172	15-8	.652	152	141	69	3.51
1994	Houston	24	148	9-6	.600	153	105	82	4.57

JEFF KING / Pittsburgh Pirates / Third Base | $27

A sore back reduced his effectiveness last year, and put him on the DL at one point. He's a very good defensive third baseman (also a good defensive *second* baseman), and he drove in 98 runs in '93. For most of his career, he hasn't been a productive hitter, and wasn't again in '94. And he's 30, so we can't expect him to get better.

YEAR	TEAM/LEVEL	G	AB	R	H	2B	3B	HR	RBI	BB	SB	AVG	OBP	SLG
1993	Pittsburgh	158	611	82	180	35	3	9	98	59	8	.295	.356	.406
1994	Pittsburgh	94	339	36	89	23	0	5	42	30	3	.263	.316	.375
1995	*Projected*	*157*	*566*	*67*	*145*	*28*	*2*	*12*	*76*	*47*	*6*	*.256*	*.313*	*.376*

KEVIN KING / Seattle Mariners / Left-handed Pitcher $13

Another installment in the Mariners' endless pitching program. King, a big, hard-throwing left-hander, was 7-16 with San Bernandino in 1992 (California League), so he was converted to the bullpen. This seemed to work, so the Mariners ripped him through the minors, apparently trying to get him to the majors before he could stop pitching well, and he's been 100 percent ineffective ever since.

YEAR	TEAM/LEVEL	G	IP	W-L	SAVES	HITS	SO	BB	ERA
1993	Seattle	13	12	0-1	0	9	8	4	6.17
1994	Calgary	25	37	1-2	1	46	29	18	5.65
1994	Seattle	19	15	0-2	0	21	6	17	7.04

MIKE KINGERY / Colorado Rockies / Center Field $24

After spending almost two full years back in the minors, Kingery made the Rockies in spring training, '94. Burks' injury made him Colorado's regular center fielder, more or less, and he had his career year, hitting .349 with lots of doubles and triples. He's not really a center fielder, or a .349 hitter, but he gives great effort, and I'm happy to see him back.

YEAR	TEAM/LEVEL	G	AB	R	H	2B	3B	HR	RBI	BB	SB	AVG	OBP	SLG
1993	Omaha AAA	116	399	61	105	19	5	10	41	36	9	.263	.325	.411
1994	Colorado	105	301	56	105	27	8	4	41	30	5	.349	.402	.532
1995	*Projected*	*113*	*327*	*40*	*89*	*16*	*3*	*4*	*30*	*27*	*6*	*.272*	*.328*	*.376*

WAYNE KIRBY / Cleveland Indians / Right Field $22

Started 34 games in right field under a platoon plan, thus getting 83 percent of his at bats against right-handed pitchers. He's a decent platoon player, a .280-to-.300 hitter (with the advantage), has good speed, a little pop in his bat, and a good arm. As an everyday player, his weaknesses would become more obvious than his strengths . . . 31 years old, limited future.

YEAR	TEAM/LEVEL	G	AB	R	H	2B	3B	HR	RBI	BB	SB	AVG	OBP	SLG
1993	Cleveland	131	458	71	123	19	5	6	60	37	17	.269	.323	.371
1994	Cleveland	78	191	33	56	6	0	5	23	13	11	.293	.341	.403
1995	*Projected*	*89*	*247*	*38*	*67*	*9*	*2*	*4*	*27*	*17*	*13*	*.271*	*.318*	*.372*

RYAN KLESKO / Atlanta Braves / Left Field $36

I believe this will be the only time in the book I use the word "awesome." Klesko's awesome power forced the Braves to wedge him into the lineup, even though they had no place for him. As a left fielder, he's a first base-man, but he has a real chance to hit 40 homers a year, maybe 45. Left-handed hitter, used for now as a platoon player.

YEAR	TEAM/LEVEL	G	AB	R	H	2B	3B	HR	RBI	BB	SB	AVG	OBP	SLG
1993	Atlanta	22	17	3	6	1	0	2	5	3	0	.353	.450	.765
1994	Atlanta	92	245	42	68	13	3	17	47	26	1	.278	.344	.563
1995	*Projected*	*128*	*437*	*60*	*108*	*21*	*2*	*19*	*63*	*42*	*2*	*.247*	*.313*	*.435*

SCOTT KLINGENBECK / Baltimore Orioles / Right-handed Starter | $16

Fifth-round 1992 draft pick from Ohio State, pitched once for Baltimore in early June, and will receive a clean shot at the rotation this year. He's 6-2, 205, could be a bit chubby, has above average fastball and break-ing pitch. Outstanding control. He looks real good, understanding that out of 100 guys who look good at Double-A, you're lucky to get five pitchers.

YEAR	TEAM/LEVEL	G	IP	W-L	PCT	HITS	SO	BB	ERA
1993	Frederick A	23	139	13-4	.765	151	146	35	2.98
1994	Bowie AA	25	144	7-5	.583	151	120	37	3.63
1994	Baltimore	1	7	1-0	1.000	6	5	4	3.86

CHUCK KNOBLAUCH / Minnesota Twins / Second Base | $69

My favorite player, a hustling second baseman who was on target for 60-plus doubles and 50-plus stolen bases . . . I don't know what the exact combination would have been, but I'm sure that nobody's ever done it before. He made three errors at second, fielding .994, and he gets to everything. The Twins used him at lead-off, but with all those doubles, he could hit third.

YEAR	TEAM/LEVEL	G	AB	R	H	2B	3B	HR	RBI	BB	SB	AVG	OBP	SLG
1993	Minnesota	153	602	82	167	27	4	2	41	65	29	.277	.354	.346
1994	Minnesota	109	445	85	139	45	3	5	51	41	35	.312	.381	.461
1995	*Projected*	*155*	*608*	*100*	*177*	*37*	*5*	*5*	*60*	*73*	*40*	*.291*	*.367*	*.393*

RANDY KNORR / Toronto Blue Jays / Catcher | $19

One of four backup catchers in baseball who could play regularly—Knorr, Hernandez, LaValliere, and Mayne. He's a solid defensive catcher, average arm, keeps his slugging percentage in the fours. Only 26, he may get a chance to be a regular, but he's four years away from free agency in an organization that has catchers, so probably will spend his best years on the bench.

YEAR	TEAM/LEVEL	G	AB	R	H	2B	3B	HR	RBI	BB	SB	AVG	OBP	SLG
1993	Toronto	39	101	11	25	3	2	4	20	9	0	.248	.309	.436
1994	Toronto	40	124	20	30	2	0	7	19	10	0	.242	.301	.427
1995	*Projected*	*76*	*231*	*26*	*59*	*10*	*0*	*9*	*29*	*17*	*0*	*.255*	*.306*	*.416*

KURT KNUDSEN / Detroit Tigers / Relief Pitcher | $14

Spent a week in the majors, otherwise spent the year pitching garbage relief at Toledo. This was his third year of splitting time between Detroit and Toledo, during which his control has not improved, his fastball has not accelerated, and his reputation has not flourished. Right-handed pitcher, gets hit so hard by left-handers (.309 career) that his value is limited.

YEAR	TEAM/LEVEL	G	IP	W-L	SAVES	HITS	SO	BB	ERA
1993	Toledo AAA	23	33	2-2	6	24	39	11	3.78
1993	Detroit	30	38	3-2	2	41	29	16	4.78
1994	Toledo AAA	37	67	2-5	4	56	64	42	4.01

KEVIN KOSLOFSKI / Kansas City Royals / Outfielder $14

A career .252 hitter in the major leagues (72 games); my guess is that that's about his true level of ability. He hit .215 at Omaha last year, but he had been discouraged by three years of beating his head against a brick wall, trying to get to Kansas City. Good outfielder, good speed, left-handed hitter, a useful bench player.

YEAR	TEAM/LEVEL	G	AB	R	H	2B	3B	HR	RBI	BB	SB	AVG	OBP	SLG
1992	Kansas City	55	133	20	33	0	2	3	13	12	2	.248	.313	.346
1993	Omaha	111	395	58	109	22	5	7	45	43	15	.276	.384	.410
1994	Omaha	93	307	43	66	8	3	6	39	37	10	.215	.299	.319

CHAD KREUTER / Detroit Tigers / Catcher $23

A switch hitter in theory, but has perhaps the widest platoon differential in the game—138 points last year (.252/.114), 109 points over the last three years (.185/.294). He can't hit left-handers. Good arm (he threw out 43 percent of opposing base stealers last year, which is outstanding). He's got to hit better than he did last year if he's going to play.

YEAR	TEAM/LEVEL	G	AB	R	H	2B	3B	HR	RBI	BB	SB	AVG	OBP	SLG
1993	Detroit	119	374	59	107	23	3	15	51	49	2	.286	.371	.484
1994	Detroit	65	170	17	38	8	0	1	19	28	0	.224	.327	.288
1995	*Projected*	*119*	*320*	*42*	*77*	*14*	*1*	*7*	*35*	*43*	*1*	*.241*	*.331*	*.356*

BILL KRUEGER / San Diego Padres / Starting Pitcher $13

A survivor, a lefty who doesn't throw hard enough to toss a salad, but posted ERAs of 3.84, 3.98, 3.60, 4.53, and 3.40 from 1989 to 1993, winning more than he lost (36-30). His luck ran out last year, and you'd have to rival Reverend Ike as a positive thinker to suppose his effectiveness will return at age 37 . . . hit .500 for Padres (6-for-12).

YEAR	TEAM/LEVEL	G	IP	W-L	PCT	HITS	SO	BB	ERA
1992	Two Teams	36	179	10-8	.556	189	99	53	4.53
1993	Detroit	32	82	6-4	.600	90	60	30	3.40
1994	Two Teams	24	61	3-4	.429	68	47	24	6.38

JOHN KRUK / Philadelphia Phillies / First Base $43

Slowed by a battle with testicular cancer and a routine injury to his right knee . . . well, actually, only the knee slowed him down; there's no evidence that the cancer affected him at all. He is always going to be able to hit, even when he's 40 years old and has to take a cab to first base. He turned 34 over the winter.

YEAR	TEAM/LEVEL	G	AB	R	H	2B	3B	HR	RBI	BB	SB	AVG	OBP	SLG
1993	Philadelphia	150	535	100	169	33	5	14	85	111	6	.316	.430	.475
1994	Philadelphia	75	255	35	77	17	0	5	38	42	4	.302	.395	.427
1995	*Projected*	*136*	*467*	*71*	*136*	*22*	*3*	*10*	*63*	*38*	*4*	*.291*	*.404*	*.415*

TIM LAKER / Montreal Expos / Catcher $17

He seemed to have established that he wasn't going to hit, but a strong season at Ottawa may have brought his career back to life. Laker is a big, strong kid who throws well, and snuck into the major leagues at age 22 be- cause the Expos were auditioning large numbers of catchers. He hit .309 with 71 RBI at Ottawa, and is only 25.

YEAR	TEAM/LEVEL	G	AB	R	H	2B	3B	HR	RBI	BB	SB	AVG	OBP	SLG
1992	Montreal	28	46	8	10	3	0	0	4	2	1	.217	.250	.283
1993	Montreal	43	86	3	17	2	1	0	7	2	2	.198	.222	.244
1994	MLE	118	408	54	115	30	1	8	56	37	8	.282	.342	.419

MARK LANGSTON / California Angels / Starting Pitcher $55

A wonderful pitcher, one of the most under-rated play- ers of our generation. He won his first start last year, but his elbow swelled up, and he had to have surgery, three bone chips removed from his elbow on April 12. This slowed him down in May and early June, but he still struck out 109 in 119 innings. He'll be back strong in '95.

YEAR	TEAM/LEVEL	G	IP	W-L	PCT	HITS	SO	BB	ERA
1992	California	32	229	13-14	.481	206	174	74	3.66
1993	California	35	256	16-11	.593	220	196	85	3.20
1994	California	18	119	7-8	.467	121	109	54	4.68

RAY LANKFORD / St. Louis Cardinals / Center Field $61

You can see many positives in the stats below, summa- rized in 89 runs scored in 109 games. It does appear that he has a serious problem with left-handed pitchers. I mentioned last year that his .233 slugging percentage against lefties was by far the worst in the NL, but even last year, having a good year, he hit .190 against the southpaws.

YEAR	TEAM/LEVEL	G	AB	R	H	2B	3B	HR	RBI	BB	SB	AVG	OBP	SLG
1993	St. Louis	127	407	64	97	17	3	7	45	81	14	.238	.366	.346
1994	St. Louis	109	416	89	111	25	5	19	57	58	11	.267	.359	.488
1995	*Projected*	*150*	*578*	*96*	*150*	*30*	*6*	*17*	*73*	*90*	*27*	*.260*	*.359*	*.420*

MIKE LANSING / Montreal Expos / Second Base/Third Base $28

Primarily a third baseman in '93, he moved more to second last year, as Sean Berry took over third, and was equally good there. His batting average was down 21 points, but the Expos were glad it wasn't down 60, plus his fielding percentage was up 27 points at second and 19 at third. No star potential, but the kind of player every team needs.

YEAR	TEAM/LEVEL	G	AB	R	H	2B	3B	HR	RBI	BB	SB	AVG	OBP	SLG
1993	Montreal	141	491	64	141	29	1	3	45	46	23	.287	.352	.369
1994	Montreal	106	394	44	105	21	2	5	35	30	12	.266	.328	.368
1995	*Projected*	*151*	*550*	*68*	*150*	*29*	*2*	*5*	*53*	*47*	*28*	*.273*	*.330*	*.360*

BARRY LARKIN / Cincinnati Reds / Shortstop $73

His average skidded to .279, ending a string of five .300 seasons, but nobody's complaining. He was 26-for-28 as a base stealer, and is 40-for-43 over the last two seasons. He established a career high in walks, 64, despite the strike, and played through the schedule without an injury for the first time since 1990. He has many good seasons left.

YEAR	TEAM/LEVEL	G	AB	R	H	2B	3B	HR	RBI	BB	SB	AVG	OBP	SLG
1993	Cincinnati	100	384	57	121	20	3	8	51	51	14	.315	.394	.445
1994	Cincinnati	110	427	78	119	23	5	9	52	64	26	.279	.369	.419
1995	*Projected*	*137*	*525*	*80*	*148*	*25*	*4*	*11*	*63*	*70*	*21*	*.282*	*.366*	*.408*

MIKE LAVALLIERE / Chicago White Sox / Catcher $19

A regular for several years with the Pirates, and once a Gold Glove winner, he has slipped into a backup role, but is still the same player that he was with Pittsburgh. With decent batting averages and a good many walks, he at least avoids wasting outs, although not many runs result because he is so terribly slow. Good defense, a little offense.

YEAR	TEAM/LEVEL	G	AB	R	H	2B	3B	HR	RBI	BB	SB	AVG	OBP	SLG
1993	Two Teams	38	102	6	26	2	0	0	8	4	0	.255	.278	.275
1994	Chicago	59	139	6	39	4	0	1	24	20	0	.281	.368	.331
1995	*Projected*	*78*	*200*	*14*	*50*	*9*	*0*	*1*	*23*	*27*	*1*	*.250*	*.339*	*.310*

TIM LEARY / Texas Rangers / Starting Pitcher $13

He started the '94 season in the Montreal system, but pitched poorly, was released, and announced his retirement. He signed with the Rangers three weeks later, and actually made three starts and three relief appearances with the Rangers, posting his fourth straight ERA of 5.05 or higher. Refused assignment to minors in October, and was declared a free agent.

YEAR	TEAM/LEVEL	G	IP	W-L	PCT	HITS	SO	BB	ERA
1992	Two Teams	26	141	8-10	.444	131	46	87	5.36
1993	Seattle	33	169	11-9	.550	202	68	58	5.05
1994	Texas	6	21	1-1	.500	26	9	11	8.14

MANUEL LEE / Texas Rangers / Shortstop $26

Had probably his best season, despite a pulled muscle in his rib cage which sidelined him in June. The Rangers, anxious to get back to the days when they had guys like Al Newman and Jeff Huson at shortstop, did not pick up his option. He's not a top-10 shortstop, but he's a pretty good solution for a team with a hole at the position.

YEAR	TEAM/LEVEL	G	AB	R	H	2B	3B	HR	RBI	BB	SB	AVG	OBP	SLG
1993	Texas	73	205	31	45	3	1	1	12	22	2	.220	.300	.259
1994	Texas	95	335	41	93	18	2	2	38	21	3	.278	.319	.361
1995	*Projected*	*127*	*399*	*50*	*102*	*12*	*2*	*3*	*37*	*40*	*5*	*.256*	*.323*	*.316*

CRAIG LEFFERTS / Released / Left-handed Pitcher $11

Released by the Angels on July 8, after the league had hit .350 against him. Just two years ago he was an effective starting pitcher, going 14-12, and I can't really understand what has happened to him since. But after two straight ugly seasons, I wouldn't want to be the GM who gave him a chance to make it three. He is 37.

YEAR	TEAM/LEVEL	G	IP	W-L	PCT	HITS	SO	BB	ERA
1992	Two Teams	32	196	14-12	.538	214	104	41	3.76
1993	Texas	52	83	3-9	.250	102	58	28	6.05
1994	California	30	35	1-1	.500	50	27	12	4.67

PHIL LEFTWICH / California Angels / Starting Pitcher $18

Had a hot streak in May (3-0, 2.51 ERA) but was utterly ineffective the rest of the season and spent some time on the DL with an inflammation in his right lower leg. Throws in the low 90s and has OK slider, but doesn't change speeds well, doesn't have effective breaking pitch. Estimated 25 to 30 percent chance of developing into a solid pitcher.

YEAR	TEAM/LEVEL	G	IP	W-L	PCT	HITS	SO	BB	ERA
1993	Vancouver AAA	20	126	7-7	.500	138	102	45	4.64
1993	California	12	81	4-6	.400	81	31	27	3.79
1994	California	20	114	5-10	.333	127	67	42	5.68

DAVE LEIPER / Oakland Athletics / Relief Pitcher $20

A 32-year-old lefty, pitched for Oakland 10 years ago, had his best year with San Diego in 1988 (2.17 ERA). Out of baseball in 1992, he developed a new pitch, got a trial in the Gulf Coast League, where he had 24 strikeouts, no walks in 21 innings. The A's signed him, he pitched well—and will continue to until an injury derails him.

YEAR	TEAM/LEVEL	G	IP	W-L	SAVES	HITS	SO	BB	ERA
1993	Carolina AA	8	30	2-1	0	26	16	5	1.48
1994	Tacoma AAA	17	26	1-1	4	25	24	8	2.05
1994	Oakland	26	19	0-0	1	13	14	6	1.93

AL LEITER / Toronto Blue Jays / Pitcher $21

He's 29, and his control remains a theory. In the last two years he has pitched 217 innings and issued 121 walks. To walk five men per game (5.02) and succeed requires some tremendous compensation, like 10 strikeouts per nine innings or 17 ground balls a game. Leiter has some positives—but he *has* to improve his control if he's going to win.

YEAR	TEAM/LEVEL	G	IP	W-L	PCT	HITS	SO	BB	ERA
1992	Syracuse AAA	27	163	8-9	.471	159	108	64	3.86
1993	Toronto	34	105	9-6	.600	93	66	56	4.11
1994	Toronto	20	112	6-7	.462	125	100	65	5.08

MARK LEITER / California Angels / Starter/Reliever $22

Signed with California as a free agent. The Angels were hoping he could start, and he was OK for a time (2-2 with a 3.71 ERA through April), but had a couple of bad outings in early May, and dropped from the rotation when Langston returned. Doesn't have as good an arm as his brother, but has better control and changes speeds better.

YEAR	TEAM/LEVEL	G	IP	W-L	PCT	HITS	SO	BB	ERA
1992	Detroit	35	112	8-5	.615	116	75	43	4.18
1993	Detroit	27	107	6-6	.500	111	70	44	4.73
1994	California	40	95	4-7	.364	99	71	35	4.72

SCOTT LEIUS / Minnesota Twins / Third Base $24

A right-handed hitter, he is at a disadvantage playing for the Twins, whose best hitters are all right-handed, and who therefore hardly ever see a left-handed pitcher. Leius, a good third baseman, had a shot at the Twins' shortstop job, but hurt his rotator cuff and returned to third. His 14 homers in '94 were out of character.

YEAR	TEAM/LEVEL	G	AB	R	H	2B	3B	HR	RBI	BB	SB	AVG	OBP	SLG
1993	Minnesota	10	18	4	3	0	0	0	2	2	0	.167	.227	.167
1994	Minnesota	97	360	57	86	16	1	14	49	37	2	.246	.318	.417
1995	*Projected*	*111*	*352*	*49*	*85*	*14*	*2*	*7*	*37*	*34*	*4*	*.241*	*.308*	*.352*

MARK LEMKE / Atlanta Braves / Second Base $31

If Mark Lemke's a .294 hitter, I'm a giant of literature, but it was that kind of year. Lemke is as good a defensive second baseman as there is, and a pesky hitter who can bunt. A year ago, it seemed that the development of Chipper Jones might take Lemke's job, but now it seems equally likely that the man to go will be Blauser.

YEAR	TEAM/LEVEL	G	AB	R	H	2B	3B	HR	RBI	BB	SB	AVG	OBP	SLG
1993	Atlanta	151	493	52	124	19	2	7	49	65	1	.252	.335	.341
1994	Atlanta	104	350	38	103	15	0	3	31	38	0	.294	.363	.363
1995	*Projected*	*152*	*550*	*55*	*135*	*16*	*2*	*7*	*47*	*69*	*2*	*.245*	*.330*	*.320*

CURTIS LESKANIC / Colorado Rockies / Starting Pitcher $24

Up to now he has made more news for being weird than for pitching, but Leskanic's 3.31 ERA at Colorado Springs is genuinely impressive. That's the Pacific Coast League, where the league batting average last year was .295, and Colorado Springs is the best hitter's park in the league. He wasn't impressive after being called up, but he wasn't awful, either. I like him.

YEAR	TEAM/LEVEL	G	IP	W-L	PCT	HITS	SO	BB	ERA
1993	Colorado	18	57	1-5	.167	59	30	27	5.37
1994	Colorado Spr. AAA	21	130	5-7	.417	129	98	54	3.31
1994	Colorado	8	22	1-1	.500	27	17	10	5.64

JESSE LEVIS / Cleveland Indians / Catcher $16

A minor league Mike LaValliere, a short, heavyset catcher who can hit singles, but can't get out of his own way. He's a *good* hitter, probably a little bit better hitter than LaValliere, and has looked OK on defense, at least while in the majors. Grade C prospect; I expect him to have a major league career.

YEAR	TEAM/LEVEL	G	AB	R	H	2B	3B	HR	RBI	BB	SB	AVG	OBP	SLG
1992	Cleveland	28	43	2	12	4	0	1	3	0	0	.279	.279	.442
1993	Cleveland	31	63	7	11	2	0	0	4	2	0	.175	.197	.206
1994	MLE	111	366	47	98	19	0	9	51	47	1	.268	.351	.393

DARREN LEWIS / San Francisco Giants / Center Field $30

One of the few Giants who played better in '94 than he had in '93. He drew almost 80 percent more walks, despite the missing games, which increased his on-base percentage by almost 40 points. Since he is a leadoff man, that's the most important thing he can do . . . outstanding defensive center fielder, led the NL in triples and could lead in stolen bases.

YEAR	TEAM/LEVEL	G	AB	R	H	2B	3B	HR	RBI	BB	SB	AVG	OBP	SLG
1993	San Francisco	136	522	84	132	17	7	2	48	30	46	.253	.302	.324
1994	San Francisco	114	451	70	116	15	9	4	29	53	30	.257	.340	.357
1995	*Projected*	*153*	*572*	*84*	*145*	*16*	*6*	*3*	*44*	*49*	*49*	*.253*	*.312*	*.318*

MARK LEWIS / Cleveland Indians / Shortstop $18

Got another shot at the Indians' shortstop job when Vizquel was hurt, but a .903 fielding percentage passed the baton back to Alvaro Espinoza. He didn't hit well, back at Charlotte, either because he was concentrating on his defense, or because he was pissed off and sulking, but in any case we know he can hit enough to be a major league shortstop. Not recommended.

YEAR	TEAM/LEVEL	G	AB	R	H	2B	3B	HR	RBI	BB	SB	AVG	OBP	SLG
1992	Cleveland	122	413	44	109	21	0	5	30	25	4	.264	.308	.351
1993	Cleveland	14	52	6	13	2	0	1	5	0	3	.250	.250	.346
1994	Cleveland	20	73	6	15	5	0	1	8	2	1	.205	.227	.315

RICHIE LEWIS / Florida Marlins / Pitcher $15

Pitched very well from the beginning of 1993 until the end of June 1994, but then was beaten severely about the earned run average. Only the strike kept his ERA under seven . . . he's had elbow surgery four times, and I suspect number five may be coming along shortly. He throws the overhand curve, which often causes elbow problems. Good arm, good curve, poor control.

YEAR	TEAM/LEVEL	G	IP	W-L	PCT	HITS	SO	BB	ERA
1992	Rochester AAA	24	159	10-9	.526	136	154	61	3.28
1993	Florida	57	77	6-3	.667	68	65	43	3.26
1994	Florida	45	54	1-4	.200	62	45	38	5.67

SCOTT LEWIS / California Angels / Pitcher $13

Actually, I'm not sure whether the Angels still own him. At season's end he was pitching for Tucson (Astros' system), but he may have been just on loan . . . had a shot at the Angels' rotation in '92, has been trying to adjust to middle relief since then, and getting progressively worse. Few pitchers can pitch well without a regular assignment.

YEAR	TEAM/LEVEL	G	IP	W-L	SAVES	HITS	SO	BB	ERA
1992	California	21	38	4-0	0	36	18	14	3.99
1993	California	15	32	1-2	0	37	10	12	4.22
1994	California	20	31	0-1	0	46	10	10	6.10

JIM LEYRITZ / New York Yankees / Utilityman $26

A Yankee in the proud tradition of Johnny Blanchard, Bob Cerv, and Cliff Johnson, a man with no speed, no fan club, and no defensive position, but God help you if you have to pitch to him. A right-handed platoon player, but over the last three years has hit much *better* the wrong way (.304 batting, .552 slugging vs. RHP, .263/.453 vs. lefties).

YEAR	TEAM/LEVEL	G	AB	R	H	2B	3B	HR	RBI	BB	SB	AVG	OBP	SLG
1993	New York	95	259	43	80	14	0	14	53	37	0	.309	.410	.525
1994	New York	75	249	47	66	12	0	17	58	35	0	.265	.365	.518
1995	*Projected*	*104*	*285*	*43*	*76*	*17*	*0*	*13*	*54*	*40*	*0*	*.267*	*.367*	*.463*

JOHN LIEBER / Pittsburgh Pirates / Starting Pitcher $29

Was expected to spend '94 in Double-A, but reached Pittsburgh in early May. He's a right-handed Greg Swindell—good size, outstanding control, superb strikeout/walk ratios; the rap on him is that he has a soft body and a tender shoulder. He was a second-round draft pick of the Royals, traded to Pittsburgh in the Stan Belinda fiasco.

YEAR	TEAM/LEVEL	G	IP	W-L	PCT	HITS	SO	BB	ERA
1994	Carolina AA	3	21	2-0	1.000	13	21	2	1.29
1994	Buffalo AAA	3	21	1-1	.500	16	21	1	1.69
1994	Pittsburgh	17	109	6-7	.462	116	71	25	3.73

MARK LIEBERTHAL / Philadelphia Phillies / Catcher $19

Lieberthal has been advertised since he was a number-one draft pick in 1990 as the Phillies' future catcher, and got his first major league playing time last July, when Daulton was out. He wasn't bad, hitting .266, but is not in any danger of taking Daulton's job. Has no power, and is inexperienced behind the plate. Probably will be Daulton's backup in '95.

YEAR	TEAM/LEVEL	G	AB	R	H	2B	3B	HR	RBI	BB	SB	AVG	OBP	SLG
1992	MLE	102	341	26	84	14	0	1	31	13	2	.246	.274	.296
1993	MLE	112	376	32	94	17	0	6	37	22	1	.250	.291	.343
1994	Philadelphia	24	79	6	21	3	1	1	5	3	0	.266	.301	.367

DEREK LILLIQUIST / Cleveland Indians / Relief Pitcher $21

Had pitched brilliantly for two years as the Indians' top left-hander in the bullpen, posting ERAs of 1.75 and 2.25. His numbers from 1994 are not good, but again, it is hard to read very much into this, since he faced only 127 batters all year. He is 29 and has a good arm. My best guess is that he'll bounce back this year.

YEAR	TEAM/LEVEL	G	IP	W-L	SAVES	HITS	SO	BB	ERA
1992	Cleveland	71	62	5-3	6	39	47	18	1.75
1993	Cleveland	56	64	4-4	10	64	40	19	2.25
1994	Cleveland	36	29	1-3	1	34	15	8	4.91

JOSE LIMA / Detroit Tigers / Starting Pitcher $16

Dominican right-hander with good control, OK fastball, best pitch is a circle change. In the minors he has had ugly won-lost records (24-45 overall) but nice strikeout/walk ratios. The Tigers do not have a good record in bringing along their young pitchers, but Lima is young (22) and promising, as opposed to old and depressing like Joe Boever and Storm Davis.

YEAR	TEAM/LEVEL	G	IP	W-L	PCT	HITS	SO	BB	ERA
1993	London AA	27	177	8-13	.381	160	138	59	4.07
1994	Toledo AAA	23	142	7-9	.438	124	117	48	3.60
1994	Detroit	3	7	0-1	.000	11	7	3	13.50

JOSE LIND / Kansas City Royals / Second Base $21

Despite the strike he reached or exceeded his norms in runs, RBI, doubles, triples, homers, walks and stolen bases. He is only 31 and in fantastic shape, so he could play regularly for several years, but as a Royals fan, I sure hope he does it somewhere else. He's a good second baseman, but not as good as his reputation, and he doesn't hit *anything*.

YEAR	TEAM/LEVEL	G	AB	R	H	2B	3B	HR	RBI	BB	SB	AVG	OBP	SLG
1993	Kansas City	136	431	33	107	13	2	0	37	13	3	.248	.303	.349
1994	Kansas City	85	290	34	78	16	2	1	31	16	9	.269	.306	.348
1995	*Projected*	*128*	*420*	*38*	*104*	*18*	*2*	*1*	*38*	*20*	*6*	*.248*	*.282*	*.307*

JIM LINDEMAN / New York Mets / Outfielder $20

Released by Houston, signed a minor league contract with the Mets, hit .366 in 32 games at Norfolk (following his .362 average at Tucson in '93), and was called up May 20. He went on to have probably his best season. His strikeout-to-walk ratios are still poor, but there is persuasive evidence that Lindeman is not the .220 hitter that he was for many years.

YEAR	TEAM/LEVEL	G	AB	R	H	2B	3B	HR	RBI	BB	SB	AVG	OBP	SLG
1993	Houston	9	23	2	8	3	0	0	0	0	0	.348	.348	.478
1994	New York	52	137	18	37	8	1	7	20	6	0	.270	.303	.496
1995	*Projected*	*68*	*189*	*21*	*49*	*8*	*0*	*4*	*23*	*13*	*1*	*.259*	*.307*	*.365*

DOUG LINTON / New York Mets / Relief Pitcher $15

Started for many years in the Toronto system, was released by Toronto and California in '93. His 1994 won-lost record and ERA could give the impression that he was OK, adequate to the middle relief assignment, but the batting average against him was .341. There is no way that anybody can keep any job in the majors with that kind of opposition average.

YEAR	TEAM/LEVEL	G	IP	W-L	PCT	HITS	SO	BB	ERA
1993	Syracuse	13	47	2-6	.250	48	42	14	5.32
1993	Two Teams	23	37	2-1	.667	46	23	23	7.36
1994	New York	32	50	6-2	.750	74	29	20	4.47

FELIPE LIRA / Detroit Tigers / Starting Pitcher $16

Like Jose Lima (previous page), Felipe Lira is a young right-handed starter in the Tigers' system. Lira throws slightly harder than Lima and is Venezuelan, not Dominican, but the two are quite similar: young Latin strike-throwers trapped with a team that can't distinguish between Ingrid and Sean Bergman. Grade C prospect, struggled some in Triple-A but could make the Tigers rotation.

YEAR	TEAM/LEVEL	G	IP	W-L	PCT	HITS	SO	BB	ERA
1992	Lakeland A	32	109	11-5	.688	95	84	16	2.39
1993	AA and AAA	27	183	11-6	.647	189	145	50	3.58
1994	Toledo AAA	26	151	7-12	.368	171	110	46	4.70

NELSON LIRIANO / Colorado Rockies / Second Base/Shortstop $23

In '93 he took over the Rockies' shortstop job after Castilla and Benavides failed, and hit well enough to hang on. Last year he got the second base job after Mejia floundered, and, again, did enough with the bat to stay around. He's a switch hitter in theory, but a vastly better left-handed hitter (.294 over the last five years left-handed, .178 right-handed).

YEAR	TEAM/LEVEL	G	AB	R	H	2B	3B	HR	RBI	BB	SB	AVG	OBP	SLG
1993	Colorado	48	151	28	46	6	3	2	15	18	4	.305	.376	.424
1994	Colorado	97	255	39	65	17	5	3	31	42	0	.255	.357	.396
1995	*Projected*	*109*	*346*	*46*	*93*	*18*	*5*	*4*	*36*	*41*	*8*	*.269*	*.346*	*.384*

PAT LISTACH / Milwaukee Brewers / Shortstop $22

Went on the DL April 25 with tendinitis in his left knee, and was never heard from again. "Tendinitis," as I write once every year, is a baseball expression which loosely translated means, "It hurts and we don't have any idea what the problem is." You would have to be a true optimist to suppose that two years of nagging injuries will suddenly go away.

YEAR	TEAM/LEVEL	G	AB	R	H	2B	3B	HR	RBI	BB	SB	AVG	OBP	SLG
1992	Milwaukee	149	579	93	168	19	6	1	47	55	54	.290	.352	.349
1993	Milwaukee	98	356	50	87	15	1	3	30	37	18	.244	.319	.317
1994	Milwaukee	16	54	8	16	3	0	0	2	3	2	.296	.333	.352

GREG LITTON / Boston Red Sox / Utilityman $18

Hit .299 for Seattle in '93, but was released, apparently because the Mariners were afraid he would win a $200 salary increase in arbitration. He signed a minor league contract with Texas, was cut, signed another one with Boston, and had a pretty good year at Pawtucket (MLE: .261 with 7 homers, 40 RBI in 74 games). A capable backup infielder, now a free agent.

YEAR	TEAM/LEVEL	G	AB	R	H	2B	3B	HR	RBI	BB	SB	AVG	OBP	SLG
1992	San Francisco	68	140	9	32	5	0	4	15	11	0	.229	.285	.350
1993	Seattle	72	174	25	52	17	0	3	25	18	0	.299	.366	.448
1994	Boston	11	21	2	2	0	0	0	1	0	0	.095	.091	.095

SCOTT LIVINGSTONE / San Diego Padres / Third Base $20

A platoon player, plays third base for the Padres against right-handed pitching. "Padres—third base" was one of the weakest positions in the majors last year. Among those who tried it: Archi Cianfrocco, Phil Clark, Keith Lockhardt, Luis Lopez, Craig Shipley, and Eddie Williams . . . Livingstone is a good third baseman, but doesn't generate any runs despite a respectable batting average.

YEAR	TEAM/LEVEL	G	AB	R	H	2B	3B	HR	RBI	BB	SB	AVG	OBP	SLG
1993	Detroit	98	304	39	89	10	2	2	39	19	1	.293	.328	.359
1994	Two Teams	72	203	11	54	13	1	2	11	7	2	.266	.289	.369
1995	*Projected*	*103*	*305*	*33*	*83*	*15*	*1*	*4*	*32*	*17*	*2*	*.272*	*.311*	*.367*

GRAEME LLOYD / Milwaukee Brewers / Relief Pitcher $19

His ERA skyrocketed although all of his other effectiveness indicators (opposition batting average, strikeouts, walks, home runs allowed, hit batsmen, wild pitches) were almost the same. I don't know what to make of this. . . . He is extremely effective against left-handers, and has a huge platoon differential—but 67 percent of the batters he has faced have been right-handers . . . will bounce back strong.

YEAR	TEAM/LEVEL	G	IP	W-L	SAVES	HITS	SO	BB	ERA
1992	Knoxville AA	49	92	4-8	14	79	65	25	1.96
1993	Milwaukee	55	64	3-4	0	64	31	13	2.83
1994	Milwaukee	43	47	2-3	3	49	31	15	5.17

KEITH LOCKHART / San Diego Padres / Third Base $16

Talk about paying your dues . . . Lockhart, a 30-year-old, left-handed hitting second/third baseman, has played 1046 minor league games. He's always been healthy, and he's not a bad hitter, as you can see below. He was in the Reds system for years, also tried Oakland and St. Louis . . . no potential, but I'd like to see him make the roster.

YEAR	TEAM/LEVEL	G	AB	R	H	2B	3B	HR	RBI	BB	SB	AVG	OBP	SLG
1993	MLE	132	448	56	121	20	1	10	58	51	2	.270	.345	.386
1994	MLE	89	307	39	82	11	2	4	27	16	1	.267	.303	.355
1994	San Diego	27	43	4	9	0	0	2	6	4	1	.209	.286	.349

KENNY LOFTON / Cleveland Indians / Center Field $85

If you don't like Kenny Lofton, you just don't like *baseball*. Sooner or later, somebody had to displace Rickey Henderson as the best leadoff man in baseball, and Lofton finally did. He's led the AL in stolen bases three straight years, also led last year in hits, and scored 100 runs despite the strike. As a center fielder, he's a walking highlight reel.

YEAR	TEAM/LEVEL	G	AB	R	H	2B	3B	HR	RBI	BB	SB	AVG	OBP	SLG
1993	Cleveland	148	569	116	185	28	8	1	42	81	70	.325	.408	.408
1994	Cleveland	112	459	105	160	32	9	12	57	52	60	.349	.412	.536
1995	*Projected*	*157*	*620*	*122*	*193*	*27*	*9*	*8*	*58*	*80*	*78*	*.311*	*.390*	*.423*

TONY LONGMIRE / Philadelphia Phillies / Outfielder $15

Is 26 years old, missed the entire 1992 season with severe shin splints, but played well for Scranton in '93, and Fregosi brought him up as part of his plan to reduce the team's on-base percentage. He started a few games in left and right, and went 8-for-31 as a pinch hitter. He's a pinch-hitter type, a left-handed line drive hitter.

YEAR	TEAM/LEVEL	G	AB	R	H	2B	3B	HR	RBI	BB	SB	AVG	OBP	SLG
1993	Scranton AAA	120	447	63	136	36	4	6	67	41	12	.304	.364	.443
1993	Philadelphia	11	13	1	3	0	0	0	1	0	0	.231	.231	.231
1994	Philadelphia	69	139	10	33	11	0	0	17	10	2	.237	.289	.317

ALBIE LOPEZ / Cleveland Indians / Starting Pitcher $31

Grade A prospect. He was rushed to the majors in '93, after half a season of Double-A, and had two impressive outings, but then struggled. Now, by my reckoning, he should be about ready. He's pitched 323 innings above A Ball, and has dominated Double-A and Triple-A . . . barrel-chested Arizona native, of Mexican descent; looks like he will have weight problems.

YEAR	TEAM/LEVEL	G	IP	W-L	PCT	HITS	SO	BB	ERA
1993	Cleveland	9	50	3-1	.750	49	25	32	5.98
1994	Charlotte AAA	22	144	13-3	.813	136	105	42	3.94
1994	Cleveland	4	17	1-2	.333	20	18	6	4.24

JAVIER LOPEZ / Atlanta Braves / Catcher $37

Outstanding young catcher, will hit much higher than his .245 average as a rookie. The only way he could miss being a star, other than injuries, is if he turns out to have fatal flaws, like Santiago, that negate most of his value. . . . The Braves carried two catchers, Lopez and O'Brien. They had 3.25 ERA with Lopez catching, 4.11 with O'Brien.

YEAR	TEAM/LEVEL	G	AB	R	H	2B	3B	HR	RBI	BB	SB	AVG	OBP	SLG
1993	Atlanta	8	16	1	6	1	1	1	2	0	0	.375	.412	.750
1994	Atlanta	80	277	27	68	9	0	13	35	17	0	.245	.299	.419
1995	*Projected*	*116*	*387*	*46*	*108*	*21*	*1*	*15*	*52*	*15*	*2*	*.279*	*.306*	*.455*

LUIS LOPEZ / San Diego Padres / Infield $22

Young middle infielder, has his feet on the ground in the majors at the age of 24. A minor league shortstop, he played 43 games at short last year, 29 at second; over time he will probably play more second, because of Gutierrez and Holbert. Very weak on the double play at this point, but could be Frank White–type second baseman. Switch hitter.

YEAR	TEAM/LEVEL	G	AB	R	H	2B	3B	HR	RBI	BB	SB	AVG	OBP	SLG
1993	San Diego	17	43	1	5	1	0	0	1	0	0	.116	.114	.140
1994	San Diego	77	235	29	85	16	1	2	20	15	3	.252	.294	.342
1995	*Projected*	*105*	*337*	*30*	*81*	*15*	*1*	*2*	*27*	*14*	*4*	*.240*	*.271*	*.309*

ANDREW LORRAINE / California Angels / Starting Pitcher $20

Perfect size for a pitcher—6-3, 195 pounds, left-handed. A fourth-round 1993 draft pick, from Stanford, he bounced through the minors in 28 easy starts, going 16-5. Throws in the high 80s, outstanding curve, changes speeds well, good athlete, intelligent. There is nothing here not to like, but it will probably be 1996, at least, before it all comes together.

YEAR	TEAM/LEVEL	G	IP	W-L	PCT	HITS	SO	BB	ERA
1993	Boise (R)	6	42	4-1	.800	33	39	6	1.29
1994	Vancouver AAA	22	142	12-4	.750	156	90	34	3.42
1994	California	4	19	0-2	.000	30	10	11	10.61

TOREY LOVULLO / California Angels / Second Base $16

Lovullo, a prospect years ago, had a good year for California in '93, but was cut anyway, because he didn't fit with their theory of the season, and the Angels always prefer a good theory to a good ballplayer. He signed with Seattle, and played well at Calgary (.294 with a .545 slugging percentage), earning a little time in the majors. Good backup infielder.

YEAR	TEAM/LEVEL	G	AB	R	H	2B	3B	HR	RBI	BB	SB	AVG	OBP	SLG
1992	MLE	131	449	54	119	29	2	16	70	50	6	.265	.339	.445
1993	California	116	367	42	92	20	0	6	30	36	7	.251	.318	.354
1994	Seattle	36	72	9	16	5	0	2	7	9	1	.222	.309	.375

SCOTT LYDY / Oakland Athletics / Outfielder $15

A big guy (6-5) who can run, Lydy got some PT with the A's in '93, when they had multiple injuries in the outfield. He struck out in 38 percent of his at bats, which sent him back to Tacoma. He shortened his stroke a little, had a good year at Tacoma, and might be able to contribute more if opportunity knocks again.

YEAR	TEAM/LEVEL	G	AB	R	H	2B	3B	HR	RBI	BB	SB	AVG	OBP	SLG
1993	Oakland	41	102	11	23	5	0	2	7	8	2	.225	.288	.333
1994	Tacoma	135	508	98	160	37	3	17	73	58	22	.315	.388	.500
1994	MLE	135	479	76	131	29	1	12	56	45	16	.273	.336	.413

JOHN MABRY / St. Louis Cardinals / Right Field $16

First point, the Cardinals need another outfielder like Tammy Fae Bakker needs more cold cream. Second point, Mabry isn't that good; he's not ready to help. He's a .240-.260 hitter who won't walk, no speed, some line drive power. He bats left, and he has a powerful throwing arm. He's only 24, and he may be a good player in two or three years.

YEAR	TEAM/LEVEL	G	AB	R	H	2B	3B	HR	RBI	BB	SB	AVG	OBP	SLG
1993	MLE	140	515	55	134	28	1	12	58	18	5	.260	.285	.388
1994	MLE	122	463	63	111	27	0	12	56	26	1	.240	.280	.376
1994	St. Louis	6	23	2	7	3	0	0	3	2	0	.304	.360	.435

MIKE MACFARLANE / Kansas City Royals / Catcher $36

Good hitter, the Royals' cleanup hitter. Crowds the plate, and is hit by pitches more than any other major league player (18 times last year, 49 times in the last three years). The Royals are moving their fences in this year, which is probably worth about three homers to Macfarlane. Very slow, average defense, average arm. Has a pencil neck.

YEAR	TEAM/LEVEL	G	AB	R	H	2B	3B	HR	RBI	BB	SB	AVG	OBP	SLG
1992	Kansas City	127	402	51	94	28	3	17	48	30	1	.234	.310	.445
1993	Kansas City	117	388	55	106	27	0	20	67	40	2	.273	.360	.497
1994	Kansas City	92	314	53	80	17	3	14	47	35	1	.255	.359	.462

QUINN MACK / Seattle Mariners / Outfield $12

Shane Mack's brother. He's 29 and his Major League Equivalents for 1992 and 1993 are just like those of 1994, which means that he is no prospect. Left-handed hitter, spent several years in the Expos system. Good outfielder, fair arm. His best attribute is an outstanding work ethic, which may get him an extra chance or two and maybe a job as a coach.

YEAR	TEAM/LEVEL	G	AB	R	H	2B	3B	HR	RBI	BB	SB	AVG	OBP	SLG
1994	Calgary AAA	114	404	63	117	30	1	5	51	31	10	.290	.341	.406
1994	MLE	114	379	40	92	26	0	3	32	20	6	.243	.281	.335
1994	Seattle	5	21	1	5	3	0	0	2	1	2	.238	.273	.381

SHANE MACK / Minnesota Twins / Center Field $49

A free agent. If he signs with another team, he might lose a few points, but in the last five years he's hit .320 in Minnesota, .299 on the road, plus he's hit 55 percent of his homers on the road, so there is nothing to suggest that his statistics will degenerate in another park. . . . He's 31; speed and throwing arm are gone, but he can hit.

YEAR	TEAM/LEVEL	G	AB	R	H	2B	3B	HR	RBI	BB	SB	AVG	OBP	SLG
1993	Minnesota	128	503	66	139	30	4	10	61	41	15	.276	.335	.412
1994	Minnesota	81	303	55	101	21	2	15	61	32	4	.333	.402	.564
1995	*Projected*	*141*	*539*	*77*	*159*	*24*	*3*	*15*	*69*	*52*	*17*	*.295*	*.357*	*.434*

GREG MADDUX / Atlanta Braves / Starting Pitcher $96

Nature's perfect pitcher, appears to be headed for the Hall of Fame. Throws a mixture of rockets, scud missiles, laser beams, and double in-shoots. Maddux had a 1.56 ERA, in a year in which *hitting* was at a high-water mark. The most amazing thing about him is that Maddux got to be the best pitcher in the league—and then he got better.

YEAR	TEAM/LEVEL	G	IP	W-L	PCT	HITS	SO	BB	ERA
1992	Chicago (N)	35	268	20-11	.645	201	199	70	2.18
1993	Atlanta	36	267	20-10	.667	228	197	52	2.36
1994	Atlanta	25	202	16-6	.727	150	156	31	1.56

MIKE MADDUX / New York Mets / Relief Pitcher $22

It must be hard, having your little brother turn into Christy Mathewson. Maddux has been a good pitcher, 1991-93, and the only thing that happened to him last year was that he gave up seven homers in 44 innings and gave up a few hits with men in scoring position; otherwise, he was OK. He'll bounce back. He's a better pitcher than Henry Mathewson.

YEAR	TEAM/LEVEL	G	IP	W-L	SAVES	HITS	SO	BB	ERA
1992	San Diego	50	80	2-2	5	71	60	24	2.37
1993	New York	58	75	3-8	5	67	57	27	3.60
1994	New York	27	44	2-1	2	45	32	13	5.11

DAVE MAGADAN / Florida Marlins / Third Base/First Base $23

Returned to the Marlins and played mostly third base (48 games), also 16 games at first. He's not any kind of a defensive player, and doesn't have the power of, say, Torey Lovullo or Nelson Liriano. On the other hand, on-base percentage is the most important individual hitting stat, and Magadan's .388 career OBP (.386 last year) makes him a useful number-two hitter.

YEAR	TEAM/LEVEL	G	AB	R	H	2B	3B	HR	RBI	BB	SB	AVG	OBP	SLG
1993	Two Teams	137	455	49	124	23	0	5	50	80	2	.273	.378	.356
1994	Florida	74	211	30	58	7	0	1	17	39	0	.275	.386	.322
1995	*Projected*	*112*	*348*	*39*	*94*	*17*	*1*	*3*	*34*	*63*	*1*	*.270*	*.382*	*.351*

MIKE MAGNANTE / Kansas City Royals / Pitcher $14

Left-handed finesse pitcher, has been consistent but not very good. He doesn't have a major league fastball or a big breaking pitch, but tries to keep hitters off-stride by changing speeds. He has a degree in Applied Math from UCLA, where he was first team Academic All-American . . . would be somewhat surprised if he is in the majors in '95.

YEAR	TEAM/LEVEL	G	IP	W-L	SAVES	HITS	SO	BB	ERA
1992	Kansas City	44	89	4-9	.308	115	35	31	4.94
1993	Kansas City	7	35	1-2	.333	37	16	11	4.08
1994	Kansas City	36	47	2-3	.400	55	21	16	4.60

JOE MAGRANE / California Angels / Starting Pitcher | $12

He has a contract for 1995 (with two option years), and there has been no announcement of his release, although I'm not sure what the Angels are waiting for. Magrane was released by the Cardinals in August 1993 but made a few good starts with California, and got a new contract. He had elbow surgery in March '94, and hasn't thrown strikes since.

YEAR	TEAM/LEVEL	G	IP	W-L	PCT	HITS	SO	BB	ERA
1992	St. Louis	5	31	1-2	.333	34	20	15	4.02
1993	Two Teams	30	164	11-12	.478	175	62	58	4.66
1994	California	20	74	2-6	.250	89	33	51	7.30

PAT MAHOMES / Minnesota Twins / Starting Pitcher | $22

Mahomes, a pitcher of great promise, battled shoulder problems last year, but wound up the year pitching very well (2.64 ERA through his last five starts). There has probably not been a good major league pitcher in the last 30 years with a strikeout/walk ratio like Mahomes' (53/62). He's going to have to improve his control to continue to win.

YEAR	TEAM/LEVEL	G	IP	W-L	PCT	HITS	SO	BB	ERA
1992	Minnesota	14	70	3-4	.429	73	44	37	5.04
1993	Minnesota	12	37	1-5	.167	47	23	16	7.71
1994	Minnesota	21	120	9-5	.643	121	53	62	4.73

MIKE MAKSUDIAN / Chicago Cubs / First Base/Catcher | $14

Refused assignment to the minor leagues in October, and claimed free agency. His value is in this: that he is a left-handed-hitting catcher who can actually hit a little. He's an emergency catcher, no defense, an emergency third baseman, a backup first baseman—but he can get on base, and occasionally drive the ball. Would have been valued when teams carried three catchers.

YEAR	TEAM/LEVEL	G	AB	R	H	2B	3B	HR	RBI	BB	SB	AVG	OBP	SLG
1992	MLE	101	326	28	82	14	0	10	43	23	2	.252	.301	.387
1993	MLE	76	255	44	74	14	5	8	38	35	3	.290	.376	.478
1994	Chicago	26	26	6	7	2	0	0	4	10	0	.269	.472	.346

JOSE MALAVE / Boston Red Sox / Left Field | $27

A longshot for the American League's Rookie of the Year Award, but a player who has the ability to be a cleanup hitter. Soon. Right-handed hitting Venezuelan, turns 24 in May, has compact swing, waits for his pitch, runs fairly well. Poor outfielder, has been criticized for his effort on defense. Williams, Yastrzemski, Rice, Greenwell, Malave . . . well, *somebody's* got to come next, don't they?

YEAR	TEAM/LEVEL	G	AB	R	H	2B	3B	HR	RBI	BB	SB	AVG	OBP	SLG
1993	Lynchburg A	82	312	42	94	27	1	8	54	36	2	.301	.374	.471
1994	New Britain AA	122	465	87	139	37	7	24	92	52	4	.299	.369	.563
1994	MLE	122	459	75	133	39	4	20	79	38	2	.290	.344	.523

CANDY MALDONADO / Cleveland Indians / Designated Hitter/Left Field $13

Declared free agency in October. He has a good agent (Tom Reich) who will move heaven and earth to find him a job, but his career is probably over, or within a few weeks of being over. He's 34, which is old for a player who wasn't a star at his peak, and has had consecutive seasons in the .200 range.

YEAR	TEAM/LEVEL	G	AB	R	H	2B	3B	HR	RBI	BB	SB	AVG	OBP	SLG
1992	Toronto	137	489	64	133	25	4	20	66	59	2	.272	.357	.462
1993	Two Teams	98	221	19	46	7	0	8	35	24	0	.208	.287	.348
1994	Cleveland	42	92	14	18	5	1	5	12	19	1	.196	.333	.435

JEFF MANTO / Baltimore Orioles / Third Base/First Base $15

Manto, 30 years old, was the American Association MVP in '94. He's not a bad player, as good a player as John Jaha or David Segui, and is often used as an example of the type of minor league journeyman who might be induced to play in a scab league for a $200,000 guarantee. Whether he would do this or not, we'll see.

YEAR	TEAM/LEVEL	G	AB	R	H	2B	3B	HR	RBI	BB	SB	AVG	OBP	SLG
1993	MLE	106	377	49	101	26	0	14	69	42	2	.268	.341	.448
1994	Two Teams AAA	131	444	81	132	31	2	31	100	70	3	.297	.404	.586
1994	MLE	131	428	66	116	25	1	25	81	59	1	.271	.359	.509

KIRT MANWARING / San Francisco Giants / Catcher $24

Established a career high for doubles last year, 17. His bat is so weak that he shouldn't play unless his glovework is authentically outstanding. He is certainly a fine defensive catcher, but whether he can save as many runs as the team passes up by playing him is debatable. Over last five years has average of .301 in May, but fades.

YEAR	TEAM/LEVEL	G	AB	R	H	2B	3B	HR	RBI	BB	SB	AVG	OBP	SLG
1993	San Francisco	130	432	48	119	15	1	5	49	41	1	.275	.345	.350
1994	San Francisco	97	316	30	79	17	1	1	29	25	1	.250	.308	.320
1995	*Projected*	*128*	*416*	*36*	*102*	*14*	*2*	*4*	*37*	*37*	*2*	*.245*	*.307*	*.317*

JOSIAS MANZANILLO / New York Mets / Pitcher $23

Manzanillo is 27 years old, but played against Lou Gehrig in the minor leagues. A native of San Pedro de Macoris and a veteran of three other systems, it was a surprise that he made the Mets in '94, and a shock that he pitched so well. He got ground balls, held right-handers to a .148 average, and got the leadoff man out consistently.

YEAR	TEAM/LEVEL	G	IP	W-L	PCT	HITS	SO	BB	ERA
1993	Norfolk AAA	14	84	1-5	.167	82	79	25	3.11
1993	Two Teams	16	29	1-1	.500	30	21	19	6.83
1994	New York	37	47	3-2	.600	34	48	13	2.66

RAVELO MANZANILLO / Pittsburgh Pirates / Left-handed Reliever $15

Josias's older brother, a left-hander. He pitched two games for the White Sox in '88, and has since pitched in Taiwan, among other places. (Or so they claim. Do we have any independent evidence that there *is* a base-ball league in Taiwan?) He has a good arm and Leyland likes him, but his control will probably cost him his job by mid-season.

YEAR	TEAM/LEVEL	G	IP	W-L	SAVES	HITS	SO	BB	ERA
1992	Taiwan			(Stats Not Available)					
1993				(Out of Baseball)					
1994	Pittsburgh	46	50	4-2	1	45	39	42	4.14

TOM MARSH / Philadelphia Phillies / Outfielder $13

Now 29 years old, a big guy who can run a little bit, great arm. The Phillies have carried him for years, hoping he would start to hit, but he never has. His best year in the minors was 1993, but he missed half of that season with various injuries. His inability to control the strike zone will ultimately prevent him from having a career.

YEAR	TEAM/LEVEL	G	AB	R	H	2B	3B	HR	RBI	BB	SB	AVG	OBP	SLG
1993	MLE	78	310	41	85	16	6	11	52	12	7	.274	.301	.471
1994	MLE	114	436	44	108	29	3	7	49	11	3	.248	.266	.376
1994	Philadelphia	8	18	3	5	1	1	0	3	1	0	.278	.316	.444

AL MARTIN / Pittsburgh Pirates / Outfielder $37

His season was ended in early July by surgery on his left wrist. Martin could be among the best outfielders in the National League in '95. He's 27, a left-handed-hitting outfielder who can hit .280-plus, he has some power and some speed, plays a solid left field and can fill in in center. He's got a lot of good years ahead of him.

YEAR	TEAM/LEVEL	G	AB	R	H	2B	3B	HR	RBI	BB	SB	AVG	OBP	SLG
1992	MLE	125	400	66	108	14	10	14	45	26	13	.270	.315	.460
1993	Pittsburgh	143	480	85	135	26	8	18	64	42	16	.281	.338	.481
1994	Pittsburgh	82	276	48	79	12	4	9	33	34	15	.286	.367	.457

NORBERTO MARTIN / Chicago White Sox / Infielder $20

Began the season at Nashville, was called up in late May, and played well the rest of the year, mostly at second base, but also some at short and third. Martin is 28 years old, a switch hitter, spent many years in the minors. He was slow to develop as a hitter, but appears to be ready to contribute, and could emerge as a regular.

YEAR	TEAM/LEVEL	G	AB	R	H	2B	3B	HR	RBI	BB	SB	AVG	OBP	SLG
1993	MLE	137	557	68	156	17	3	7	58	20	21	.280	.305	.359
1993	Chicago	8	14	3	5	0	0	0	2	1	0	.357	.400	.357
1994	Chicago	45	131	19	36	7	1	1	16	9	4	.275	.317	.366

DAVE MARTINEZ / San Francisco Giants / Outfield/First Base $23

Filled in for Giants at their 1994 trouble spots, right field and first base. Refused assignment to the minor leagues at season's end, and declared free agency. His stats for his two years in San Francisco are oddly similar—58 hits each year, 27 RBI each year, percentages almost the same. He is only 30 years old, and may have better years ahead of him.

YEAR	TEAM/LEVEL	G	AB	R	H	2B	3B	HR	RBI	BB	SB	AVG	OBP	SLG
1993	San Francisco	91	241	28	58	12	1	5	27	27	6	.241	.317	.361
1994	San Francisco	97	235	23	58	9	3	4	27	21	3	.247	.314	.362
1995	*Projected*	*131*	*358*	*42*	*97*	*16*	*6*	*8*	*38*	*39*	*10*	*.271*	*.341*	*.394*

DENNIS MARTINEZ / Cleveland Indians / Starting Pitcher $40

Apart from the fact that he is 40 years old, or will be 40 in May, there is very little to suggest that he won't win 15 or 16 games again this year. He has had winning records four years in a row, seven times in the last eight years, since emerging from a mid-career crisis. Outstanding control; often struggles in April.

YEAR	TEAM/LEVEL	G	IP	W-L	PCT	HITS	SO	BB	ERA
1992	Montreal	32	226	16-11	.593	172	147	60	2.47
1993	Montreal	35	225	15-9	.625	211	138	64	3.85
1994	Cleveland	24	177	11-6	.647	166	92	44	3.52

DOMINGO MARTINEZ / Toronto Blue Jays / First Base $14

An extraordinary player—extraordinarily consistent, unusually slow, unusually durable. He's only 27, but he's been in Triple-A for four years, in Double-A for three years before that, hitting .270 every year with 21 to 24 homers. In the majors, he'd hit around .250 with low on-base percentages, but significant power. He deserves a chance to fail in the major leagues.

YEAR	TEAM/LEVEL	G	AB	R	H	2B	3B	HR	RBI	BB	SB	AVG	OBP	SLG
1992	MLE	116	421	40	103	19	0	17	46	24	4	.254	.323	.354
1993	MLE	127	456	43	118	23	1	22	68	26	3	.259	.299	.458
1994	MLE	131	458	47	114	19	1	18	67	31	1	.249	.297	.413

EDGAR MARTINEZ / Seattle Mariners / Third Base $39

Martinez is among the best hitters in baseball, but the Mariners let him rot in the minors for several years after he was ready, and he's had a couple of injury years, so the clock is running. He's 32, poor defense—but a legitimate .300 hitter, with power and walks and some speed. He can hit leadoff, third, or fourth, and help the team.

YEAR	TEAM/LEVEL	G	AB	R	H	2B	3B	HR	RBI	BB	SB	AVG	OBP	SLG
1993	Seattle	42	135	20	32	7	0	4	13	28	0	.237	.366	.378
1994	Seattle	89	326	47	93	23	1	13	51	53	6	.285	.387	.482
1995	*Projected*	*137*	*481*	*74*	*145*	*32*	*1*	*16*	*62*	*63*	*8*	*.301*	*.382*	*.472*

JOSE MARTINEZ / San Diego Padres / Right-handed Pitcher $12

Thin Dominican, 24 years old. Martinez was outstanding for three years in the Mets system, highlighted by a 20-4 record, 1.49 ERA in 1991. He doesn't throw hard, so the Mets let him go in the expansion draft, and he moved on to San Diego in the Sheffield trade. Has not pitched well in recent years, and most people have written him off.

YEAR	TEAM/LEVEL	G	IP	W-L	PCT	HITS	SO	BB	ERA
1993	Two Teams AAA	27	115	8-7	.533	148	45	39	6.01
1994	Wichita AA	25	134	4-11	.267	154	68	50	5.12
1994	San Diego	4	12	0-2	.000	18	7	5	6.75

PEDRO A. MARTINEZ / San Diego Padres / Left-handed Reliever $22

A starter in the minors, Martinez moved to the bullpen when he reached San Diego. He has a live arm, nothing spectacular, but mixes his pitches well and had been—I guess has been—consistently successful. His ERA last year stayed low, but his control was just awful. Nothing great is in store for him, but if he can find home plate he'll be around.

YEAR	TEAM/LEVEL	G	IP	W-L	PCT	HITS	SO	BB	ERA
1993	Las Vegas AAA	15	88	3-5	.375	94	65	40	4.72
1993	San Diego	32	37	3-1	.750	23	32	13	2.43
1994	San Diego	48	68	3-2	.600	52	52	49	2.90

PEDRO J. MARTINEZ / Montreal Expos / Right-handed Pitcher $57

There is every reason to believe that Pedro will be one of the best pitchers in baseball over the next few years. His future is unlimited. Many of you will note that, when his brother was the same age, we would have said the same thing about him, but that didn't happen, in part, because Lasorda pushed Ramon too hard when he was too young.

YEAR	TEAM/LEVEL	G	IP	W-L	PCT	HITS	SO	BB	ERA
1992	Los Angeles	2	8	0-1	.000	6	8	1	2.25
1993	Los Angeles	65	107	10-5	.667	76	119	57	2.61
1994	Montreal	24	145	11-5	.688	115	142	45	3.42

RAMON MARTINEZ / Los Angeles Dodgers / Starting Pitcher $33

He increased his strikeout rate, improved his control, posted a winning record, and finished the season pitching very well. This makes a solid argument that his career is moving in the right direction, after three years of drifting. His record shows "fatigue" all over it. He pitches better on long rest, fades in August, and is ineffective if he stays in the game too long.

YEAR	TEAM/LEVEL	G	IP	W-L	PCT	HITS	SO	BB	ERA
1992	Los Angeles	25	151	8-11	.421	141	101	69	4.00
1993	Los Angeles	32	212	10-12	.455	202	127	104	3.44
1994	Los Angeles	24	170	12-7	.632	160	119	56	3.97

TINO MARTINEZ / Seattle Mariners / First Base $28

His 1993 season was ended by a knee injury, which was supposed to haunt him last year. He started slowly in '94, but then got with the spirit of the season, hitting .348 with 11 homers in 31 games after July 1. I am inclined to dismiss this as a lively ball fluke, and suspect that his performance may return in '95 to previous norms.

YEAR	TEAM/LEVEL	G	AB	R	H	2B	3B	HR	RBI	BB	SB	AVG	OBP	SLG
1993	Seattle	109	408	48	108	25	1	17	60	45	0	.265	.343	.456
1994	Seattle	97	329	42	88	21	0	20	61	29	1	.261	.320	.508
1995	*Projected*	*155*	*550*	*66*	*145*	*30*	*1*	*23*	*83*	*58*	*2*	*.264*	*.334*	*.447*

ROGER MASON / New York Mets / Relief Pitcher $21

A 6-6 right-hander, was a hot prospect many years ago, finally settled into a middle relief role in his early thirties. He is now 36 years old, and the decline in his strikeout rate last year might be a tipoff that the end is near for him. On the other hand, what middle reliever *can* you count on to have a good year?

YEAR	TEAM/LEVEL	G	IP	W-L	SAVES	HITS	SO	BB	ERA
1992	Pittsburgh	65	88	5-7	8	80	56	33	4.09
1993	Two Teams	68	100	5-12	0	90	71	34	4.06
1994	Two Teams	47	60	3-5	1	55	33	25	3.75

MIKE MATHENY / Milwaukee Brewers / Catcher $14

A big catcher with good defensive skills, including a strong arm and leadership qualities. Eighth round draft pick, 1991, from the University of Michigan. He hasn't hit anywhere above Rookie ball. No power, no walks, no speed, doesn't hit for average. He can't survive as a regular, but his defense may keep him in play for years as a backup and Triple-A catcher.

YEAR	TEAM/LEVEL	G	AB	R	H	2B	3B	HR	RBI	BB	SB	AVG	OBP	SLG
1993	MLE	107	327	31	74	18	1	1	22	11	0	.226	.251	.297
1994	New Orleans	57	177	20	39	10	1	4	21	16	1	.220	.299	.356
1994	Milwaukee	28	53	3	12	3	0	1	2	3	0	.226	.293	.340

TERRY MATHEWS / Florida Marlins / Right-handed Pitcher $20

Is 30 years old, a starter in the Texas system, reached the majors in 1991. He dropped to the minors after an injury in '92, signed with Florida in November 1993, and got back to the majors by pitching well. If he stays healthy, he will continue to pitch well . . . a first baseman in college, has gone 3-for-6 as a major league hitter.

YEAR	TEAM/LEVEL	G	IP	W-L	SAVES	HITS	SO	BB	ERA
1992	Texas	40	42	0-0	0	48	26	31	5.95
1993	Tucson AAA	16	33	0-2	2	40	34	11	3.55
1994	Florida	24	43	2-1	0	45	21	9	3.35

FRANCISCO MATOS / Oakland Athletics / Second Base $14

Signed as a 17-year-old in 1987, he spent almost seven years in the A's system without making the 40-man roster, but was called to the majors last summer to try to help the A's get by Gates' injury. He could hit .250 in the majors, and is supposed to be a good second baseman, but with sub-.300 on-base and slugging percentages.

YEAR	TEAM/LEVEL	G	AB	R	H	2B	3B	HR	RBI	BB	SB	AVG	OBP	SLG
1994	Tacoma AAA	86	336	40	103	10	1	0	30	14	16	.307	.331	.342
1994	MLE	86	318	31	85	7	0	0	23	10	12	.267	.290	.289
1994	Oakland	14	28	1	7	1	0	0	2	1	1	.250	.267	.286

DON MATTINGLY / New York Yankees / First Base $27

Slowed last year by tendinitis in his right wrist. He was 88 percent better than an average American League hitter in 1986, 20 percent better in 1993, 15 percent better last year . . . became the sixth player to get 2000 hits as a Yankee, joining Gehrig, Ruth, Mantle, Berra, and DiMaggio. He is third on the Yankee list in doubles, among the top 10 in homers and RBI.

YEAR	TEAM/LEVEL	G	AB	R	H	2B	3B	HR	RBI	BB	SB	AVG	OBP	SLG
1993	New York	134	530	78	154	27	2	17	86	61	0	.291	.364	.445
1994	New York	97	372	62	113	20	1	6	51	60	0	.304	.397	.411
1995	*Projected*	*142*	*558*	*83*	*163*	*35*	*1*	*15*	*82*	*63*	*1*	*.292*	*.364*	*.439*

TIM MAUSER / San Diego Padres / Relief Pitcher $22

Missed part of the season with a knee injury, but pitched well when healthy. He was originally in the Phillies' system (1988-93), where he was mostly a) a starting pitcher, and b) not very good. He got a lot better when he moved to the bullpen, has been an effective major league pitcher for a year and a half, and should continue to be.

YEAR	TEAM/LEVEL	G	IP	W-L	SAVES	HITS	SO	BB	ERA
1993	Scranton AAA	19	21	2-0	10	10	25	5	0.87
1993	Two Teams	36	54	0-1	0	51	46	24	4.00
1994	San Diego	35	49	2-4	2	50	32	19	3.49

DERRICK MAY / Chicago Cubs / Left Field $28

Symptomatic of the Cubs' problems. He usually hits fourth or fifth for Chicago, but his .280-to-.300 batting average covers a multitude of weaknesses. He isn't fast, has limited power, isn't a good outfielder. His on-base percentages are poor for an outfielder. He'd be an OK platoon player, but the Cubs have better outfielders that they don't even play.

YEAR	TEAM/LEVEL	G	AB	R	H	2B	3B	HR	RBI	BB	SB	AVG	OBP	SLG
1993	Chicago	128	465	62	137	25	2	10	77	31	10	.295	.336	.422
1994	Chicago	100	345	43	98	19	2	8	51	30	3	.284	.340	.420
1995	*Projected*	*141*	*457*	*58*	*132*	*24*	*1*	*10*	*66*	*29*	*6*	*.289*	*.331*	*.411*

BRENT MAYNE / Kansas City Royals / Catcher $21

Has made some progress as a hitter, improving his secondary average from .099 in 1992 to .194 last year. A left-handed hitter, a better defensive catcher than Mike Macfarlane, and a valued reserve. After four years in the majors he is making no obvious progress toward becoming a regular. Behind the plate, he looks very much like Bob Boone, the Royals' new manager.

YEAR	TEAM/LEVEL	G	AB	R	H	2B	3B	HR	RBI	BB	SB	AVG	OBP	SLG
1993	Kansas City	71	205	22	52	9	1	2	22	18	3	.254	.317	.337
1994	Kansas City	46	144	19	37	5	1	2	20	14	1	.257	.323	.347
1995	*Projected*	*86*	*234*	*24*	*58*	*10*	*1*	*2*	*25*	*19*	*2*	*.248*	*.304*	*.325*

DAVE MCCARTY / Minnesota Twins / Outfielder/First Base $18

The retirement of Kent Hrbek may give him a chance to play, or may not; after years of doing this, I have learned that it is folly to anticipate Tom Kelly. McCarty's qualifications for the job are very similar to those of Steve Dunn. They're about the same age, same size, similar minor league batting records. Dunn bats left, and may have more power.

YEAR	TEAM/LEVEL	G	AB	R	H	2B	3B	HR	RBI	BB	SB	AVG	OBP	SLG
1992	MLE	137	475	70	129	17	2	15	75	45	4	.272	.335	.411
1993	Minnesota	98	350	36	75	15	2	2	21	19	2	.214	.257	.286
1994	Minnesota	44	131	21	34	6	2	1	12	7	2	.260	.322	.374

KIRK MCCASKILL / Chicago White Sox / Starting Pitcher $20

The White Sox answer to Storm Davis. Had a 2.49 ERA until just before the strike, then got the holy hell beat out of him in two games. He pitched better last year than he had pitched since 1990. His history has always been that he was unable to build on success, and since he is now 34, I wouldn't bet on that to change.

YEAR	TEAM/LEVEL	G	IP	W-L	PCT	HITS	SO	BB	ERA
1992	Chicago	34	209	12-13	.480	193	109	95	4.18
1993	Chicago	30	114	4-8	.333	144	65	36	5.23
1994	Chicago	40	53	1-4	.200	51	37	22	3.42

LLOYD MCCLENDON / Pittsburgh Pirates / Outfield/Pinch Hitter $15

A heavyset right-handed hitter who has had good years off the bench. Unlike most modern managers, Jim Leyland likes to stick with his bench players. If a reserve doesn't hit in 100 at bats he'll figure, correctly, that you can't necessarily base a decision on that. Still, McClendon is 36, overweight, and coming off of *two* rather poor seasons.

YEAR	TEAM/LEVEL	G	AB	R	H	2B	3B	HR	RBI	BB	SB	AVG	OBP	SLG
1992	Pittsburgh	84	190	26	48	8	1	3	20	28	1	.253	.350	.353
1993	Pittsburgh	88	181	21	40	11	1	2	19	23	0	.221	.306	.326
1994	Pittsburgh	51	92	9	22	4	0	4	12	4	0	.239	.276	.413

RAY MCDAVID / San Diego Padres / Outfielder $16

The Warren Newson of the future. He's bigger than Newson, but has similar skills—a left-handed hitter who probably won't hit enough to play every day, but whose combination of speed, walks, and a little power would make him valuable off the bench. He is young enough to improve, and thus could be a regular, but also looks like he might put on weight.

YEAR	TEAM/LEVEL	G	AB	R	H	2B	3B	HR	RBI	BB	SB	AVG	OBP	SLG
1994	Las Vegas AAA	128	476	85	129	24	6	13	62	67	24	.271	.370	.429
1994	MLE	128	447	54	100	18	2	9	39	42	14	.224	.290	.333
1994	San Diego	9	28	2	7	1	0	0	2	1	1	.250	.276	.286

BEN MCDONALD / Baltimore Orioles / Starting Pitcher $45

Posted a winning record for the first time since 1990, when he was just out of LSU. He hasn't made anybody forget Jim Palmer, but after 40 wins in three years, it is time to stop talking about his potential. Note to Phil Regan: He needs five days between starts. In his career his ERA is 4.26 on four days' rest, but 2.86 on five.

YEAR	TEAM/LEVEL	G	IP	W-L	PCT	HITS	SO	BB	ERA
1992	Baltimore	35	227	13-13	.500	213	158	74	4.24
1993	Baltimore	34	220	13-14	.482	185	171	86	3.39
1994	Baltimore	24	157	14-7	.667	151	94	54	4.06

JACK MCDOWELL / Chicago White Sox / Starting Pitcher $74

After several vicious salary battles he is expected to be a free agent, but may not qualify if the players don't get comp time. Many people suspect that his best years are behind him at age 29. He may not be able to win 20 games with another team, but I see no real evidence that his skills are anything less than they have been.

YEAR	TEAM/LEVEL	G	IP	W-L	PCT	HITS	SO	BB	ERA
1992	Chicago	34	261	20-10	.667	247	178	75	3.18
1993	Chicago	34	257	22-10	.688	261	158	69	3.37
1994	Chicago	25	181	10-9	.526	186	127	42	3.73

ODDIBE MCDOWELL / Texas Rangers / Prodigal Son $22

Oddibe played well, despite two serious injuries, but was designated for assignment in early October, just after Kennedy was fired. With 28 walks and 14 stolen bases in limited playing time, he scored runs at a rate equivalent to 100 runs in 540 at bats, but he didn't finish strong, and Rusty Greer has taken over the job that McDowell was signed to do.

YEAR	TEAM/LEVEL	G	AB	R	H	2B	3B	HR	RBI	BB	SB	AVG	OBP	SLG
1993	Tulsa AA	34	114	26	39	7	1	8	31	19	3	.342	.437	.632
1994	Ok. City AAA	16	52	9	14	3	1	0	2	8	2	.269	.377	.365
1994	Texas	59	183	34	48	5	1	1	15	28	14	.262	.355	.317

ROGER MCDOWELL / Los Angeles Dodgers / Relief Pitcher $13

Stick a fork in him. McDowell still throws ground balls, but his control is gone, and he is so ineffective against left-handers that he just has to intentionally walk any lefty who can beat him. His 2.25 ERA of '93 was a fluke, caused by the fact that half the runs he allowed were scored as unearned. He hasn't pitched well since 1991.

YEAR	TEAM/LEVEL	G	IP	W-L	SAVES	HITS	SO	BB	ERA
1992	Los Angeles	65	84	6-10	14	103	50	42	4.09
1993	Los Angeles	54	68	5-3	2	76	27	30	2.25
1994	Los Angeles	32	41	0-3	0	50	29	22	5.23

CHUCK MCELROY / Cincinnati Reds / Left-handed Relief Pitcher $21

His '94 season breaks down into two parts. He was enormously effective from opening day until June 21, when he had pitched 29 times with an ERA of 0.91, but wasn't at all effective the rest of the year. This leaves him more or less where he has been for several years. It is not clear whether he has harnessed his considerable ability.

YEAR	TEAM/LEVEL	G	IP	W-L	SAVES	HITS	SO	BB	ERA
1992	Chicago	72	84	4-7	6	73	83	51	3.55
1993	Chicago	49	47	2-2	0	51	31	25	4.56
1994	Cincinnati	52	58	1-2	5	52	38	15	2.34

WILLIE MCGEE / San Francisco Giants (Free Agent) / Right Field $27

His season was ended in early June by a torn left Achilles' tendon. After the season he refused assignment to the minor leagues, and became a free agent. Willie is 36, and doesn't run particularly well anymore (stolen base totals over the last five years: 31, 17, 13, 10, 3. Triples: 7, 3, 2, 1, 0). He'd still be an OK fifth outfielder.

YEAR	TEAM/LEVEL	G	AB	R	H	2B	3B	HR	RBI	BB	SB	AVG	OBP	SLG
1993	San Francisco	130	475	53	143	28	1	4	46	38	10	.301	.353	.389
1994	San Francisco	45	156	19	44	3	0	5	23	15	3	.282	.337	.397
1995	*Projected*	*97*	*329*	*35*	*91*	*16*	*3*	*3*	*31*	*25*	*7*	*.277*	*.328*	*.371*

FRED MCGRIFF / Atlanta Braves / First Base $80

Doing everything he can to refute the stupid notion that modern stars aren't as consistent as those of other generations. He had his seventh consecutive 30-homer season in '94, making him the ninth player ever to do that. The others are Jimmie Foxx (12 straight), Gehrig, Schmidt, and Eddie Mathews (9 each), Ruth and Mantle (8 each), and Aaron and Kiner (7 each).

YEAR	TEAM/LEVEL	G	AB	R	H	2B	3B	HR	RBI	BB	SB	AVG	OBP	SLG
1993	Two Teams	151	557	111	162	29	2	37	101	76	5	.291	.375	.549
1994	Atlanta	113	424	81	135	25	1	34	94	50	7	.318	.389	.623
1995	*Projected*	*153*	*558*	*95*	*163*	*27*	*1*	*36*	*103*	*82*	*7*	*.292*	*.383*	*.538*

TERRY MCGRIFF / St. Louis Cardinals / Catcher $14

Played for Cincinnati in 1987-88, but didn't hit, and had been in the minors except for a few innings a year since 1988. He had his best minor league season with Edmonton in '93, which got the attention of the Car-dinals, who signed him to a minor league contract. He made the opening-day roster, and spent the entire season with the Cardinals.

YEAR	TEAM/LEVEL	G	AB	R	H	2B	3B	HR	RBI	BB	SB	AVG	OBP	SLG
1993	Edmonton AAA	105	339	62	117	29	2	7	55	49	2	.345	.426	.504
1993	Florida	3	7	0	0	0	0	0	0	1	0	.000	.125	.000
1994	St. Louis	42	114	10	25	6	0	0	13	13	0	.219	.308	.272

MARK MCGWIRE / Oakland Athletics / First Base $29

He has battled a problem with his heel for two years; it only seems like 20. Logic argues that he will come back. He is not old (31), and there is little evidence that his skills have deteriorated. He is not prone to miscel-laneous nagging injuries, like Eric Davis; he just has a problem with his heel. He's a formidable hitter, and an excellent fielder.

YEAR	TEAM/LEVEL	G	AB	R	H	2B	3B	HR	RBI	BB	SB	AVG	OBP	SLG
1993	Oakland	27	84	16	28	6	0	9	24	21	0	.333	.467	.726
1994	Oakland	47	135	26	34	3	0	9	25	37	0	.252	.413	.474
1995	*Projected*	*127*	*438*	*74*	*106*	*18*	*0*	*29*	*81*	*96*	*1*	*.242*	*.378*	*.482*

JEFF MCKNIGHT / New York Mets / Utilityman $14

Got some major league playing time because . . . well, now that you mention it, I'm not sure *why* he was in the majors. Of his 27 at bats, 26 were as a pinch hitter, but he didn't hit, which isn't surprising, since his minor league career average is .265. He's 32, and will have to do something amazing in the minors to get back to the majors.

YEAR	TEAM/LEVEL	G	AB	R	H	2B	3B	HR	RBI	BB	SB	AVG	OBP	SLG
1992	New York	31	85	10	23	3	1	2	13	2	0	.271	.287	.400
1993	New York	105	164	19	42	3	1	2	13	13	0	.256	.311	.323
1994	New York	31	27	1	4	1	0	0	2	4	0	.148	.250	.185

MARK MCLEMORE / Baltimore Orioles / Second Base $26

A surprising career. McLemore was California's second baseman in 1987, didn't hit, and dropped out of the majors. He had a terrific comeback in 1992—as a right fielder. He moved back to second last year, continued to play pretty well, with a .354 on-base percentage, 20 steals in 25 tries, and solid defense . . . switch hitter, but a far better hitter left-handed.

YEAR	TEAM/LEVEL	G	AB	R	H	2B	3B	HR	RBI	BB	SB	AVG	OBP	SLG
1993	Baltimore	148	581	81	165	27	5	4	72	64	21	.284	.353	.368
1994	Baltimore	104	343	44	88	11	1	3	29	51	20	.257	.354	.321
1995	*Projected*	*137*	*449*	*60*	*114*	*16*	*3*	*3*	*46*	*53*	*18*	*.254*	*.333*	*.323*

GREG MCMICHAEL / Atlanta Braves / Relief Pitcher $31

The batting average against him jumped from .206 to .280, and he tied for the major league lead in blown saves, with 10. He gave up only one home run and his control remained good, but the Braves will certainly *consider* finding another closer in '95. Throws a changeup that breaks right or left, depending on the spin, also a pretty good slider.

YEAR	TEAM/LEVEL	G	IP	W-L	SAVES	HITS	SO	BB	ERA
1992	AA and AAA	34	137	10-7	3	126	139	47	3.36
1993	Atlanta	74	92	2-3	19	68	89	29	2.06
1994	Atlanta	51	59	4-6	21	66	47	19	3.84

BRIAN MCRAE / Kansas City Royals / Center Field $34

In 1994, for the first time, he was a fine player. A Gold Glove quality center fielder (although his arm is weak), he increased his walk rate by 98 percent, established career highs in stolen bases and stolen base percentage, and was on target to score 100 runs. He came up young, and has just matured . . . is still a much better right-handed hitter than left.

YEAR	TEAM/LEVEL	G	AB	R	H	2B	3B	HR	RBI	BB	SB	AVG	OBP	SLG
1993	Kansas City	153	627	78	177	28	9	12	69	37	23	.282	.325	.413
1994	Kansas City	114	436	71	119	22	6	4	40	54	28	.273	.359	.378
1995	*Projected*	*159*	*614*	*84*	*161*	*30*	*8*	*9*	*63*	*54*	*25*	*.262*	*.322*	*.381*

KEVIN MCREYNOLDS / New York Mets / Left Field $17

Reported to the Mets in better shape, but visited the disabled list three times, for a bulging disc, a strained groin (or maybe it was a strained disc and a bulging groin), and cartilage damage in his knee. He can't play the outfield anymore, can't run. The only thing he can still do is that he can still hit a left-handed pitcher.

YEAR	TEAM/LEVEL	G	AB	R	H	2B	3B	HR	RBI	BB	SB	AVG	OBP	SLG
1992	Kansas City	109	373	45	92	25	0	13	49	67	7	.247	.357	.418
1993	Kansas City	110	351	44	86	22	4	11	42	37	2	.245	.316	.425
1994	New York	51	180	23	46	11	2	4	21	20	2	.256	.328	.406

RUSTY MEACHAM / Kansas City Royals / Relief Pitcher $20

Released by KC last March, he re-signed with them, and in May and June was the same marvelous pitcher that he had been in 1992. His elbow started to act up again, then, and he was ineffective over the last five weeks of the shortened schedule . . . he's a lot of fun to watch, very intense, works quick, attacks the hitter with everything he's got.

YEAR	TEAM/LEVEL	G	IP	W-L	SAVES	HITS	SO	BB	ERA
1992	Kansas City	64	102	10-4	2	88	64	21	2.74
1993	Kansas City	15	21	2-2	0	31	13	5	5.57
1994	Kansas City	36	51	3-3	4	51	36	12	3.73

PAT MEARES / Minnesota Twins / Shortstop $25

Shared the Twins shortstop job with Jeff Reboulet, another right-handed hitter. Neither player took the job as the season wore on, and it is unclear, at this writing, who will play the position in 1995. Meares is a pretty good hitter for a shortstop, and played well enough in the field that it would not surprise me to see him get the everyday job.

YEAR	TEAM/LEVEL	G	AB	R	H	2B	3B	HR	RBI	BB	SB	AVG	OBP	SLG
1993	Minnesota	111	346	33	87	14	3	0	33	7	4	.251	.266	.309
1994	Minnesota	80	229	29	61	12	1	2	24	14	5	.266	.310	.354
1995	*Projected*	*126*	*394*	*44*	*104*	*21*	*2*	*2*	*36*	*15*	*6*	*.264*	*.291*	*.343*

ROBERTO MEJIA / Colorado Rockies / Second Base $26

Right-handed-hitting second baseman with power and speed, like Juan Samuel. Mejia, who is very young, was taken from the Dodgers in the expansion draft, and is regarded as a player who may have enormous value in a few years. He doesn't look too bad at second base, but he strikes out in almost 30 percent of his at bats. He'll be 23 in April.

YEAR	TEAM/LEVEL	G	AB	R	H	2B	3B	HR	RBI	BB	SB	AVG	OBP	SLG
1993	Colorado	65	229	31	53	14	5	5	20	13	4	.231	.275	.402
1994	Colorado	38	116	11	28	8	1	4	14	15	3	.241	.326	.431
1995	*Projected*	*137*	*438*	*60*	*115*	*28*	*4*	*14*	*52*	*30*	*10*	*.263*	*.310*	*.441*

JOSE MELENDEZ / Boston Red Sox / Relief Pitcher $15

He has been injured for almost all of the last two seasons, which makes it anyone's guess whether he will return, when he will return, and whether he will be able to pitch if he does return. The Red Sox designated him for reassignment in October, so I think it is likely he will be somewhere else when his time comes.

YEAR	TEAM/LEVEL	G	IP	W-L	SAVES	HITS	SO	BB	ERA
1992	San Diego	56	89	6-7	0	82	82	20	2.92
1993	Boston	9	16	2-1	0	10	14	5	2.25
1994	Boston	10	16	0-1	0	20	9	8	6.06

BOB MELVIN / Chicago White Sox / Catcher $12

Is 33 years old, and is almost out of the league. He played for the Yankees and White Sox in '94, Boston in '93, Kansas City in '92, Baltimore in '91 . . . sooner or later, he's going to run out of teams. His offense isn't much and his defense isn't much better, but he can hit a little against a left-handed pitcher.

YEAR	TEAM/LEVEL	G	AB	R	H	2B	3B	HR	RBI	BB	SB	AVG	OBP	SLG
1992	Kansas City	32	70	5	22	5	0	0	6	5	0	.314	.351	.386
1993	Boston	77	176	13	39	7	0	3	23	7	0	.222	.251	.313
1994	Two Teams	20	33	5	7	0	0	1	4	1	0	.212	.235	.303

TONY MENENDEZ / Pittsburgh Pirates / Relief Pitcher $15

You have to root for this guy. He's the Jeff Manto of pitchers, has been in the minors since 1984, pitching for almost everybody, has been released numerous times. A Cuban-born right-hander, 30 years old, he posted a 2.42 ERA for Buffalo in '93, with 24 saves, and a 2.22 ERA for Phoenix in '94, with more strikeouts than innings.

YEAR	TEAM/LEVEL	G	IP	W-L	SAVES	HITS	SO	BB	ERA
1993	Pittsburgh	14	21	2-0	0	20	13	4	3.00
1994	Phoenix AAA	28	28	0-2	12	24	31	11	2.22
1994	San Francisco	6	3	0-1	0	8	2	2	21.60

ORLANDO MERCED / Pittsburgh Pirates / Right Field $27

Merced has a career batting average of .327 in May, but .235 in August. This is a fairly common pattern, and suggests to me that the player could benefit from a little less playing time . . . played part or all of 68 games in right field in '94, 55 games at first. Lack of power and speed prevents him from filling a key offensive role.

YEAR	TEAM/LEVEL	G	AB	R	H	2B	3B	HR	RBI	BB	SB	AVG	OBP	SLG
1993	Pittsburgh	137	447	68	140	26	4	8	70	77	3	.313	.414	.443
1994	Pittsburgh	108	386	48	105	21	3	9	51	42	4	.272	.343	.412
1995	*Projected*	*152*	*550*	*75*	*154*	*27*	*4*	*11*	*76*	*82*	*5*	*.280*	*.373*	*.404*

JOSE MERCEDES / Milwaukee Brewers / Right-handed Reliever $14

Mercedes was signed by Baltimore in 1989, but didn't make their roster after posting a 4.78 ERA for Bowie in '92. The Brewers took him under Rule 5, and gave him a few innings. He has a good arm, no breaking pitch, no control. The 2.32 ERA last year means nothing; he isn't ready to pitch, and won't be for at least two or three years.

YEAR	TEAM/LEVEL	G	IP	W-L	SAVES	HITS	SO	BB	ERA
1992	Kane County A	8	47	3-2	0	40	45	15	2.66
1993	Bowie AA	26	147	6-8	0	170	75	65	4.78
1994	Milwaukee	19	31	2-0	0	22	11	16	2.32

KENT MERCKER / Atlanta Braves / Relief Pitcher $41

One can never be sure, but I believe that Kent Mercker is going to be a great pitcher. His no-hitter, 111 strikeouts in 112 innings, four straight winning records, blazing fastball—these are all important assets. Add in that his arm has *not* been abused in his formative years, that he has had the experience of pitching behind Maddux, et al. . . . he looks great.

YEAR	TEAM/LEVEL	G	IP	W-L	PCT	HITS	SO	BB	ERA
1992	Atlanta	53	68	3-2	.600	51	49	35	3.42
1993	Atlanta	43	66	3-1	.750	52	59	36	2.86
1994	Atlanta	20	112	9-4	.692	90	111	45	3.45

BRETT MERRIMAN / Minnesota Twins / Relief Pitcher $12

I see no evidence that this man is a major league pitcher. He had good ERAs in the minors from 1991 to 1993, but his strikeout/walk ratios and opposition batting averages were *not* good, and he also gave up high numbers of *un*-earned runs in those years. He doesn't throw hard, by major league standards, doesn't have good control.

YEAR	TEAM/LEVEL	G	IP	W-L	SAVES	HITS	SO	BB	ERA
1993	Portland AAA	39	48	5-0	15	46	29	18	3.00
1993	Minnesota	19	27	1-1	0	36	14	23	9.67
1994	Minnesota	15	17	0-1	0	18	10	14	6.35

MATT MERULLO / Cleveland Indians / Catcher/Designated Hitter $16

A 29-year-old left-handed hitter, and he can actually hit. His opportunity to play in the majors was 1991, and he didn't hit then, in 140 at bats, which has damaged his career enormously, since he can't run and isn't a brilliant defensive player. His major league at bats have gone down in oddly regular increments (140, 50, 20, 10)—but he *can* play.

YEAR	TEAM/LEVEL	G	AB	R	H	2B	3B	HR	RBI	BB	SB	AVG	OBP	SLG
Major L Totals		147	301	18	61	3	1	6	32	18	0	.203	.245	.279
1993	MLE	103	336	39	101	25	0	9	51	22	0	.301	.344	.455
1994	MLE	112	406	45	114	19	4	10	64	21	1	.281	.316	.421

JOSE MESA / Cleveland Indians / Starting Pitcher $22

He was the Indians' best starting pitcher in '93, which is saying almost nothing, but moved to the bullpen in '94, when the Indians acquired some real starting pitchers. He pitched well, in the bullpen, and should continue to do so. Throws hard, throws a big curve, hasn't had a major injury since 1989. His best years should be ahead of him.

YEAR	TEAM/LEVEL	G	IP	W-L	PCT	HITS	SO	BB	ERA
1992	Two Teams	28	161	7-12	.368	169	62	70	4.59
1993	Cleveland	34	209	10-12	.455	232	118	62	4.92
1994	Cleveland	51	73	7-5	.583	71	63	26	3.82

DANNY MICELI / Pittsburgh Pirates / Relief Pitcher $24

The Kansas City Royals' Minor League Player of the Year in 1992, he was traded to Pittsburgh in '93 as partial payment for Stan Belinda. He throws hard (reportedly 95), and he throws strikes. His second pitch is a slider, and he is making progress on changing speeds. I like any young pitcher who has 27 strikeouts and 11 walks in 27 innings.

YEAR	TEAM/LEVEL	G	IP	W-L	SAVES	HITS	SO	BB	ERA
1993	Pittsburgh	9	5	0-0	0	6	4	3	5.06
1994	Buffalo AAA	19	24	1-1	2	15	31	6	1.88
1994	Pittsburgh	28	27	2-1	2	28	27	11	5.93

MATT MIESKE / Milwaukee Brewers / Outfield $23

Will emerge as a good platoon player. He started 69 games in right field for the Brewers, and was devastating against left-handed pitchers (.299, .657 slugging percentage), but ineffective against normal people (.245/.354). In the minors in '93 it was the same thing—.337 against left-handed pitchers, .208 against right-handers. Defense is pretty good, runs fairly well.

YEAR	TEAM/LEVEL	G	AB	R	H	2B	3B	HR	RBI	BB	SB	AVG	OBP	SLG
1993	Milwaukee	23	58	9	14	0	0	3	7	4	0	.241	.290	.397
1994	Milwaukee	84	259	39	67	13	1	10	38	21	3	.259	.320	.432
1995	*Projected*	*92*	*300*	*42*	*73*	*15*	*2*	*10*	*38*	*24*	*5*	*.243*	*.299*	*.407*

BOB MILACKI / Kansas City Royals / Starting Pitcher $13

In the last two years he has been released by Baltimore, Oakland, Cleveland, and Kansas City twice. The Royals signed him to a minor league contract, released him, re-signed him, sent him to Omaha, called him up . . . he's now a free agent. He wasn't as bad, for the Royals, as his 0-5 record and 6.14 ERA would suggest, but he's probably out of chances.

YEAR	TEAM/LEVEL	G	IP	W-L	PCT	HITS	SO	BB	ERA
1993	Cleveland	5	16	1-1	.500	19	7	11	3.38
1994	Omaha AAA	16	86	4-3	.571	91	59	42	5.02
1994	Kansas City	10	56	0-5	.000	68	17	20	6.14

KURT MILLER / Florida Marlins / Starting Pitcher $12

A big right-hander originally drafted by Pittsburgh, Miller has regressed massively since 1992, when he went 7-5 at Tulsa. He was called up by Florida for four starts, although he was having a dreadful season at Edmonton. He has no breaking pitch that works, and I see no likelihood of his being a successful pitcher in the next three to four years.

YEAR	TEAM/LEVEL	G	IP	W-L	PCT	HITS	SO	BB	ERA
1993	Edmonton AAA	9	48	3-3	.500	42	19	34	4.50
1994	Edmonton AAA	23	126	7-13	.350	164	58	64	6.88
1994	Florida	4	20	1-3	.250	26	11	7	8.10

ORLANDO MILLER / Houston Astros / Shortstop $14

A 26-year-old Panamanian, acquired by the Astros from the Yankees in 1990, in exchange for Dave Silvestri. He is supposed to be a good defensive shortstop, but won't hit enough to have a significant major league career. His best year in the minors was 1993, when he hit .304 with 16 homers, 89 RBI at Tucson, but with 20 walks, 95 strikeouts.

YEAR	TEAM/LEVEL	G	AB	R	H	2B	3B	HR	RBI	BB	SB	AVG	OBP	SLG
1992	MLE	122	437	54	109	23	8	9	56	12	1	.249	.269	.400
1993	MLE	93	318	34	67	12	3	5	35	10	2	.211	.235	.314
1994	Houston	16	40	3	13	0	1	2	9	2	1	.325	.386	.525

RANDY MILLIGAN / Montreal Expos / First Base $14

Home run totals over the last five years: 20, 16, 11, 6, 2. What is the next number in this sequence? Milligan is a big right-handed power hitter, overweight. His game is to sort out pitches until he finds one he can hit for distance, which creates an ancillary value, in many walks. But since he's lost his power, it doesn't work anymore.

YEAR	TEAM/LEVEL	G	AB	R	H	2B	3B	HR	RBI	BB	SB	AVG	OBP	SLG
1992	Baltimore	137	462	71	111	21	1	11	53	106	0	.240	.383	.361
1993	Two Teams	102	281	37	84	18	1	6	36	60	0	.299	.423	.434
1994	Montreal	47	82	10	19	2	0	2	12	14	0	.232	.337	.329

ALAN MILLS / Baltimore Orioles / Relief Pitcher $21

His 5.16 ERA last year is not, to me, a big item; since he pitched only 45 innings, his stats aren't a reliable indicator of his ability. There are few reliable middle relievers, and he might be one of the few. But I *would* be concerned about the hypersensitive nature of the Orioles' system, in which anyone who isn't outstanding is a candidate to be released.

YEAR	TEAM/LEVEL	G	IP	W-L	SAVES	HITS	SO	BB	ERA
1992	Baltimore	35	103	10-4	2	78	60	54	2.61
1993	Baltimore	45	100	5-4	4	80	68	51	3.23
1994	Baltimore	47	45	3-3	2	43	44	24	5.16

NATE MINCHEY / Boston Red Sox / Starting Pitcher $22

He is not a hot prospect, and you won't read about him in *Baseball America* or *The Baseball Weekly*, but nonetheless Minchey gives every indication of being almost ready to pitch in the majors. A 6-7 right-hander, fastball not outstanding, but motion is hard to read, control is good, has been healthy and effective in the minors. I like him.

YEAR	TEAM/LEVEL	G	IP	W-L	PCT	HITS	SO	BB	ERA
1993	Boston	5	33	1-2	.333	35	18	8	3.55
1994	Pawtucket AAA	23	151	11-5	.688	128	93	51	3.03
1994	Boston	6	23	2-3	.400	44	15	14	8.61

BLAS MINOR / Pittsburgh Pirates / Relief Pitcher $17

The league hit .351 against him, which wouldn't have been so bad except that most of it was extra base hits (14 of the 27 hits he allowed were for extra bases) . . . this sent him to the minors, after a rookie season (1993) in which he often pitched well. He recovered his effectiveness at Buffalo, and as long as he's healthy will receive several more chances.

YEAR	TEAM/LEVEL	G	IP	W-L	SAVES	HITS	SO	BB	ERA
1993	Pittsburgh	65	94	8-6	2	94	84	26	4.10
1994	Pittsburgh	17	19	0-1	1	27	17	9	8.05
1994	Buffalo AAA	33	51	1-2	3	47	61	12	2.98

ANGEL MIRANDA / Milwaukee Brewers / Starting Pitcher $25

Tore a ligament in his knee in spring training, which prevented him from following through on a solid rookie season. He was just getting back into form in early August, when the strike hit. Miranda throws a good fastball, 89-91, and an excellent screwball, and he throws strikes. That's a combination that has always worked, from Carl Hubbell to Scott McGregor. I like him.

YEAR	TEAM/LEVEL	G	IP	W-L	PCT	HITS	SO	BB	ERA
1993	New Orleans AAA	9	18	0-1	.000	11	24	10	3.44
1993	Milwaukee	22	120	4-5	.444	100	88	52	3.30
1994	Milwaukee	8	46	2-5	.286	39	24	27	5.28

KEITH MITCHELL / Seattle Mariners / Outfielder $15

Refused assignment to the minors, and is now a free agent. A cousin of Kevin Mitchell, he had a trial with Atlanta in 1991, hitting .318 in 48 games. His career ruptured after that on a series of behavior problems, and he spent two years in the minors, hitting like a middle infielder. He is only 25, played all three outfield positions with the Mariners.

YEAR	TEAM/LEVEL	G	AB	R	H	2B	3B	HR	RBI	BB	SB	AVG	OBP	SLG
1993	Richmond AAA	110	353	59	82	23	1	4	44	48	9	.232	.318	.337
1994	Seattle	46	128	21	29	2	0	5	15	18	0	.227	.324	.359
1995	*Projected*	*55*	*159*	*22*	*38*	*6*	*0*	*9*	*20*	*22*	*3*	*.239*	*.299*	*.407*

KEVIN MITCHELL / Cincinnati Reds / Left Field $53

Mitchell turned 33 over the winter, which means that he has reached the age at which we would normally expect his production as a hitter to become less reliable. He hasn't played more than 113 games in a season since 1991, since he is fat and prone to injuries. On the other hand, .330 hitters with .600 slugging percentages have never been easy to find.

YEAR	TEAM/LEVEL	G	AB	R	H	2B	3B	HR	RBI	BB	SB	AVG	OBP	SLG
1993	Cincinnati	93	323	56	110	21	3	19	64	25	1	.341	.385	.601
1994	Cincinnati	95	310	57	101	18	1	30	77	59	2	.326	.429	.681
1995	*Projected*	*118*	*399*	*61*	*114*	*21*	*2*	*21*	*74*	*54*	*1*	*.286*	*.371*	*.506*

MIKE MOHLER / Oakland Athletics / Left-handed Pitcher $16

In last year's book, I criticized the A's organization for bringing Mohler to the majors before he pitched well at Double-A or Triple-A, saying that "I don't really see how he can expect to develop unless he has some success." He did pitch well at Tacoma last year, and may be closer to contributing. A left-hander, doesn't throw hard. Grade C prospect.

YEAR	TEAM/LEVEL	G	IP	W-L	SAVES	HITS	SO	BB	ERA
1992	Huntsville AA	44	80	3-8	3	72	56	39	3.59
1993	Oakland	42	64	1-6	0	57	42	44	5.60
1994	Tacoma AAA	17	64	1-3	0	66	50	21	3.53

PAUL MOLITOR / Toronto Blue Jays / Designated Hitter/First Base $59

He is 38, going on 25. He has been almost 100 percent healthy now for four years, six of the last seven years. He is playing unbelievably well, and will probably continue to do so. He was 20-for-20 as a base stealer last year, the first player in history to do that. With a little luck, he'll get his 3000th hit in September 1996.

YEAR	TEAM/LEVEL	G	AB	R	H	2B	3B	HR	RBI	BB	SB	AVG	OBP	SLG
1993	Toronto	160	636	121	211	37	5	22	111	77	22	.332	.402	.509
1994	Toronto	115	454	86	155	30	4	14	75	55	20	.341	.410	.518
1995	*Projected*	*146*	*574*	*86*	*173*	*29*	*4*	*13*	*80*	*69*	*23*	*.301*	*.376*	*.434*

RAUL MONDESI / Los Angeles Dodgers / Right Field $57

Mondesi is regarded as being in the Clemente mold, in the same sense that Manny Ramirez is in the Henry Aaron mold, and Matt Williams is in the Mike Schmidt mold. I remain somewhat skeptical that he will get there. His arm is tremendous, but his speed, I think, will leave him quickly, and I'm not sure he's going to hit .300 every year.

YEAR	TEAM/LEVEL	G	AB	R	H	2B	3B	HR	RBI	BB	SB	AVG	OBP	SLG
1993	Los Angeles	42	86	13	25	3	1	4	10	4	4	.291	.322	.488
1994	Los Angeles	112	434	63	133	27	8	16	56	16	11	.306	.333	.516
1995	*Projected*	*156*	*561*	*71*	*155*	*25*	*6*	*15*	*65*	*19*	*14*	*.276*	*.300*	*.422*

RICH MONTELEONE / San Francisco Giants / Relief Pitcher $21

Was out for a month with a stress fracture of the right metatarsal, returned June 16 and pitched exceptionally well the rest of the year (2.10 ERA in 25 appearances). He's been steady in a role in which not many pitchers can be counted on . . . usually pitches when his team is behind. Like many relievers, pitches his best when he works on short rest.

YEAR	TEAM/LEVEL	G	IP	W-L	SAVES	HITS	SO	BB	ERA
1992	New York	47	93	7-3	0	82	62	27	3.30
1993	New York	42	86	7-4	0	85	50	35	4.94
1994	San Francisco	39	45	4-3	0	43	16	13	3.18

JEFF MONTGOMERY / Kansas City Royals / Closer $59

After five seasons of extraordinarily consistent work, he opened last year pitching badly, carrying an ERA over six and a half into late June. An MRI in mid-June revealed bursitis in his shoulder, and he took a few days off to get a cortisone shot. When he returned he was as devastating as ever, allowing only one run the rest of the season.

YEAR	TEAM/LEVEL	G	IP	W-L	SAVES	HITS	SO	BB	ERA
1992	Kansas City	65	83	1-6	39	61	69	27	2.18
1993	Kansas City	69	87	7-5	45	65	66	23	2.27
1994	Kansas City	42	45	2-3	27	48	50	15	4.03

MARCUS MOORE / Colorado Rockies / Pitcher $26

Currently facing criminal charges. If Coors Field is better for a pitcher, as is expected, and if the ball isn't quite as lively in '95, and if the team develops a little, then *some* Rockies pitchers will show tremendous individ-ual improvement in their stats. Those who are most likely to improve will be those who are young and have ability, like Marcus Moore.

YEAR	TEAM/LEVEL	G	IP	W-L	PCT	HITS	SO	BB	ERA
1993	Colo. Sp. AAA	30	44	1-5	.167	54	38	29	4.47
1993	Colorado	27	26	3-1	.750	30	13	20	6.84
1994	Colorado	29	34	1-1	.500	33	33	21	6.15

MIKE MOORE / Detroit Tigers / Starting Pitcher $23

Has posted winning records for four straight seasons, and has, oh, I don't know, maybe a 3 percent chance of making it five straight. He led the league in walks last year, in home runs allowed the year before. To have a winning record despite this is amazing, but I evaluate him rather like a bank robber. He's going to get caught, sooner or later.

YEAR	TEAM/LEVEL	G	IP	W-L	PCT	HITS	SO	BB	ERA
1992	Oakland	36	223	17-12	.586	229	117	103	4.12
1993	Detroit	36	214	13-9	.590	227	89	89	5.22
1994	Detroit	25	154	11-10	.524	152	62	89	5.42

MICKEY MORANDINI / Philadelphia Phillies / Second Base $27

One of the few Phillies to have a better year in '94 than he had in '93, as he cut his strikeouts in half. Morandini hit .235 against left-handed pitchers last year (12-for-51), lifting his career average against southpaws to .202. Pretty good defensive second baseman, excellent baserunner despite average speed, and a fine number-two hitter against a right-handed pitcher.

YEAR	TEAM/LEVEL	G	AB	R	H	2B	3B	HR	RBI	BB	SB	AVG	OBP	SLG
1993	Philadelphia	120	425	57	105	19	9	3	33	34	13	.247	.309	.355
1994	Philadelphia	87	274	40	80	16	5	2	26	34	10	.292	.378	.409
1995	*Projected*	*135*	*449*	*56*	*119*	*19*	*7*	*4*	*38*	*39*	*12*	*.263*	*.322*	*.363*

MIKE MORDECAI / Atlanta Braves / Shortstop $14

The only regular at Richmond who *wasn't* regarded as a major prospect, but had a fine season, and played four games for Atlanta. He's 27, a switch hitter, runs pretty well, and can play shortstop. At a minimum, he has a chance to take Rafael Belliard's job, and if his improved hitting stats last year reflect real improvement, could actually become a player.

YEAR	TEAM/LEVEL	G	AB	R	H	2B	3B	HR	RBI	BB	SB	AVG	OBP	SLG
1993	Richmond AAA	72	205	29	55	8	1	2	14	14	10	.268	.318	.346
1994	Richmond AAA	99	382	67	107	25	1	14	57	35	14	.280	.340	.481
1994	MLE	99	368	50	93	21	0	11	43	26	9	.253	.302	.399

MIKE MORGAN / Chicago Cubs / Starting Pitcher $19

His 2-10 log in '94 gives him 11 losing records in the majors, to go with two winning records and one season of 1-1. It wasn't the first time he's gone 2-10; he had that record before, 1979. Left-handed batters hit .386 against him. . . . Needs five more wins for 100 in his career, but just two more to catch Milt Gaston.

YEAR	TEAM/LEVEL	G	IP	W-L	PCT	HITS	SO	BB	ERA
1992	Chicago	34	240	16-8	.667	203	123	79	2.55
1993	Chicago	32	208	10-15	.400	206	111	74	4.03
1994	Chicago	15	81	2-10	.167	111	57	35	6.69

RUSS MORMAN / Florida Marlins / First Base $15

He hit .350 last year at Edmonton, 19 homers, 82 RBI. His best years are behind him at 33, and he has spent them all in the minor leagues, but he's been just as good a player as many of the guys who have had major league careers, like Dave Magadan, Randy Milligan, Ricky Jordan, Dave Martinez. Right-handed hitter, fine defensive first baseman.

YEAR	TEAM/LEVEL	G	AB	R	H	2B	3B	HR	RBI	BB	SB	AVG	OBP	SLG
1993	MLE	119	392	59	114	30	1	20	58	38	0	.291	.353	.526
1994	MLE	114	377	45	113	24	1	12	53	24	5	.300	.342	.464
1994	Florida	13	33	2	7	0	1	1	2	2	0	.212	.278	.364

HAL MORRIS / Cincinnati Reds / First Base $47

High on the list of things I was wrong about last year was Hal Morris' chance of moving from platoon player to regular. Morris has never hit left-handers, and I thought this would drag him down if he played every day. What happened was that he still didn't hit the lefties (.255 with no homers), but hit so well against right-handers that nobody cared.

YEAR	TEAM/LEVEL	G	AB	R	H	2B	3B	HR	RBI	BB	SB	AVG	OBP	SLG
1993	Cincinnati	101	379	48	120	18	0	7	49	34	2	.317	.371	.420
1994	Cincinnati	112	438	60	146	30	4	10	78	34	6	.335	.385	.491
1995	*Projected*	*144*	*523*	*65*	*162*	*29*	*3*	*11*	*81*	*52*	*6*	*.310*	*.372*	*.440*

JACK MORRIS / Released / Wheat Farmer $8

Released by the Indians just before the strike, apparently in a disagreement about his attention to baseball. He had left the team a number of times since mid-July to return to his ranch in Montana, helping with the wheat harvest, and the Indians concluded that he had lost interest in baseball. He can still pitch if he wants to, but I suspect he doesn't.

YEAR	TEAM/LEVEL	G	IP	W-L	PCT	HITS	SO	BB	ERA
1992	Toronto	34	241	21-6	.778	222	132	80	4.04
1993	Toronto	27	153	7-12	.368	189	103	65	6.19
1994	Cleveland	23	141	10-6	.625	163	100	67	5.60

JAMES MOUTON / Houston Astros / Right Field $24

An interesting player; you can see how he *might* become a good player. He doesn't have a right fielder's arm, and hasn't proven he can hit the way a right fielder is supposed to hit. But he is very fast, he can hit *some*, and he is surrounded by Houston players like Bagwell, Caminiti, and Drabek, who work hard, and will help to bring him along.

YEAR	TEAM/LEVEL	G	AB	R	H	2B	3B	HR	RBI	BB	SB	AVG	OBP	SLG
1993	Tucson AAA	134	546	126	172	42	12	16	92	72	40	.315	.397	.524
1993	MLE	134	505	79	131	33	6	9	57	45	26	.259	.320	.402
1994	Houston	99	310	43	76	11	0	2	16	27	24	.245	.315	.300

JAMIE MOYER / Baltimore Orioles / Starting Pitcher $27

Started slowly but pitched well in the six weeks just before the strike. His excellent control was negated, for most of the year, by his inability to get outs with men in scoring position (.333 average). Since he has no history of that problem, and since he seemed to fix it about July 1, I wouldn't worry about that. The Orioles are unpredictable.

YEAR	TEAM/LEVEL	G	IP	W-L	PCT	HITS	SO	BB	ERA
1992	Toledo AAA	21	139	10-8	.556	128	80	37	2.86
1993	Baltimore	25	152	12-9	.571	154	90	38	3.43
1994	Baltimore	23	149	5-7	.417	158	87	38	4.77

TERRY MULHOLLAND / New York Yankees / Starting Pitcher $25

A free agent. His statistics won't tell us what went wrong last year. His strikeout and walk data were stable. He allowed no stolen bases all year, consistent with his history. But a) left-handed hitters, whom he had completely stymied in previous years, hit .338 against him, and b) when he got behind in the count, he just got clobbered.

YEAR	TEAM/LEVEL	G	IP	W-L	PCT	HITS	SO	BB	ERA
1992	Philadelphia	32	229	13-11	.542	227	125	46	3.81
1993	Philadelphia	29	191	12-9	.571	177	116	40	3.25
1994	New York	24	121	6-7	.462	150	72	37	6.49

BOBBY MUNOZ / Philadelphia Phillies / Relief Pitcher $41

One of three players traded to the Phillies in exchange for Terry Mulholland, he moved into the Phillies rotation in late May, and was among the better pitchers in the National League. A 6-7 right-hander from Puerto Rico, throws hard. Now 27; arm was not abused in his formative years. There is every reason to expect him to have a very good career.

YEAR	TEAM/LEVEL	G	IP	W-L	PCT	HITS	SO	BB	ERA
1993	Columbus AAA	22	31	3-1	.750	24	16	8	1.44
1993	New York	38	46	3-3	.500	48	33	26	5.32
1994	Philadelphia	21	104	7-5	.583	101	59	35	2.67

MIKE MUNOZ / Colorado Rockies / Relief Pitcher $17

He pitched well as a left-handed middle reliever, as he did in '92, but without showing any improvement in his control. He throws a hard sinking fastball, and he is *not* easy to hit. But he's walked 5.51 men per nine innings in his career, 6.11 last year. He's 29. I can't see that he's ever going to be a pitcher you can count on.

YEAR	TEAM/LEVEL	G	IP	W-L	SAVES	HITS	SO	BB	ERA
1992	Detroit	63	47	1-2	2	44	23	24	3.67
1993	Two Teams	29	21	2-2	0	25	17	15	4.71
1994	Colorado	57	46	4-2	1	37	32	31	3.74

PEDRO MUNOZ / Minnesota Twins / Left Field $27

He is still young (26), and a proven hitter, with a .430 career slugging percentage. He has lost his speed and still strikes out too much, but then, so does Andres Galarraga. Not much of an outfielder. Kelly has not been anxious to get him into the lineup—but he's a strong platoon player at worst, and could well drive in 100 runs a year.

YEAR	TEAM/LEVEL	G	AB	R	H	2B	3B	HR	RBI	BB	SB	AVG	OBP	SLG
1993	Minnesota	104	326	34	76	11	1	13	38	25	1	.233	.294	.393
1994	Minnesota	75	244	35	72	15	2	11	36	19	0	.295	.348	.508
1995	*Projected*	*122*	*391*	*48*	*108*	*22*	*2*	*14*	*57*	*25*	*2*	*.276*	*.320*	*.450*

ROB MURPHY / New York Yankees / Relief Pitcher $18

Pitched most of the year with the Cardinals, who let him go on waivers; he was claimed by the Yankees. He pitched better last year than he has in most recent seasons, but he gave up nine homers while facing only 174 batters. His control is good, and he gave up less than one hit per inning for the first time in several years.

YEAR	TEAM/LEVEL	G	IP	W-L	SAVES	HITS	SO	BB	ERA
1992	Houston	58	55	3-1	0	56	42	21	4.07
1993	St. Louis	73	65	5-7	1	73	41	20	4.87
1994	Two Teams	53	42	4-3	2	38	25	13	4.29

EDDIE MURRAY / Cleveland Indians / First Base $36

If the season starts on schedule, he will get his 3000th hit this summer, probably in July. He is still a productive hitter at 39, although no longer one of the best. He would probably have driven in 100 runs last year, without the strike. His alienation from the press will *not* keep him out of the Hall of Fame. The reporters aren't that immature.

YEAR	TEAM/LEVEL	G	AB	R	H	2B	3B	HR	RBI	BB	SB	AVG	OBP	SLG
1993	New York	154	610	77	174	28	1	27	100	40	2	.285	.325	.467
1994	Cleveland	108	433	57	110	21	1	17	76	31	6	.254	.302	.425
1995	*Projected*	*135*	*473*	*54*	*126*	*21*	*1*	*16*	*76*	*39*	*4*	*.266*	*.322*	*.416*

MIKE MUSSINA / Baltimore Orioles / Starting Pitcher $72

I wonder how many pitchers in baseball history have gone 48-16 over three seasons? Mussina is one of the best pitchers in baseball, but his years of effectiveness are probably limited. He's 26, but pitches more like he's 33. He'll run out of gas within four years, when guys like Cone and Randy Johnson, who are older than he is, are still going strong.

YEAR	TEAM/LEVEL	G	IP	W-L	PCT	HITS	SO	BB	ERA
1992	Baltimore	32	241	18-5	.783	212	130	48	2.54
1993	Baltimore	25	168	14-6	.700	163	117	44	4.46
1994	Baltimore	24	176	16-5	.762	163	99	42	3.06

JEFF MUTIS / Florida Marlins / Lefty $14

Failed as a starter in '93, and was waived by Cleveland. He signed with the Marlins, was assigned to the ever-popular left-handed short reliever role, but wasn't any better there, allowing a .331 batting average. Sent to the minors just before the strike, he posted an 8.44 ERA in 27 innings at Edmonton. He has an arm, and that's about all.

YEAR	TEAM/LEVEL	G	IP	W-L	PCT	HITS	SO	BB	ERA
1993	Charlotte AAA	12	76	6-0	1.000	64	59	25	2.62
1993	Cleveland	17	81	3-6	.333	93	29	33	5.78
1994	Florida	35	38	1-0	1.000	51	30	15	5.40

GREG MYERS / California Angels / Catcher $22

Started '94 playing quite a bit, but a serious knee injury in late April took him out for sixty days. When he returned he was the Angels' number-one catcher against right-handed pitchers. He wasn't awful at bat, and threw out 46 percent of opposing base stealers, one of the best percentages in baseball. Might keep his job, or might surrender it to Jorge Fabregas.

YEAR	TEAM/LEVEL	G	AB	R	H	2B	3B	HR	RBI	BB	SB	AVG	OBP	SLG
1992	Two Teams	30	78	4	18	7	0	1	13	5	0	.231	.271	.359
1993	California	108	290	27	74	10	0	7	40	17	3	.255	.298	.362
1994	California	45	126	10	31	6	0	2	8	10	0	.246	.299	.341

RANDY MYERS / Chicago Cubs / Closer $46

His 1994 earned run averages, by months: 1.13 in April, 1.80 in May, 2.16 in June, 7.36 in July, 9.00 in August. Something was clearly wrong, but whether eight months' rest will fix it or make it worse is, in my experience, a 50-50 proposition. Watch him closely in spring training, before you draft him.

YEAR	TEAM/LEVEL	G	IP	W-L	SAVES	HITS	SO	BB	ERA
1992	San Diego	65	77	2-6	38	83	61	32	4.46
1993	Chicago	73	75	2-4	53	65	86	26	3.11
1994	Chicago	38	40	1-5	21	40	32	16	3.79

CHRIS NABHOLZ / Boston Red Sox / Starting Pitcher | $16

Traded to Cleveland last February, he had an 11.45 ERA for the Indians, being placed on the DL because, hell, there had to be *something* wrong. Sent to Charlotte to rehab, he pitched great, and was traded to the Red Sox, where his ERA was 6.64. Something of a comeback is likely. There are no Cy Young Awards in his future.

YEAR	TEAM/LEVEL	G	IP	W-L	PCT	HITS	SO	BB	ERA
1992	Montreal	32	195	11-12	.478	176	130	74	3.32
1993	Montreal	26	117	9-8	.529	100	74	63	4.09
1994	Two Teams	14	53	3-5	.375	67	28	38	7.64

TIM NAEHRING / Boston Red Sox / Infielder | $34

Started 45 games at second, 7 to 10 at each of the other infield positions. He spent a month on the DL, and was essentially a regular the rest of the year. I was quite impressed with him as a second baseman, particularly the way he hangs in on the double play. He's 28 now, but if he can stay healthy, he's going to be a valuable player.

YEAR	TEAM/LEVEL	G	AB	R	H	2B	3B	HR	RBI	BB	SB	AVG	OBP	SLG
1993	Boston	39	127	14	42	10	0	1	17	10	1	.331	.377	.433
1994	Boston	80	297	41	82	18	1	7	42	30	1	.276	.349	.414
1995	*Projected*	*112*	*369*	*45*	*100*	*22*	*0*	*8*	*46*	*41*	*1*	*.272*	*.345*	*.397*

CHARLES NAGY / Cleveland Indians / Starting Pitcher | $36

Completed his comeback from 1993 shoulder surgery, and by the end of July was throwing 120 pitches a start again. I don't think this is a good idea, but then, nobody asked me . . . doesn't throw hard, but has good sinking fastball, and knows how to use it. He doesn't walk people, and he gets grounders . . . a right-hander, but very tough on left-handed batters.

YEAR	TEAM/LEVEL	G	IP	W-L	PCT	HITS	SO	BB	ERA
1992	Cleveland	33	252	17-10	.630	245	169	57	2.96
1993	Cleveland	9	49	2-6	.250	66	30	13	6.29
1994	Cleveland	23	169	10-8	.556	175	108	48	3.45

ROB NATAL / Florida Marlins / Catcher | $15

Not a bad player, a backup catcher who isn't an awful hitter and isn't an awful defensive player. He looks worse than he is—looks awkward behind the plate, although he throws OK, looks slow, but actually runs better than many catchers. He's a right-handed hitter, 29 years old. I would expect him to be up and down over the next five years.

YEAR	TEAM/LEVEL	G	AB	R	H	2B	3B	HR	RBI	BB	SB	AVG	OBP	SLG
1992	MLE	96	325	36	85	16	1	7	36	20	2	.262	.304	.382
1993	Florida	41	117	3	25	4	1	1	6	6	1	.214	.273	.291
1994	Florida	10	29	2	8	2	0	0	2	5	1	.276	.382	.345

JAIME NAVARRO / Milwaukee Brewers / Starting Pitcher $19

Here's another case of the "tired arm" syndrome; after he pitched 460 innings in 1992-93, sportswriters said he had a tired arm. Well, if your arm is tired, rest it for a week. If it doesn't come back in a week, that's not fatigue, that's an injury ... has made some adjustments, and probably will start on the road back this year.

YEAR	TEAM/LEVEL	G	IP	W-L	PCT	HITS	SO	BB	ERA
1992	Milwaukee	34	246	17-11	.607	224	100	64	3.33
1993	Milwaukee	35	214	11-12	.478	254	114	73	5.33
1994	Milwaukee	29	90	4-9	.308	115	65	35	6.62

DENNY NEAGLE / Pittsburgh Pirates / Left-handed Pitcher $26

I am torn between recommending him because 1) his strikeout/walk ratio is great, 2) everybody says he has good stuff, and 3) he pitched well in the minors, and not recommending him because he's not making any progress. His ERA was going up last year as the schedule ran. The strikeout/walk is still the best indicator, so I guess I'll go with that.

YEAR	TEAM/LEVEL	G	IP	W-L	PCT	HITS	SO	BB	ERA
1992	Pittsburgh	55	86	4-6	.400	81	77	43	4.48
1993	Pittsburgh	50	81	3-5	.375	82	73	37	5.31
1994	Pittsburgh	24	137	9-10	.474	135	122	49	5.12

TROY NEEL / Oakland Athletics / Designated Hitter/First Base $34

A big Texan who can really hit, he'll be in the majors for many years. He hits left, but has career average of .355 (!) against left-handers, .256 against right-handers. He is viewed as a weak defensive first baseman, although I have not seen evidence of that ... missed three weeks in '94 with a broken hand. Will have 100-RBI seasons.

YEAR	TEAM/LEVEL	G	AB	R	H	2B	3B	HR	RBI	BB	SB	AVG	OBP	SLG
1993	Oakland	123	427	59	124	21	0	19	63	49	3	.290	.367	.473
1994	Oakland	83	278	43	74	13	0	15	48	38	2	.266	.357	.475
1995	*Projected*	*146*	*529*	*68*	*142*	*28*	*0*	*20*	*75*	*66*	*4*	*.268*	*.350*	*.435*

JEFF NELSON / Seattle Mariners / Right-handed Relief Pitcher $21

After pitching in 71 games in 1993, not very effectively, he bounced between Seattle and Calgary in '94, but pitched much better, the best ball of his career. He's not going to be the closer in Seattle, because Ayala has that role, but Nelson is regarded as having closer material—a hard slider, a good fastball, and an aggressive attitude.

YEAR	TEAM/LEVEL	G	IP	W-L	SAVES	HITS	SO	BB	ERA
1992	Seattle	65	80	1-7	5	71	45	44	3.49
1993	Seattle	71	60	5-3	1	57	61	34	4.35
1994	Seattle	28	42	0-0	0	35	44	20	2.76

ROBB NEN / Florida Marlins / Right-handed Pitcher $37

He took over the assignment of being Florida's closer, and performed so well that it may not be easy for Bryan Harvey to get the job back. Harvey is an amazing pitcher, but Nen had 15 saves in 15 chances, and you can't do much better than that. He throws *very* hard, and he throws strikes, or at least did in '94.

YEAR	TEAM/LEVEL	G	IP	W-L	SAVES	HITS	SO	BB	ERA
1993	Ok. City AAA	6	28	0-2	0	45	12	18	6.67
1993	Two Teams	24	56	2-1	0	63	39	46	6.75
1994	Florida	44	58	5-5	15	46	60	17	2.95

MARC NEWFIELD / Seattle Mariners / Outfield $28

Also hit .184 in a 12-game callup, not shown below. Newfield, the sixth player taken in the 1990 draft, is the best *hitting* prospect in the Seattle system, one of the best in baseball. He's big and strong, but doesn't strike out, hits line drives. Slow; has no obvious defensive position. He's only 22; will be an MVP candidate in five years.

YEAR	TEAM/LEVEL	G	AB	R	H	2B	3B	HR	RBI	BB	SB	AVG	OBP	SLG
1993	Seattle	22	66	5	15	3	0	1	7	2	0	.227	.257	.318
1994	Calgary	107	430	89	150	44	2	19	83	42	0	.349	.413	.593
1994	MLE	107	398	56	118	38	1	11	53	27	0	.296	.341	.480

WARREN NEWSON / Chicago White Sox / Right Field/Designated Hitter $20

The White Sox lead the league in short players—Newson (5-7), Cora, Grebeck, Raines, LaValliere. Newson has been in Chicago for four years as a backup outfielder, which is not common. He stays around because he contributes. He's a .270 hitter with almost as many walks as hits, runs well, has a little power. Never bats against a lefty. Doesn't have a right fielder's arm.

YEAR	TEAM/LEVEL	G	AB	R	H	2B	3B	HR	RBI	BB	SB	AVG	OBP	SLG
1993	Chicago	26	40	9	12	0	0	2	6	9	0	.300	.429	.450
1994	Chicago	63	102	16	26	5	0	2	7	14	1	.255	.345	.363
1995	*Projected*	*90*	*185*	*32*	*51*	*8*	*0*	*4*	*21*	*38*	*3*	*.276*	*.399*	*.384*

DAVID NIED / Colorado Rockies / Starting Pitcher $30

A 4.80 ERA in Mile High Stadium, which inflates runs by 43 percent, is equivalent to about 3.75 in a normal park. The National League ERA was 4.21, so Nied's ERA, in context, is consistent with his won-lost record. He was a better-than-average pitcher. Since he is young and developing, I would expect him to be better than that this year. **Draft him.**

YEAR	TEAM/LEVEL	G	IP	W-L	PCT	HITS	SO	BB	ERA
1992	Atlanta	6	23	3-0	1.000	10	19	5	1.17
1993	Colorado	16	87	5-9	.357	99	46	42	5.17
1994	Colorado	22	122	9-7	.563	137	74	47	4.80

MELVIN NIEVES / San Diego Padres / Outfield $26

The Padres, after trading Fred McGriff and acquiring Nieves, have allowed him to languish in the minors for almost two seasons, for no apparent reason. He was ready to play in the majors two years ago. A big switch hitter, overswings, will lead the league in strikeouts, but will pay off in power. He is 23 now; it is time to give him a job.

YEAR	TEAM/LEVEL	G	AB	R	H	2B	3B	HR	RBI	BB	SB	AVG	OBP	SLG
1994	MLE	111	380	51	99	12	2	19	58	37	0	.261	.326	.453
1994	San Diego	10	19	2	5	1	0	1	4	3	0	.263	.364	.474
1995	Projected	137	463	63	128	19	2	21	67	44	4	.272	.335	.458

DAVE NILSSON / Milwaukee Brewers / Catcher $36

Was one of the best-hitting catchers in baseball, batting fifth for Milwaukee. This is not a fluke; he will continue to hit in '95, and could hit better. He doesn't throw well—threw out only 10 baserunners in 64 tries, although of course the pitchers are partially responsible. He's no Gold Glove, but he's going to make a lot of money with his bat.

YEAR	TEAM/LEVEL	G	AB	R	H	2B	3B	HR	RBI	BB	SB	AVG	OBP	SLG
1993	Milwaukee	100	296	35	76	10	2	7	40	37	3	.257	.336	.375
1994	Milwaukee	109	397	51	109	28	3	12	69	34	1	.275	.326	.451
1995	Projected	155	550	72	159	34	4	13	85	53	7	.289	.352	.436

OTIS NIXON / Boston Red Sox / Center Field $26

Signed a two-year contract with the Sox, and did everything he could have been expected to do, or a little bit more. Third Red Sox player in the last 70 years to steal 40 bases, others being Billy Werber (1934) and Tommy Harper (1973).... According to the media guide, he has a child named "Genesis." Do you suppose that's a boy or a girl?

YEAR	TEAM/LEVEL	G	AB	R	H	2B	3B	HR	RBI	BB	SB	AVG	OBP	SLG
1993	Atlanta	134	461	77	124	12	3	1	24	61	47	.269	.351	.315
1994	Boston	103	398	60	109	15	1	0	25	55	42	.274	.360	.317
1995	Projected	126	463	65	119	9	1	1	21	53	41	.255	.331	.285

JUNIOR NOBOA / Free Agent / Infielder $15

His "two teams" last year were Oakland, for which he played 17 games, and Pittsburgh, for which he batted twice. He played second base for Oakland, but not very well, also played 67 games for Buffalo. He was cut after the season, of course, and has virtually no chance of ever making anybody's 40-man roster in normal times. Only 30, can hit line drives.

YEAR	TEAM/LEVEL	G	AB	R	H	2B	3B	HR	RBI	BB	SB	AVG	OBP	SLG
1992	New York (N)	46	47	7	7	0	0	0	3	3	0	.149	.212	.149
1993	Indianapolis AAA	45	180	27	51	11	1	0	14	14	0	.283	.337	.356
1994	Two Teams	19	42	3	13	1	1	0	16	3	1	.310	.341	.381

MATT NOKES / New York Yankees / Designated Hitter/Catcher $23

The highlights of his season include a .595 slugging percentage, a broken hand, a shouting and/or shoving match with Yankees' pitching coach Billy Connors, and reaching free agency. Nokes has a career slugging per-centage of .445, and there aren't many left-handed-hitting catchers who do better. This is the sum of his positive contributions.

YEAR	TEAM/LEVEL	G	AB	R	H	2B	3B	HR	RBI	BB	SB	AVG	OBP	SLG
1993	New York	76	217	25	54	8	0	10	35	16	0	.249	.303	.424
1994	New York	28	79	11	23	3	0	7	19	5	0	.291	.329	.595
1995	*Projected*	*104*	*306*	*37*	*74*	*11*	*0*	*15*	*50*	*26*	*0*	*.242*	*.299*	*.425*

EDWIN NUNEZ / Free Agent / Relief Pitcher $12

After going through the Mariners, Mets, Tigers, Brewers, and Rangers at a rate accelerating to one team per season, he had a pretty decent 1993 season with Oakland, pitching middle relief. He's a huge man, throws very hard, has a reputation for having a terrible temper. He started badly last year, and refused assignment to the minors, making him a free agent. Nobody called.

YEAR	TEAM/LEVEL	G	IP	W-L	SAVES	HITS	SO	BB	ERA
1992	Texas	49	59	1-3	3	63	49	22	4.85
1993	Oakland	56	76	3-6	1	89	58	29	3.81
1994	Oakland	15	15	0-0	0	26	15	10	12.00

SHERMAN OBANDO / Baltimore Orioles / Outfield/Designated Hitter $19

The Orioles got him from the Yankees under Rule 5, and he opened the '93 season playing part-time in the Orioles' outfield. He played OK, but had repeated hamstring pulls, and Jeffrey Hammonds took that job away, so Obando is back in the minors, with no way out. Is 25 years old, big, not fast, can hit. He's comparable to Pedro Munoz.

YEAR	TEAM/LEVEL	G	AB	R	H	2B	3B	HR	RBI	BB	SB	AVG	OBP	SLG
1993	Baltimore	31	92	8	25	2	0	3	15	4	0	.272	.309	.391
1994	Rochester	109	403	67	133	36	7	20	69	30	1	.330	.379	.603
1994	MLE	109	384	53	114	30	4	16	54	23	0	.297	.337	.521

CHARLIE O'BRIEN / Atlanta Braves / Catcher $18

Right-handed hitting backup catcher, 34 years old. His career is a year-to-year project, but he has hit better the last two years than he had ever hit before, and consequently his position seems fairly solid. He has a repu-tation as a defensive wizard. The Mets got him, in part, to work with Hundley, and the Braves, to work with Lopez.

YEAR	TEAM/LEVEL	G	AB	R	H	2B	3B	HR	RBI	BB	SB	AVG	OBP	SLG
1993	New York	67	188	15	48	11	0	4	23	14	1	.255	.312	.378
1994	Atlanta	51	152	24	37	11	0	8	28	15	0	.243	.322	.474
1995	*Projected*	*76*	*201*	*20*	*45*	*11*	*0*	*4*	*22*	*18*	*1*	*.224*	*.288*	*.339*

JOSE OFFERMAN / Los Angeles Dodgers / Shortstop $31

He has improved his fielding percentage from .935 in '92 to .950 in '93 to .966 last year. This didn't do him any good when he stopped hitting and stopped running; the Dodgers sent him to Albuquerque, "to regain his stroke." He has been among the better offensive shortstops in the NL, and, since he is only 26, probably will be again.

YEAR	TEAM/LEVEL	G	AB	R	H	2B	3B	HR	RBI	BB	SB	AVG	OBP	SLG
1993	Los Angeles	158	590	77	159	21	6	1	62	71	30	.269	.346	.331
1994	Los Angeles	72	243	27	51	8	4	1	25	38	2	.210	.314	.288
1995	*Projected*	*127*	*450*	*66*	*119*	*13*	*4*	*2*	*41*	*55*	*18*	*.264*	*.345*	*.324*

CHAD OGEA / Cleveland Indians / Right-handed Starter $23

Louisiana native, pitched in three College World Series for LSU. You never know if a young pitcher will develop, but Ogea seems like one to bet on. He is said to have a feel for what he is doing on the mound, which is reflected in his winning records and excellent K/W ratios. Throws trailing fastball, changeup is his best pitch. Grade B prospect.

YEAR	TEAM/LEVEL	G	IP	W-L	PCT	HITS	SO	BB	ERA
1993	Charlotte AAA	29	182	13-8	.619	169	135	54	3.81
1994	Charlotte AAA	24	164	9-10	.474	146	113	34	3.85
1994	Cleveland	4	16	0-1	.000	21	11	10	6.06

GREG O'HALLORAN / Florida Marlins / Catcher/Third Base $14

A left-handed hitter from the Blue Jays' system, 27 years old, batted 11 times for Florida. His best asset is the ability to play all over the field (catcher, third base, first base, the outfield). He's not a particularly good fielder at any of them, and his bat is certainly nothing special: no power, no speed, doesn't walk much, doesn't hit for a high average.

YEAR	TEAM/LEVEL	G	AB	R	H	2B	3B	HR	RBI	BB	SB	AVG	OBP	SLG
1993	MLE	109	315	27	79	13	2	3	30	11	1	.251	.276	.324
1994	Portland AA	104	388	52	102	22	6	7	53	37	2	.263	.331	.405
1994	MLE	104	372	38	86	19	3	5	38	23	1	.231	.276	.339

TROY O'LEARY / Milwaukee Brewers / Outfield $18

A 25-year-old left-handed hitter, has been in the Milwaukee system since 1987. He could hit .270 in the majors with 15 to 25 stolen bases, which would be enough to get him playing time if there were a little power mixed in. He will receive trials as a regular, and could hold on to a regular job if he plays well.

YEAR	TEAM/LEVEL	G	AB	R	H	2B	3B	HR	RBI	BB	SB	AVG	OBP	SLG
1992	MLE	135	469	61	132	22	4	3	52	33	18	.281	.329	.365
1993	Milwaukee	19	41	3	12	3	0	0	3	5	0	.293	.370	.366
1994	Milwaukee	27	66	8	18	1	1	2	7	5	1	.273	.329	.409

JOHN OLERUD / Toronto Blue Jays / First Base $58

He had a streak, from mid-May to early July, when he hit around .230 for six weeks. The rest of the year he hit .330, making an overall average of .297, which is also his career average. His '94 on-base percentage and slugging percentage were also very near to his career norms. Who will have a better career: Olerud or Mo Vaughn?

YEAR	TEAM/LEVEL	G	AB	R	H	2B	3B	HR	RBI	BB	SB	AVG	OBP	SLG
1993	Toronto	158	551	109	200	54	2	24	107	114	0	.363	.473	.599
1994	Toronto	108	384	47	114	29	2	12	67	61	1	.297	.393	.477
1995	*Projected*	*158*	*555*	*88*	*177*	*38*	*1*	*24*	*96*	*98*	*1*	*.319*	*.421*	*.521*

JOSE OLIVA / Atlanta Braves / Third Base $24

Oliva emerged as a prospect in the Texas system, came to Atlanta in the Charlie Leibrandt deal. He has apparently stagnated since coming over, as his best MLE was in 1991, when he was 20 years old. He was called to the majors last June 29, while Pendleton was out, and shot lights out for six weeks, going back down August 1. Grade B prospect.

YEAR	TEAM/LEVEL	G	AB	R	H	2B	3B	HR	RBI	BB	SB	AVG	OBP	SLG
1993	MLE	125	403	54	88	18	4	18	56	30	0	.218	.273	.417
1994	MLE	99	359	39	82	14	0	19	48	18	1	.228	.265	.426
1994	Atlanta	19	59	9	17	5	0	6	11	7	0	.288	.364	.678

OMAR OLIVARES / St. Louis Cardinals / Pitcher $20

Career is in steady regression. He pitched fairly well in '92, as a starter, but moved to the bullpen in '93. That bombed, and he started '94 at Louisville, re-converting to a starter. He pitched OK at Louisville, but was ineffective when he returned to St. Louis. Good hitter; career average of .229. Avoid him in '95. How often does a river run uphill?

YEAR	TEAM/LEVEL	G	IP	W-L	PCT	HITS	SO	BB	ERA
1992	St. Louis	32	197	9-9	.500	189	124	63	3.84
1993	St. Louis	59	119	5-3	.625	134	63	54	4.17
1994	St. Louis	14	74	3-4	.429	84	26	37	5.74

DARREN OLIVER / Texas Rangers / Relief Pitcher $29

Slender left-hander, held left-handed batters to a .119 average in '94. Has above-average fastball, mixes it with a wide slider which is almost a curve. Originally a starter, he tore up his shoulder, and missed almost all of the 1990 and '91 seasons, re-emerging as a reliever. Control isn't great, but then, most good pitchers don't start off as control pitchers.

YEAR	TEAM/LEVEL	G	IP	W-L	SAVES	HITS	SO	BB	ERA
1993	Tulsa AA	46	73	7-5	6	51	77	41	1.96
1993	Texas	2	3	0-0	0	2	4	1	2.70
1994	Texas	43	50	4-0	2	40	50	35	3.42

JOE OLIVER / Cincinnati Reds / Catcher $21

He had what was originally thought to be a sprained
ankle, and had to take a day off. The Reds didn't think
it was serious enough to put him on the DL, but it just
didn't heal. For two months he was a week away from
coming back, and eventually missed the season with
"swelling in his knees and ankles." A marginal player
if healthy, has been released.

YEAR	TEAM/LEVEL	G	AB	R	H	2B	3B	HR	RBI	BB	SB	AVG	OBP	SLG
1992	Cincinnati	143	485	42	131	25	1	10	57	35	2	.270	.316	.388
1993	Cincinnati	139	482	40	115	28	0	14	75	27	0	.239	.276	.384
1994	Cincinnati	6	19	1	4	0	0	1	5	2	0	.211	.286	.368

GREGG OLSON / Atlanta Braves / Closer $13

He threw too many curveballs, too early in his career,
and his arm is probably shot. He is only 28, and obviously he is an extremely fine pitcher if his arm will let
him show it. He'll have several snatches of fame left, a
few weeks here and there of brilliant pitching. My best
guess it that he'll never be back.

YEAR	TEAM/LEVEL	G	IP	W-L	SAVES	HITS	SO	BB	ERA
1992	Baltimore	60	61	1-5	36	46	58	24	2.05
1993	Baltimore	50	45	0-2	29	37	44	18	1.60
1994	Atlanta	16	15	0-2	1	19	10	13	9.20

PAUL O'NEILL / New York Yankees / Right Field $52

What has made him so effective the last two years is his
uncanny ability to jump on the first pitch, or else get
ahead in the count. When he hit the first pitch last year,
he hit .489 (23-for-47). When he was ahead in the
count he hit .424. Behind in the count, he hit .265. . . .
Made only one error in right field.

YEAR	TEAM/LEVEL	G	AB	R	H	2B	3B	HR	RBI	BB	SB	AVG	OBP	SLG
1993	New York	141	498	71	155	34	1	20	75	44	2	.311	.367	.504
1994	New York	103	368	68	132	25	1	21	83	72	5	.359	.460	.603
1995	*Projected*	*144*	*505*	*73*	*143*	*28*	*1*	*20*	*80*	*70*	*5*	*.283*	*.370*	*.461*

STEVE ONTIVEROS / Oakland Athletics / Relief Pitcher $35

Question: Who led the American League in ERA? If
you said "Steve Ontiveros," you *were* paying attention.
He started a remarkable comeback with Seattle in '93,
signed with Oakland as a free agent. In the bullpen
until late May, posted 5.58 ERA in 14 games, moved to
rotation and had 1.59 ERA in 13 starts. I like his
chances to keep it going.

YEAR	TEAM/LEVEL	G	IP	W-L	PCT	HITS	SO	BB	ERA
1992	(Out of Baseball—Everybody Gave Up on Him)								
1993	Seattle	14	18	0-2	.000	18	13	6	1.00
1994	Oakland	27	115	6-4	.600	93	56	26	2.65

JOSE OQUENDO / St. Louis Cardinals / Utility Infielder $18

Has been with the Cardinals for nine years. He was never fast, and time and several years of battling a bone spur on his heel have left him actually slow, almost too slow to be useful as a middle infielder. On the other hand, he's a .260 hitter, and has had more walks than strikeouts every year since 1987. OK backup infielder/pinch hitter.

YEAR	TEAM/LEVEL	G	AB	R	H	2B	3B	HR	RBI	BB	SB	AVG	OBP	SLG
1992	St. Louis	14	35	3	9	3	1	0	3	5	0	.257	.350	.400
1993	St. Louis	46	73	7	15	0	0	0	4	12	0	.205	.314	.205
1994	St. Louis	55	129	13	34	2	2	0	9	21	1	.264	.364	.310

MIKE OQUIST / Baltimore Orioles / Starting Pitcher $18

A .500 pitcher at Rochester (22-22 over two-plus years), he was able to stay even at Baltimore. There is nothing really impressive about him, standard repertoire, but he has been able to rack up innings. I have always believed that *most* pitchers would eventually succeed if they could pitch 200 innings a year and stay healthy, but very few can.

YEAR	TEAM/LEVEL	G	IP	W-L	PCT	HITS	SO	BB	ERA
1993	Rochester AAA	28	149	9-8	.529	144	128	41	3.50
1993	Baltimore	5	12	0-0	.000	12	8	4	3.86
1994	Baltimore	15	58	3-3	.500	75	39	30	6.17

JESSE OROSCO / Milwaukee Brewers / Reliever $19

He is 38 and didn't pitch well, but as I said before, you can't read too much into his numbers, since he faced only 174 batters. He is sixth among active pitchers in career games (754), fifth in ERA (2.95), fifth in opposition batting average (.224), eighth in strikeouts/nine innings (7.99). Left-handed, but is tougher on *right*-handed batters.

YEAR	TEAM/LEVEL	G	IP	W-L	SAVES	HITS	SO	BB	ERA
1992	Milwaukee	59	39	3-1	1	33	40	13	3.23
1993	Milwaukee	57	57	3-5	8	47	67	17	3.18
1994	Milwaukee	40	39	3-1	0	32	36	26	5.08

JOE ORSULAK / New York Mets / Right Field $22

He's been as consistent as cement for 10 years, but his numbers went down one click last year, when most of the other hitters were going up. He grounded into 11 double plays; that was a career high. His on-base percentage was .299; that matched his career low. He's 33 in May; probably has a couple of years left, with declining playing time.

YEAR	TEAM/LEVEL	G	AB	R	H	2B	3B	HR	RBI	BB	SB	AVG	OBP	SLG
1993	New York	134	409	59	116	15	4	8	35	28	5	.284	.331	.399
1994	New York	98	292	39	76	3	0	8	42	18	4	.260	.299	.353
1995	*Projected*	*101*	*302*	*38*	*80*	*12*	*2*	*5*	*30*	*19*	*4*	*.265*	*.308*	*.368*

JUNIOR ORTIZ / Texas Rangers / Catcher $14

A career backup catcher, refused assignment to the minor leagues at season's end, and became a free agent. He's a right-handed hitter from Puerto Rico, but has spent almost his entire career backing up other right-handed-hitting Latin catchers—Tony Pena in Pittsburgh, Sandy Alomar in Cleveland, Rodriguez in Texas.

YEAR	TEAM/LEVEL	G	AB	R	H	2B	3B	HR	RBI	BB	SB	AVG	OBP	SLG
1992	Cleveland	86	244	20	61	7	0	0	24	12	1	.250	.296	.279
1993	Cleveland	95	249	19	55	13	0	0	20	11	1	.221	.267	.273
1994	Texas	29	76	3	21	2	0	0	9	5	0	.276	.328	.303

LUIS ORTIZ / Boston Red Sox / Outfield/Designated Hitter $20

Also played a few games in the majors, not shown below. Ortiz, a 23-year-old Dominican, is a *good* major league hitter. . . 1994 was his second year at Pawtucket, and he showed improvement, particularly in controlling the strike zone. He will have a good career. However, the man he has to beat out of a job, Jose Malave, had a *great* year at New Britain.

YEAR	TEAM/LEVEL	G	AB	R	H	2B	3B	HR	RBI	BB	SB	AVG	OBP	SLG
1993	MLE	102	389	34	105	28	0	13	61	9	0	.270	.286	.442
1994	Pawtucket	81	317	47	99	15	3	8	36	29	1	.312	.370	.435
1994	MLE	81	310	39	92	15	1	5	30	24	0	.297	.347	.400

DONOVAN OSBORNE / St. Louis Cardinals / Starting Pitcher $13

The sore shoulder which ended his 1993 season a month early turned out to be a serious injury, and he had reconstructive surgery last winter. He probably won't throw again until spring training, 1995. There is no way of knowing when or if he will return, or how effective he will be. He was well on his way to being a good pitcher.

YEAR	TEAM/LEVEL	G	IP	W-L	PCT	HITS	SO	BB	ERA
1992	St. Louis	34	179	11-9	.550	193	104	38	3.77
1993	St. Louis	26	156	10-7	.588	153	83	47	3.76
1994	St. Louis			(On Disabled List)					

AL OSUNA / Los Angeles Dodgers / Relief Pitcher $17

Spent most of 1994 at Albuquerque, where he pitched extremely well (2.82 ERA, excellent strikeout/walk ratio. Albquerque, as most of you know, is a tough place to pitch). Osuna, a gangly left-hander, throws an 88-mph fastball, slider, change, and split-fingered fastball. He pitched well in '91 and '93, well in the minors in '94. His career will have more moments.

YEAR	TEAM/LEVEL	G	IP	W-L	SAVES	HITS	SO	BB	ERA
1992	Houston	66	62	6-3	0	52	37	38	4.23
1993	Houston	44	25	1-1	2	17	21	13	3.20
1994	Los Angeles	15	9	2-0	0	13	7	4	6.23

ANTONIO OSUNA / Los Angeles Dodgers / Relief Pitcher $31

Probably will be the Dodgers' closer by 1996, and could be a Rookie of the Year candidate in 1995. He's a small Mexican right-handed pitcher with a 95-mph heater, once struck out 15 consecutive batters in the Mexican Winter League. He's 22 years old, was 16-7 as a starter in the Mexican League in 1992, moved to the bullpen in '93.

YEAR	TEAM/LEVEL	G	IP	W-L	SAVES	HITS	SO	BB	ERA
1993	Bakersfield A	14	18	0-2	2	19	20	5	4.91
1994	San Antonio AA	35	46	1-2	19	19	53	18	0.98
1994	Albuquerque AAA	6	6	0-0	4	5	8	1	0.00

DAVE OTTO / Chicago Cubs / Relief Pitcher $19

A 6-7, 30-year-old left-hander, had chances to establish himself every year from 1987 to 1993. When he was released by Pittsburgh in 1993 I figured he was probably done. He signed a minor league contract with the Cubs, *wasn't* invited to spring training, but earned another shot with a 1.02 ERA at Iowa—and had his best major league season.

YEAR	TEAM/LEVEL	G	IP	W-L	PCT	HITS	SO	BB	ERA
1992	Cleveland	18	80	5-9	.357	110	32	33	7.06
1993	Pittsburgh	28	68	3-4	.429	85	30	28	5.03
1994	Chicago	36	45	0-1	.000	49	19	22	3.80

SPIKE OWEN / California Angels / Third Base $25

His .418 on-base percentage was 99 points better than his previous career average, and 69 points better than his previous best. He is 34, slow, and has no power, so his career will end quickly if he stops hitting. You never know, but that might be several years away. He's not a shortstop anymore, which means that he can concentrate on the other side of his game.

YEAR	TEAM/LEVEL	G	AB	R	H	2B	3B	HR	RBI	BB	SB	AVG	OBP	SLG
1993	New York	103	334	41	78	16	2	2	20	29	3	.234	.294	.311
1994	California	82	268	30	83	17	2	3	37	49	2	.310	.418	.422
1995	*Projected*	*121*	*393*	*45*	*97*	*17*	*3*	*4*	*34*	*52*	*5*	*.247*	*.335*	*.336*

JAYHAWK OWENS / Colorado Rockies / Catcher $15

A 26-year-old catcher, might hit enough to stay in the majors as a backup catcher, but more likely won't. Originally in the Twins' system, he was an outfielder 1990-91, moved to catcher in 1992, and was taken in the first round of the expansion draft that November. Cincinnati native, runs better than many catchers, often hit by pitches.

YEAR	TEAM/LEVEL	G	AB	R	H	2B	3B	HR	RBI	BB	SB	AVG	OBP	SLG
1993	Colorado	33	86	12	18	5	0	3	6	6	1	.209	.277	.372
1994	Col. Sp. AAA	77	257	32	69	11	7	8	44	32	3	.268	.359	.436
1994	Colorado	6	12	4	3	0	1	0	1	3	0	.250	.400	.417

TOM PAGNOZZI / St. Louis Cardinals / Catcher $29

Neither rain nor strike nor knee surgery shall keep this sturdy warrior from hitting seven homers and driving in 40 runs. I wrote last year that he "has a multi-year record of hitting poorly in Busch Stadium," and in '94 he again hit 50 points better on the road (.295/.246). A regular for four-plus years, and will be for several more.

YEAR	TEAM/LEVEL	G	AB	R	H	2B	3B	HR	RBI	BB	SB	AVG	OBP	SLG
1993	St. Louis	92	330	31	85	15	1	7	41	19	1	.258	.296	.373
1994	St. Louis	70	243	21	66	12	1	7	40	21	0	.272	.327	.416
1995	*Projected*	*117*	*396*	*31*	*100*	*18*	*1*	*7*	*42*	*27*	*1*	*.253*	*.300*	*.356*

LANCE PAINTER / Colorado Rockies / Starting Pitcher $16

See comments on Marcus Moore and David Nied. Painter's stats last year are much better than the 6.11 ERA would suggest, and there is a possibility that his performance could dramatically improve in 1995. He is a corner Painter, not Randy Johnson, but if he can get 300 innings under his belt and stay off the DL, his career might take off.

YEAR	TEAM/LEVEL	G	IP	W-L	PCT	HITS	SO	BB	ERA
1993	Col. Sp. AAA	23	138	9-7	.563	165	91	44	4.30
1993	Colorado	10	39	2-2	.500	52	16	9	6.00
1994	Colorado	15	74	4-6	.400	91	41	26	6.11

VICENTE PALACIOS / St. Louis Cardinals / Starter/Reliever $24

Palacios led the Pacific Coast League in ERA in 1987, and bounced between Buffalo and Pittsburgh from then until 1992. He often pitched well in Pittsburgh, and generally pitched brilliantly at Buffalo, but could never establish Leyland's confidence. A shoulder injury in '92 sent him to the Mexican League, and he made the Cardinals out of spring training. He's not a bad pitcher.

YEAR	TEAM/LEVEL	G	IP	W-L	PCT	HITS	SO	BB	ERA
1992	Pittsburgh	20	53	3-2	.600	56	33	27	4.25
1993	Two Teams/Mexico	38	59	4-4	.500	47	57	40	3.94
1994	St. Louis	31	118	3-8	.273	104	95	43	4.44

DONN PALL / Chicago Cubs / Relief Pitcher $16

A veteran pitcher, good control. His "two teams" below in 1994 were the Yankees and Cubs; in 1993 they were the White Sox and Phillies. It is probably fair to say that he didn't pitch as well as his 3.69 ERA would suggest, as a) the average against him was .311, b) he allowed 43 percent of inherited runners to score, and c) the Yankees released him in July.

YEAR	TEAM/LEVEL	G	IP	W-L	SAVES	HITS	SO	BB	ERA
1992	Chicago (A)	39	73	5-2	1	79	27	27	4.93
1993	Two Teams	47	76	3-3	1	77	40	14	3.07
1994	Two Teams	28	39	1-2	0	51	23	10	3.69

ORLANDO PALMEIRO / California Angels / Outfielder $15

If the Angels are lonesome for Luis Polonia, Palmeiro has some of the same skills. He's small (155 pounds), bats left, doesn't throw well. If he ran as well as Polonia he would have a career, but he doesn't, although he can run a little. He can hit .280 in the majors, which throws him into the mix with Garret Anderson and Jim Edmonds.

YEAR	TEAM/LEVEL	G	AB	R	H	2B	3B	HR	RBI	BB	SB	AVG	OBP	SLG
1993	Midland AA	131	535	85	163	19	5	0	64	42	18	.305	.356	.359
1994	Vancouver AAA	117	458	79	150	28	4	1	47	58	21	.328	.402	.413
1994	MLE	117	432	59	124	22	2	0	35	42	13	.287	.350	.347

RAFAEL PALMEIRO / Baltimore Orioles / First Base $65

He has hit 183 doubles since 1990, the most of any major league player; he is also among the major league leaders in hits and extra base hits during the 90s. He is one of the most durable players in baseball, playing at least 95 percent of his team's games every year since 1988. . . . His son is named Patrick Ryne, after Ryne Sandberg.

YEAR	TEAM/LEVEL	G	AB	R	H	2B	3B	HR	RBI	BB	SB	AVG	OBP	SLG
1993	Texas	160	597	124	176	40	2	37	105	73	22	.295	.371	.554
1994	Baltimore	111	436	82	139	32	0	23	78	54	7	.319	.392	.550
1995	*Projected*	*160*	*611*	*103*	*172*	*36*	*3*	*25*	*92*	*77*	*12*	*.282*	*.362*	*.473*

DEAN PALMER / Texas Rangers / Third Base $32

His batting average has gone up every year since his first at bat in 1989: .105, .187, .229, .245, .246. Despite this, the Rangers are more than a little frustrated with him. He made 22 errors, the most of any major league third baseman, and started only eight double plays. His .302 on-base percentage last year was his worst in three years.

YEAR	TEAM/LEVEL	G	AB	R	H	2B	3B	HR	RBI	BB	SB	AVG	OBP	SLG
1993	Texas	148	519	88	127	31	2	33	96	53	11	.245	.321	.503
1994	Texas	93	342	50	84	14	2	19	59	26	3	.246	.302	.465
1995	*Projected*	*138*	*492*	*76*	*121*	*23*	*2*	*28*	*80*	*51*	*9*	*.246*	*.317*	*.472*

ERIK PAPPAS / St. Louis Cardinals / Catcher $13

Pappas seemed to have his career turned around last year, when he hit .276 and earned a surprising amount of playing time during Pagnozzi's injuries. An .091 batting average and a rash of unsightly defensive plays sent him back to the minors early last year, and he hit .199 at Louisville. First-round draft pick from 1984; most of his career has been a struggle.

YEAR	TEAM/LEVEL	G	AB	R	H	2B	3B	HR	RBI	BB	SB	AVG	OBP	SLG
1992	Two Teams AAA	82	236	35	57	12	1	5	28	39	8	.242	.349	.364
1993	St. Louis	82	228	25	63	12	0	1	28	35	1	.276	.368	.342
1994	St. Louis	15	44	8	4	1	0	0	5	10	0	.091	.259	.114

CRAIG PAQUETTE / Oakland Athletics / Third Base $14

Last year I wrote that he is "also known as Phil Hiatt," since their play seemed interchangeable. Well, last year they both did the same thing: They went back to the minors, and they showed real improvement. Paquette didn't improve as much as Hiatt did, but the A's are still looking for a third baseman, and he's in the picture. Grade D prospect.

YEAR	TEAM/LEVEL	G	AB	R	H	2B	3B	HR	RBI	BB	SB	AVG	OBP	SLG
1993	Oakland	105	393	35	86	20	4	12	46	14	4	.219	.245	.382
1994	MLE	65	232	30	57	9	1	12	37	10	2	.246	.277	.448
1994	Oakland	14	49	0	7	2	0	0	0	0	1	.143	.143	.184

MARK PARENT / Chicago Cubs / Catcher $19

A big, lumbering, right-handed-hitting catcher who throws very well, doesn't do anything else often enough to be a regular. He's 33, but '93 and '94 have been the two best seasons of his career. He backed up Rick Wilkins last year, but played better than Wilkins did, and by the end of the schedule was playing most of the time against left-handers.

YEAR	TEAM/LEVEL	G	AB	R	H	2B	3B	HR	RBI	BB	SB	AVG	OBP	SLG
1993	Baltimore	22	54	7	14	2	0	4	12	3	0	.259	.293	.519
1994	Chicago	44	99	8	26	4	0	3	16	13	0	.263	.348	.394
1995	*Projected*	*50*	*123*	*12*	*29*	*6*	*0*	*4*	*16*	*11*	*0*	*.236*	*.299*	*.382*

CHAN HO PARK / Los Angeles Dodgers / Right-handed Pitcher $25

He was the big whoop last spring, as the Dodgers somehow persuaded and/or bribed the South Korean government to let Park come play in the States. His fastball is impressive, about like his 1994 strikeout total (100), but he has a lot of things to work on, and Double-A seemed to be the right level for him. His story is just beginning.

YEAR	TEAM/LEVEL	G	IP	W-L	PCT	HITS	SO	BB	ERA
1993	Han Yang University—South Korea								
1994	San Antonio AA	20	101	5-7	.417	91	100	57	3.55
1994	Los Angeles	2	4	0-0	.000	5	6	5	11.25

DEREK PARKS / Minnesota Twins / Catcher $16

Had a chance to be the Twins' catcher, but Parks and Walbeck had a stink-up-the-joint contest, and I think Parks won; he stunk worse than Walbeck did. It wasn't easy. Parks is capable of playing better, but since he was a first-round draft pick in 1986 and still isn't established, this isn't the first time he has punted an opportunity, either.

YEAR	TEAM/LEVEL	G	AB	R	H	2B	3B	HR	RBI	BB	SB	AVG	OBP	SLG
1992	MLE	79	243	26	55	11	0	9	38	20	0	.226	.285	.383
1993	MLE	107	348	47	98	21	0	12	53	36	0	.282	.349	.445
1994	Minnesota	31	89	6	17	6	0	1	9	4	0	.191	.242	.292

LANCE PARRISH / Pittsburgh Pirates / Catcher $20

Released by Cleveland in May 1993, he signed a minor league contract with the Pirates, and got a major league job when Goff didn't play well. Parrish played *very* well, posting his highest batting average in nine years, the highest on-base percentage of his career. He throws better than Slaught, and the Pirates had a better ERA with Parrish catching than with Slaught.

YEAR	TEAM/LEVEL	G	AB	R	H	2B	3B	HR	RBI	BB	SB	AVG	OBP	SLG
1993	Cleveland	10	20	2	4	1	0	1	2	4	1	.200	.333	.400
1994	Pittsburgh	40	126	10	34	5	0	3	16	18	1	.270	.363	.381
1995	*Projected*	*74*	*196*	*17*	*44*	*10*	*1*	*6*	*20*	*23*	*1*	*.224*	*.306*	*.378*

DAN PASQUA / Chicago White Sox / Outfield/First Base $12

Surprisingly enough, Pasqua hasn't been released as of this writing; the White Sox are still holding him. He's hit .211, .205, and .217 the last three years, and missed most of the 1994 season following knee surgery. It is difficult to imagine that he is going to come out of this three-year slump, at age 33 and following knee surgery, as a productive player.

YEAR	TEAM/LEVEL	G	AB	R	H	2B	3B	HR	RBI	BB	SB	AVG	OBP	SLG
1992	Chicago	93	265	26	56	16	1	6	33	36	0	.211	.305	.347
1993	Chicago	78	176	22	36	10	1	5	20	26	2	.205	.302	.358
1994	Chicago	11	23	2	5	2	0	2	4	0	0	.217	.217	.565

BOB PATTERSON / California Angels / Left-Handed Spot Pitcher $19

Cut by the Rangers after the 1993 season, he had to go to spring training and earn a job with the Angels. He did, and pitched reasonably well, holding both left-handers and right-handers to a batting average of .229. Standard repertoire, best pitch is probably a slow curve . . . he has never been charged with an error in the major leagues.

YEAR	TEAM/LEVEL	G	IP	W-L	SAVES	HITS	SO	BB	ERA
1992	Pittsburgh	60	65	6-3	9	59	43	23	2.92
1993	Texas	52	53	2-4	1	59	46	11	4.78
1994	California	47	42	2-3	1	35	30	15	4.07

JOHN PATTERSON / San Francisco Giants / Second Base $20

He was one of the key reasons for the Giants' disappointing season. With Robbie Thompson out Patterson platooned at second base with Steve Scarsone. He played well defensively (for a converted outfielder coming off a serious knee injury), but didn't hit much . . . a switch hitter in theory, but has career average of .156 batting right-handed. He may have better years.

YEAR	TEAM/LEVEL	G	AB	R	H	2B	3B	HR	RBI	BB	SB	AVG	OBP	SLG
1993	San Francisco	16	16	1	3	0	0	1	2	0	0	.188	.188	.375
1994	San Francisco	85	240	36	57	10	1	3	32	16	13	.237	.315	.325
1995	*Projected*	*96*	*294*	*35*	*72*	*16*	*3*	*3*	*32*	*18*	*11*	*.245*	*.288*	*.350*

ROGER PAVLIK / Texas Rangers / Starting Pitcher $19

Those dreaded words: partially torn rotator cuff. Pavlik, like a lot of pitchers, would be headed to Cooperstown if he could just stay off the disabled list. He was seen, going into 1994, as the Rangers' number-two starter, but had more trips to the DL (three) than wins (two). He'll probably never be the same, and if he is it won't be this year.

YEAR	TEAM/LEVEL	G	IP	W-L	PCT	HITS	SO	BB	ERA
1992	Texas	13	62	4-4	.500	66	45	34	4.21
1993	Texas	26	166	12-6	.667	151	131	80	3.41
1994	Texas	11	50	2-5	.286	61	31	30	7.69

BILL PECOTA / Atlanta Braves / Utility Player $16

A utility infielder, but played almost entirely at third base, while Pendleton was hurt. He's an outstanding third baseman, but his .214 average is a) not what you're looking for at that position, and b) closer to his true ability than the .323 average of 1993. Probably will keep his job with Atlanta. Probably will get the same job somewhere else if he doesn't.

YEAR	TEAM/LEVEL	G	AB	R	H	2B	3B	HR	RBI	BB	SB	AVG	OBP	SLG
1992	New York (N)	117	269	28	61	13	0	2	26	25	9	.227	.293	.297
1993	Atlanta	72	62	17	20	2	1	0	5	2	1	.323	.344	.387
1994	Atlanta	64	112	11	24	5	0	2	16	16	1	.214	.310	.313

STEVE PEGUES / Pittsburgh Pirates / Outfield $14

Is 27 years old, strong, fast. A second-round draft pick of the Tigers (1987), he was a top prospect until he separated his shoulder. He's gone from Detroit to the Padres to the Reds to the Pirates, the latter being the "two teams" below. He's a good outfielder and a .280 hitter, but he walks as often as Rush Limbaugh gives money to a Democrat.

YEAR	TEAM/LEVEL	G	AB	R	H	2B	3B	HR	RBI	BB	SB	AVG	OBP	SLG
1993	MLE	68	249	33	74	15	2	6	32	4	7	.297	.308	.446
1994	MLE	63	237	30	63	14	7	5	24	5	7	.266	.281	.447
1994	Two Teams	18	36	2	13	2	0	0	2	2	1	.361	.395	.417

RUDY PEMBERTON / Detroit Tigers / Outfield $15

A 26-year-old Dominican, could be loosely described as being in the Eric Davis mold—a right-handed-hitting outfielder who steals some bases, hits some homers, strikes out quite a bit, and has been known to get hurt. He doesn't do any of those four things nearly as often as Eric Davis does. *Nothing* is being written about him, but he can play.

YEAR	TEAM/LEVEL	G	AB	R	H	2B	3B	HR	RBI	BB	SB	AVG	OBP	SLG
1993	London AA	124	471	70	130	22	4	15	67	24	14	.276	.325	.435
1994	Toledo AAA	99	360	49	109	13	3	12	58	18	30	.303	.341	.456
1994	MLE	99	355	48	104	11	2	12	57	18	24	.293	.327	.437

ALEJANDRO PENA / Released / Relief Pitcher $12

How many roads must a man walk down/Before they call him a man? And how many chances/Does Alejandro get/Before he is forever canned? . . . Sorry; my '60s are showing there. Pena re-injured his elbow last June, and the Pirates released him. But if he can lob the ball to home plate, he'll probably find somebody to pay his salary.

YEAR	TEAM/LEVEL	G	IP	W-L	SAVES	HITS	SO	BB	ERA
1992	Atlanta	41	42	1-6	15	40	34	13	4.07
1993	Pittsburgh				(On Disabled List)				
1994	Pittsburgh	22	29	3-2	7	22	27	10	5.02

GERONIMO PEÑA / St. Louis Cardinals / Second Base $26

Switch hitter, he decided to hit right-handed in '94. This didn't work at all, and he was hitting .172 by the end of May. He went back to switch hitting, hit the snot out of the ball for two months, and seemed finally to have claimed the Cardinals' second base job, about August 1. So John Wetteland broke his arm with a fastball, and . . .

YEAR	TEAM/LEVEL	G	AB	R	H	2B	3B	HR	RBI	BB	SB	AVG	OBP	SLG
1993	St. Louis	74	254	34	65	19	2	5	30	25	13	.256	.330	.406
1994	St. Louis	83	213	33	54	13	1	11	34	24	9	.254	.344	.479
1995	*Projected*	*101*	*305*	*43*	*80*	*17*	*2*	*9*	*39*	*34*	*16*	*.262*	*.336*	*.420*

TONY PEÑA / Cleveland Indians / Catcher $18

Like Lance Parrish, he gave a convincing imitation of a dead mackerel when he was trying to stay in the lineup in '92 and '93, but played extremely well in '94, cut back to 40 games. His .295 batting average was his best since 1983; his .438 slugging percentage, believe it or not, was a career high. Is 38 years old, extremely well liked.

YEAR	TEAM/LEVEL	G	AB	R	H	2B	3B	HR	RBI	BB	SB	AVG	OBP	SLG
1993	Boston	126	304	20	55	11	0	4	19	25	1	.181	.246	.257
1994	Cleveland	40	112	18	33	8	1	2	10	9	0	.295	.341	.438
1995	*Projected*	*58*	*143*	*13*	*34*	*5*	*0*	*2*	*12*	*10*	*1*	*.238*	*.288*	*.315*

TERRY PENDLETON / Atlanta Braves / Third Base $26

His contract ran out with the 1994 season, and he will not return to Atlanta in '95. He is 34 years old, he looks overweight, and he is coming off a lousy season. On the other hand, he was *such* a good player, from '91 to '93, that it's hard to believe he doesn't have anything left. My guess is he'll be somebody's third baseman in '95.

YEAR	TEAM/LEVEL	G	AB	R	H	2B	3B	HR	RBI	BB	SB	AVG	OBP	SLG
1993	Atlanta	161	633	81	172	33	1	17	84	36	5	.272	.311	.408
1994	Atlanta	77	309	25	78	18	3	7	30	12	2	.252	.280	.398
1995	*Projected*	*144*	*570*	*65*	*149*	*27*	*2*	*13*	*68*	*30*	*4*	*.261*	*.298*	*.384*

BRAD PENNINGTON / Baltimore Orioles / Relief Pitcher $14

The Steve Dalkowski of the '90s, a man whose fastball explodes, but usually not close enough to the strike zone for anybody to get hurt when it does. I wrote last year that *"eventually* Pennington may be good, but eventually might be five or seven years away.'' The only thing that has changed is that now it's four to six years.

YEAR	TEAM/LEVEL	G	IP	W-L	SAVES	HITS	SO	BB	ERA
1993	Baltimore	34	33	3-2	4	34	39	25	6.55
1994	Rochester AAA	35	86	6-8	3	68	89	74	5.32
1994	Baltimore	8	6	0-1	0	9	7	8	12.00

EDUARDO PEREZ / California Angels / First Base $25

Started 1994 as the Angels' first baseman, but was sent to Vancouver in June. His father (Tony) was a third baseman who had to move to first; so is the son. His father came up at the same age, and wasn't impressive for two seasons, but drove in 102 runs at age 25. Eduardo is 25. He won't be as good as his father, but he might be good enough.

YEAR	TEAM/LEVEL	G	AB	R	H	2B	3B	HR	RBI	BB	SB	AVG	OBP	SLG
1993	MLE	96	342	46	90	17	2	9	49	19	12	.263	.302	.404
1993	California	52	180	16	45	6	2	4	30	9	5	.250	.292	.372
1994	California	38	129	10	27	7	0	5	16	12	3	.209	.275	.380

MELIDO PEREZ / New York Yankees / Starting Pitcher $33

The only thing that was different about him, in the statistics, is that he was much better with runners in scoring position. The rest of his stats—his strikeouts, walks, home runs allowed, performance with no one on base—that was all about the same. He threw his wild pitches. But he cut his batting average, with runners in scoring position, from .347 to .269.

YEAR	TEAM/LEVEL	G	IP	W-L	PCT	HITS	SO	BB	ERA
1992	New York	33	248	13-16	.448	212	218	93	2.87
1993	New York	25	163	6-14	.300	173	148	64	5.19
1994	New York	22	151	9-4	.692	134	109	58	4.10

MIKE PEREZ / St. Louis Cardinals / Relief Pitcher $25

In 1992 he pitched 77 times with a 1.84 ERA, and had *no* saves. Last year he pitched 36 times with an 8.71 ERA, but had 12 saves. . . . He pitched very well in April (six saves in six chances, 1.29 ERA), but strained his shoulder in early May, and . . . well, the word "ineffective" seems grossly inadequate. Thirty percent chance of a comeback in '95.

YEAR	TEAM/LEVEL	G	IP	W-L	SAVES	HITS	SO	BB	ERA
1992	St. Louis	77	93	9-3	0	70	46	32	1.84
1993	St. Louis	65	73	7-2	7	65	58	20	2.48
1994	St. Louis	36	31	2-3	12	52	20	10	8.71

ROBERTO PEREZ / Toronto Blue Jays / Left Field $15

Also played four games with Toronto, not shown below . . . in another organization, Perez might be a prized prospect. His physical tools are impressive, and he'll hit .280. Strong, but hasn't hit a lot of homers; fast, but not a base stealer. Never walks. He would have to beat back Delgado and Shawn Green to play regularly in '95, and that's unlikely. Grade C prospect.

YEAR	TEAM/LEVEL	G	AB	R	H	2B	3B	HR	RBI	BB	SB	AVG	OBP	SLG
1993	MLE	138	513	62	143	25	8	11	55	20	10	.279	.306	.423
1994	Syracuse AAA	128	510	63	155	28	3	10	65	27	4	.304	.336	.429
1994	MLE	128	498	55	143	27	2	9	57	23	3	.287	.319	.404

YORKIS PEREZ / Florida Marlins / Lefty Reliever $21

Dominican, signed by the Twins at age 15 (1983). He wasn't ready to pitch by the time he ran out of options, so he has searched for the strike zone in the Montreal system, Braves system, with the Cubs, in Japan, with the Expos again, and finally with the Marlins. He finally found it, and is now a reasonably valuable property. Throws hard, good slider.

YEAR	TEAM/LEVEL	G	IP	W-L	SAVES	HITS	SO	BB	ERA
1993	Harrisburg AA	34	44	4-2	3	49	58	20	3.45
1993	Ottawa AAA	20	20	0-1	5	14	17	7	3.60
1994	Florida	44	41	3-0	0	33	41	14	3.54

GERALD PERRY / St. Louis Cardinals / Pinch Hitter $18

He was 12-for-40 as a pinch hitter. He has had two terrific seasons as a pinch hitter, and you wouldn't believe how rare that is in the history of baseball. As a regular he was weak against left-handed pitchers, but in his current role he rarely sees one. I give Joe Torre credit for finding a way to get something out of him.

YEAR	TEAM/LEVEL	G	AB	R	H	2B	3B	HR	RBI	BB	SB	AVG	OBP	SLG
1992	St. Louis	87	143	13	34	8	0	1	18	15	3	.238	.311	.315
1993	St. Louis	96	98	21	33	5	0	4	16	18	1	.337	.440	.510
1994	St. Louis	60	77	15	25	7	0	3	18	15	1	.325	.435	.532

HERB PERRY / Cleveland Indians / Third Base/First Base $20

Played quarterback at the University of Florida. Has potential as a hitter for both power and average and runs pretty well. Hard-nosed, crowds the plate, and gets hit by pitches 10 times a year. He also has a chronically sore shoulder which limits his defense. He can hit, but may end up like Jeff Manto or Russ Morman, without a position. Grade B prospect.

YEAR	TEAM/LEVEL	G	AB	R	H	2B	3B	HR	RBI	BB	SB	AVG	OBP	SLG
1993	MLE	89	316	42	77	18	0	7	44	25	4	.244	.299	.367
1994	Charlotte	102	376	67	123	20	4	13	70	41	9	.327	.397	.505
1994	MLE	102	365	58	112	19	2	11	60	35	6	.307	.369	.460

ROBERTO PETAGINE / Houston Astros / First Base $22

Petagine had a great year at Jackson in '93, but broke a bone in his wrist last year, when he cued a shot off the end of his bat (the vibration in the bat broke the bone).

He didn't play as well when he returned. Left-handed hitter, 24 years old; a terrific prospect but Lord knows when he'll get to play, with Bagwell ahead of him.

YEAR	TEAM/LEVEL	G	AB	R	H	2B	3B	HR	RBI	BB	SB	AVG	OBP	SLG
1993	MLE	128	417	59	126	32	1	10	72	57	4	.302	.386	.456
1994	Tucson AAA	65	247	53	78	19	0	10	44	35	3	.316	.399	.514
1994	MLE	65	229	34	60	15	0	5	28	22	1	.262	.327	.393

J. R. PHILLIPS / San Francisco Giants / First Base $23

Phillips was expected to step into Will Clark's shoes last year, which wouldn't have been easy if he was a *good* player. He did have a better year at Phoenix (.300, 27

homers in 95 games), and the Giants didn't find a first baseman during the season, so he may be able to hold the job in '95. Low average, power hitter.

YEAR	TEAM/LEVEL	G	AB	R	H	2B	3B	HR	RBI	BB	SB	AVG	OBP	SLG
1994	MLE	95	338	47	86	23	2	18	54	30	2	.254	.315	.494
1994	San Francisco	15	38	1	5	0	0	1	3	1	1	.132	.150	.211
1995	*Projected*	*112*	*386*	*45*	*91*	*23*	*2*	*15*	*55*	*26*	*3*	*.236*	*.284*	*.422*

TONY PHILLIPS / Detroit Tigers / Utilityman $60

With Gomez, Trammell, Fryman, and Whitaker rotating around the infield he played mostly left field in '94. Let's see . . . he's a switch hitter who hits for a pretty good average, runs well, walks 100 times a year, has

some power, and plays five defensive positions very well. He's 36, but he's one of the best players in baseball. He'll score 110 runs again this year.

YEAR	TEAM/LEVEL	G	AB	R	H	2B	3B	HR	RBI	BB	SB	AVG	OBP	SLG
1993	Detroit	151	566	113	177	27	0	7	57	132	16	.313	.443	.398
1994	Detroit	114	438	91	123	19	3	19	61	95	13	.281	.409	.468
1995	*Projected*	*147*	*553*	*110*	*141*	*22*	*2*	*10*	*53*	*121*	*14*	*.255*	*.389*	*.356*

STEVE PHOENIX / Oakland A's / Reliever $19

An undrafted free agent from Grand Canyon University, Phoenix has a fastball in the low- to mid-80s. He changes speeds well, throws strikes, has an OK slider and a very good split-finger fastball. He has pitched

well enough at every level of the minors to keep moving up, and last year moved into the closer role, where he was enormously effective. Grade B prospect.

YEAR	TEAM/LEVEL	G	IP	W-L	SAVES	HITS	SO	BB	ERA
1993	AA and AAA	22	50	2-4	1	55	36	32	4.83
1994	Huntsville AA	38	49	0-2	20	42	40	16	1.29
1994	Tacoma AAA	20	22	6-2	9	16	16	4	1.23

MIKE PIAZZA / Los Angeles Dodgers / Catcher | $84

What would *prevent* Mike Piazza from becoming a Hall of Famer? Why would that not happen? A) Injuries. (Can always happen, particularly to a catcher.) B) An abuse syndrome. (Doesn't seem likely.) C) Just stops hitting. (Can't see it.) D) His game develops a fatal defect. (He's slow now and will get slower, but so what?) E) If his career is too short. (Could happen.)

YEAR	TEAM/LEVEL	G	AB	R	H	2B	3B	HR	RBI	BB	SB	AVG	OBP	SLG
1993	Los Angeles	149	547	81	174	24	2	35	112	46	3	.318	.370	.561
1994	Los Angeles	107	405	64	129	18	0	24	92	33	1	.319	.370	.541
1995	*Projected*	*152*	*550*	*77*	*175*	*28*	*1*	*30*	*107*	*47*	*2*	*.318*	*.372*	*.536*

HIPOLITO PICHARDO / Kansas City Royals / Starting Pitcher | $25

He may benefit from working with the Royals' new manager, Bob Boone. There are two things standing between Pichardo and major league success: the lack of a good breaking pitch, and the lack of a regular work schedule. In his career he is 16-12 as a starting pitcher, 3.98 ERA, but has 4.86 ERA as a reliever.

YEAR	TEAM/LEVEL	G	IP	W-L	PCT	HITS	SO	BB	ERA
1992	Kansas City	31	144	9-6	.600	148	59	49	3.95
1993	Kansas City	30	165	7-8	.467	183	70	53	4.04
1994	Kansas City	45	68	5-3	.625	82	36	24	4.92

GREG PIRKL / Seattle Mariners / Designated Hitter/First Base | $15

A huge converted catcher; they list him at 240 pounds, but I'm not sure whether they are weighing the piano. He was in the majors for a few games last May and June and hit six homers, but got sent back down anyway (I guess Piniella didn't like his defense at DH). Right-handed hitter, slow, low OBP, will have major league career.

YEAR	TEAM/LEVEL	G	AB	R	H	2B	3B	HR	RBI	BB	SB	AVG	OBP	SLG
1994	Calgary AAA	87	353	69	112	21	0	22	72	24	1	.317	.367	.564
1994	MLE	87	328	44	87	18	0	13	46	15	0	.265	.297	.439
1994	Seattle	19	53	7	14	3	0	6	11	1	0	.264	.286	.660

ERIK PLANTENBERG / Seattle Mariners / Left-handed Relief Pitcher | $12

Lefty taken from the Red Sox system in the Rule 5 draft. He has worked mostly as a starting pitcher in the minors, exclusively as a reliever in the majors. Not big, doesn't throw real hard, doesn't have particularly good control. Best minor league season was 1991, 11-5 at Lynchburg, but had elbow problems in 1992. Grade D prospect.

YEAR	TEAM/LEVEL	G	IP	W-L	SAVES	HITS	SO	BB	ERA
1993	Seattle	20	10	0-0	1	11	3	12	6.52
1994	Calgary AAA	19	102	6-7	0	122	69	62	5.84
1994	Seattle	6	7	0-0	0	4	1	7	0.00

PHIL PLANTIER / San Diego Padres / Left Field $27

A year ago I wrote that his batting average against left-handed pitchers, .185, was the lowest of any (1993) NL regular. Last year it went *down*, to .152. He does have an odd batting stance, and you can see how it could interfere with his ability to hit a left-hander. He is still young, but he doesn't have young player's skills.

YEAR	TEAM/LEVEL	G	AB	R	H	2B	3B	HR	RBI	BB	SB	AVG	OBP	SLG
1993	San Diego	138	462	67	111	20	1	34	100	61	4	.240	.335	.509
1994	San Diego	96	341	44	75	21	0	18	41	36	3	.220	.302	.440
1995	*Projected*	*135*	*440*	*64*	*114*	*22*	*1*	*25*	*71*	*58*	*4*	*.259*	*.345*	*.484*

DAN PLESAC / Chicago Cubs / Relief Pitcher $19

Left-handed reliever, outstanding control, gets ground balls, very tough on left-handed hitters. He still throws hard, but his fastball is straight, and he gives up home-runs. He gets hit hard when he is behind in the count, and he is not effective when he works a lot; he's more effective with a day or two off between appearances.

YEAR	TEAM/LEVEL	G	IP	W-L	SAVES	HITS	SO	BB	ERA
1992	Milwaukee	44	79	5-4	1	64	54	35	2.96
1993	Chicago	57	63	2-1	0	74	47	21	4.74
1994	Chicago	54	55	2-3	1	61	53	13	4.61

ERIC PLUNK / Cleveland Indians / Middle Relief $27

Has pitched well for two years in the Indians' bullpen. He's always been a decent pitcher—posted ERAs of 3.28 or better in five of the last seven seasons, and 3.64 is not exactly Jim DeShaies territory. In his career he has almost one strikeout per inning, more strikeouts than hits. Still, he has moved around, making periodic trips to the minors.

YEAR	TEAM/LEVEL	G	IP	W-L	SAVES	HITS	SO	BB	ERA
1992	Cleveland	58	72	9-6	4	61	50	38	3.64
1993	Cleveland	70	71	4-5	15	61	77	30	2.79
1994	Cleveland	41	71	7-2	3	61	73	37	2.54

LUIS POLONIA / New York Yankees / Left Field $29

Hit .300 for the first time in four years; his lifetime average is still .295. He established career highs in both on-base percentage (.383) and slugging percentage (.414). The Yankees platooned him, which makes sense because he's always hit 80 points better against right-handers. Not as fast as he once was; never was a good outfielder, but a quality leadoff hitter.

YEAR	TEAM/LEVEL	G	AB	R	H	2B	3B	HR	RBI	BB	SB	AVG	OBP	SLG
1993	California	152	576	75	156	17	6	1	32	48	55	.271	.328	.326
1994	New York	95	350	62	109	21	6	1	36	37	20	.311	.383	.414
1995	*Projected*	*142*	*540*	*83*	*156*	*19*	*7*	*2*	*42*	*46*	*46*	*.289*	*.347*	*.361*

JIM POOLE / Baltimore Orioles / Relief Pitcher $16

As terrific as he was in 1993, that's how bad he was in '94. He was called in to face left-handers, and left-handers hit .421 against him (16-for-38), plus of course there are an ocean of candidates for the role that he plays (left-handed reliever). I've always liked him, but wouldn't bet on him to keep his job.

YEAR	TEAM/LEVEL	G	IP	W-L	SAVES	HITS	SO	BB	ERA
1992	Baltimore	6	3	0-0	0	3	3	1	0.00
1993	Baltimore	55	50	2-1	2	30	29	21	2.15
1994	Baltimore	38	20	1-0	0	32	18	11	6.64

MARK PORTUGAL / San Francisco Giants / Starting Pitcher $34

He did what the Giants could have expected. He won more than he lost. There is nothing remarkable about Portugal, but he mixes his pitches well, and has had 100 decisions in the last six years, winning 62 of them. Over the last five years has 37-16 record, 2.74 ERA on artificial turf, but 18-21, 4.66 on grass fields.

YEAR	TEAM/LEVEL	G	IP	W-L	PCT	HITS	SO	BB	ERA
1992	Houston	18	101	6-3	.667	76	62	41	2.66
1993	Houston	33	208	18-4	.812	194	131	77	2.77
1994	San Francisco	21	137	10-8	.555	135	87	45	3.93

PORK CHOP POUGH / Cleveland Indians / Outfielder $14

A cousin of Tom Gordon, Royals' starter, he was on Cleveland's 40-man roster three years ago, but dropped off after failing to master Double-A. He's a good fastball hitter, but it threw him when they started tossing him junk; he'd chase it and get himself out. He's back now and looking good. He's 25 years old; the Indians have no place to play him.

YEAR	TEAM/LEVEL	G	AB	R	H	2B	3B	HR	RBI	BB	SB	AVG	OBP	SLG
1993	Kinston A	120	418	66	113	18	1	13	57	59	8	.270	.364	.411
1994	Canton AA	105	379	69	113	24	3	20	66	43	3	.298	.372	.536
1994	MLE	121	411	60	112	26	2	18	60	37	2	.273	.333	.477

ROSS POWELL / Houston Astros / Left-handed Pitcher $14

His minor league record isn't very good, either for 1994 or for any other year, but he has pitched well enough in his major league trials that he will probably be back in the majors this year. He's usually been a starting pitcher in the minors (career record, 46-48), and has been vulnerable to the long ball. Grade D prospect.

YEAR	TEAM/LEVEL	G	IP	W-L	PCT	HITS	SO	BB	ERA
1993	Cincinnati	9	16	0-3	.000	13	17	6	4.41
1994	Two Teams AAA	20	77	5-3	.625	97	56	38	6.05
1994	Houston	12	7	0-0	.000	6	5	5	1.23

TODD PRATT / Philadelphia Phillies / Catcher $19

Looking at his stats, my first assumption was that he didn't hit while Daulton was out. Actually, though, Pratt hit pretty well at that time; he just hardly had a hit the rest of the season, when he was a bench player. One-way catcher from the Red Sox system, didn't start to hit until it was too late for him to become a regular.

YEAR	TEAM/LEVEL	G	AB	R	H	2B	3B	HR	RBI	BB	SB	AVG	OBP	SLG
1993	Philadelphia	33	87	8	25	6	0	5	13	5	0	.287	.330	.529
1994	Philadelphia	28	102	10	20	6	1	2	9	12	0	.196	.281	.333
1995	*Projected*	67	186	22	49	11	0	6	27	25	0	.263	.351	.419

TOM PRINCE / Los Angeles Dodgers / Backup Catcher $13

Released by Pittsburgh after the 1993 season, he signed with the Dodgers, and was in the majors for three games in April. He has played 180 major league games with a batting average of .179, which is awfully good evidence that he'll never hit, but he did have an interesting year at Albuquerque. He hit .285, and 56 percent of his hits were for extra bases.

YEAR	TEAM/LEVEL	G	AB	R	H	2B	3B	HR	RBI	BB	SB	AVG	OBP	SLG
1993	Pittsburgh	66	179	14	35	14	0	2	24	13	1	.196	.272	.307
1994	Albuquerque AAA	103	330	61	94	31	2	20	54	51	2	.285	.396	.573
1994	MLE	103	305	36	69	21	0	11	32	30	1	.226	.296	.403

KIRBY PUCKETT / Minnesota Twins / Right Field $75

We should note that Kirby, despite his peculiar build, has been durable and has conceded very little to age (he is now 34). It was often written, when he was young, that his body type would slow him down by the time he was 30 . . . now has the Twins' record for career hits, and still has a chance to get 3000 before the year 2000.

YEAR	TEAM/LEVEL	G	AB	R	H	2B	3B	HR	RBI	BB	SB	AVG	OBP	SLG
1993	Minnesota	156	622	89	184	39	3	22	89	47	8	.296	.349	.474
1994	Minnesota	108	439	79	139	32	3	20	112	28	6	.317	.362	.540
1995	*Projected*	151	603	87	181	34	3	18	101	42	10	.300	.346	.456

TIM PUGH / Cincinnati Reds / Starting Pitcher $14

Was sent to Indianapolis on May 31, and may have been hurt, as he made only seven starts after being demoted. He didn't pitch very well—in fact, now that you mention it, he hasn't pitched very well anywhere in years, since he got to Double-A. I'm not sure why the Reds put him in their rotation. His next shot will be in middle relief.

YEAR	TEAM/LEVEL	G	IP	W-L	PCT	HITS	SO	BB	ERA
1992	Cincinnati	7	45	4-2	.667	47	18	13	2.58
1993	Cincinnati	31	164	10-15	.400	200	94	59	5.26
1994	Cincinnati	10	48	3-3	.500	60	24	26	6.04

CARLOS PULIDO / Minnesota Twins / Starter/Reliever $15

Little Venezuelan left-hander, listed at 6-0, 180, but looks smaller. No one thought he was a prospect until he went 11-1, 2.24 in the Venezuelan Winter League. He followed that with a solid spring training and made the team. Below-average fastball, average slider, pretty good screwball. Pitched very poorly as a starter (6.68 ERA) but better as a reliever (2.87).

YEAR	TEAM/LEVEL	G	IP	W-L	PCT	HITS	SO	BB	ERA
1992	Orlando AA	52	100	6-2	.750	99	87	37	4.40
1993	Portland AAA	33	146	10-6	.625	169	79	45	4.19
1994	Minnesota	19	84	3-7	.300	87	32	40	5.98

BILL PULSIPHER / New York Mets / Starting Pitcher $28

A hard-throwing left-hander, the Mets' second-round draft pick in 1991. His fastball is in the mid-90s with outstanding movement, plus he has a good curve and a deceptive delivery. He has pitched well everywhere since he signed, and is unquestionably a **Grade A prospect.** The odds are that he'll hurt his arm, but if he doesn't, he'll be outstanding.

YEAR	TEAM/LEVEL	G	IP	W-L	PCT	HITS	SO	BB	ERA
1993	Capital City A	6	43	2-3	.400	34	29	12	2.08
1993	St. Lucie A	13	96	7-3	.700	63	102	39	2.24
1994	Binghamton AA	28	201	14-9	.609	179	171	89	3.22

EDDIE PYE / Los Angeles Dodgers / Infielder $15

Got his first 10 major league at bats last summer; had been at Albuquerque since 1991, hitting .433 (13-for-30), .302, .329, and .335. He could hit .270 in the majors, although not with enough power, speed, or defense to force his way into the lineup. A right-handed hitter from Tennessee, 27 years old; best position is second base.

YEAR	TEAM/LEVEL	G	AB	R	H	2B	3B	HR	RBI	BB	SB	AVG	OBP	SLG
1993	Albuquerque AAA	101	365	53	120	21	7	7	66	32	5	.329	.391	.482
1994	Albuquerque AAA	100	361	79	121	19	6	2	42	48	11	.335	.419	.438
1994	MLE	100	330	47	90	13	2	1	25	28	6	.273	.330	.333

PAUL QUANTRILL / Philadelphia Phillies / Right-handed Pitcher $19

He hasn't been able to get established in the majors, but there's a lot to like here. Good arm; throws hard slider and a sinking fastball. Has exceptional control. Keeps hitters back off the plate. Likes to throw every day; doesn't mind starting or relief, or both. He needs a strikeout pitch, and he needs regular work.

YEAR	TEAM/LEVEL	G	IP	W-L	SAVES	HITS	SO	BB	ERA
1992	Boston	27	49	2-3	1	55	24	15	2.19
1993	Boston	49	138	6-12	1	151	66	44	3.91
1994	Bos. & Phil.	35	53	3-3	1	64	28	15	4.92

TOM QUINLAN / Philadelphia Phillies / Third Base $14

Acquired from the Toronto organization. Quinlan would like Kim Batiste's job, an assignment which, as I understand it, involves striking out a lot and making crucial errors. As a hitter, he's probably about a match for Batiste—a .200 hitter with a little power, never walks, will strike out even more than Batiste. As a third baseman, he'd *have* to be an improvement.

YEAR	TEAM/LEVEL	G	AB	R	H	2B	3B	HR	RBI	BB	SB	AVG	OBP	SLG
1993	Syracuse AAA	141	461	63	109	20	5	16	53	56	6	.236	.339	.406
1994	Scranton AAA	76	262	38	63	12	2	9	23	28	4	.240	.322	.405
1994	Philadelphia	24	35	6	7	2	0	1	3	3	0	.200	.263	.343

SCOTT RADINSKY / Chicago White Sox / Relief Pitcher $28

Radinsky missed the 1994 season after being diagnosed with Hodgkin's disease, which is a form of lymphatic cancer. The disease was detected early, and at last report Radinsky was doing well, and is expected to be ready to pitch by spring training. Radinsky has (or had) a tremendous arm, but was getting mixed results. If he's 100 percent, he remains a potential closer.

YEAR	TEAM/LEVEL	G	IP	W-L	SAVES	HITS	SO	BB	ERA
1992	Chicago	68	59	3-7	15	54	48	34	2.73
1993	Chicago	73	55	8-2	4	61	44	19	4.28
1994	Chicago			(Out with Hodgkin's Disease)					

BRAD RADKE / Minnesota Twins / Starting Pitcher $18

An eighth-round draft pick in 1991; nobody thinks he's a prospect, and nothing is written about him in the papers, because his best fastball is only about 85. He has, however, been getting people out all along the line with a curve and change, and he's now 22 and at Triple-A. If he pitches well there, he'll receive a look late in the season.

YEAR	TEAM/LEVEL	G	IP	W-L	PCT	HITS	SO	BB	ERA
1993	Fort Myers A	14	92	3-5	.375	85	69	21	3.82
1993	Nashville AA	13	76	2-6	.250	81	76	16	4.62
1994	Nashville AA	29	186	12-9	.571	167	123	34	2.66

TIM RAINES / Chicago White Sox / Left Field $46

Raines is one of the five best leadoff men in the history of baseball, but has received little credit for this because his career runs parallel to that of the greatest leadoff man ever, Rickey Henderson. He is now 35 years old, but would have scored 110 runs last year if the season had run its course. Intelligent, well-liked by his teammates.

YEAR	TEAM/LEVEL	G	AB	R	H	2B	3B	HR	RBI	BB	SB	AVG	OBP	SLG
1993	Chicago	115	415	75	127	16	4	16	54	64	21	.306	.401	.480
1994	Chicago	101	364	80	102	15	5	10	52	61	13	.266	.365	.409
1995	*Projected*	*132*	*489*	*89*	*137*	*23*	*5*	*9*	*54*	*74*	*26*	*.280*	*.375*	*.403*

MANNY RAMIREZ / Cleveland Indians / Right Field $65

History shows us that there is at least one and normally are two rookies in every crop who will wind up in Cooperstown. My bets from the 1994 rookies: Manny Ramirez and Ryan Klesko. Manny had a terrible slump last May, hitting .132, but hit .300 or better in every other month, hit .361 against left-handers, and played surprisingly well in right field.

YEAR	TEAM/LEVEL	G	AB	R	H	2B	3B	HR	RBI	BB	SB	AVG	OBP	SLG
1993	Cleveland	22	53	5	9	1	0	2	5	2	0	.170	.200	.302
1994	Cleveland	91	290	51	78	22	0	17	60	42	4	.269	.357	.521
1995	*Projected*	*152*	*555*	*100*	*164*	*44*	*1*	*36*	*111*	*69*	*4*	*.295*	*.373*	*.573*

PAT RAPP / Florida Marlins / Pitcher $27

Rapp has never pitched badly anywhere since he signed with the Giants in 1989, and is near the point at which the money will start coming in. He didn't pitch badly last year, but he didn't pitch as well as he might have. He had big trouble getting out left-handers, and began walking them to avoid getting hit. He needs to make an adjustment.

YEAR	TEAM/LEVEL	G	IP	W-L	PCT	HITS	SO	BB	ERA
1993	Edmonton AAA	17	108	8-3	.727	89	93	34	3.43
1993	Florida	16	94	4-6	.400	101	57	39	4.02
1994	Florida	24	133	7-8	.467	132	75	69	3.85

LUIS (QUOTH THE) RAVEN / California Angels / Third Base $13

A 26-year-old Venezuelan, signed as a free agent in 1988. A year ago he was no prospect, but he hit 31 homers and drove in 116 runs, and even though it was a lively ball season and he was playing in places where the home runs fly, this draws some attention. Has played mostly first; Angels are trying him at third. Grade D prospect.

YEAR	TEAM/LEVEL	G	AB	R	H	2B	3B	HR	RBI	BB	SB	AVG	OBP	SLG
1994	Midland AA	47	191	41	58	8	5	18	57	5	4	.304	.327	.681
1994	Vancouver AAA	85	328	66	100	13	4	13	59	22	7	.305	.344	.488
1994	MLE	132	492	78	131	16	4	23	84	18	6	.266	.292	.455

RANDY READY / Philadelphia Phillies / Utilityman $16

He spent the first half of the year at Ottawa (Expos system) but was cut by them after hitting .205. Signed by the Phillies, he played second base against left-handed pitchers, and played well, perhaps well enough to extend his career another season. He's not exactly Bill Mazeroski, but he can hit lefties.

YEAR	TEAM/LEVEL	G	AB	R	H	2B	3B	HR	RBI	BB	SB	AVG	OBP	SLG
1992	Oakland	61	125	17	25	2	0	3	17	25	1	.200	.329	.288
1993	Montreal	40	134	22	34	8	1	1	10	23	2	.254	.367	.351
1994	Philadelphia	17	42	5	16	1	0	1	3	8	0	.381	.480	.476

JEFF REBOULET / Minnesota Twins / Utility Infielder $19

Right-handed hitter, not fast, a good defensive shortstop who is used by the Twins at short and third, and a little bit here and there. Attended the same junior college as Kirby Puckett, then went to LSU, where he was a teammate of Mark Guthrie. In the minors (1986-92) he didn't look like he would hit, but he has so far.

YEAR	TEAM/LEVEL	G	AB	R	H	2B	3B	HR	RBI	BB	SB	AVG	OBP	SLG
1993	Minnesota	109	240	33	62	8	0	1	15	35	5	.258	.356	.304
1994	Minnesota	74	189	28	49	11	1	3	23	18	0	.259	.327	.376
1995	*Projected*	*107*	*241*	*30*	*57*	*14*	*1*	*2*	*22*	*35*	*3*	*.237*	*.333*	*.328*

GARY REDUS / Texas Rangers / First Base/Outfield $12

Redus is 38 years old, and missed most of the 1994 season with a pulled hamstring and bone chips in his elbow. The manager who brought him to Texas, Kevin Kennedy, has been fired, and the general manager as well. This is not a propitious situation, but Redus remains a player who can get on base and score runs. No defense.

YEAR	TEAM/LEVEL	G	AB	R	H	2B	3B	HR	RBI	BB	SB	AVG	OBP	SLG
1992	Pittsburgh	76	176	26	45	7	3	3	12	17	11	.256	.321	.381
1993	Texas	77	222	28	64	12	4	6	31	23	4	.288	.351	.459
1994	Texas	18	33	2	9	1	0	0	2	4	0	.273	.351	.303

JEFF REED / San Francisco Giants / Catcher $17

A backup catcher, as bad a hitter as Manwaring. He hits left and Manwaring right, so they form a kind of a platoon, although Manwaring plays 80 percent of the time, rather than 35 percent as he would in a true platoon. Reed has always been known as a defensive catcher, but he doesn't throw as well as he once did. His position is not secure.

YEAR	TEAM/LEVEL	G	AB	R	H	2B	3B	HR	RBI	BB	SB	AVG	OBP	SLG
1992	Cincinnati	15	25	2	4	0	0	0	2	1	0	.160	.192	.160
1993	San Francisco	66	119	10	31	3	0	6	12	16	0	.261	.346	.437
1994	San Francisco	50	103	11	18	3	0	1	7	11	0	.175	.254	.233

JODY REED / Milwaukee Brewers / Second Base $25

Coming off his best season since 1991. Reed is slow and has no power, so he needs to do two things: a) get on base, and b) play second base better than the .260 hitters like Todd Haney and Jeff Gardner, who are always looking for jobs. He did those things in 1994, turning 72 double plays with only three errors, and posting a .362 on-base percentage.

YEAR	TEAM/LEVEL	G	AB	R	H	2B	3B	HR	RBI	BB	SB	AVG	OBP	SLG
1993	Los Angeles	132	445	48	123	21	2	2	31	38	1	.276	.333	.346
1994	Milwaukee	108	399	48	108	22	0	2	37	57	5	.271	.362	.341
1995	*Projected*	*142*	*521*	*63*	*139*	*33*	*1*	*4*	*44*	*60*	*5*	*.267*	*.343*	*.357*

RICK REED / Cincinnati Reds / Starting Pitcher $14

Kevin Kennedy gave opportunities last spring to a number of minor league veterans, and he'd have been smart to have stuck with this one. Reed, cut by Texas in May, signed with the Reds and had another good Triple-A season (10-6). He's not Greg Maddux, but on the worst day of his life he's a better pitcher than Brian Bohanon or Hector Fajardo.

YEAR	TEAM/LEVEL	G	IP	W-L	PCT	HITS	SO	BB	ERA
1992	Kansas City	19	100	3-7	.300	105	49	20	3.68
1993	Two Teams AAA	24	163	12-7	.632	159	79	16	3.32
1994	Texas	4	17	1-1	.500	17	12	7	5.94

STEVE REED / Colorado Rockies / Relief Pitcher $25

Draft him. Moving through the minors, he was enormously effective, plus he was consistently healthy. In his two years with Colorado, he's had ERAs of 1.60 and 1.76 on the road, but 6.39 and 5.94 in Mile High Stadium. The Rockies are moving *out* of Mile High Stadium, into a better park for a pitcher. His ERA may drop by two runs.

YEAR	TEAM/LEVEL	G	IP	W-L	SAVES	HITS	SO	BB	ERA
1992	San Francisco	18	16	1-0	0	13	11	3	2.30
1993	Colorado	64	84	9-5	3	80	51	30	4.48
1994	Colorado	61	64	3-2	3	79	51	26	3.94

MIKE REMLINGER / New York Mets / Left-handed Pitcher $16

A prospect with the Giants in the late 1980s, Remlinger's career was almost destroyed by elbow injuries and a loss of self-confidence. Signed by the Mets as a minor league free agent, he pitched well at Norfolk, and wound up the year in the Mets rotation. He is probably just keeping the seat warm for Pulsipher or Isringhausen. Not much fastball, good curve.

YEAR	TEAM/LEVEL	G	IP	W-L	PCT	HITS	SO	BB	ERA
1993	Calgary AAA	19	85	4-3	.571	100	51	52	5.53
1994	Norfolk AAA	12	63	2-4	.333	57	45	25	3.14
1994	New York	10	55	1-5	.167	55	33	35	4.61

RICH RENTERIA / Florida Marlins / Second Base $13

Renteria has not been released at this moment, but he is the most marginal of players, and also missed most of the 1994 season with an injury to his hamstring. He missed the 1990 season with an injury, was cut by the Mariners, and played 1991-92 in Mexico, hitting .442 with 106 RBI for Jalisco in 1991. His career is day to day.

YEAR	TEAM/LEVEL	G	AB	R	H	2B	3B	HR	RBI	BB	SB	AVG	OBP	SLG
1992	Jalisco MX	113	420	86	142	26	4	13	83	49	17	.338	.412	.512
1993	Florida	103	263	27	67	9	2	2	30	21	0	.255	.314	.327
1994	Florida	28	49	5	11	0	0	2	4	1	0	.224	.269	.347

CARLOS REYES / Oakland Athletics / Reliever/Starter $18

A Rule 5 draft from Atlanta. Began the season in the bullpen, moved to the rotation, made nine starts with a good 3.48 ERA. He failed to win a single start, because the A's didn't score for him, and he would come out of the games after about five innings. Even so, he went on the DL in July with a muscle strain. He has some ability.

YEAR	TEAM/LEVEL	G	IP	W-L	SAVES	HITS	SO	BB	ERA
1993	Greenville AA	33	70	8-1	2	64	57	24	2.06
1993	Richmond AAA	18	29	1-0	1	30	30	11	3.77
1994	Oakland	27	78	0-3	1	71	57	44	4.15

HAROLD REYNOLDS / California Angels / Second Base $15

A free agent, having been waived by the Angels in October. He signed a minor league contract with San Diego a year ago, went to California in a trade, and was a platoon second baseman the first two and a half months of the season, a bench player after that. He can't hit left-handers, and his base stealing is now a negative.

YEAR	TEAM/LEVEL	G	AB	R	H	2B	3B	HR	RBI	BB	SB	AVG	OBP	SLG
1992	Seattle	140	458	55	113	23	3	3	33	45	15	.247	.316	.330
1993	Baltimore	145	485	64	122	20	4	4	47	66	12	.252	.343	.334
1994	California	74	207	33	48	10	1	0	11	23	10	.232	.310	.290

SHANE REYNOLDS / Houston Astros / Starting Pitcher $32

Meaning no disrespect to Drabek, Swindell, or Harnisch, all of whom are fine pitchers, Shane Reynolds is probably the best pitcher on the Houston staff. A third-round 1989 draft, he struggled with his control for three years. Since he found the strike zone in '92, he's been nothing but outstanding. Moved into the rotation in May, had 2.54 ERA as a starter.

YEAR	TEAM/LEVEL	G	IP	W-L	PCT	HITS	SO	BB	ERA
1993	Tucson AAA	25	139	10-6	.625	147	106	21	3.62
1993	Houston	5	11	0-0	.000	11	10	6	0.82
1994	Houston	33	124	8-5	.615	128	110	21	3.05

ARMANDO REYNOSO / Colorado Rockies / Starting Pitcher $29

The Rockies' best pitcher in 1993, he snapped his ulnar collateral ligament throwing a pitch last May 20, and had to have the Tommy John surgery. It will probably be a couple of years, at least, until he is ready to pitch well again. He's 29 years old, was a star for years in the Mexican League, where he went 20-3 in 1990.

YEAR	TEAM/LEVEL	G	IP	W-L	PCT	HITS	SO	BB	ERA
1992	Richmond AAA	28	169	12-9	.571	156	108	52	2.66
1993	Colorado	30	189	12-11	.522	206	117	63	4.00
1994	Colorado	9	52	3-4	.429	54	25	22	4.82

ARTHUR RHODES / Baltimore Orioles / Starting Pitcher — $28

I continue to believe that Rhodes has Cy Young potential. This is no consolation to those of you who drafted him the last two years. His career has been ugly, but at the same age, we would have said the same thing about Randy Johnson or Sandy Koufax. There are few pitchers who have that kind of ability, and this is one of the few.

YEAR	TEAM/LEVEL	G	IP	W-L	PCT	HITS	SO	BB	ERA
1992	Baltimore	15	94	7-5	.583	87	77	38	3.63
1993	Baltimore	17	86	5-6	.455	91	49	49	6.51
1994	Baltimore	10	53	3-5	.375	51	47	30	5.81

KARL (TUFFY) RHODES / Chicago Cubs / Outfield — $18

Rhodes initiated the 1994 home run party with three on opening day, and hit .313 through April with six homers. He fell into a slump in May, and by season's end was hardly playing. The Cubs had him leading off because he's small, fast, and a selective hitter, so his .234 batting average was unwelcome. He's a better player than Derrick May.

YEAR	TEAM/LEVEL	G	AB	R	H	2B	3B	HR	RBI	BB	SB	AVG	OBP	SLG
1993	MLE	123	461	80	127	36	1	19	63	40	11	.275	.333	.482
1993	Hous. & Chi.	20	54	12	15	2	1	3	7	11	2	.278	.400	.519
1994	Chicago	95	269	39	63	17	0	8	19	33	6	.234	.318	.387

DAVE RIGHETTI / Toronto Blue Jays / Relief Pitcher — $7

He was released by San Francisco in '93, Oakland in April, and Toronto in October, probably bringing his career to an end. He had ERAs of 3.79 or lower every year from 1979 to 1991, and 24 or more saves every year from 1984 to 1991. Historical footnote: He was the first *successful* starter to be converted to relief in mid-career.

YEAR	TEAM/LEVEL	G	IP	W-L	SAVES	HITS	SO	BB	ERA
1992	San Francisco	54	78	2-7	3	79	47	36	5.06
1993	San Francisco	51	47	1-1	1	58	31	17	5.70
1994	Two Teams	20	20	0-1	0	22	14	19	10.18

JOSE RIJO / Cincinnati Reds / Starting Pitcher — $78

An amazing pitcher, the closest thing there is to a safe pick. He has had seven straight winning seasons, six of those with winning percentages over .600. His 3.08 ERA last year was his *highest* in seven years. He has led the league in starts twice in a row, 1993 and '94. He turns 30 in May, and his strikeout rates are still going up.

YEAR	TEAM/LEVEL	G	IP	W-L	PCT	HITS	SO	BB	ERA
1992	Cincinnati	33	211	15-10	.600	185	171	44	2.56
1993	Cincinnati	36	257	14-9	.609	218	227	62	2.48
1994	Cincinnati	26	172	9-6	.600	177	171	52	3.08

BILLY RIPKEN / Texas Rangers / Second Base $14

A free agent. He had numerous opportunities over the last two years to win the Rangers' second base job, but kept dropping onto the DL with hamstring pulls and a bruised hip. His career average is .243, and it's a quiet .243, with no power, no speed, no walks. But his defense and his .309 average in 32 games will probably get him a job.

YEAR	TEAM/LEVEL	G	AB	R	H	2B	3B	HR	RBI	BB	SB	AVG	OBP	SLG
1992	Baltimore	111	330	35	76	15	0	4	36	18	2	.230	.275	.312
1993	Texas	50	132	12	25	4	0	0	11	11	0	.189	.270	.220
1994	Texas	32	81	9	25	5	0	0	6	3	2	.309	.333	.370

CAL RIPKEN / Baltimore Orioles / Shortstop $48

Hit .300 for the fourth time in his career last year, his highest average in three years, also his highest on-base and slugging percentages. He also played exceptionally well at shortstop, leading all major league shortstops in both double plays (70) and fielding percentage (.985). Grounded into 17 more double plays, giving him 240 in his career. The career record is 328.

YEAR	TEAM/LEVEL	G	AB	R	H	2B	3B	HR	RBI	BB	SB	AVG	OBP	SLG
1993	Baltimore	162	641	87	165	26	3	24	90	65	1	.257	.329	.420
1994	Baltimore	112	444	71	140	19	3	13	75	32	1	.315	.364	.459
1995	*Projected*	*162*	*639*	*86*	*170*	*32*	*2*	*21*	*93*	*61*	*2*	*.266*	*.330*	*.421*

BILL RISLEY / Seattle Mariners / Pitcher $27

Continues his rise from non-prospect status. A 14th-round draft pick for Cincinnati, he went to Montreal as a throw-in in the Wetteland trade. He pitched well for Ottawa, but was squeezed out by the wealth of pitching talent there, and found himself last April in Calgary. Is 28 years old, throws 89-mph fastball, slider, change. Look at the strikeouts and hits.

YEAR	TEAM/LEVEL	G	IP	W-L	PCT	HITS	SO	BB	ERA
1992	Indianapolis AAA	25	96	5-8	.385	105	64	47	6.40
1993	Ottawa AAA	41	64	2-4	.333	51	74	34	2.54
1994	Seattle	37	52	9-6	.600	31	61	19	3.44

KEVIN RITZ / Colorado Rockies / Starting Pitcher $21

A big 29-year-old right-hander, had several trials with Detroit. Taken by the Rockies in the expansion draft, he was expected to be in their rotation, but missed the '93 season after an injury. He went 5-0 at Colorado Springs early in '94, 1.29 ERA, which got him back in the rotation, and he wasn't too bad.

YEAR	TEAM/LEVEL	G	IP	W-L	PCT	HITS	SO	BB	ERA
1992	Detroit	23	80	2-5	.286	88	57	44	5.60
1993	Colorado			(Injured—Did Not Pitch)					
1994	Colorado	15	74	5-6	.455	88	53	35	5.62

BEN RIVERA / Philadelphia Phillies / Starting Pitcher $16

One of many Phillies who failed to follow through on fine 1993 seasons. He opened the season pitching poorly, and went on the DL with a "strained shoulder" in early May. He was out two and a half months, but wasn't any better when he returned. . . . A big guy who throws hard but was never a finished pitcher. I wouldn't expect much from him.

YEAR	TEAM/LEVEL	G	IP	W-L	PCT	HITS	SO	BB	ERA
1992	Two Teams	28	117	7-4	.636	99	77	45	3.07
1993	Philadelphia	30	163	13-9	.591	175	123	85	5.02
1994	Philadelphia	9	38	3-4	.429	40	19	22	6.87

LUIS RIVERA / New York Mets / Shortstop $16

A regular for several years in Boston, he signed with the Mets as a free agent, did a good job backing up Vizcaino and Kent and was 6-for-17 as a pinch hitter. Right-handed hitter, not fast, a .230 hitter. Good bunter, OK defensive shortstop. Doesn't have a contract for '95, but will probably keep his job since he played well.

YEAR	TEAM/LEVEL	G	AB	R	H	2B	3B	HR	RBI	BB	SB	AVG	OBP	SLG
1992	Boston	102	288	17	62	11	1	0	29	26	4	.215	.287	.260
1993	Boston	62	130	13	27	8	1	1	7	11	1	.208	.273	.308
1994	New York	32	43	11	12	2	1	3	5	4	0	.279	.367	.591

KEVIN ROBERSON / Chicago Cubs / Outfield $15

A big, strong switch hitter who can run OK, although it takes him a long time to get his momentum established. If he's going to make it as a major league player, which is unlikely, it will be as a power hitter. He has 13 home runs in 235 major league at bats, a rate of 30 homers/season, but has far more strikeouts than hits.

YEAR	TEAM/LEVEL	G	AB	R	H	2B	3B	HR	RBI	BB	SB	AVG	OBP	SLG
1993	MLE	67	252	34	69	17	0	13	35	13	1	.274	.309	.496
1993	Chicago	62	180	23	34	4	1	9	27	12	0	.189	.251	.372
1994	Chicago	44	55	8	12	4	0	4	9	2	0	.218	.271	.509

SID ROBERSON / Milwaukee Brewers / Starting Pitcher $18

A small left-hander, 5-foot-9, 170 pounds. He was a 29th-round draft pick in 1992, but has led the California League and the Texas League in earned run average the last two seasons, being named Texas League Pitcher of the Year. Best pitch is a curve, which he will throw behind in the count. Is near a degree in accounting.

YEAR	TEAM/LEVEL	G	IP	W-L	PCT	HITS	SO	BB	ERA
1992	Helena R	9	65	4-4	.500	68	65	18	3.46
1993	Stockton A	24	166	12-8	.600	157	87	34	2.60
1994	El Paso AA	25	181	15-8	.652	190	119	48	2.83

BIP ROBERTS / San Diego Padres / Second Base $40

A free agent; also played a little in left and center for the Padres. He's comparable to Tony Phillips, in that he's a fine player who has had trouble finding a position, and plays all over the field. Doesn't have Tony's power, but hits for higher averages. Switch hitter, a better hitter left-handed. Usually doesn't hit well in April.

YEAR	TEAM/LEVEL	G	AB	R	H	2B	3B	HR	RBI	BB	SB	AVG	OBP	SLG
1993	Cincinnati	83	292	46	70	13	0	1	18	38	26	.240	.330	.295
1994	San Diego	105	403	52	129	15	5	2	31	39	21	.320	.383	.397
1995	*Projected*	*131*	*473*	*69*	*137*	*21*	*3*	*4*	*37*	*56*	*34*	*.290*	*.365*	*.372*

CHRIS ROBERTS / New York Mets / Starting Pitcher $21

One of the young pitchers who is supposed to have the Mets back in the race by 1996. He is a left-hander, doesn't throw exceptionally hard, but is compared to Jimmy Key and Tom Glavine—poised, always in control of the situation. He was an All-American at Florida State, a first-round draft pick in 1992, and may reach New York this summer.

YEAR	TEAM/LEVEL	G	IP	W-L	PCT	HITS	SO	BB	ERA
1992	Florida State	14	100	8-4	.667	81	84	43	2.34
1993	St. Lucie A	25	173	13-5	.722	162	111	36	2.75
1994	Binghamton AA	27	175	13-8	.619	164	128	77	3.29

RICH ROBERTSON / Pittsburgh Pirates / Left-handed Pitcher $11

Tall and skinny, has worked as a starting pitcher in the minors, but relief in two major league trials. He hasn't been devastating at any level in the minors, has never had an ERA below three, and has a career record of 32-40. He's 26 and there isn't any reason to think he'll be good. But as long as he stays healthy, there's a chance.

YEAR	TEAM/LEVEL	G	IP	W-L	PCT	HITS	SO	BB	ERA
1993	Buffalo AAA	23	132	9-8	.529	141	71	52	4.28
1994	Buffalo AAA	18	119	5-10	.333	112	71	36	3.11
1994	Pittsburgh	8	16	0-0	.000	20	8	10	6.89

ALEX RODRIGUEZ / Seattle Mariners / Shortstop $24

A 19-year-old shortstop, the first player taken in the 1993 draft. He was called to the majors after tearing through the Midwest and Southern leagues, but was overmatched, and was sent back down just before the strike. He has the range and arm to be a Gold Glove shortstop once he learns how; what he will hit is anybody's guess. **Grade A prospect.**

YEAR	TEAM/LEVEL	G	AB	R	H	2B	3B	HR	RBI	BB	SB	AVG	OBP	SLG
1994	Appleton A	79	295	55	93	21	7	15	63	34	17	.315	.386	.586
1994	AA and AAA	49	178	29	54	11	5	7	29	18	4	.303	.371	.539
1994	Seattle	17	54	4	11	0	0	0	2	3	3	.204	.241	.204

CARLOS RODRIGUEZ / Boston Red Sox / Shortstop $16

A Mexican shortstop trapped in the Yankee system, he became a six-year free agent a year ago, and the Red Sox signed him to keep alive the memory of Luis Rivera. A switch hitter and could hit some singles, but slow, no power, and will probably struggle to keep his on-base percentage over .300. A good bunter, good shortstop. Comparable to David Howard.

YEAR	TEAM/LEVEL	G	AB	R	H	2B	3B	HR	RBI	BB	SB	AVG	OBP	SLG
1993	MLE	95	293	32	82	19	0	0	33	24	2	.280	.334	.345
1994	Boston	57	174	15	50	14	1	1	13	11	1	.287	.330	.397
1995	*Projected*	*90*	*288*	*25*	*79*	*17*	*1*	*2*	*28*	*19*	*2*	*.262*	*.308*	*.350*

HENRY RODRIGUEZ / Los Angeles Dodgers / Outfielder $20

He had been on the Dodgers' bench for several years, but the flameout of Darryl Strawberry gave him a chance to play every game against right-handed pitchers. He was fair. He hit over .300 until mid-June, but under .200 the last two months. If Billy Ashley takes left field, as is expected, Rodriguez will go back to the bench.

YEAR	TEAM/LEVEL	G	AB	R	H	2B	3B	HR	RBI	BB	SB	AVG	OBP	SLG
1993	Los Angeles	76	176	20	39	10	0	8	23	11	1	.222	.266	.415
1994	Los Angeles	104	306	33	82	14	2	8	49	17	0	.268	.307	.405
1995	*Projected*	*116*	*345*	*35*	*82*	*16*	*2*	*9*	*43*	*20*	*1*	*.279*	*.326*	*.424*

IVAN RODRIGUEZ / Texas Rangers / Catcher $64

He is younger than either Raul Mondesi or Bob Hamelin, and he's already arguably the best catcher the Rangers have ever had. He came up at 19, and the fear has been that, like Butch Wynegar and Tony Pena, he would stall out, not develop as a hitter. But every season of his career, he has established career highs in on-base and slugging pecentage.

YEAR	TEAM/LEVEL	G	AB	R	H	2B	3B	HR	RBI	BB	SB	AVG	OBP	SLG
1993	Texas	137	473	56	129	28	4	10	66	29	8	.273	.315	.412
1994	Texas	99	363	56	108	19	1	16	57	31	6	.298	.360	.488
1995	*Projected*	*145*	*516*	*64*	*144*	*26*	*2*	*15*	*69*	*36*	*6*	*.279*	*.326*	*.424*

RICH RODRIGUEZ / St. Louis Cardinals / Relief Pitcher $20

A serviceable, consistent middle reliever, has been able to work 60-70 times a year without getting hurt. He throws several pitches, which makes him extremely effective when he's ahead in the count. Is 32 years old, left-handed, good control, usually works above the belt. He had 15 holds last year, third in the league.

YEAR	TEAM/LEVEL	G	IP	W-L	SAVES	HITS	SO	BB	ERA
1992	San Diego	61	91	6-3	0	77	64	29	2.37
1993	Two Teams	70	76	2-4	3	73	43	33	3.79
1994	St. Louis	56	60	3-5	0	62	43	26	4.03

KENNY ROGERS / Texas Rangers / Starting Pitcher $39

Has been a solid starter for two seasons, which makes him the ace of the Rangers' staff, since Pavlik got hurt and Brown hasn't pitched well. He is comparable to Tom Browning (who, oddly enough, also threw a per- fect game) except that he throws harder, and cuts off the running game better. Was among the league leaders in doubles and homers allowed (38 and 24).

YEAR	TEAM/LEVEL	G	IP	W-L	PCT	HITS	SO	BB	ERA
1992	Texas	81	79	3-6	.333	80	70	26	3.09
1993	Texas	35	208	16-10	.615	210	140	71	4.10
1994	Texas	24	167	11-8	.579	169	120	52	4.46

KEVIN ROGERS / San Francisco Giants / Left-handed Pitcher $15

After a fine rookie season, entered 1994 as a key to the Giants bullpen. In mid-April he complained about a funny feeling in his arm. It was initially diagnosed as too much caffeine and cigarettes, but eventually discov- ered to be a blood clot in his shoulder, requiring sur- gery. He should be back for 1995, but he'll lose a couple of years of effectiveness.

YEAR	TEAM/LEVEL	G	IP	W-L	PCT	HITS	SO	BB	ERA
1992	San Francisco	6	34	0-2	.000	37	26	13	4.24
1993	San Francisco	64	81	2-2	.500	71	62	28	2.68
1994	San Francisco	9	10	0-0	.000	10	7	6	3.48

MEL ROJAS / Montreal Expos / Relief Pitcher $38

An outstanding set-up man, the best in baseball. Rojas' manager (and uncle) Felipe Alou is the quickest hook in the majors. Also, unlike most managers, he'll bring in his closer in the eighth inning. This creates so much work for the closer that no one man could han- dle it, and Rojas will get two or three saves a month, even when Wetteland is healthy.

YEAR	TEAM/LEVEL	G	IP	W-L	SAVES	HITS	SO	BB	ERA
1992	Montreal	68	101	7-1	10	71	70	34	1.43
1993	Montreal	66	88	5-8	10	80	48	30	2.95
1994	Montreal	58	84	3-2	16	71	84	21	3.32

JOHN ROPER / Cincinnati Reds / Starting Pitcher $23

He has been regarded for years as the Reds' best pitch- ing prospect, and in 1994 we began to see why. To this point in his career he has been absurdly ineffective against left-handed hitters (they've hit .341 against him, .581 slugging percentage), and will have to find some way to fix that if he's going to be good. Best pitch is a big curve.

YEAR	TEAM/LEVEL	G	IP	W-L	PCT	HITS	SO	BB	ERA
1993	Cincinnati	16	80	2-5	.286	92	54	36	5.63
1994	Indianapolis AAA	8	58	7-0	1.000	48	33	10	2.17
1994	Cincinnati	16	92	6-2	.750	90	51	30	4.50

RICH ROWLAND / Boston Red Sox / Catcher $23

A strong backup catcher, as I've written for years—hits about like Rob Deer, and has a fine arm. I wouldn't *recommend* him as an everyday catcher, but if he gets a chance to play, he might be comparable to Ron Kark- ovice; probably doesn't throw quite as well, but has more power. He'll drive in twice as many runs, per at bat, as Damon Berryhill.

YEAR	TEAM/LEVEL	G	AB	R	H	2B	3B	HR	RBI	BB	SB	AVG	OBP	SLG
1993	MLE	96	319	55	81	21	1	21	56	48	0	.254	.351	.524
1993	Detroit	21	46	7	17	4	0	0	5	11	0	.205	.295	.253
1994	Boston	46	118	14	27	3	0	9	20	11	0	.229	.295	.483

STAN ROYER / Boston Red Sox / First/Third Base $10

The league caught up with him last year, after three straight seasons in which he had hit better than he ought to in a few at bats a year. His 1994 strikeout to walk ratio: 21 to 0. A slow right-handed-hitting first baseman, he probably has a better chance of taking Mo Vaughn's job than you or I, but it would be close.

YEAR	TEAM/LEVEL	G	AB	R	H	2B	3B	HR	RBI	BB	SB	AVG	OBP	SLG
1992	St. Louis	13	31	6	10	2	0	2	9	1	0	.323	.333	.581
1993	St. Louis	24	46	4	14	2	0	1	8	2	0	.304	.333	.413
1994	Two Teams	43	66	3	11	5	0	1	3	0	0	.167	.167	.288

KIRK RUETER / Montreal Expos / Left-handed Starting Pitcher $24

His career record is 15-3, but I don't know anybody who believes he is that good. He was slowed last season by a pulled groin muscle and the death of his mother, but was still in the rotation at season's end, in some ways pitching better than in '93. Alou babies him, gets him out of the game after four or five innings.

YEAR	TEAM/LEVEL	G	IP	W-L	PCT	HITS	SO	BB	ERA
1993	AA and AAA	16	103	9-2	.818	93	63	10	1.92
1993	Montreal	14	86	8-0	1.000	85	31	18	2.73
1994	Montreal	20	92	7-3	.700	106	50	23	5.17

SCOTT RUFFCORN / Chicago White Sox / Starting Pitcher $30

Ruffcorn is thought to be the next star pitcher to come out of the White Sox factory, following McDowell, Fernandez, Alvarez, and Bere. He throws hard and throws strikes, and has dominated every level in the minors. He's been completely intimidated by major league hitters in his four starts to this point, which is interesting but probably not meaningful. I suspect he'll be outstanding.

YEAR	TEAM/LEVEL	G	IP	W-L	PCT	HITS	SO	BB	ERA
1993	Chicago	3	10	0-2	.000	9	2	10	8.10
1994	Nashville AAA	24	166	15-3	.833	139	144	40	2.72
1994	Chicago	2	6	0-2	.000	15	3	5	12.79

BRUCE RUFFIN / Colorado Rockies / Left-handed Pitcher $34

A failed starter, Ruffin began 1993 in the Rockies' rotation, got hit hard, and moved to the bullpen, where he was flat-out outstanding for four months. He opened '94 pitching backup relief, and was again outstanding.

When Darren Holmes faded, Ruffin moved into the closer role. He wasn't as good there, but wasn't bad, and opens the '95 season as Colorado's closer.

YEAR	TEAM/LEVEL	G	IP	W-L	SAVES	HITS	SO	BB	ERA
1992	Milwaukee	25	58	1-6	0	66	45	41	6.67
1993	Colorado	59	140	6-5	2	145	126	69	3.87
1994	Colorado	56	56	4-5	16	55	65	30	4.04

JOHNNY RUFFIN / Cincinnati Reds / Right-handed Pitcher $34

Ruffin pitched long relief for the Reds, usually coming in when the Reds were behind. He was outstanding, among the best relievers (non-closers) in baseball. He has an outstanding arm, 93-mph fastball with a lot of movement, and it is expected that he will eventually be a closer. He is only 23; the Reds got him from the White Sox for Tim Belcher.

YEAR	TEAM/LEVEL	G	IP	W-L	SAVES	HITS	SO	BB	ERA
1993	Two Teams AAA	32	67	4-5	2	51	75	18	3.11
1993	Cincinnati	21	38	2-1	2	36	30	11	3.58
1994	Cincinnati	51	70	7-2	1	57	44	27	3.09

JEFF RUSSELL / Cleveland Indians / Relief Pitcher $19

Russell saved 143 games, 1989-93, despite frequent elbow and ankle injuries, and opened 1994 as the Sox closer. He had eight saves in April but a high ERA, and fell out of the closer role. Boston traded him to the Indians, who tried him as a closer, and that didn't work, either. It is unlikely that he will get the closer job again.

YEAR	TEAM/LEVEL	G	IP	W-L	SAVES	HITS	SO	BB	ERA
1992	Two Teams	59	66	4-3	30	55	48	25	1.63
1993	Boston	51	47	1-4	33	39	45	14	2.70
1994	Two Teams	42	41	1-6	17	43	28	16	5.09

KEN RYAN / Boston Red Sox / Closer $35

Ryan was a minor league closer, and pitched well as a rookie in '93. He opened '94 in the minors due to a spring training injury, but was back by mid-April, and had a 0.00 ERA through 18 outings, inheriting the big-money job when Russell failed. He's a pure power pitcher—a big, wide right-hander who lives and dies on his fastball.

YEAR	TEAM/LEVEL	G	IP	W-L	SAVES	HITS	SO	BB	ERA
1992	Boston	7	7	0-0	0	4	5	5	6.43
1993	Boston	47	50	7-2	1	43	49	29	3.60
1994	Boston	42	48	2-3	13	46	32	17	2.44

BRET SABERHAGEN / New York Mets / Starting Pitcher $58

He was in the hunt for his third Cy Young Award when the strike stopped the season. In his last nine starts he had gone 7-0 with a 1.51 ERA. As I suppose you read, his strikeout/walk ratio was the best in the history of baseball. He breaks down quite a bit, but he's an amazing pitcher when he's healthy.

YEAR	TEAM/LEVEL	G	IP	W-L	PCT	HITS	SO	BB	ERA
1992	New York	17	98	3-5	.375	84	81	27	3.50
1993	New York	19	139	7-7	.500	131	93	17	3.29
1994	New York	24	177	14-4	.778	169	143	13	2.74

CHRIS SABO / Baltimore Orioles / Third Base $27

Refused assignment to the minors in October, and is a free agent for the second consecutive winter. He is 33 and his best years are behind him, but he is still capable of hitting 20 homers and driving in 85. Ankle and foot injuries have taken his speed; back trouble and a poor arm have reduced his value as a third baseman.

YEAR	TEAM/LEVEL	G	AB	R	H	2B	3B	HR	RBI	BB	SB	AVG	OBP	SLG
1993	Cincinnati	148	552	86	143	33	2	21	82	43	6	.259	.315	.440
1994	Baltimore	69	258	41	66	15	2	11	42	20	1	.256	.320	.465
1995	*Projected*	*119*	*428*	*60*	*106*	*28*	*11*	*14*	*58*	*34*	*4*	*.249*	*.303*	*.416*

BRIAN SACKINSKY / Baltimore Orioles / Starting Pitcher $16

Sackinsky attended Stanford, where he was a teammate of Mike Mussina, Jeffrey Hammonds, and Paul Carey. The Orioles drafted him in the second round, and were worried a year ago that they might have wasted the pick, but he had a good year at Bowie, and will receive a look this year if he continues to make progress. Changes speeds well, doesn't throw exceptionally hard.

YEAR	TEAM/LEVEL	G	IP	W-L	PCT	HITS	SO	BB	ERA
1993	Albany A	9	51	3-4	.429	50	41	16	3.20
1993	Frederick A	18	121	6-8	.429	117	112	37	3.20
1994	Bowie AA	28	177	11-7	.611	165	145	39	3.36

OLMEDO SAENZ / Chicago White Sox / Third Base $14

A 24-year-old right-handed hitter from Panama; established himself as a prospect by hitting .347 in 49 games at Birmingham (1993). He is regarded as the best third baseman the Sox have in their system, and might develop enough to be a major league third baseman, but has no future in Chicago as long as Ventura is there.

YEAR	TEAM/LEVEL	G	AB	R	H	2B	3B	HR	RBI	BB	SB	AVG	OBP	SLG
1994	Nashville AAA	107	383	48	100	27	2	12	59	30	3	.261	.326	.436
1994	MLE	107	372	40	89	23	1	10	49	24	2	.239	.285	.387
1994	Chicago	5	14	2	2	0	1	0	0	0	0	.143	.143	.286

A. J. SAGER / San Diego Padres / Right-handed Pitcher $9

A 10th-round draft pick in 1988, Sager wandered list-lessly through the Padres' system until 1993, when he pitched well at Wichita (Double-A), then at Las Vegas. He got a spring-training invitation out of that and showed enough to make the team, but didn't do anything once the regular season began. Grade D prospect; no reason to expect much from him.

YEAR	TEAM/LEVEL	G	IP	W-L	PCT	HITS	SO	BB	ERA
1993	Las Vegas AAA	21	90	6-5	.545	91	58	18	3.70
1994	Las Vegas AAA	23	41	1-4	.200	57	23	8	4.43
1994	San Diego	22	47	1-4	.200	62	26	16	5.98

ROGER SALKELD / Seattle Mariners / Starting Pitcher $15

After an epic minor league career in which he has at times been compared to Roger Clemens and at times to Bob Milacki, Salkeld reached the majors in September 1993, and pitched well, in September '93 and April '94 (2.13 ERA). Then he got hit hard a couple of times, lost all confidence, and began walking everybody. Grade C prospect; has time to recover.

YEAR	TEAM/LEVEL	G	IP	W-L	PCT	HITS	SO	BB	ERA
1993	Seattle	3	14	0-0	.000	13	13	4	2.51
1994	Seattle	13	59	2-5	.286	76	45	46	7.17
1994	Calgary AAA	13	67	3-7	.300	74	54	39	6.15

TIM SALMON / California Angels / Right Field $62

Is 26 years old; there is every reason to believe that he will be better in '95 than he has been the last two years, and he's been awfully good so far. Right-handed hitter, but has career batting average of .241 against left-handed pitchers, .286 against right-handers. Very slow; probably will have to move to first base within a few years.

YEAR	TEAM/LEVEL	G	AB	R	H	2B	3B	HR	RBI	BB	SB	AVG	OBP	SLG
1993	California	142	515	93	146	35	1	31	95	82	5	.283	.382	.536
1994	California	100	373	67	107	18	2	23	70	54	1	.287	.382	.531
1995	*Projected*	*155*	*550*	*103*	*159*	*29*	*2*	*34*	*103*	*94*	*6*	*.289*	*.393*	*.535*

JUAN SAMUEL / Detroit Tigers / Utilityman $18

Sparky used him mostly in center field, in combination with Eric Davis and Milt Cuyler, and, because he played so well, began platooning him with Lou Whitaker later in the year. He hit .309 and didn't make an error in center field, which is kind of amazing if you've seen him play the outfield. Now 34; needs to be spotted carefully.

YEAR	TEAM/LEVEL	G	AB	R	H	2B	3B	HR	RBI	BB	SB	AVG	OBP	SLG
1993	Cincinnati	103	261	31	60	10	4	4	26	23	9	.230	.298	.345
1994	Detroit	59	136	32	42	9	5	5	21	10	5	.309	.364	.559
1995	*Projected*	*101*	*246*	*35*	*62*	*17*	*4*	*5*	*32*	*19*	*7*	*.252*	*.306*	*.415*

REY SANCHEZ / Chicago Cubs / Second Base $27

Moved into the second base spot following the retirement of Sandberg, more or less (he also played some third, and spelled Dunston at short). He is quick but slow, if you know what I mean. He has a good first step, but doesn't actually run well. He'll never be Ryne Sandberg, but middle infielders who hit .280 have a certain value.

YEAR	TEAM/LEVEL	G	AB	R	H	2B	3B	HR	RBI	BB	SB	AVG	OBP	SLG
1993	Chicago	105	344	35	97	11	2	0	28	15	1	.282	.316	.326
1994	Chicago	96	291	26	83	13	1	0	24	20	2	.285	.345	.337
1995	*Projected*	*134*	*448*	*45*	*123*	*16*	*3*	*2*	*37*	*23*	*4*	*.275*	*.310*	*.337*

RYNE SANDBERG / Chicago Cubs / Retired   Unknown

I may be completely wrong, but don't be shocked if he comes out of retirement. From the facts that a) he announced his retirement to spend time with his family, and b) his wife filed for divorce a week later, we might infer that he retired in the midst of a family crisis. He can still play, not only now but for several years yet.

YEAR	TEAM/LEVEL	G	AB	R	H	2B	3B	HR	RBI	BB	SB	AVG	OBP	SLG
1992	Chicago	158	612	100	186	32	8	26	87	68	17	.304	.371	.510
1993	Chicago	117	456	78	141	20	0	9	45	37	9	.309	.359	.412
1994	Chicago	57	223	36	53	9	5	5	24	23	2	.238	.312	.390

DEION SANDERS / Cincinnati Reds / Center Field $30

Deion has played 92 to 97 games in each of the last three seasons, and has driven in exactly 28 runs each year. Do you think Deion's publicity persona actually appeals to anyone, or do you think he just gets advertising dollars because the world is screwed up? I personally don't know anybody who doesn't detest him, but maybe he has his own market.

YEAR	TEAM/LEVEL	G	AB	R	H	2B	3B	HR	RBI	BB	SB	AVG	OBP	SLG
1993	Atlanta	95	272	42	75	18	6	6	28	16	19	.276	.321	.452
1994	Two Teams	92	375	58	106	17	4	4	28	32	38	.283	.342	.381
1995	*Projected*	*142*	*527*	*87*	*152*	*22*	*10*	*12*	*51*	*39*	*47*	*.288*	*.337*	*.436*

REGGIE SANDERS / Cincinnati Reds / Right Field $38

A consistent hitter, can kill a left-hander. He's been reasonably healthy for two seasons, plus he has settled in as a right fielder, after a couple of years shuttling among the outfield spots. He has power and speed, hits for a fairly good average and walks some, although he also strikes out too much. He's a solid, quality player, 27 years old.

YEAR	TEAM/LEVEL	G	AB	R	H	2B	3B	HR	RBI	BB	SB	AVG	OBP	SLG
1993	Cincinnati	138	496	90	136	16	4	20	83	51	27	.274	.343	.444
1994	Cincinnati	107	400	66	105	20	8	17	62	41	21	.262	.332	.480
1995	*Projected*	*152*	*563*	*93*	*151*	*25*	*6*	*22*	*78*	*63*	*28*	*.268*	*.342*	*.451*

SCOTT SANDERS / San Diego Padres / Starting Pitcher $27

Survived the season in the Padres' rotation, despite leading the league in wild pitches (10), and that is noteworthy, as how many pitchers who get a shot at the rotation will make it through their first year? He throws a fastball and a hard slider (which sometimes gets away), changes speeds. May not be quite on the same level as Hamilton, but I like him.

YEAR	TEAM/LEVEL	G	IP	W-L	PCT	HITS	SO	BB	ERA
1993	Las Vegas AAA	24	152	5-10	.333	170	161	62	4.96
1993	San Diego	9	52	3-3	.500	54	37	23	4.13
1994	San Diego	23	111	4-8	.333	103	109	48	4.78

SCOTT SANDERSON / Chicago White Sox / Starting Pitcher $17

A 38-year-old veteran who survives by not walking anybody, won 33 games in 1990-91 with Oakland and New York. He signed a minor league contract with the White Sox, made the team, and filled in as a "staff stabilizer," an extra starting pitcher who went into and out of the rotation as needed. He was OK, and he'll probably keep that job.

YEAR	TEAM/LEVEL	G	IP	W-L	PCT	HITS	SO	BB	ERA
1992	New York (A)	33	193	12-11	.522	220	104	64	4.93
1993	Two Teams	32	184	11-13	.458	201	102	34	4.21
1994	Chicago	18	92	8-4	.667	110	36	12	5.09

MO SANFORD / Minnesota Twins / Starting Pitcher $18

A hot prospect with the Reds four years ago, but something went wrong, and he's in the minors at 28. I wrote last year that "he has a comeback in him, a big comeback, but it probably doesn't start until '95." That is still what I believe. He struck out 141 in 126 innings for Salt Lake City, and was added to the Twins roster.

YEAR	TEAM/LEVEL	G	IP	W-L	PCT	HITS	SO	BB	ERA
1993	Colo. Sp. AAA	20	105	3-6	.333	103	104	57	5.23
1993	Colorado	11	36	1-2	.333	37	36	27	5.30
1994	Salt Lake AAA	37	126	7-5	.583	121	141	52	4.87

BENITO SANTIAGO / Florida Marlins / Catcher $25

Benito threw out 43 percent of opposing base stealers last year, the best percentage in the league. He hit .273, his highest average since he hit .300 as a rookie, and had a .424 slugging percentage, also his highest since 1987. He is a free agent, and it is generally assumed that the Marlins don't want him back, because of Charles Johnson. Average catcher at best.

YEAR	TEAM/LEVEL	G	AB	R	H	2B	3B	HR	RBI	BB	SB	AVG	OBP	SLG
1993	Florida	139	469	49	108	19	6	13	50	37	10	.230	.291	.380
1994	Florida	101	337	35	92	14	2	11	41	25	1	.273	.322	.424
1995	*Projected*	*137*	*466*	*48*	*118*	*20*	*3*	*13*	*52*	*33*	*6*	*.253*	*.303*	*.393*

DOUG SAUNDERS / New York Mets / Infield $9

Saunders was projected as the Mets' second baseman of the future before they acquired Jeff Kent; Kent's development has trapped him in the minor leagues. He's a Jose Lind-type, a good field/no hit second baseman, but he had a good year at Binghamton in '94, and may see a little daylight in '95. Grade D prospect.

YEAR	TEAM/LEVEL	G	AB	R	H	2B	3B	HR	RBI	BB	SB	AVG	OBP	SLG
1993	New York (N)	28	67	8	14	2	0	0	0	3	0	.209	.243	.239
1994	Binghamton AA	96	338	48	96	19	4	8	45	43	3	.284	.361	.435
1994	MLE	96	325	38	83	16	2	6	35	29	2	.255	.316	.372

STEVE SAX / Oakland Athletics / Utilityman $7

Refused assignment to the minors in October, becoming a free agent. He was released by the White Sox a year ago; the A's signed him to cover second during an injury to Brent Gates, but he played a few games and then went out with a sore heel, which kept him on the DL the rest of the year. A comeback is not (quite) impossible.

YEAR	TEAM/LEVEL	G	AB	R	H	2B	3B	HR	RBI	BB	SB	AVG	OBP	SLG
1992	Chicago	143	567	74	134	26	4	4	47	43	30	.236	.290	.317
1993	Chicago	57	119	20	28	5	0	1	8	8	7	.235	.283	.303
1994	Oakland	7	24	2	6	0	1	0	1	0	0	.250	.250	.333

BOB SCANLAN / Milwaukee Brewers / Relief Pitcher $21

After almost two years of ineffective relief he moved into the Brewers' starting rotation about the first of June, and pitched well, posting a 3.68 ERA through 12 starts. He is, in my opinion, better suited to starting than relief, because he's a four-pitch pitcher and needs to use all his pitches, since none of them is all that good. Limited future.

YEAR	TEAM/LEVEL	G	IP	W-L	SAVES	HITS	SO	BB	ERA
1992	Chicago	69	87	3-6	14	76	42	30	2.89
1993	Chicago	70	75	4-5	0	79	44	28	4.54
1994	Milwaukee	30	103	2-6	2	117	65	28	4.11

STEVE SCARSONE / San Francisco Giants / Infielder $17

A 29-year-old, spent eight years in the minor leagues. It has been several years since anyone projected him to be a regular, but after Thompson's injury he shared the second base job with John Patterson, and played far better both ways than Patterson did. Right-handed hitter, slow, can't play shortstop. Playing time will probably increase a little if he continues to play well.

YEAR	TEAM/LEVEL	G	AB	R	H	2B	3B	HR	RBI	BB	SB	AVG	OBP	SLG
1993	San Francisco	44	103	16	26	9	0	2	15	4	0	.252	.278	.398
1994	San Francisco	52	103	21	28	8	0	2	13	10	0	.272	.330	.408
1995	*Projected*	*87*	*239*	*31*	*60*	*13*	*1*	*5*	*28*	*17*	*4*	*.251*	*.301*	*.377*

RICH SCHIED / Florida Marlins / Starting Pitcher $11

A 30-year-old lefty, originally signed by the Brooklyn Dodgers. He was winning at Edmonton when the Marlins needed a starter, so they brought him up, and he pitched well. Obviously, the odds are that he'll never have more than a few weeks here and there in the majors, but if you asked for convincing evidence that he *can't* pitch, I don't have it.

YEAR	TEAM/LEVEL	G	IP	W-L	PCT	HITS	SO	BB	ERA
1993	Edmonton AAA	38	110	5-7	.417	130	84	38	5.07
1994	Edmonton AAA	17	102	9-4	.692	110	86	41	4.05
1994	Florida	8	32	1-3	.250	35	17	8	3.34

CURT SCHILLING / Philadelphia Phillies / Starting Pitcher $38

One of the best pitchers in the National League in '92 and '93, he was 0-7 in mid-May, when he went on the DL with a bone spur in his elbow. Reactivated in late July, he pitched well in four starts before the strike. His proven ability and strong late-season performance makes him an excellent bet to come back strong in '95.

YEAR	TEAM/LEVEL	G	IP	W-L	PCT	HITS	SO	BB	ERA
1992	Philadelphia	42	226	14-11	.560	165	147	59	2.35
1993	Philadelphia	34	235	16-7	.696	234	186	57	4.02
1994	Philadelphia	13	82	2-8	.200	87	58	28	4.48

DICK SCHOFIELD / Toronto Blue Jays / Shortstop $21

A year ago, it seemed unlikely that he would ever play regularly again. Alex Gonzalez's poor start put him back in the lineup, and he matched his career high in average, at .255, and did his usual more-than-competent job at short. He is only 32, but living on borrowed time, as a regular. The Blue Jays' poor season may cost him his job.

YEAR	TEAM/LEVEL	G	AB	R	H	2B	3B	HR	RBI	BB	SB	AVG	OBP	SLG
1992	Two Teams	143	423	52	87	18	2	4	36	61	11	.206	.311	.286
1993	Toronto	36	110	11	21	1	2	0	5	16	3	.191	.294	.236
1994	Toronto	95	325	38	83	14	1	4	32	34	7	.255	.332	.342

PETE SCHOUREK / Cincinnati Reds / Left-handed Pitcher $20

Schourek pitched well for the Mets in 1992, but struggled most of the season in '93, and was let go on waivers at the end of spring training. Cincinnati claimed him, and I think they got a bargain. They helped him make some adjustments, put him in the rotation in June, and he was good. And he may pitch well for the next 10 years.

YEAR	TEAM/LEVEL	G	IP	W-L	PCT	HITS	SO	BB	ERA
1992	New York	22	136	6-8	.429	137	60	44	3.64
1993	New York	41	128	5-12	.417	168	72	45	5.96
1994	Cincinnati	22	81	7-2	.778	90	69	29	4.09

STEVE SCHRENK / Chicago White Sox / Starting Pitcher $14

Schrenk was a prospect in the late '80s, but lost most of '91 and '92 to arm and shoulder injuries, and doesn't throw as hard as he once did. He went 15-2 at Sarasota in '92, however, and has been battling back since then. Best pitch is a sinking fastball, good control, regarded as very competitive. Works hard. Grade C prospect.

YEAR	TEAM/LEVEL	G	IP	W-L	PCT	HITS	SO	BB	ERA
1992	Sarasota A	25	154	15-2	.882	130	113	40	2.05
1993	AA and AAA	29	184	11-9	.550	148	129	54	2.98
1994	Nashville AAA	29	179	14-6	.700	175	134	69	3.48

ERIC SCHULLSTRUM / Minnesota Twins / Relief Pitcher $19

No prospect a year ago, Schullstrum started the season pitching long relief in Double-A. He was OK, the closer got promoted, he got to close games, did well, got sent to Triple-A, did well there, and was in the Twins' bullpen by mid-July. 1) Tom Kelly is good with relievers. 2) I like any pitcher with a 51/9 strikeout/walk ratio.

YEAR	TEAM/LEVEL	G	IP	W-L	SAVES	HITS	SO	BB	ERA
1993	Two Teams AA	28	123	6-10	1	135	108	51	4.33
1994	AA and AAA	34	52	1-3	10	48	51	9	2.92
1994	Minnesota	9	13	0-0	1	13	13	5	2.77

JEFF SCHWARZ / California Angels / Relief Pitcher $14

I can't understand why in the hell he is in the majors. He'll be 31 in May, and he throws hard, but his control is laughable—60 walks in 69 major league innings—and what's the thinking here? He's going to start throwing strikes all of a sudden, at age 30? For heaven's sake, send him to the minors. Let him find his control *there*.

YEAR	TEAM/LEVEL	G	IP	W-L	SAVES	HITS	SO	BB	ERA
1992	AA and AAA	44	75	3-4	9	42	95	40	2.05
1993	Chicago	41	51	2-2	0	35	41	38	3.71
1994	California	13	18	0-0	0	14	18	22	5.50

DARRYL SCOTT / Yokohama BayStars / Relief Pitcher $13

Scott refused assignment to the minor leagues last spring, and signed to play in Japan. I know I'm missing something here, but I don't know what it is. Scott's credentials as a major league pitcher are better than those of several guys the Angels have tried as closers, but they were unwilling in his case even to clear a spot in long relief. I suspect he'll return.

YEAR	TEAM/LEVEL	G	IP	W-L	SAVES	HITS	SO	BB	ERA
1993	Vancouver AAA	46	52	7-1	15	35	57	19	2.09
1993	California	16	20	1-2	0	19	13	11	5.85
1994	Yokohama JPN	—	32	0-1	—	—	27	—	2.51

TIM SCOTT / Montreal Expos / Relief Pitcher $23

One of many relievers who have thrived in Felipe Alou's system, which insures regular work for the bullpen. Scott had the Tommy John surgery in 1987, when he was 21, and took several years to fully recover. In '93 he allowed 55 percent of inherited runners to score, the worst percentage in the league, but last year allowed only two inherited runners to score all year.

YEAR	TEAM/LEVEL	G	IP	W-L	SAVES	HITS	SO	BB	ERA
1992	San Diego	34	38	4-1	0	39	30	21	5.26
1993	Two Teams	56	72	7-2	1	69	65	34	3.01
1994	Montreal	40	53	5-2	1	51	37	18	2.70

RUDY SEANEZ / Los Angeles Dodgers / Right-handed Reliever $15

A year ago I said that Seanez was "roughly speaking, the worst pitching prospect in the history of the world." Seanez pitched well in a few major league innings, and this description, which may have been hyperbolic anyway, is probably not accurate now. He throws hard, but has battled his control, has been hurt, and has little if any history of success before 1994.

YEAR	TEAM/LEVEL	G	IP	W-L	SAVES	HITS	SO	BB	ERA
1993	Las Vegas AAA	14	20	0-1	0	24	14	11	6.41
1993	San Diego	3	3	0-0	0	8	1	2	13.50
1994	Los Angeles	17	24	1-1	0	24	18	9	2.66

DAVID SEGUI / New York Mets / First Base/Left Field $16

Rico Brogna took the Mets' first base job in July, and opens the season as the Mets' first baseman. Brogna is a left-handed hitter; Segui is a switch hitter but a better hitter left-handed, so that won't help him. Segui is a marginal regular, comparable to Sid Bream or Todd Benzinger, but probably a better player than Brogna.

YEAR	TEAM/LEVEL	G	AB	R	H	2B	3B	HR	RBI	BB	SB	AVG	OBP	SLG
1993	Baltimore	146	450	54	123	27	0	10	60	58	2	.273	.351	.400
1994	New York	92	336	46	81	17	1	10	43	33	0	.241	.308	.387
1995	Projected	110	276	35	70	15	0	5	33	34	1	.254	.335	.362

KEVIN SEITZER / Milwaukee Brewers / Third Base/First Base $22

Hit .300 for the first time since 1988, also had .400-plus slugging percentage for first time since 1988. With runners in scoring position he hit .403. The development of Jeff Cirillo probably seals him off third base, at least with the Brewers, which will put even more pressure on him to hit. He is *capable* of hitting enough to hold on to his playing time.

YEAR	TEAM/LEVEL	G	AB	R	H	2B	3B	HR	RBI	BB	SB	AVG	OBP	SLG
1993	Two Teams	120	417	45	112	16	2	11	57	44	7	.269	.338	.396
1994	Milwaukee	80	309	44	97	24	2	5	49	30	2	.314	.375	.453
1995	Projected	134	488	62	137	25	2	7	65	53	9	.281	.351	.383

AARON SELE / Boston Red Sox / Starting Pitcher $34

After a strong performance in the second half '93 he opened '94 pitching the same way—3-0 in April, 2.56 ERA. He had a sinking spell after that and had to make some adjustments, but finished the season fairly strong, and his outlook is still good—maybe better than it was, since he has survived the transition. Should win 15 or more.

YEAR	TEAM/LEVEL	G	IP	W-L	PCT	HITS	SO	BB	ERA
1993	Pawtucket AAA	14	94	8-2	.800	74	87	23	2.19
1993	Boston	18	112	7-2	.778	100	93	48	2.74
1994	Boston	22	143	8-7	.533	140	105	60	3.83

FRANK SEMINARA / New York Mets / Starting Pitcher $11

Right-hander with a funny motion, pitched well for San Diego in '92, but was given up on quickly in '93. He has slipped into the role of Triple-A starter for an organization that has many pitching prospects, so his future is cloudy. He is 12-9 in the majors, and there is little evidence that he *couldn't* continue to pitch .500 ball.

YEAR	TEAM/LEVEL	G	IP	W-L	PCT	HITS	SO	BB	ERA
1992	San Diego	19	100	9-4	.692	98	61	46	3.68
1993	San Diego	18	46	3-3	.500	53	22	21	4.47
1994	San Diego	10	17	0-2	.000	20	7	8	5.82

SCOTT SERVAIS / Houston Astros / Catcher $18

The trade of his platoon partner, Taubensee, devastated him. Servais has a career average of .266 against left-handers, .183 against right-handers. In '93, when 54 percent of his at bats were against left-handers. He was fairly effective. In '94, sharing the job with another right-handed hitter (Eusebio), 73 percent of his at bats were against right-handers, which drove his average down sharply.

YEAR	TEAM/LEVEL	G	AB	R	H	2B	3B	HR	RBI	BB	SB	AVG	OBP	SLG
1992	Houston	77	205	12	49	9	0	0	15	11	0	.239	.294	.283
1993	Houston	85	258	24	63	11	0	11	32	22	0	.244	.313	.415
1994	Houston	78	251	27	49	15	1	9	41	10	0	.195	.235	.371

SCOTT SERVICE / Cincinnati Reds / Relief Pitcher $15

Big right-hander, has had previous trials with Philadelphia (1988), Montreal (1992), and Colorado (1993). He pitched well in Triple-A in '94, as he often has before, plus in 66 innings in the majors, he has 65 strike-outs and only 25 walks, and he's only 28. But his chance of having a career is inversely related to the number of trials he has failed.

YEAR	TEAM/LEVEL	G	IP	W-L	SAVES	HITS	SO	BB	ERA
1993	Two Teams	29	46	2-2	2	44	43	16	4.30
1994	Indianapolis AAA	40	58	5-5	13	35	67	27	2.31
1994	Cincinnati	6	7	1-2	0	8	5	3	7.36

JON SHAVE / Texas Rangers / Second Base $11

At the start of spring training ('94) he was a candidate for the Rangers' second base job, but he suffered a fractured larynx in spring training, and was unable to start the season. Jeff Frye, who is a comparable talent, has taken the Rangers' second base job, and Shave played poorly at Oklahoma City, so his future is in doubt.

YEAR	TEAM/LEVEL	G	AB	R	H	2B	3B	HR	RBI	BB	SB	AVG	OBP	SLG
1992	Tulsa AA	118	453	57	130	23	5	2	36	37	6	.287	.343	.373
1993	Texas	17	47	3	15	2	0	0	7	0	1	.319	.306	.362
1994	Ok. City	95	332	29	73	15	2	1	31	14	6	.220	.258	.286

JEFF SHAW / Montreal Expos / Starting Pitcher $20

A failed starter from the Cleveland organization, Shaw has become one of Felipe Alou's five crucial right-handed relievers (Wetteland, Rojas, Scott, Shaw, and Heredia). Among the five he is the most vulnerable to left-handed hitters, who have a career average of .309 against him. His strikeout rate has been increasing steadily, and his control improving slightly.

YEAR	TEAM/LEVEL	G	IP	W-L	PCT	HITS	SO	BB	ERA
1992	Cleveland	2	8	0-1	.000	7	3	4	8.22
1993	Montreal	55	96	2-7	.222	91	50	32	4.14
1994	Montreal	46	67	5-2	.714	67	47	15	3.88

DANNY SHEAFFER / Colorado Rockies / Catcher $14

Waived by the Rockies in October; will be lucky to be in the majors in '95. He's a 33-year-old right-handed hitter who was in the minors from 1981 through 1992, got a chance to play because of expansion, and extended that by a year by hitting about 80 points over his head in the Rockies' first season.

YEAR	TEAM/LEVEL	G	AB	R	H	2B	3B	HR	RBI	BB	SB	AVG	OBP	SLG
1992	Portland AAA	116	442	54	122	23	4	5	56	21	3	.276	.309	.380
1993	Colorado	82	216	26	60	9	1	4	32	8	2	.278	.299	.384
1994	Colorado	44	110	11	24	4	0	1	12	10	0	.218	.283	.282

GARY SHEFFIELD / Florida Marlins / Right Field $53

In the tradition of Dick Allen, Rogers Hornsby, Pete Browning, Goose Goslin—a tremendous hitter who moves from team to team because he's a poor fielder and a big pain. At some point in his career, Sheffield will win an MVP Award. He'll have a year where he behaves himself, works hard, and stays healthy. There is no reason 1995 couldn't be the year.

YEAR	TEAM/LEVEL	G	AB	R	H	2B	3B	HR	RBI	BB	SB	AVG	OBP	SLG
1993	Two Teams	140	494	67	145	20	5	20	73	47	17	.294	.361	.476
1994	Florida	87	322	61	89	16	1	27	78	51	12	.276	.380	.584
1995	*Projected*	*142*	*518*	*78*	*152*	*28*	*2*	*26*	*88*	*59*	*13*	*.293*	*.366*	*.506*

CRAIG SHIPLEY / San Diego Padres / Third Base $19

A career .238 hitter going into the 1994 season, he hit .300 or better in every month of the schedule, and by season's end was more or less the Padres' third base-man. Baseball players do *not* learn to hit at age 31, and we should expect that the pitchers will adjust to him in '95. Didn't play well at third, but is capable enough there.

YEAR	TEAM/LEVEL	G	AB	R	H	2B	3B	HR	RBI	BB	SB	AVG	OBP	SLG
1993	San Diego	105	230	25	54	9	0	4	22	10	12	.235	.275	.326
1994	San Diego	81	240	32	80	14	4	4	30	9	6	.333	.362	.475
1995	*Projected*	*105*	*258*	*28*	*68*	*11*	*1*	*3*	*23*	*10*	*8*	*.264*	*.291*	*.349*

BRIAN SHOUSE / Pittsburgh Pirates / Left-handed Relief Pitcher $13

A left-handed middle reliever in the minors. The Pirates had a bullpen ERA of 5.36, and the top lefty was Rav-elo Manzanillo, so I would think that there was oppor-tunity for Shouse to move up. A 13th-round draft pick, short, does not impress the radar guns, but has pitched well enough at every minor league level to earn a shot.

YEAR	TEAM/LEVEL	G	IP	W-L	SAVES	HITS	SO	BB	ERA
1993	Buffalo AAA	48	52	1-0	2	54	25	17	3.83
1993	Pittsburgh	6	4	0-0	0	7	3	2	9.00
1994	Buffalo AAA	43	52	3-4	0	44	31	15	3.63

PAUL SHUEY / Cleveland Indians / Relief Pitcher $15

Big right-hander, throws very hard, looks overweight. A first-round draft pick in 1992, he was a starting pitcher in '92 and '93, and pitched poorly. Converting to the bullpen in late '93, he pitched fairly well in April, while the Indians were desperate for a closer, so he got called up to do that, with predictable results. No rela-tion to Mark Dewey.

YEAR	TEAM/LEVEL	G	IP	W-L	SAVES	HITS	SO	BB	ERA
1994	Kinston A	13	12	1-0	8	10	16	3	3.75
1994	Cleveland	14	12	0-1	5	14	16	12	8.49
1994	Charlotte AAA	20	23	2-1	10	15	25	10	1.93

TERRY SHUMPERT / Kansas City Royals / Second Base $22

It is expected that his playing time will increase in '95, because a) he's a better hitter than Jose Lind, and b) Hal McRae, who didn't want to play anybody younger than 35, has been fired. Defensively, Shumpert looks very good to me, but apparently I'm seeing things dif-ferently than most people in the Kansas City area. Could be Kansas City's regular second baseman.

YEAR	TEAM/LEVEL	G	AB	R	H	2B	3B	HR	RBI	BB	SB	AVG	OBP	SLG
1992	Kansas City	36	94	6	14	5	1	1	11	3	2	.149	.175	.255
1993	MLE	111	394	51	105	26	0	8	43	29	24	.266	.317	.393
1994	Kansas City	64	183	28	44	6	2	8	24	13	18	.240	.289	.426

RUBEN SIERRA / Oakland Athletics / Right Field $66

He's a switch hitter and a better defensive player than Carter, but basically he's very similar to Joe Carter—a power hitter and a tremendous RBI producer, also runs well, but his overall value is limited by his low on-base percentage. Hits 40 points better on the road than he does in Oakland. Still only 29 years old; signed in Oakland through 1997.

YEAR	TEAM/LEVEL	G	AB	R	H	2B	3B	HR	RBI	BB	SB	AVG	OBP	SLG
1993	Oakland	158	630	77	147	23	5	22	101	52	25	.233	.288	.390
1994	Oakland	110	426	71	114	21	1	23	92	23	8	.268	.298	.484
1995	*Projected*	*159*	*626*	*88*	*169*	*33*	*5*	*25*	*109*	*47*	*18*	*.270*	*.321*	*.458*

DAVE SILVESTRI / New York Yankees / Second Base $18

Like Russ Davis, a decent major league player trapped in Triple-A. He's an odd player for a middle infielder, a low-average power hitter; from looking at his minor league records I would assume he lifts weights. Grade C prospect, overdue for playing time at 27. Takes a lot of pitches looking for one he can pull.

YEAR	TEAM/LEVEL	G	AB	R	H	2B	3B	HR	RBI	BB	SB	AVG	OBP	SLG
1993	MLE	120	413	62	100	23	2	16	53	56	4	.242	.333	.424
1994	MLE	114	383	62	88	17	1	21	72	71	13	.230	.350	.444
Totals in majors		26	52	10	12	1	3	2	7	9	0	.231	.339	.481

MIKE SIMMS / Houston Astros / First Base/Outfield $7

Simms hit 39 homers for Asheville in 1987, when he was just 20. Since then he has been consistently healthy, has played 1000-plus minor league games, driving in almost 700 runs. He's had a few major league at bats and has tried two other systems (San Diego and Pittsburgh), but is back in Houston now, trying to play right field. Limited future.

YEAR	TEAM/LEVEL	G	AB	R	H	2B	3B	HR	RBI	BB	SB	AVG	OBP	SLG
1993	Las Vegas AAA	129	414	74	111	25	2	24	80	67	1	.268	.375	.512
1994	Two Teams AAA	118	428	86	120	39	6	24	93	55	9	.280	.371	.568
1994	MLE	118	401	57	93	31	3	13	60	35	5	.232	.294	.421

DON SLAUGHT / Pittsburgh Pirates / Catcher $33

A high-average hitter, for a catcher. There are fewer than 10 catchers in the last 50 years who have hit .280 or better in 1200-game careers. In recent years, he's begun to walk a little, last year setting a career high in walks, despite playing only 76 games. He's not as quick as he once was, and he never did have a strong arm.

YEAR	TEAM/LEVEL	G	AB	R	H	2B	3B	HR	RBI	BB	SB	AVG	OBP	SLG
1993	Pittsburgh	113	377	34	113	19	2	10	55	29	2	.300	.356	.440
1994	Pittsburgh	76	240	21	69	7	0	2	21	34	0	.287	.381	.342
1995	*Projected*	*111*	*334*	*30*	*91*	*20*	*2*	*6*	*41*	*35*	*1*	*.272*	*.341*	*.398*

HEATHCLIFF SLOCUMB / Philadelphia Phillies / Relief Pitcher $19

Coming off his best season, his first full major league season, with no trip to the minors. Fregosi assigned him to long relief, usually working the seventh/eighth innings when the Phillies were tied or behind. He pitched OK, not as well as his 2.86 ERA would suggest. Has dramatically improved his ability to hold runners, also uses his off-speed pitches more effectively.

YEAR	TEAM/LEVEL	G	IP	W-L	SAVES	HITS	SO	BB	ERA
1992	Chicago	30	36	0-3	1	52	27	21	6.50
1993	Two Teams	30	38	4-1	0	35	22	20	4.03
1994	Philadelphia	52	72	5-1	0	75	58	28	2.86

JOHN SMILEY / Cincinnati Reds / Starting Pitcher $38

He has always been a fine pitcher, with the exception of his two injury seasons, 1990 (broken hand) and 1993 (bone spur on his elbow); otherwise his career record is 78-51. Usually throws his fastball on the first pitch, gets ahead of the hitter, then sets to work with slider, overhand curve, change. He's tough. Probably has several good seasons left.

YEAR	TEAM/LEVEL	G	IP	W-L	PCT	HITS	SO	BB	ERA
1992	Minnesota	34	241	16-9	.640	205	163	65	3.21
1993	Cincinnati	18	106	3-9	.250	117	60	31	5.62
1994	Cincinnati	24	159	11-10	.524	169	112	37	3.86

DAN SMITH / Texas Rangers / Left-handed Pitcher $9

Smith was a Grade B prospect in 1992, when he went 11-7 with a 2.52 ERA for Tulsa. Since then his transaction log looks like a phone book—at least three trips to the disabled list, countless callups and options. He may come back, but he's pitched only 80 innings in the last two years, and it's unlikely this has accelerated his development.

YEAR	TEAM/LEVEL	G	IP	W-L	SAVES	HITS	SO	BB	ERA
1993	Ok. City AAA	3	15	1-2	0	16	12	5	4.70
1994	Ok. City AAA	10	25	2-1	2	27	15	9	2.84
1994	Texas	13	15	1-5	0	18	9	12	4.30

DWIGHT SMITH / Baltimore Orioles / Outfield $27

Well, at least he's in the right league. Smith is a born DH, an awful outfielder but a lifetime .284 hitter with some power. He finally got to the American League last year, where he could in theory DH, but played for California, which has a strong switch-hitting DH, and Baltimore, which has a strong left-handed DH (Baines). He's a role player.

YEAR	TEAM/LEVEL	G	AB	R	H	2B	3B	HR	RBI	BB	SB	AVG	OBP	SLG
1993	Chicago	111	300	51	93	17	5	11	35	25	8	.300	.355	.494
1994	Two Teams	73	196	31	55	7	2	8	30	12	2	.281	.324	.459
1995	*Projected*	*116*	*274*	*38*	*77*	*14*	*2*	*7*	*32*	*19*	*7*	*.281*	*.328*	*.423*

LEE SMITH / Baltimore Orioles / Closer $47

Had an eight-plus ERA over the last six weeks of the season, and thus enters the '95 season as he has entered the last two: trying to prove he can still do the job. Smith is such a complex character that any comment shorter than a novel risks over-simplification, but my guess is that he may have two years left as a closer.

YEAR	TEAM/LEVEL	G	IP	W-L	SAVES	HITS	SO	BB	ERA
1992	St. Louis	70	75	4-9	43	62	60	26	3.12
1993	Two Teams	63	58	2-4	46	53	60	14	3.88
1994	Baltimore	41	38	1-4	33	34	42	11	3.29

LONNIE SMITH / Baltimore Orioles / Designated Hitter $8

Lonnie is 39 years old, was injured a substantial part of the '94 season, and hit only .203 when he was healthy. He did not get a hit all year against a right-handed pitcher (0-for-17). He hasn't been released as of yet, but it would be a surprise to see his career continue for more than another month or two.

YEAR	TEAM/LEVEL	G	AB	R	H	2B	3B	HR	RBI	BB	SB	AVG	OBP	SLG
1992	Atlanta	84	158	23	39	8	2	6	33	17	4	.247	.324	.437
1993	Two Teams	102	223	43	62	6	4	8	27	51	9	.278	.420	.448
1994	Baltimore	35	59	13	12	3	0	0	2	11	1	.203	.333	.254

OZZIE SMITH / St. Louis Cardinals / Shortstop $38

Ozzie wants to get 2500 hits, apparently to insure that he won't be remembered as a one-way shortstop. He has 2365 hits so far. There is every reason to think he can get the remaining 135 this season. He is 40 years old, still an above-average defensive shortstop, compensating for a weak arm with exceptional quickness. Good OBP, rarely strikes out.

YEAR	TEAM/LEVEL	G	AB	R	H	2B	3B	HR	RBI	BB	SB	AVG	OBP	SLG
1992	St. Louis	132	518	73	153	20	2	0	31	59	43	.295	.367	.342
1993	St. Louis	141	545	75	157	22	6	1	53	43	21	.288	.337	.356
1994	St. Louis	98	381	51	100	18	3	3	30	38	6	.262	.326	.349

PETE SMITH / New York Mets / Starting Pitcher $22

Has a losing record every season in his career except 1992, when he was 7-0; his career record is 34-58. He has pitched most of his career with awful teams, and I used to believe he could win with better luck. I'm less convinced now, and in any case the Mets' many young pitchers may deprive him of further opportunities to try the issue.

YEAR	TEAM/LEVEL	G	IP	W-L	PCT	HITS	SO	BB	ERA
1992	Atlanta	12	79	7-0	1.000	63	43	28	2.05
1993	Atlanta	20	91	4-8	.333	92	53	36	4.37
1994	New York	21	131	4-10	.286	145	62	42	5.55

WILLIE SMITH / St. Louis Cardinals / Reliever $19

A huge right-handed reliever, 6-6, 250, looks like Lee Smith on the mound. He throws very hard, but has been in several systems, and had shoulder and elbow injuries before receiving a trial with the Cardinals. 1994 was his best professional season, with twice as many strikeouts as hits allowed, and the Cardinals do need a closer.

YEAR	TEAM/LEVEL	G	IP	W-L	SAVES	HITS	SO	BB	ERA
1993				(Injured—Did Not Pitch)					
1994	Louisville	44	47	2-3	29	25	54	25	2.31
1994	St. Louis	8	7	1-1	0	9	7	3	9.00

ZANE SMITH / Pittsburgh Pirates / Starting Pitcher $34

Had 306 ground ball outs in '94, only 118 fly ball outs, the highest ground-ball/fly-ball ratio in the National League, other than Greg Maddux. This was his first full season back from shoulder surgery, and it is likely he may be a little bit better this season, '95. Very tough on left-handed hitters, pitches best in cool weather.

YEAR	TEAM/LEVEL	G	IP	W-L	PCT	HITS	SO	BB	ERA
1992	Pittsburgh	23	141	8-8	.500	138	56	19	3.06
1993	Pittsburgh	14	83	3-7	.300	97	32	22	4.55
1994	Pittsburgh	25	157	10-8	.556	162	57	34	3.27

JOHN SMOLTZ / Atlanta Braves / Starting Pitcher $46

He pitched so-so early in the year, and got worse in mid-summer, dropping from the rotation in July. He had surgery after the strike to remove a bone spur from his elbow, and I would guess that he will come back as strong as before, that not being a career-threatening operation. Turns 28 in May, should have five good years left.

YEAR	TEAM/LEVEL	G	IP	W-L	PCT	HITS	SO	BB	ERA
1992	Atlanta	35	247	15-12	.556	206	215	80	2.85
1993	Atlanta	35	244	15-11	.577	208	208	100	3.62
1994	Atlanta	21	135	6-10	.375	120	113	48	4.14

J. T. SNOW / California Angels / First Base $24

Started 1994 at Vancouver, where he drove in 43 runs in 53 games, leading to his recall on June 3. He was the Angels' everyday first baseman the rest of the year, wasn't very good. His defense is an asset; he just needs to be more consistent at bat. I don't think he has All-Star potential, but he could hit a solid .280.

YEAR	TEAM/LEVEL	G	AB	R	H	2B	3B	HR	RBI	BB	SB	AVG	OBP	SLG
1993	California	129	419	60	101	18	2	16	57	55	3	.241	.328	.408
1994	California	61	223	22	49	4	0	8	30	19	0	.220	.289	.345
1995	*Projected*	*99*	*333*	*44*	*85*	*15*	*1*	*11*	*47*	*40*	*1*	*.255*	*.335*	*.405*

CORY SNYDER   /   Los Angeles Dodgers   /   Outfielder/Utility $13

Refused assignment to the minors in October, and is now a free agent. For the Dodgers he was mostly a platoon left fielder, also started one or more games at each infield position and in right field. This "versatility" and his sporadic power will no doubt get him a major league job for '95 . . . hits behind in the count more than 75 percent of the time.

YEAR	TEAM/LEVEL	G	AB	R	H	2B	3B	HR	RBI	BB	SB	AVG	OBP	SLG
1992	San Francisco	124	390	48	105	22	2	14	57	23	4	.269	.311	.444
1993	Los Angeles	143	516	61	137	33	1	11	56	47	4	.266	.331	.397
1994	Los Angeles	73	153	18	36	6	0	6	18	14	1	.235	.300	.392

LUIS SOJO   /   Seattle Mariners   /   Second Base $19

Sojo had a shot as California's second baseman in '91 and '92, and failed the audition, for reasons I didn't really understand. Anyway, he signed a minor league contract with Seattle a year ago, got called up when Amaral started his error-of-the-day plan, and played some second and some short for the Mariners. He certainly *hit* well enough.

YEAR	TEAM/LEVEL	G	AB	R	H	2B	3B	HR	RBI	BB	SB	AVG	OBP	SLG
1992	California	106	368	37	100	12	3	7	43	14	7	.272	.299	.378
1993	Toronto	19	47	5	8	2	0	0	6	4	0	.170	.231	.213
1994	Seattle	63	213	32	59	9	2	6	22	8	2	.277	.308	.423

PAUL SORRENTO   /   Cleveland Indians   /   First Base $28

Criticized before last year for not hitting left-handers and not hitting in the clutch, he hit .270 against left-handers and .360 with runners in scoring position, among the American League's best. He also cut his strikeout rate. . . . Not a cleanup hitter or an All-Star, but a valuable man in the six-seven spots in the order. A very consistent player.

YEAR	TEAM/LEVEL	G	AB	R	H	2B	3B	HR	RBI	BB	SB	AVG	OBP	SLG
1993	Cleveland	148	463	75	119	26	1	18	65	58	3	.257	.340	.434
1994	Cleveland	95	322	43	90	14	0	14	62	34	0	.280	.345	.453
1995	*Projected*	*142*	*453*	*63*	*118*	*26*	*1*	*17*	*65*	*56*	*2*	*.260*	*.342*	*.435*

SAMMY SOSA   /   Chicago Cubs   /   Right Field $53

Had his best major league season in '93, and was on his way to topping it last year, hitting .300, on target for 100 RBI and another 30/30 combo. Has a strong arm and excellent range in right, although he does make errors. He is regarded as hard-working, and is admired by his teammates. Only 26; his run is just beginning.

YEAR	TEAM/LEVEL	G	AB	R	H	2B	3B	HR	RBI	BB	SB	AVG	OBP	SLG
1993	Chicago	159	598	92	156	25	5	33	93	38	36	.261	.309	.485
1994	Chicago	105	426	59	128	17	6	25	70	25	22	.300	.339	.545
1995	*Projected*	*154*	*603*	*90*	*168*	*23*	*6*	*30*	*88*	*40*	*37*	*.279*	*.323*	*.486*

TIM SPEHR / Montreal Expos / Catcher $16

Felipe Alou is one of the few managers left who carries a third catcher—maybe the only one, I don't know. Spehr has been the third man for two years, and played well in '94. He probably does *not* have the ability to move up, but will be around for years. Has good speed, often comes in as pinch runner and catches the last couple of innings.

YEAR	TEAM/LEVEL	G	AB	R	H	2B	3B	HR	RBI	BB	SB	AVG	OBP	SLG
1992	Kansas City	37	74	7	14	5	0	3	14	9	1	.189	.282	.378
1993	Montreal	53	87	14	20	6	0	2	10	6	2	.230	.281	.368
1994	Montreal	52	36	8	9	3	1	0	5	4	2	.250	.325	.389

BILL SPIERS / New York Mets / Infielder $17

A left-handed hitter, one of few middle infielders who platoons, or at least rarely plays against lefties (against whom he has hit .151 over the last three years.) A second baseman in '93, he played mostly short and third last year, wasn't great but wasn't bad. He was 7-for-8 as a base stealer.

YEAR	TEAM/LEVEL	G	AB	R	H	2B	3B	HR	RBI	BB	SB	AVG	OBP	SLG
1992	Milwaukee	12	16	2	5	2	0	0	2	1	1	.313	.353	.438
1993	Milwaukee	113	340	43	81	8	4	2	36	29	9	.238	.302	.303
1994	Milwaukee	73	214	27	54	10	1	0	17	19	7	.252	.316	.308

PAUL SPOLJARIC / Toronto Blue Jays / Left-handed Starting Pitcher $16

A native Canadian who is sporadically, or spoljarically, regarded as the Blue Jays' top pitching prospect. A big, hard-throwing left-hander, fair control, decent curve but sometimes gets beat with it. Lost the 1991 season with a bad elbow. A career .500 pitcher in the minors (35-35); won't be better in the majors.

YEAR	TEAM/LEVEL	G	IP	W-L	PCT	HITS	SO	BB	ERA
1993	Syracuse AAA	18	95	8-7	.533	97	88	52	5.29
1994	Syracuse AAA	8	47	1-5	.167	47	38	28	5.70
1994	Knoxville AA	17	102	6-5	.545	88	79	48	3.62

JERRY SPRADLIN / Florida Marlins / Relief Pitcher $15

An overgrown finesse pitcher, pitched well for the Reds in '93, but nonetheless opened '94 at Indianapolis, and got only a couple of very quick chances to show what he could do in the majors. The Reds asked waivers on him in early August, and the Marlins claimed him. His lack of a fastball limits his future, but he hasn't proven that he *can't* pitch.

YEAR	TEAM/LEVEL	G	IP	W-L	SAVES	HITS	SO	BB	ERA
1993	Cincinnati	37	49	2-1	2	44	24	9	3.49
1994	Two Teams AAA	34	84	4-3	4	99	52	20	3.62
1994	Cincinnati	6	8	0-0	0	12	4	2	10.13

ED SPRAGUE / Toronto Blue Jays / Third Base $22

I am not convinced that Sprague deserves a regular position. He has a fine arm and he has some power potential, but he is slow, has limited range, makes errors, grounds into double plays, doesn't get on base much, and has yet to post a .400 slugging percentage in the majors. May have his best season in '95 if he stays in the lineup.

YEAR	TEAM/LEVEL	G	AB	R	H	2B	3B	HR	RBI	BB	SB	AVG	OBP	SLG
1992	Toronto	22	47	6	11	2	0	1	7	3	0	.234	.280	.340
1993	Toronto	150	546	50	142	31	1	12	73	32	1	.260	.310	.386
1994	Toronto	109	405	38	97	19	1	11	44	23	1	.240	.296	.373

RUSS SPRINGER / California Angels / Starting Pitcher $18

Springer, a part of the Jim Abbott trade, has pitched consistently well in Triple-A, first with the Yankees, then with California. He has not been able to get established in the majors, and the Angels have almost lost confidence in him. I haven't. I believe that once he gets past the 200-inning mark in the majors, he's got a chance to be good.

YEAR	TEAM/LEVEL	G	IP	W-L	PCT	HITS	SO	BB	ERA
1993	California	14	60	1-6	.143	73	31	32	7.20
1994	Vancouver AAA	12	83	7-4	.636	77	58	19	3.04
1994	California	18	46	2-2	.500	53	28	14	5.52

SCOTT STAHOVIAK / Minnesota Twins / Third Base/First Base $13

Left-handed hitter, 25 years old, attended Creighton University. Similar as a hitter to Dave Magadan or Jim Eisenreich, might improve a little. His defense at third is not good, and will probably force him to move to first, where he will challenge Steve Dunn and Dave McCarty for the open spot created by Hrbek's retirement. Grade B prospect.

YEAR	TEAM/LEVEL	G	AB	R	H	2B	3B	HR	RBI	BB	SB	AVG	OBP	SLG
1993	Minnesota	20	57	1	11	4	0	0	1	3	0	.193	.233	.263
1994	Salt Lake AAA	123	437	96	139	41	6	13	94	70	6	.318	.413	.529
1994	MLE	123	415	65	117	36	4	8	63	48	4	.282	.356	.446

MATT STAIRS / Montreal Expos / DH/Left Field $9

Stairs disappeared from the radar screen a couple of years ago, but has been discovered hibernating in a cave under the polar ice cap, and will probably be back in the majors for another shot in '95. He can hit; he could hit .300 in the majors with a little luck, and it's not an empty .300. Defense and bad luck have held him back.

YEAR	TEAM/LEVEL	G	AB	R	H	2B	3B	HR	RBI	BB	SB	AVG	OBP	SLG
1993	Montreal	6	8	1	3	1	0	0	2	0	0	.375	.375	.500
1994	New Brit. AA	93	317	44	98	25	2	9	61	53	10	.309	.407	.486
1994	MLE	93	315	38	96	26	1	7	52	39	6	.305	.381	.460

ANDY STANKIEWICZ / Houston Astros / Utility Infielder $18

Stankiewicz came to Houston in the Domingo Jean/Xavier Hernandez trade, and was the only guy involved who did anything. He made the Astros as a reserve infielder, which means reserve shortstop, since Cam-initi and Biggio never leave the lineup. He made no errors in 17 games at shortstop, and had a .400 on-base percentage. Over-qualified as a reserve.

YEAR	TEAM/LEVEL	G	AB	R	H	2B	3B	HR	RBI	BB	SB	AVG	OBP	SLG
1992	New York (A)	116	400	52	107	22	2	2	25	38	9	.268	.338	.348
1993	Columbus AAA	90	331	45	80	12	5	0	32	29	12	.242	.306	.308
1994	Houston	37	54	10	14	3	0	1	5	12	1	.259	.403	.370

MIKE STANLEY / New York Yankees / Catcher $38

After his big season in '93 he started slowly, hitting .222 through 30 games, then going on the DL with a strained hamstring. When he got back he was an animal, hitting .346 the rest of the year. He threw out 35 percent of base stealers, which is good, and made only three errors. His time is limited, because he waited so long to start hitting.

YEAR	TEAM/LEVEL	G	AB	R	H	2B	3B	HR	RBI	BB	SB	AVG	OBP	SLG
1993	New York	130	423	70	129	17	1	26	84	57	1	.305	.389	.534
1994	New York	82	290	54	87	20	0	17	57	39	0	.300	.384	.545
1995	*Projected*	*113*	*350*	*54*	*95*	*14*	*0*	*15*	*58*	*52*	*0*	*.271*	*.366*	*.440*

MIKE STANTON / Atlanta Braves / Relief Pitcher $24

Stanton throws about as hard as anybody in baseball, but has blown several chances to be the Braves' closer, and may get stuck in the lefty-relief role. He doesn't change speeds well or use his curve well enough to get strikeouts, and his control is so-so. If he takes a step forward in middle relief, he'll get another shot at the closer job.

YEAR	TEAM/LEVEL	G	IP	W-L	SAVES	HITS	SO	BB	ERA
1992	Atlanta	65	64	5-4	8	59	44	20	4.10
1993	Atlanta	63	52	4-6	27	51	43	29	4.67
1994	Atlanta	49	46	3-1	3	41	35	26	3.55

DAVE STATON / San Diego Padres / First Base $8

A Rob Deer-type hitter, tries to compensate for low average and frequent strikeouts with a homer a week. Staton began the '94 season as the Padres' first baseman, was sent down May 20 and spent most of the season at Las Vegas. Very slow, 27 years old, not a good first baseman, injury prone. Grade D prospect; might develop into a platoon player.

YEAR	TEAM/LEVEL	G	AB	R	H	2B	3B	HR	RBI	BB	SB	AVG	OBP	SLG
1993	San Diego	17	42	7	11	3	0	5	9	3	0	.262	.326	.690
1994	San Diego	29	66	6	12	2	0	4	6	10	0	.182	.289	.394
1994	Las Vegas AAA	79	271	39	75	10	2	12	47	44	0	.277	.382	.461

TERRY STEINBACH / Oakland Athletics / Catcher $36

He has the same stats every year. In his eight major league seasons he's hit between .273 and .285 six times, hit 9 to 12 homers five times. Excellent defensive catcher, threw out 40 percent of base stealers last year, best in the American League. He is 33, and his hitting may begin to decline this year, and will decline within a couple of years.

YEAR	TEAM/LEVEL	G	AB	R	H	2B	3B	HR	RBI	BB	SB	AVG	OBP	SLG
1992	Oakland	128	438	48	122	20	1	12	53	45	2	.279	.345	.411
1993	Oakland	104	389	47	111	19	1	10	43	25	3	.285	.333	.416
1994	Oakland	103	369	51	105	21	2	11	57	26	2	.285	.327	.442

DAVE STEVENS / Minnesota Twins / Relief Pitcher $12

Originally in the Cubs' system, where he was a starting pitcher, with unimpressive results. He moved to the bullpen in mid-1993, and was traded to the Twins as part of the Banks/Walbeck trade. A good half-season at Salt Lake City got him to the majors. He throws hard, has a good slider, poor control, no off-speed pitch. Grade C prospect.

YEAR	TEAM/LEVEL	G	IP	W-L	SAVES	HITS	SO	BB	ERA
1993	Iowa AAA	24	34	4-0	4	24	29	14	4.19
1994	Salt Lake AAA	23	43	6-2	3	41	30	16	1.67
1994	Minnesota	24	45	5-2	0	55	24	23	6.80

DAVE STEWART / Toronto Blue Jays / Starting Pitcher $12

Has left Toronto as a free agent. Stewart has talked frequently about retiring, plus he is 38 years old, coming off his first losing season since 1985, and has just posted the highest earned run average of his career. On the other hand, his strikeout rate was also the highest of his career, and if he wants to come back I wouldn't bet against him.

YEAR	TEAM/LEVEL	G	IP	W-L	PCT	HITS	SO	BB	ERA
1992	Oakland	31	199	12-10	.545	175	130	79	3.66
1993	Toronto	26	162	12-8	.600	146	96	72	4.44
1994	Toronto	22	133	7-8	.467	151	111	62	5.87

PHIL STIDHAM / Detroit Tigers / Relief Pitcher $12

A 17th-round pick in 1991, out of the University of Arkansas. Stidham throws sidearm and doesn't throw hard, tries to get right-handers to swing at pitches in the dirt outside and works lefties in on the fists. He probably won't be a major league closer, but could have a good career as a set-up man and ground-ball specialist.

YEAR	TEAM/LEVEL	G	IP	W-L	SAVES	HITS	SO	BB	ERA
1993	London AA	33	34	2-2	2	40	39	19	2.38
1994	AA and AAA	55	75	3-3	6	52	63	31	2.88
1994	Detroit	5	4	0-0	0	12	4	4	24.92

KELLY STINNETT / New York Mets / Catcher $18

A 25-year-old catcher, drafted from Cleveland under Rule 5, and stuck with the Mets as Hundley's backup. 5-11, 195 pounds, strong, good arm, good defense. He's not helpless at bat. He's at least as good a player as Brad Ausmus or Joe Girardi, potentially better. Solid backup, won't hurt the team if he has to go into the lineup due to an injury.

YEAR	TEAM/LEVEL	G	AB	R	H	2B	3B	HR	RBI	BB	SB	AVG	OBP	SLG
1993	MLE	98	276	32	67	8	1	4	25	13	0	.243	.277	.322
1994	New York	47	150	20	38	6	2	2	14	11	2	.253	.323	.360
1995	*Projected*	*76*	*218*	*25*	*56*	*7*	*1*	*4*	*21*	*11*	*3*	*.257*	*.293*	*.353*

KEVIN STOCKER / Philadelphia Phillies / Shortstop $34

He missed a month with torn ligaments in his right wrist, but played extremely well the rest of the season. Through 152 major league games he has hit .298, with a .396 on-base percentage. I doubt that he will be a career .298 hitter, but he is the best shortstop the Phillies have had since Larry Bowa. Not yet a Gold Glove shortstop.

YEAR	TEAM/LEVEL	G	AB	R	H	2B	3B	HR	RBI	BB	SB	AVG	OBP	SLG
1993	Philadelphia	70	259	46	84	12	3	2	31	30	5	.324	.409	.417
1994	Philadelphia	82	271	38	74	11	2	2	28	44	2	.273	.383	.351
1995	*Projected*	*134*	*457*	*67*	*125*	*20*	*2*	*4*	*41*	*52*	*11*	*.274*	*.348*	*.352*

TODD STOTTLEMYRE / Toronto Blue Jays / Starting Pitcher $21

He's a free agent now, and as such he serves as a kind of IQ test for general managers. If he pitches .500 ball with the Blue Jays, how will he do with your team? If he has a career ERA of 4.39 in his twenties, what will it be in his thirties? Trust me: You *don't* want to pay $8 or $10 million to find out.

YEAR	TEAM/LEVEL	G	IP	W-L	PCT	HITS	SO	BB	ERA
1992	Toronto	28	174	12-11	.522	175	98	63	4.50
1993	Toronto	30	177	11-12	.478	204	98	69	4.84
1994	Toronto	26	141	7-7	.500	149	105	48	4.22

DOUG STRANGE / Texas Rangers / Second Base/Utility Player $19

After years of waiting, he became Texas' second baseman by default in 1993, when Frye and Ripken and Shave were all unable to play. He had a good year, and started '94 as the Rangers' second baseman, but didn't hit, then had an injury of his own, a knee injury, during which time Jeff Frye took over the job. Good backup infielder, no regular.

YEAR	TEAM/LEVEL	G	AB	R	H	2B	3B	HR	RBI	BB	SB	AVG	OBP	SLG
1993	Texas	145	484	58	124	29	0	7	60	43	6	.256	.318	.360
1994	Texas	73	226	26	48	12	1	5	26	15	1	.212	.268	.341
1995	*Projected*	*94*	*273*	*31*	*67*	*16*	*1*	*4*	*30*	*20*	*3*	*.245*	*.297*	*.355*

DARRYL STRAWBERRY / San Francisco Giants / Right Field $24

Got into 29 games with the Giants, and played well. He has fully recovered from his back injury. Of course he is always going to be a risk, and at 33 his upside potential is not what it once was. But I would bet on him to play 130-140 games this year, and I don't think it is impossible that he might drive in 90 or 100 runs.

YEAR	TEAM/LEVEL	G	AB	R	H	2B	3B	HR	RBI	BB	SB	AVG	OBP	SLG
1993	Los Angeles	32	100	12	14	2	0	5	12	16	1	.140	.267	.310
1994	San Francisco	29	92	13	22	3	1	4	17	19	0	.239	.363	.424
1995	*Projected*	*129*	*413*	*52*	*102*	*18*	*2*	*19*	*72*	*70*	*5*	*.247*	*.356*	*.438*

B. J. SURHOFF / Milwaukee Brewers / Third Base/Catcher/Outfield $21

A free agent, coming off an injury year (sore shoulder, strained abdominal muscle, abdominal surgery). A seven-year regular, he was always marginal as an everyday player, either at catcher or third base. But he's a consistent .260 to .270 hitter, runs fairly well, has good work habits, and can play several positions. That should make him a dynamite bench player.

YEAR	TEAM/LEVEL	G	AB	R	H	2B	3B	HR	RBI	BB	SB	AVG	OBP	SLG
1993	Milwaukee	148	552	66	151	38	3	7	79	36	12	.274	.318	.391
1994	Milwaukee	40	134	20	35	11	2	5	22	16	0	.261	.336	.485
1995	*Projected*	*98*	*340*	*42*	*88*	*16*	*2*	*4*	*43*	*29*	*8*	*.259*	*.317*	*.353*

RICK SUTCLIFFE / St. Louis Cardinals / Starting Pitcher $7

He finally staggered out of the Cardinals' rotation in late July, due to an injured rotator cuff, and he is expected to retire (but look at it this way: If you could make just a few hundred thousand a year playing baseball, would *you* retire?) His career record in 171-139—about thirty wins short of the worst guys in the Hall of Fame.

YEAR	TEAM/LEVEL	G	IP	W-L	PCT	HITS	SO	BB	ERA
1992	Baltimore	36	237	16-15	.516	251	109	74	4.47
1993	Baltimore	29	166	10-10	.500	212	80	74	5.75
1994	St. Louis	16	68	6-4	.600	93	26	32	6.52

DALE SVEUM / Seattle Mariners / Strikeout Artist $2

He hit 22 homers at Calgary, which got him back to Seattle to post another sub-.200 batting average, his third in a row and fourth in five years. Since he's a switch hitter, once played shortstop and once drove in 95 runs, baseball men are always tempted to see if maybe he can do *something* to help. He can't. He does everything, but badly.

YEAR	TEAM/LEVEL	G	AB	R	H	2B	3B	HR	RBI	BB	SB	AVG	OBP	SLG
1992	Two Teams	94	249	28	49	13	0	4	28	28	1	.197	.273	.297
1993	Oakland	30	79	12	14	2	1	2	6	16	0	.177	.316	.304
1994	Seattle	10	27	3	5	0	0	1	2	2	0	.185	.241	.296

RUSS SWAN / Cleveland Indians / Relief Pitcher $6

Swan is a left-hander, one of countless Seattle Mariners who was tried as a closer. Released by the Mariners a year ago, he signed with Cleveland and pitched 12 times for them in April (and boy, was that ugly). He spent the rest of the year at Charlotte, where his ERA was 7.09. His career is all but over at 31.

YEAR	TEAM/LEVEL	G	IP	W-L	SAVES	HITS	SO	BB	ERA
1992	Seattle	55	104	3-10	9	104	45	45	4.74
1993	Seattle	23	20	3-3	0	25	10	18	9.15
1994	Cleveland	12	8	0-1	0	13	2	7	11.25

BILL SWIFT / San Francisco Giants / Starting Pitcher $49

A free agent. He is prone to minor injuries which limit his innings, such as the inflamed muscle in his side in '94. Healthy, he is among the best pitchers in baseball. His sinking fastball gets him more ground balls than any other major league pitcher, and he has other pitches to come back with if he needs them. Has career batting average of .215.

YEAR	TEAM/LEVEL	G	IP	W-L	PCT	HITS	SO	BB	ERA
1992	San Francisco	30	165	10-4	.714	144	77	43	2.08
1993	San Francisco	34	233	21-8	.724	195	157	55	2.82
1994	San Francisco	17	109	8-7	.533	109	62	31	3.38

GREG SWINDELL / Houston Astros / Starting Pitcher $34

I have always liked Swindell, because strikeout/walk ratio is the best indicator of future success in a pitcher, and Swindell's strikeout/walk ratios have always been (and still are) outstanding. Every other indicator of future success for him is going downhill rapidly, and you would have to be concerned. Pitches best when he can get an extra day's rest.

YEAR	TEAM/LEVEL	G	IP	W-L	PCT	HITS	SO	BB	ERA
1992	Cincinnati	31	214	12-8	.600	210	138	41	2.70
1993	Houston	31	190	12-13	.480	215	124	40	4.16
1994	Houston	24	148	8-9	.471	175	74	26	4.37

JEFF (SMOKIN') TABAKA / San Diego Padres / Left-handed Reliever $13

Minor league veteran, 31 years of age, had a real good year with El Paso in 1992, and has been looking for a chance to prove himself as a lefty one-out guy. He pitched five times for the Pirates in April, got hit hard, went to the Padres on waivers, and pitched fairly well in San Diego (3.89 ERA). Limited future.

YEAR	TEAM/LEVEL	G	IP	W-L	SAVES	HITS	SO	BB	ERA
1993	New Orleans AAA	53	58	6-6	1	50	63	30	3.24
1994	Buffalo AAA	9	5	1-0	1	3	4	4	3.38
1994	Two Teams	39	41	3-1	1	32	32	27	5.27

JEFF TACKETT / Baltimore Orioles / Catcher $14

Bob Melvin-type backup catcher, good defense, doesn't hit much, will never be a regular. There is something funny about him, as a hitter. He has a career average of .308 against left-handers, .190 against right-handers, although not enough at bats against lefties that you'd want to rely on that, but against right-handers he just dribbles ground balls.

YEAR	TEAM/LEVEL	G	AB	R	H	2B	3B	HR	RBI	BB	SB	AVG	OBP	SLG
1992	Baltimore	65	179	21	43	8	1	5	24	17	0	.240	.307	.380
1993	Baltimore	39	87	8	15	3	0	0	9	13	0	.172	.277	.207
1994	Baltimore	26	53	5	12	3	1	2	9	5	0	.226	.317	.434

KEVIN TAPANI / Minnesota Twins / Starting Pitcher $28

The Twins' best starting pitcher, because a) he never walks anybody, and b) their other starters are really, really awful. The ERA of Twins' starters last year was 5.84; without Tapani it was way over six. The average against Tapani was .291, and he leads the American League every year in doubles allowed—44 last year, 56 the year before. Can pitch better.

YEAR	TEAM/LEVEL	G	IP	W-L	PCT	HITS	SO	BB	ERA
1992	Minnesota	34	220	16-11	.593	226	138	48	3.97
1993	Minnesota	36	226	12-15	.444	243	150	57	4.43
1994	Minnesota	24	156	11-7	.611	181	91	39	4.62

TONY TARASCO / Atlanta Braves / Outfield $29

This guy is too good to be riding the bench. He got into 87 games last (51 of them as a pinch hitter), and played awfully well, but actually lost playing time as the season went on, due to Ryan Klesko's power. He's going to be a fine major league player, probably comparable to Reggie Sanders, Moises Alou, or Jeff Conine, but left-handed.

YEAR	TEAM/LEVEL	G	AB	R	H	2B	3B	HR	RBI	BB	SB	AVG	OBP	SLG
1993	Atlanta	24	35	6	8	2	0	0	2	0	0	.229	.243	.286
1994	Atlanta	87	132	16	36	6	0	5	19	9	5	.273	.313	.432
1995	*Projected*	*107*	*307*	*44*	*88*	*13*	*1*	*9*	*36*	*17*	*12*	*.287*	*.324*	*.429*

DANNY TARTABULL / New York Yankees / Designated Hitter $38

Tartabull rarely attempts to play the outfield anymore, which helps to keep him healthy, and also shelters him from the criticism that inevitably follows his defensive misadventures. He's a legitimate cleanup hitter, has never had a season when he wouldn't have driven in 95 runs if he got the at bats. There are rumors that the Yankees may move him.

YEAR	TEAM/LEVEL	G	AB	R	H	2B	3B	HR	RBI	BB	SB	AVG	OBP	SLG
1992	New York	123	421	72	112	19	0	25	85	103	2	.266	.409	.489
1993	New York	138	513	87	128	33	2	31	102	92	0	.250	.363	.503
1994	New York	104	399	68	102	24	1	19	67	66	1	.256	.360	.464

JIM TATUM / Colorado Rockies / Pinch Hitter/Catcher $16

Tatum is an outstanding hitter, but he is slow and doesn't have a defensive position, and he hasn't caught a break yet. The Rockies have sent him to the Arizona Fall League to try to make him a catcher, which will probably take years to pay off even if it works, and Tatum is 27. But he's a hell of a lot better hitter than Joe Girardi.

YEAR	TEAM/LEVEL	G	AB	R	H	2B	3B	HR	RBI	BB	SB	AVG	OBP	SLG
1993	Colorado	92	98	7	20	5	0	1	12	5	0	.204	.245	.286
1994	Colo. Sp. AAA	121	439	76	154	43	1	21	97	44	2	.351	.408	.597
1994	MLE	121	421	53	136	37	0	16	68	32	1	.323	.371	.525

EDDIE TAUBENSEE / Cincinnati Reds / Catcher $30

Taubensee had the misfortune to be traded for Kenny Lofton, so the Astros were always disappointed in him, no matter how well he played. The Reds, needing a catcher after Oliver's injury, traded for Taubensee and platooned him with Brian Dorsett, and he had a slugging percentage of almost .500 after the trade. Only 26, an above-average defensive catcher, and a solid left-handed hitter.

YEAR	TEAM/LEVEL	G	AB	R	H	2B	3B	HR	RBI	BB	SB	AVG	OBP	SLG
1993	Houston	94	288	26	72	11	1	9	42	21	1	.250	.299	.389
1994	Two Teams	66	187	29	53	8	2	8	21	15	2	.283	.333	.476
1995	*Projected*	*116*	*339*	*38*	*91*	*18*	*2*	*10*	*43*	*30*	*2*	*.268*	*.328*	*.422*

JESUS TAVAREZ / Florida Marlins / Outfield $15

A 24-year-old Dominican, taken from Seattle in the first round of the expansion draft. He's a switch hitter, fast, good defensive outfielder. He is expected to develop, if he develops, as a leadoff hitter. He'll take a walk, and might hit for a good average in time. The Marlins already have a crowded outfield, and 1995 will probably be Tavarez' Triple-A season.

YEAR	TEAM/LEVEL	G	AB	R	H	2B	3B	HR	RBI	BB	SB	AVG	OBP	SLG
1993	High Desert A	109	444	104	130	21	8	7	71	57	47	.293	.375	.423
1994	Portland AA	89	353	60	101	11	8	2	32	35	20	.286	.351	.380
1994	Florida	17	39	4	7	0	0	0	4	1	1	.179	.200	.179

JULIAN TAVAREZ / Cleveland Indians / Starting Pitcher $20

Rushed to the majors as a 20-year-old in 1993, didn't pitch well, and spent 1994 back at Charlotte. Thin, looks like he will blow away with the breeze, but throws a live fastball and a sharp breaking pitch, with good control. He had a terrific year in Triple-A, and he might eventually be a fine pitcher, but probably not before 1997.

YEAR	TEAM/LEVEL	G	IP	W-L	PCT	HITS	SO	BB	ERA
1993	Canton-Akr. AA	3	19	2-1	.667	14	11	1	0.95
1993	Cleveland	8	37	2-2	.500	53	19	13	6.57
1994	Charlotte AAA	26	176	15-6	.714	167	102	43	3.48

BILLY TAYLOR / Oakland Athletics / Relief Pitcher $27

Is 33 years old, a 6-8, 200-pound stringbean. He's been pitching professionally since 1980, was ineffective as a starter most of his career, but converted to relief in 1989 and has been outstanding since. The A's signed him as a free agent, and he struck out more than one per inning, holding batters to a .220 average. He'll continue to pitch well.

YEAR	TEAM/LEVEL	G	IP	W-L	SAVES	HITS	SO	BB	ERA
1992	Richmond AAA	47	79	2-3	12	72	82	27	2.28
1993	Richmond AAA	59	68	2-4	26	56	81	26	1.98
1994	Oakland	41	46	1-3	1	38	48	18	3.50

KERRY TAYLOR / San Diego Padres / Right-handed Pitcher $16

After jumping from A Ball to the majors in 1993 (he was a Rule 5 draftee from the Twins), Taylor went down to Triple-A for the 1994 season. He wasn't awful. A 5.54 earned run average at Las Vegas is like a 4.30 mark in other Triple-A parks. Throws hard, has a curve, is learning to throw strikes. Grade C prospect.

YEAR	TEAM/LEVEL	G	IP	W-L	PCT	HITS	SO	BB	ERA
1992	Kenosha A	27	170	10-9	.526	150	158	68	2.75
1993	San Diego	36	68	0-5	.000	72	45	49	6.45
1994	Las Vegas AAA	27	156	9-9	.500	175	142	81	5.54

ANTHONY TELFORD / Atlanta Braves / Right-handed Pitcher $14

Telford is probably a major league pitcher, but never got a clear shot with the Orioles, and signed with Atlanta as a minor league free agent. Atlanta doesn't exactly have frequent openings on their pitching staff, and has better candidates than Telford to fill any that may develop. Shoulder injuries have taken his fastball, but he knows how to use what he has.

YEAR	TEAM/LEVEL	G	IP	W-L	PCT	HITS	SO	BB	ERA
1992	Rochester AAA	27	181	12-7	.632	183	129	64	4.18
1993	Rochester AAA	38	91	7-7	.500	98	66	33	4.27
1994	Richmond AAA	38	143	10-6	.625	148	111	41	4.23

DAVE TELGHEDER / New York Mets / Right-handed Pitcher $15

Spent most of '93 with the Mets and opened '94 in New York, but returned in April to Norfolk, where he pitched fairly well. He's 28, graduated from U-Mass before entering baseball. The Mets have many young pitching prospects who throw harder, and Telgheder is unlikely to receive another chance to be a starting pitcher.

YEAR	TEAM/LEVEL	G	IP	W-L	PCT	HITS	SO	BB	ERA
1993	New York	24	76	6-2	.750	82	35	21	4.76
1994	New York	6	10	0-1	.000	11	4	8	7.20
1994	Norfolk AAA	23	159	8-10	.444	156	83	26	3.40

MICKEY TETTLETON / Detroit Tigers / Catcher/Utility Regular　　$39

Is 34 years old, played mainly at catcher last season (53 games at catcher, 24 at first, 18 in the outfield) after moving all around in 1993. His defense behind the plate is better than his reputation, although he doesn't have a strong arm. But he puts a ton of runs on the scoreboard with his power and walks, and shows no signs of growing old.

YEAR	TEAM/LEVEL	G	AB	R	H	2B	3B	HR	RBI	BB	SB	AVG	OBP	SLG
1992	Detroit	157	525	82	125	25	0	32	83	122	0	.238	.379	.469
1993	Detroit	152	522	79	128	25	4	32	110	109	3	.245	.372	.492
1994	Detroit	107	339	57	84	18	2	17	51	97	0	.248	.419	.463

BOB TEWKSBURY / St. Louis Cardinals / Starting Pitcher　　$31

An archetype, a repository of extreme characteristics. One of the best control pitchers ever, but has led the National League in hits allowed the last two years. There is a theory that the lively ball hurts control pitchers most, because they put the ball in play. I don't know whether I believe this or not, but Tewksbury is 50-50 to come back strong.

YEAR	TEAM/LEVEL	G	IP	W-L	PCT	HITS	SO	BB	ERA
1992	St. Louis	33	233	16-5	.762	217	91	20	2.16
1993	St. Louis	32	214	17-10	.630	258	97	20	3.83
1994	St. Louis	24	156	12-10	.545	190	79	22	5.32

BOBBY THIGPEN / Released / Relief Pitcher　　$9

Piniella thought he could turn him around, but after allowing 17 baserunners in eight innings he was released. He still throws hard, and as long as he is healthy, there is always the chance he could develop a new pitch and make a comeback. I would rather take my chances on someone else, like John Tudor, Luis Tiant, or Catfish Hunter.

YEAR	TEAM/LEVEL	G	IP	W-L	SAVES	HITS	SO	BB	ERA
1992	Chicago	55	55	1-3	22	58	45	33	4.75
1993	Two Teams	42	54	3-1	1	74	29	21	5.83
1994	Seattle	7	8	0-2	0	12	4	5	9.39

FRANK THOMAS / Chicago White Sox / First Base　　$98

Babe Ruth, Ted Williams, Frank Thomas . . . maybe the three best hitters God ever made. Gets on base half the time, has tremendous power, hits .350 . . . what more could you want? He works hard, stays healthy, never slumps. Only weaknesses are his glove and speed. When the White Sox picked him seventh overall in the 1989 draft, they were widely ridiculed by the scouting community.

YEAR	TEAM/LEVEL	G	AB	R	H	2B	3B	HR	RBI	BB	SB	AVG	OBP	SLG
1993	Chicago	153	549	106	174	36	0	41	128	112	4	.317	.426	.607
1994	Chicago	113	399	106	141	34	1	38	101	109	2	.353	.487	.729
1995	*Projected*	*159*	*565*	*122*	*188*	*39*	*2*	*40*	*128*	*136*	*4*	*.333*	*.462*	*.621*

JIM THOME / Cleveland Indians / Third Base $40

One of the best-hitting third basemen in baseball, and still several years away from his prime. His two main weaknesses are left-handed pitching (hit .167 against them last year) and his glove. He arrived with a good defensive reputation, but didn't play well. The Indians may give the third base job to David Bell, with Thome moving to first or the outfield.

YEAR	TEAM/LEVEL	G	AB	R	H	2B	3B	HR	RBI	BB	SB	AVG	OBP	SLG
1993	Cleveland	47	154	28	41	11	0	7	22	29	2	.266	.385	.474
1994	Cleveland	98	321	58	86	20	1	20	52	46	3	.268	.359	.523
1995	*Projected*	*135*	*452*	*75*	*129*	*27*	*2*	*18*	*74*	*69*	*3*	*.279*	*.373*	*.463*

MARK THOMPSON / Colorado Rockies / Starting Prospect $23

Thompson was Colorado's second round pick in 1992, a hard thrower from the University of Kentucky, and will get a chance to make the majors in 1995. His performance in Triple-A last year was not impressive on the surface, but Colorado Springs is an awful place to pitch, worse than Mile High. Grade B prospect. Few young pitchers slip easily into major league success.

YEAR	TEAM/LEVEL	G	IP	W-L	PCT	HITS	SO	BB	ERA
1993	Colo. Spr. AAA	4	33	3-0	1.000	31	22	11	2.70
1994	Colo. Spr. AAA	23	140	8-9	.471	169	82	57	4.49
1994	Colorado	2	9	1-1	.500	16	5	8	9.00

MILT THOMPSON / Houston Astros / Left Field $21

Quality reserve outfielder, picked up by the Astros for the pennant drive that never was. Good line drive hitter, still pretty fast, shows few signs of slipping although he is now 36. Left-handed hitter, 77 percent base stealer in his career. Usually plays left because his arm is marginal for the other positions, but can play center or right if needed.

YEAR	TEAM/LEVEL	G	AB	R	H	2B	3B	HR	RBI	BB	SB	AVG	OBP	SLG
1993	Philadelphia	129	340	42	89	14	2	4	44	40	9	.262	.341	.350
1994	Two Teams	96	241	34	66	7	0	4	33	24	9	.274	.346	.353
1995	*Projected*	*107*	*246*	*33*	*65*	*12*	*2*	*3*	*30*	*25*	*10*	*.264*	*.332*	*.366*

ROBBY THOMPSON / San Francisco Giants / Second Base $23

Missed most of the season with a sore shoulder, eventually diagnosed as a torn rotator cuff; he had surgery to repair it in mid-July, and his status to begin the 1995 season is uncertain. My best guess is that his bat will put him back in the lineup at first base, but that he'll never be able to play second again.

YEAR	TEAM/LEVEL	G	AB	R	H	2B	3B	HR	RBI	BB	SB	AVG	OBP	SLG
1993	San Francisco	128	494	85	154	30	2	19	65	45	10	.312	.375	.496
1994	San Francisco	35	129	13	27	8	2	2	7	15	3	.209	.290	.349
1995	*Projected*	*129*	*449*	*58*	*116*	*23*	*3*	*12*	*45*	*44*	*8*	*.258*	*.325*	*.403*

RYAN THOMPSON / New York Mets / Center Field | $25

In 622 at bats over two seasons he has hit 29 homers and driven in 85. He strikes out so much, however, that his average is low, and seems to be going lower. He may also be suffering from Ed Whitson's Disease, the inability to perform in New York City—anyway, he hit .305 on the road last year, but .134 in New York.

YEAR	TEAM/LEVEL	G	AB	R	H	2B	3B	HR	RBI	BB	SB	AVG	OBP	SLG
1993	New York	80	288	34	72	19	2	11	26	19	2	.250	.302	.444
1994	New York	98	334	39	75	14	1	18	59	28	1	.225	.301	.434
1995	*Projected*	*155*	*550*	*71*	*128*	*24*	*3*	*21*	*63*	*45*	*7*	*.239*	*.291*	*.402*

MIKE TIMLIN / Toronto Blue Jays / Relief Pitcher | $23

Got off to a terrible start, with earned run averages of 8.10 in April and 7.56 in May. He pitched very well the rest of the year, and I would be vaguely optimistic that he might be ready to emerge from whatever cloud has been following him for three years, since his fine rookie season (1991). Throws hard, throws a great slider.

YEAR	TEAM/LEVEL	G	IP	W-L	SAVES	HITS	SO	BB	ERA
1992	Toronto	26	44	0-2	1	45	35	20	4.12
1993	Toronto	54	56	4-2	1	63	49	27	4.63
1994	Toronto	34	40	0-1	2	41	38	20	5.18

RON TINGLEY / Chicago White Sox / Catcher | $13

Released by California, Tingley signed with the Marlins, refused assignment to the minors in late June, became a free agent, and signed with the White Sox, where he spent the remainder of the season. Turns 36 in May; has tendinitis in his shoulder, which is not a good thing to have if you are a decent defensive catcher who can't hit. Career is almost over.

YEAR	TEAM/LEVEL	G	AB	R	H	2B	3B	HR	RBI	BB	SB	AVG	OBP	SLG
1992	California	71	127	15	25	2	1	3	8	13	2	.197	.282	.299
1993	California	58	90	7	18	7	0	0	12	9	1	.200	.277	.278
1994	Two Teams	24	57	4	9	3	1	1	2	5	0	.158	.226	.298

LEE TINSLEY / Boston Red Sox / Outfielder | $19

When Dan Duquette took over the Red Sox, he vowed to bring more speed to Fenway, and Tinsley was one of his first acquistions. Tinsley put in an OK season off the bench, stole 13 bases in 13 tries. He runs well, fields well, is a switch hitter with a little power, will take a walk. He won't hit enough to be a regular outfielder.

YEAR	TEAM/LEVEL	G	AB	R	H	2B	3B	HR	RBI	BB	SB	AVG	OBP	SLG
1993	MLE	111	424	64	110	20	10	7	43	34	22	.259	.314	.403
1993	Seattle	11	19	2	3	1	0	1	2	2	0	.158	.238	.368
1994	Boston	78	144	27	32	4	0	2	14	19	13	.222	.315	.292

ANDY TOMBERLIN / Boston Red Sox / Outfield $16

Tomberlin can play a little, a left-handed hitter, a former pitcher who still throws well, can run, hits line drives and occasional homers, good plate discipline. He's as capable a major league player as Wayne Kirby, Mitch Webster, Thomas Howard, or Mike Felder, better than some. Now 28, could surprise a lot of people if he gets the playing time.

YEAR	TEAM/LEVEL	G	AB	R	H	2B	3B	HR	RBI	BB	SB	AVG	OBP	SLG
1993	Buffalo AAA	68	221	41	63	11	6	12	45	18	3	.285	.347	.552
1993	Pittsburgh	27	42	4	12	0	1	1	5	2	0	.286	.333	.405
1994	Pawtucket AAA	54	189	38	63	12	2	13	39	22	11	.333	.407	.624

RANDY TOMLIN / Pittsburgh Pirates / Starting Pitcher $12

Tomlin pitches like a man tossing eggs, so there was always skepticism about him, even when he pitched well from 1990 through 1992. He had tendinitis and a bone spur on his elbow in 1993, and has lost his fine edge. He may come back, like Jamie Moyer or Bob Tewksbury, after a couple of years in the minors. He's a poor gamble for 1995.

YEAR	TEAM/LEVEL	G	IP	W-L	PCT	HITS	SO	BB	ERA
1992	Pittsburgh	35	209	14-9	.609	226	90	42	3.41
1993	Pittsburgh	18	98	4-8	.333	109	44	15	4.85
1994	Pittsburgh	10	21	0-3	.000	23	17	10	3.92

DILSON TORRES / Kansas City Royals / Right-handed Pitcher $19

A big Venezuelan, 6-3, 200. The Royals took him from the Blue Jays in the minor league Rule 5, and he pitched exceptionally well for two farm clubs, going 13-2, with a 96/25 strikeout/walk ratio in 118 innings. His performance didn't suffer when he moved to Double-A. Turns 25 on May 31; will start the season at Omaha.

YEAR	TEAM/LEVEL	G	IP	W-L	PCT	HITS	SO	BB	ERA
1993	St. Catharines A	17	23	1-4	.200	21	23	6	3.13
1994	Wilmington A	15	59	7-2	.778	47	49	15	1.37
1994	Memphis AA	10	59	6-0	1.000	47	47	10	1.83

SALOMON TORRES / San Francisco Giants / Right-handed Starting Pitcher $22

Torres started and lost the pennant-losing game of 1993, which carried over into 1994. He tried to leave the team, saying that he "didn't have the stuff to pitch at this level" and that his religion (Jehovah's Witness) was more important than baseball. Dusty Baker talked him into returning, but he didn't improve, and was sent to Phoenix in July. A risk for 1995.

YEAR	TEAM/LEVEL	G	IP	W-L	PCT	HITS	SO	BB	ERA
1993	San Francisco	8	45	3-5	.375	37	23	27	4.03
1994	San Francisco	16	84	2-8	.200	95	42	34	5.44
1994	Phoenix AAA	13	79	5-6	.455	85	64	31	4.22

STEVE TRACHSEL / Chicago Cubs / Right-handed Starting Pitcher $42

Everything about him is consistent with the expectation that he will have a brilliant future, that he will be one of the premier pitchers of the next 10 years. Throws an excellent forkball, a very good curve, an average fastball. Missed a little time with a blister on his finger. The only real question about him is whether he'll stay healthy.

YEAR	TEAM/LEVEL	G	IP	W-L	PCT	HITS	SO	BB	ERA
1993	Iowa AAA	27	171	13-6	.684	170	135	45	3.96
1993	Chicago	3	20	0-2	.000	16	14	3	4.58
1994	Chicago	22	146	9-7	.563	133	108	54	3.21

ALAN TRAMMELL / Detroit Tigers / Shortstop $28

Still playing well at 37. He is exclusively a shortstop again, after a couple of years moving around making room for Fryman. He has been the Tigers' shortstop for half of his life, and is clearly the best shortstop the Tigers have ever had, probably one of the 15 best shortstops in baseball history. Now shares the position with Chris Gomez.

YEAR	TEAM/LEVEL	G	AB	R	H	2B	3B	HR	RBI	BB	SB	AVG	OBP	SLG
1993	Detroit	112	401	72	132	25	3	12	60	38	12	.329	.388	.496
1994	Detroit	76	292	38	78	17	1	8	28	16	3	.267	.307	.414
1995	*Projected*	*96*	*337*	*43*	*89*	*17*	*1*	*7*	*36*	*28*	*6*	*.264*	*.321*	*.383*

JEFF TREADWAY / Los Angeles Dodgers / Utility Infield/Pinch Hitter $20

Hit .303 with Cleveland in '93, but was released anyway. He signed a minor league contract with the Dodgers, made the team, and hit about .300 again, including 13-for-27 as a pinch hitter. He's a second baseman who can't really play second, can't throw, but hits better than most *regular* second basemen, let alone backups. Ability to pinch hit will keep him around.

YEAR	TEAM/LEVEL	G	AB	R	H	2B	3B	HR	RBI	BB	SB	AVG	OBP	SLG
1993	Cleveland	97	221	25	67	14	1	2	27	14	1	.303	.347	.403
1994	Los Angeles	52	67	14	20	3	0	0	5	5	1	.299	.351	.343
1995	*Projected*	*61*	*97*	*11*	*26*	*8*	*1*	*1*	*9*	*7*	*1*	*.268*	*.317*	*.402*

RICKY TRLICEK / Boston Red Sox / Relief Pitcher $16

Has been turned loose by Philadelphia, Atlanta, Toronto, and Los Angeles, always for the same reason: He can't pitch. He throws hard, so he keeps getting chances, and he's only 26, so things may eventually work out for him. A big guy, 6-3, 200 pounds, collects baseball cards. His name is pronounced Trill-Chek.

YEAR	TEAM/LEVEL	G	IP	W-L	SAVES	HITS	SO	BB	ERA
1993	Los Angeles	41	64	1-2	1	59	41	21	4.08
1994	AA and AAA	17	52	2-2	0	31	32	19	1.73
1994	Boston	12	22	1-1	0	32	7	16	8.06

MIKE TROMBLEY / Minnesota Twins / Reliever/Starter $17

A Mike Boddicker-type, throws a big slurve, which I think means sloppy curve. Is 28 years old, no fastball, good control. Tom Kelly didn't give him a start last year, although a) he's been an effective minor league starter, b) his career record in 17 major league starts isn't bad, and c) the Twins starting pitchers were mostly on a suicide watch. Needs to pitch.

YEAR	TEAM/LEVEL	G	IP	W-L	PCT	HITS	SO	BB	ERA
1992	Minnesota	10	46	3-2	.600	43	38	17	3.30
1993	Minnesota	44	114	6-6	.500	131	85	41	4.88
1994	Minnesota	24	48	2-0	1.000	56	32	18	6.33

MIKE TUCKER / Kansas City Royals / Left Field/Second Base $23

The Royals' first-round pick in 1992, from a small college in Virginia. Originally a shortstop, he was moved to second base and then to left, where he is likely to play for KC in 1995. Thought to be a potential batting champion when drafted, he hasn't shown that, but has developed more power than anticipated. Left-handed hitter, turns 24 in June, quick bat.

YEAR	TEAM/LEVEL	G	AB	R	H	2B	3B	HR	RBI	BB	SB	AVG	OBP	SLG
1993	Memphis AA	72	244	38	68	7	4	9	35	42	12	.279	.392	.451
1994	Omaha AAA	132	485	75	134	16	7	21	77	69	11	.276	.366	.468
1994	MLE	132	465	55	114	15	6	12	57	50	7	.245	.318	.381

SCOOTER TUCKER / Houston Astros / Catcher $13

Tucker lost his battle with Scott Servais over a share of the Astros' catching job. He returned to Tucson, and had his career year in 1994, at age 27. If he could hit at this level he would have a major league career, but his '94 season is far better than what he's done before, so that's questionable. But he's earned another trial.

YEAR	TEAM/LEVEL	G	AB	R	H	2B	3B	HR	RBI	BB	SB	AVG	OBP	SLG
1993	Houston	9	26	1	5	1	0	0	3	2	0	.192	.250	.231
1994	Tucson AAA	113	408	64	131	38	1	14	80	48	3	.321	.396	.522
1994	MLE	113	378	41	101	30	0	8	51	30	1	.267	.321	.410

BRIAN TURANG / Seattle Mariners / Outfielder $16

Small right-handed hitter, primarily an outfielder but can also play second and third. He played well in 1993, poorly in 1994, but returned to Calgary and hit .343 in 65 games (MLE shown below). The free agent departure of Jay Buhner and the disappointing performance of Eric Anthony could give him an opening, and it is not impossible that he could be a regular.

YEAR	TEAM/LEVEL	G	AB	R	H	2B	3B	HR	RBI	BB	SB	AVG	OBP	SLG
1993	Seattle	40	140	22	35	11	1	0	7	17	6	.250	.340	.343
1994	MLE	68	268	32	77	15	2	3	25	11	3	.287	.315	.392
1994	Seattle	38	112	9	21	5	1	1	8	7	3	.188	.242	.277

CHRIS TURNER / California Angels / Catcher $18

Opened the season as the Angels' catcher, but a .114 average in April pitched him into a time-sharing arrangement with Myers, Fabregas, and Dalesandro. He is a good defensive catcher and runs well for a catcher, but is unlikely to hit enough to play 130 games a year. I'd compare him to Jeff Reed or Kirt Manwaring.

YEAR	TEAM/LEVEL	G	AB	R	H	2B	3B	HR	RBI	BB	SB	AVG	OBP	SLG
1993	California	25	75	9	21	5	0	1	13	9	1	.280	.360	.387
1994	California	58	149	23	36	7	1	1	12	10	3	.242	.290	.322
1995	*Projected*	*71*	*189*	*26*	*46*	*8*	*0*	*2*	*24*	*22*	*2*	*.243*	*.322*	*.317*

MATT TURNER / Cleveland Indians / Right-handed Pitcher $19

Traded from Florida to the Indians in spring training, Turner opened the year in the Indians bullpen, but developed lymphatic cancer. His chemotherapy has gone well, and he is expected to return in 1995. The Indians released him during the strike so he could continue drawing his salary; he is expected to re-sign once the labor situation is resolved. Good if healthy.

YEAR	TEAM/LEVEL	G	IP	W-L	SAVES	HITS	SO	BB	ERA
1992	Tucson AAA	63	100	2-8	14	93	84	40	3.51
1993	Florida	55	68	4-5	0	55	59	26	2.91
1994	Cleveland	9	13	1-0	1	13	5	7	2.13

TOM URBANI / St. Louis Cardinals / Left-handed Pitcher $18

He was in the Cardinals' rotation at season's end, but not pitching very well, so his role is still uncertain. Is 27 years old, fastball is a little short, but he mixes his pitches well, and has the phenomenal control that Joe Torre favors. Had 28 strikeouts, only 5 walks after June 1. In the mix with Cormier, Olivares, Osborne, trying to crack the rotation.

YEAR	TEAM/LEVEL	G	IP	W-L	PCT	HITS	SO	BB	ERA
1993	Louisville AAA	18	95	9-5	.643	86	65	23	2.47
1993	St. Louis	18	62	1-3	.250	73	33	26	4.65
1994	St. Louis	20	80	3-7	.300	98	43	21	5.15

UGUETH URBINA / Montreal Expos / Starting Pitcher $20

A 21-year-old Venezuelan right-hander, exploded onto the scene in 1993, dominating the Midwest League much the same way Salomon Torres did four years ago, and held his own after a promotion to Double-A. Throws hard, throws strikes. Grade B prospect. Will probably pitch Triple-A in 1995, but could move up if the Expos develop holes in their pitching staff.

YEAR	TEAM/LEVEL	G	IP	W-L	PCT	HITS	SO	BB	ERA
1993	Burlington A	16	108	10-1	.909	78	107	36	1.99
1993	Harrisburg AA	11	70	4-5	.444	66	45	32	3.99
1994	Harrisburg AA	21	121	9-3	.750	96	86	43	3.28

ISMAEL VALDES / Los Angeles Dodgers / Right-handed Pitcher $25

Tall, thin, Mexican right-hander, in the majors at 21, with virtually no experience. He has a great arm and good control, and he is in the best pitchers' park in baseball. He will have very good numbers, when healthy, over the next five years, but injuries limited him to 38 innings in 1992 and 13 innings in 1993, so his health is a concern.

YEAR	TEAM/LEVEL	G	IP	W-L	PCT	HITS	SO	BB	ERA
1994	San Antonio AA	8	53	2-3	.400	54	55	9	3.38
1994	Albuquerque AAA	4	26	3-0	1.000	21	24	6	2.77
1994	Los Angeles	21	28	3-1	.750	21	28	10	3.18

SERGIO VALDEZ / Boston Red Sox / Relief Pitcher $15

There is something here we don't know. Valdez has a good arm and has pitched well, but rarely gets more than a week here and there in the majors. In 1992 he had a 2.41 ERA for Montreal, equally good supporting stats, but was cut the next spring. He is tagged as no prospect, and fair or not, the designation appears to be terminal.

YEAR	TEAM/LEVEL	G	IP	W-L	PCT	HITS	SO	BB	ERA
1993	Ottawa AAA	30	84	5-3	.625	77	53	22	3.12
1994	Pawtucket AAA	26	99	1-2	.333	94	67	29	3.26
1994	Boston	12	14	0-1	.000	25	4	8	8.16

JOHN VALENTIN / Boston Red Sox / Shortstop $32

Lost a month to a knee injury, otherwise had a good season, at bat and in the field. The best-hitting shortstop in the American League, unless Cal Ripken has a good year; the question now is why he didn't hit in the minors. Is 28 years old; was a teammate of Mo Vaughn at Seton Hall, and a high school basketball teammate of David Rivers.

YEAR	TEAM/LEVEL	G	AB	R	H	2B	3B	HR	RBI	BB	SB	AVG	OBP	SLG
1993	Boston	144	468	50	130	40	3	11	66	49	3	.278	.346	.447
1994	Boston	84	301	53	95	26	2	9	49	42	3	.316	.400	.505
1995	*Projected*	*142*	*479*	*59*	*130*	*34*	*1*	*12*	*58*	*58*	*3*	*.271*	*.350*	*.422*

JOSE VALENTIN / Milwaukee Brewers / Shortstop $26

Took control of the shortstop job after Listach got hurt. He's a switch hitter in theory, but hit just .135 right-handed. He had an excellent .361 secondary average—good power, 38 walks, 12 stolen bases in 15 attempts. Terrific range at shortstop, but led the American League in errors. Struck out 75 times; will have to cut that or his average will nose-dive.

YEAR	TEAM/LEVEL	G	AB	R	H	2B	3B	HR	RBI	BB	SB	AVG	OBP	SLG
1993	Milwaukee	19	53	10	13	1	2	1	7	7	1	.245	.344	.396
1994	Milwaukee	97	285	47	68	19	0	11	46	38	12	.239	.330	.421
1995	*Projected*	*117*	*364*	*52*	*87*	*18*	*3*	*8*	*43*	*41*	*8*	*.239*	*.316*	*.371*

FERNANDO VALENZUELA / Philadelphia Phillies / Starting Pitcher $22

A free agent. Signed by Philadelphia in June to patch their injury-riddled rotation, he pitched well in eight starts before the strike. He's a good pitcher and I'd like to have him, but he has sharp limits: He *needs* rest.

There are several things in his record that reveal this, including his ERA on five days' rest (4.18) opposed to four (4.96).

YEAR	TEAM/LEVEL	G	IP	W-L	PCT	HITS	SO	BB	ERA
1992	Jalisco (Mex.)	22	156	10-9	.526	154	98	51	3.86
1993	Baltimore	32	179	8-10	.444	179	78	79	4.94
1994	Philadelphia	8	45	1-2	.333	42	19	7	3.00

DAVE VALLE / Milwaukee Brewers / Catcher $17

The Red Sox signed him to solve their catching problems (huh?). He hit .158 for Boston, and lost the job to Damon Berryhill, then was traded to Milwaukee for Tom Brunansky, because the Sox decided they wanted a slow, washed-up outfielder instead of a slow, washed-up catcher. Now a free agent, again; probably due for a good year as a backup.

YEAR	TEAM/LEVEL	G	AB	R	H	2B	3B	HR	RBI	BB	SB	AVG	OBP	SLG
1993	Seattle	135	423	48	109	19	0	13	63	48	1	.258	.354	.395
1994	Two Teams	46	112	14	26	8	1	2	10	18	0	.232	.348	.375
1995	*Projected*	*63*	*161*	*16*	*36*	*7*	*0*	*4*	*17*	*17*	*0*	*.224*	*.298*	*.342*

JOHN VANDERWAL / Colorado Rockies / Pinch Hitter/First Base $18

A fairly productive hitter. He has 599 major league at bats, yeilding 15 homers, 71 runs, 73 RBI, 8 triples and 68 walks. His average isn't good (.235), but he pinch hits a lot (58 times last year), and that's a tough job. He won't move into the lineup, but he's a valuable role player, and will have his Gerald Perry season sooner or later.

YEAR	TEAM/LEVEL	G	AB	R	H	2B	3B	HR	RBI	BB	SB	AVG	OBP	SLG
1992	Montreal	105	213	21	51	8	2	4	20	24	3	.239	.316	.352
1993	Montreal	106	215	34	50	7	4	5	30	27	6	.233	.320	.372
1994	Colorado	91	110	12	27	3	1	5	15	16	2	.245	.339	.427

TIM VANEGMOND / Boston Red Sox / Starting Pitcher $22

Right-hander, a 17th round draft pick in 1991. Vanegmond was MVP of the Division II College World Series in both 1990 AND 1991. He throws a decent fastball, an excellent curve, and a good changeup, with good control. There is nothing that stands out about him, plus I always avoid Red Sox pitchers, unless they're Roger Clemens or Aaron Sele. Grade D prospect.

YEAR	TEAM/LEVEL	G	IP	W-L	PCT	HITS	SO	BB	ERA
1993	New Britain AA	29	190	6-12	.333	182	163	44	3.97
1994	Pawtucket AAA	20	119	9-5	.643	110	87	42	3.77
1994	Boston	7	38	2-3	.400	38	22	21	6.34

WILLIAM VANLANDINGHAM / San Francisco Giants / Starting Pitcher $28

So wild at the University of Kentucky that he seldom pitched, VanLandingham was drafted in the fifth round on the theory that he might harness his control some-day. He throws hard, low 90s with movement, has a wicked slider that he busts in on the fists. He doesn't look like a finished pitcher to me, and I suspect that he is headed for adjustment problems.

YEAR	TEAM/LEVEL	G	IP	W-L	PCT	HITS	SO	BB	ERA
1993	San Jose A	27	163	14-8	.636	167	171	87	5.12
1994	AA & AAA	13	80	5-4	.556	62	74	25	2.69
1994	San Francisco	16	84	8-2	.800	70	56	43	3.54

TODD VAN POPPEL / Oakland Athletics / Starting Pitcher $18

If he's making any progress, I don't see it. He pitched poorly at home, on the road, in all months of the season, in grass parks and turf parks. He led the league in walks, and he must be the only pitcher in baseball who is no more effective when he gets ahead in the count than he is when behind. A younger Bobby Witt.

YEAR	TEAM/LEVEL	G	IP	W-L	PCT	HITS	SO	BB	ERA
1993	Tacoma AAA	16	79	4-8	.333	67	71	54	5.83
1993	Oakland	16	84	6-6	.500	76	47	62	5.04
1994	Oakland	23	117	7-10	.412	108	83	89	6.09

ANDY VAN SLYKE / Pittsburgh Pirates / Center Field $27

A free agent, will not return to the Pirates, who are rebuilding. I suspect that he drove his average down by staying in the lineup with some injuries, but he was 33 last year, which is the most common age for a hitter to suddenly lose it. He will have more good seasons, but he'll never again be a player you can count on.

YEAR	TEAM/LEVEL	G	AB	R	H	2B	3B	HR	RBI	BB	SB	AVG	OBP	SLG
1993	Pittsburgh	83	323	42	100	13	4	8	50	24	11	.310	.357	.449
1994	Pittsburgh	105	374	41	92	18	3	6	30	52	7	.246	.340	.358
1995	*Projected*	*131*	*501*	*65*	*138*	*23*	*5*	*11*	*59*	*52*	*11*	*.275*	*.344*	*.407*

GARY VARSHO / Pittsburgh Pirates / Utility Outfielder/Pinch Hitter $15

Returned to Pittsburgh in 1994 after a year with Cincinnati. An adequate left-handed line drive hitter, used as a pinch hitter and defensive substitute. Is 33 years old, was designated for assignment in October, but probably will return to the roster in spring training, since Leyland likes to work with a veteran bench.

YEAR	TEAM/LEVEL	G	AB	R	H	2B	3B	HR	RBI	BB	SB	AVG	OBP	SLG
1992	Pittsburgh	103	162	22	36	6	3	4	22	10	5	.222	.266	.370
1993	Cincinnati	77	95	8	22	6	0	2	11	9	1	.232	.302	.358
1994	Pittsburgh	67	82	15	21	6	3	0	5	4	0	.256	.307	.402

GREG VAUGHN / Milwaukee Brewers / Designated Hitter/Left Field $34

Had shoulder surgery after the strike, which may prevent him from playing the field, and also might affect his hitting (on the other hand, many hitters, like Shane Mack, have gotten *better* after shoulder surgery).

Vaughn is 29, and still trying to push his career average to .250, but he produces runs. Has career average of .189 in the late innings of close games.

YEAR	TEAM/LEVEL	G	AB	R	H	2B	3B	HR	RBI	BB	SB	AVG	OBP	SLG
1993	Milwaukee	154	569	97	152	28	2	30	97	89	10	.267	.369	.482
1994	Milwaukee	95	370	59	94	24	1	19	55	51	9	.254	.345	.478
1995	*Projected*	*155*	*555*	*88*	*133*	*28*	*2*	*26*	*89*	*79*	*13*	*.240*	*.334*	*.438*

MO VAUGHN / Boston Red Sox / First Base $59

The 10th Red Sox first baseman to drive in 100 runs in a season—Buck Freeman, Jimmie Foxx, Rudy York, Walt Dropo, Vic Wertz, Dick Stuart, Tony Perez, Buckner, Esasky, and Vaughn, also Yastrzemski and Evans

in seasons they split between first and the outfield . . . had a great year against left-handed pitchers; has career average of .327 with men in scoring position.

YEAR	TEAM/LEVEL	G	AB	R	H	2B	3B	HR	RBI	BB	SB	AVG	OBP	SLG
1993	Boston	152	539	86	160	34	1	29	101	79	4	.297	.390	.525
1994	Boston	111	394	65	122	25	1	26	82	57	4	.310	.408	.576
1995	*Projected*	*157*	*558*	*80*	*154*	*31*	*1*	*29*	*101*	*79*	*4*	*.276*	*.366*	*.491*

RANDY VELARDE / New York Yankees / Infielder $23

Before Showalter came, Velarde was regarded as a disappointment, because he's not a very good defensive shortstop. Showalter, like all good managers, focused on what Velarde *can* do, and has made him a key mem-

ber of the best bench in the majors. If Jeter develops rapidly that will squeeze Velarde's playing time, but a hitter this good isn't going to disappear.

YEAR	TEAM/LEVEL	G	AB	R	H	2B	3B	HR	RBI	BB	SB	AVG	OBP	SLG
1993	New York	85	226	28	68	13	2	7	24	18	2	.301	.360	.469
1994	New York	77	280	47	78	16	1	9	34	22	4	.279	.338	.439
1995	*Projected*	*118*	*371*	*50*	*97*	*17*	*1*	*9*	*39*	*33*	*6*	*.261*	*.322*	*.385*

ROBIN VENTURA / Chicago White Sox / Third Base $68

Probably the best third baseman in the league, although the margin between Ventura and Fryman is thin, and Thome is probably a better hitter. Ventura is very slow, and he had a poor year in the field in '94 (18 errors,

.934 fielding percentage). Nobody in baseball is any more consistent with the bat, and his best years *might* still be ahead of him.

YEAR	TEAM/LEVEL	G	AB	R	H	2B	3B	HR	RBI	BB	SB	AVG	OBP	SLG
1993	Chicago	157	554	85	145	27	1	22	94	105	1	.262	.379	.433
1994	Chicago	108	401	57	113	15	1	18	78	61	3	.282	.373	.459
1995	*Projected*	*156*	*571*	*83*	*155*	*27*	*1*	*21*	*92*	*98*	*3*	*.271*	*.378*	*.433*

DAVE VERES / Houston Astros / Right-handed Pitcher $19

Minor league veteran, has been pitching professionally since 1986. Age 28, has pitched in the Oakland, Los Angeles, and Houston systems. A starting pitcher from 1986 to 1990, he walked five men a game and lost more than he won. His control got much better when he moved to the bullpen in '91. I expect him to continue to pitch well.

YEAR	TEAM/LEVEL	G	IP	W-L	PCT	HITS	SO	BB	ERA
1993	Tucson AAA	43	130	6-10	.375	156	122	32	4.90
1994	Tucson AAA	16	24	1-1	.500	17	19	10	1.88
1994	Houston	32	41	3-3	.500	39	28	7	2.41

RANDY VERES / Chicago Cubs / Right-handed Pitcher $15

Similar to Dave Veres (above), although they are not related. This Veres is 29, a professional since 1985, in the Brewers, Braves, Giants, and Indians systems. He reached the majors with the Brewers in 1989 and 1990, posting a 3.78 earned run average in 50 innings, has fought his way back by converting to relief. May get a shot in middle relief for someone.

YEAR	TEAM/LEVEL	G	IP	W-L	PCT	HITS	SO	BB	ERA
1993	Canton-Akron AA	13	57	1-5	.167	59	49	19	4.89
1994	Iowa AAA	33	55	5-6	.455	43	42	11	2.93
1994	Chicago	10	10	1-1	.500	12	5	2	5.59

FERNANDO VINA / New York Mets / Infielder $17

Left-handed hitter, 26 years old, runs well, and can play all the infield positions plus a little outfield. The Mets don't need him at second or short, and his bat isn't strong enough for third, so they are using him as a utility player and pinch runner. Doesn't drive the ball, but makes contact. Gets hit by pitches a lot. Won't be a regular.

YEAR	TEAM/LEVEL	G	AB	R	H	2B	3B	HR	RBI	BB	SB	AVG	OBP	SLG
1993	Seattle	24	45	5	10	2	0	0	2	4	6	.222	.327	.267
1993	Norfolk AAA	73	287	24	66	6	4	4	27	7	16	.230	.258	.321
1994	New York	79	124	20	31	6	0	0	6	12	3	.250	.372	.298

FRANK VIOLA / Boston Red Sox (Released) / Starting Pitcher $17

Arthroscopic elbow surgery ended his 1993 campaign, and his 1994 season ended in May when the elbow blew out completely. He's now had the Tommy John surgery, and has been released by the Red Sox. If he comes back strong—and he is, after all, 35—it will probably be in a couple of years. He's had a grand career, and I'll miss him.

YEAR	TEAM/LEVEL	G	IP	W-L	PCT	HITS	SO	BB	ERA
1992	Boston	35	238	13-12	.520	214	121	89	3.44
1993	Boston	29	184	11-8	.579	180	91	72	3.14
1994	Boston	6	31	1-1	.500	34	9	17	4.65

JOSE VIZCAINO / New York Mets / Shortstop $32

The return of Shawon Dunston left the Cubs with two shortstops, and they traded Vizcaino for Anthony Young. He was OK, the best shortstop the Mets have had in the last few years. He was 1-for-12 as a base stealer, and his average dropped 31 points, most of which is just the difference between Wrigley Field and Shea Stadium.

YEAR	TEAM/LEVEL	G	AB	R	H	2B	3B	HR	RBI	BB	SB	AVG	OBP	SLG
1993	Chicago	151	551	74	158	19	4	4	54	46	12	.287	.340	.358
1994	New York	103	410	47	105	13	3	3	33	33	1	.256	.310	.324
1995	Projected	153	564	65	151	18	3	4	47	44	8	.268	.321	.332

OMAR VIZQUEL / Cleveland Indians / Shortstop $32

The Indians got him from the Mariners for Felix Fermin. They wanted Vizquel to anchor their infield defense, which had been shaky in previous years, and he did that quite well, but missed much of the season with a severe knee injury. A Gold Glove quality fielder, chips in occasionally on the offense. Switch hitter, 28 years old.

YEAR	TEAM/LEVEL	G	AB	R	H	2B	3B	HR	RBI	BB	SB	AVG	OBP	SLG
1993	Seattle	158	560	68	143	14	2	2	31	50	12	.255	.319	.298
1994	Cleveland	69	286	39	78	10	1	1	33	23	13	.273	.325	.325
1995	Projected	138	494	56	128	14	2	2	35	41	14	.259	.316	.309

JACK VOIGT / Baltimore Orioles / Outfielder $20

He crushes left-handers—.352 against them in '93, .293 last year, career average of .333 against left-handers with 10 doubles and eight homers in 132 at bats. He has a good on-base percentage and is a defensive sub in the outfield, so if he can continue to hit lefties at anything like the same pace, his playing time will probably increase.

YEAR	TEAM/LEVEL	G	AB	R	H	2B	3B	HR	RBI	BB	SB	AVG	OBP	SLG
1993	Baltimore	64	152	32	45	11	1	6	23	25	1	.296	.395	.500
1994	Baltimore	59	141	15	34	5	0	3	20	18	0	.241	.327	.340
1995	Projected	87	246	36	63	12	1	7	32	32	3	.256	.342	.398

ED VOSBERG / Oakland Athletics / Relief Pitcher $16

Once a prospect, got a few innings with the Padres in 1986 and the Giants in 1990, then was out of baseball for two years. He came back to the game in 1993, and is now trying to get a job as (stop me if this sounds familiar) a left-handed-one-out guy. He's with the right team . . . LaRussa likes to keep several of these guys around.

YEAR	TEAM/LEVEL	G	IP	W-L	SAVES	HITS	SO	BB	ERA
1993	Iowa AAA	52	63	5-1	3	67	64	22	3.57
1994	Tacoma AAA	26	54	4-2	3	39	54	19	3.35
1994	Oakland	16	14	0-2	0	16	12	5	3.95

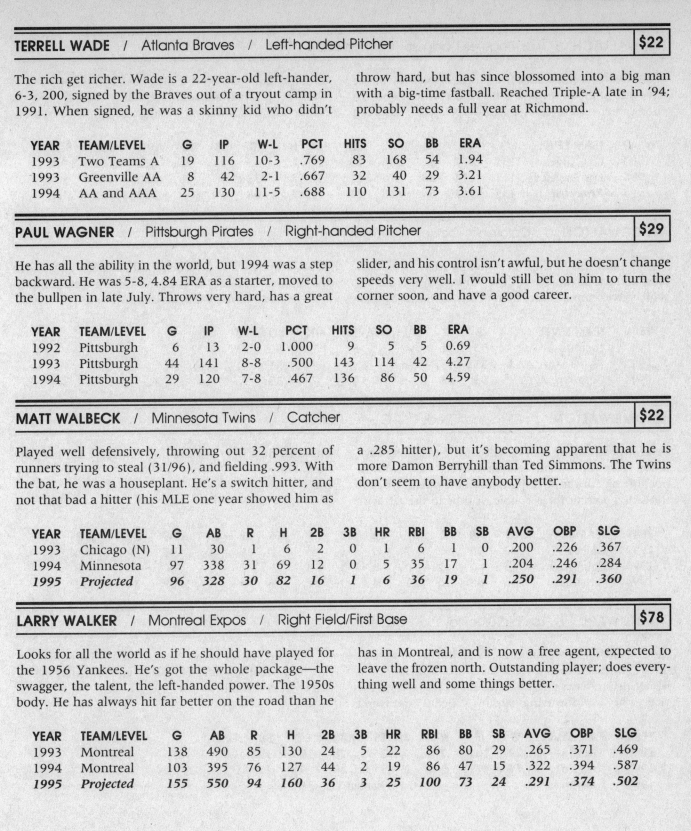

TERRELL WADE / Atlanta Braves / Left-handed Pitcher **$22**

The rich get richer. Wade is a 22-year-old left-hander, 6-3, 200, signed by the Braves out of a tryout camp in 1991. When signed, he was a skinny kid who didn't throw hard, but has since blossomed into a big man with a big-time fastball. Reached Triple-A late in '94; probably needs a full year at Richmond.

YEAR	TEAM/LEVEL	G	IP	W-L	PCT	HITS	SO	BB	ERA
1993	Two Teams A	19	116	10-3	.769	83	168	54	1.94
1993	Greenville AA	8	42	2-1	.667	32	40	29	3.21
1994	AA and AAA	25	130	11-5	.688	110	131	73	3.61

PAUL WAGNER / Pittsburgh Pirates / Right-handed Pitcher **$29**

He has all the ability in the world, but 1994 was a step backward. He was 5-8, 4.84 ERA as a starter, moved to the bullpen in late July. Throws very hard, has a great slider, and his control isn't awful, but he doesn't change speeds very well. I would still bet on him to turn the corner soon, and have a good career.

YEAR	TEAM/LEVEL	G	IP	W-L	PCT	HITS	SO	BB	ERA
1992	Pittsburgh	6	13	2-0	1.000	9	5	5	0.69
1993	Pittsburgh	44	141	8-8	.500	143	114	42	4.27
1994	Pittsburgh	29	120	7-8	.467	136	86	50	4.59

MATT WALBECK / Minnesota Twins / Catcher **$22**

Played well defensively, throwing out 32 percent of runners trying to steal (31/96), and fielding .993. With the bat, he was a houseplant. He's a switch hitter, and not that bad a hitter (his MLE one year showed him as a .285 hitter), but it's becoming apparent that he is more Damon Berryhill than Ted Simmons. The Twins don't seem to have anybody better.

YEAR	TEAM/LEVEL	G	AB	R	H	2B	3B	HR	RBI	BB	SB	AVG	OBP	SLG
1993	Chicago (N)	11	30	1	6	2	0	1	6	1	0	.200	.226	.367
1994	Minnesota	97	338	31	69	12	0	5	35	17	1	.204	.246	.284
1995	*Projected*	*96*	*328*	*30*	*82*	*16*	*1*	*6*	*36*	*19*	*1*	*.250*	*.291*	*.360*

LARRY WALKER / Montreal Expos / Right Field/First Base **$78**

Looks for all the world as if he should have played for the 1956 Yankees. He's got the whole package—the swagger, the talent, the left-handed power. The 1950s body. He has always hit far better on the road than he has in Montreal, and is now a free agent, expected to leave the frozen north. Outstanding player; does everything well and some things better.

YEAR	TEAM/LEVEL	G	AB	R	H	2B	3B	HR	RBI	BB	SB	AVG	OBP	SLG
1993	Montreal	138	490	85	130	24	5	22	86	80	29	.265	.371	.469
1994	Montreal	103	395	76	127	44	2	19	86	47	15	.322	.394	.587
1995	*Projected*	*155*	*550*	*94*	*160*	*36*	*3*	*25*	*100*	*73*	*24*	*.291*	*.374*	*.502*

TIM WALLACH / Los Angeles Dodgers / Third Base $24

Wow. Wallach came back from three dismal seasons to have one of the best years of his career. And it's been a good career—a Brooks Robinson-type career, although he's not quite as good as Brooks. I thought he was washed up a year ago, and I certainly wouldn't bet on him to top .240 this year . . . still a good third baseman.

YEAR	TEAM/LEVEL	G	AB	R	H	2B	3B	HR	RBI	BB	SB	AVG	OBP	SLG
1993	Los Angeles	133	477	42	106	19	1	12	62	32	0	.222	.271	.342
1994	Los Angeles	113	414	68	116	21	1	23	78	46	0	.280	.356	.502
1995	*Projected*	*139*	*503*	*56*	*118*	*27*	*1*	*14*	*68*	*45*	*1*	*.235*	*.297*	*.376*

BRUCE WALTON / Colorado Rockies / Relief Pitcher $13

Signed with the Rockies after failing trials with Oakland and Montreal. He got five innings in the majors, which gives him a career total of 34. He doesn't throw 90, but rarely walks anybody, and has been effective in the minors. But he's now 32, and he's running out of time to build a major league career.

YEAR	TEAM/LEVEL	G	IP	W-L	SAVES	HITS	SO	BB	ERA
1992	Tacoma AAA	35	81	8-2	8	76	60	21	2.77
1993	Two Teams AAA	53	58	6-4	23	44	54	11	1.25
1994	Colo. Sp. AAA	51	58	3-4	13	74	39	16	4.84

JEROME WALTON / Cincinnati Reds / Center Field $17

Left for dead a year ago, he got a spring training invitation from Cincinnati, and played very well from the opening day of spring training until the opening day of the strike, except for a couple of trips to the DL with bunions. He is only 29, and he has ability. But then, he had ability in 1992, when he hit .127, and he was 26 then.

YEAR	TEAM/LEVEL	G	AB	R	H	2B	3B	HR	RBI	BB	SB	AVG	OBP	SLG
1992	Chicago (N)	30	55	7	7	0	1	0	1	9	1	.127	.273	.164
1993	California	5	2	2	0	0	0	0	0	1	1	.000	.333	.000
1994	Cincinnati	46	68	10	21	4	0	1	9	4	1	.309	.347	.412

DUANE WARD / Toronto Blue Jays / Closer? $34

Developed "bicep tendinitis" in spring training. For three months he was a week away from pitching, but he decided to have surgery instead, and was out for the year. If he's not throwing hard by March 25, he won't be 100 percent for three years. If he is, the injury still might re-occur anytime. But he's a great pitcher, so you can't write him off.

YEAR	TEAM/LEVEL	G	IP	W-L	SAVES	HITS	SO	BB	ERA
1992	Toronto	79	101	7-4	12	76	103	39	1.95
1993	Toronto	71	72	2-3	45	49	97	25	2.13
1994	Toronto			(On Disabled List)					

TURNER WARD / Milwaukee Brewers / Outfielder $19

I said last year that he "will never be a regular", but I sometimes underestimate the stupidity of major league decision-makers. Ward hit .313 in April, but then remembered who he was, and hit under .200 in June, July, and August, pushing his season's average near his career norm. A regular? Hell, he's not even a good fifth outfielder.

YEAR	TEAM/LEVEL	G	AB	R	H	2B	3B	HR	RBI	BB	SB	AVG	OBP	SLG
1993	Toronto	72	167	20	32	4	2	4	28	23	3	.192	.287	.311
1994	Milwaukee	102	367	55	85	15	2	9	45	52	6	.232	.328	.357
1995	*Projected*	*92*	*281*	*41*	*68*	*12*	*1*	*6*	*30*	*42*	*6*	*.242*	*.341*	*.356*

JOHN WASDIN / Oakland Athletics / Starting Pitcher $18

Right-hander, the Athletics' first round pick in the 1993 draft, 25th overall, out of Florida State. A three pitch pitcher: upper 80s fastball, excellent slider, developing a changeup, all with very good control. Intelligent and coachable, will be given a chance to make the A's rotation. **Grade A prospect,** probably needs a year in Triple-A, but the A's also need pitching.

YEAR	TEAM/LEVEL	G	IP	W-L	PCT	HITS	SO	BB	ERA
1993	Two Teams A	12	65	2-6	.250	47	51	13	2.37
1994	Modesto A	6	27	3-1	.750	17	30	5	1.69
1994	Huntsville AA	21	142	12-3	.800	126	108	29	3.43

ALLEN WATSON / St. Louis Cardinals / Left-handed Starting Pitcher $24

He reminds me a little bit of a young Danny Jackson, not in his delivery, but in other ways. He throws hard, and when he gets on a roll he is nearly impossible to beat, as Jackson was at his age. But he doesn't really have a strikeout pitch, and if the umpire isn't giving him one of his pitches, he can't adjust. Still has star potential.

YEAR	TEAM/LEVEL	G	IP	W-L	PCT	HITS	SO	BB	ERA
1993	Louisville AAA	17	121	5-4	.556	101	86	31	2.91
1993	St. Louis	16	86	6-7	.462	90	49	28	4.60
1994	St. Louis	22	116	6-5	.545	130	74	53	5.52

GARY WAYNE / Los Angeles Dodgers / Left-handed Relief Pitcher $13

Released by the Rockies, he signed with Los Angeles and began the year as their main lefty one-out guy. He held left-handers to a .233 average, but was mediocre overall and was sent to Albuquerque in June. He wasn't good at Albuquerque, either (4.93 ERA). Is 32 years old; major league career now depends on catching breaks.

YEAR	TEAM/LEVEL	G	IP	W-L	SAVES	HITS	SO	BB	ERA
1992	Minnesota	41	48	3-3	0	46	29	19	2.63
1993	Colorado	65	62	5-3	1	68	49	26	5.05
1994	Los Angeles	19	17	1-3	0	19	10	6	4.67

DAVE WEATHERS / Florida Marlins / Starting Pitcher | $22

Big right-hander, 6-3, 205, throws heavy sinker and slider. Made the Marlins' rotation in spring training, started out hot and was 7-6, 3.41 ERA in 103 innings through the end of June. The last six weeks, then, were real ugly (11.25 ERA), which means that he was either hurt or tired. If he was just tired, he's a valuable young pitcher.

YEAR	TEAM/LEVEL	G	IP	W-L	PCT	HITS	SO	BB	ERA
1993	Edmonton AAA	22	141	11-4	.733	150	117	47	3.83
1993	Florida	14	46	2-3	.400	57	34	13	5.12
1994	Florida	24	135	8-12	.400	166	72	59	5.27

LENNY WEBSTER / Montreal Expos / Backup Catcher | $18

He lost his job as the Twins' backup catcher after a poor year, but was traded to Montreal, where he was able to play mostly against left-handed pitchers (as Darrin Fletcher bats left). In his role, he's outstanding. He's a good defensive catcher, and in 427 major league at bats has 26 doubles, 10 homers, 46 walks, 53 RBI, and a .260 average.

YEAR	TEAM/LEVEL	G	AB	R	H	2B	3B	HR	RBI	BB	SB	AVG	OBP	SLG
1993	Minnesota	49	106	14	21	2	0	1	8	11	1	.198	.274	.245
1994	Montreal	57	143	13	39	10	0	5	23	16	0	.273	.370	.448
1995	*Projected*	*95*	*223*	*25*	*56*	*17*	*0*	*4*	*25*	*20*	*1*	*.251*	*.313*	*.381*

MITCH WEBSTER / Los Angeles Dodgers / Utility Outfielder | $15

Turns 36 in May, trying to hold on as a reserve outfielder. He's still a useful player: a switch hitter, good defense, has some power, and will take a walk, but has lost most of his speed. Lasorda used him mainly as a pinch hitter/defensive sub (he was 9 for 31 pinch hitting.) A free agent, will re-sign or catch on somewhere.

YEAR	TEAM/LEVEL	G	AB	R	H	2B	3B	HR	RBI	BB	SB	AVG	OBP	SLG
1992	Los Angeles	135	262	33	70	12	5	6	35	27	11	.267	.334	.420
1993	Los Angeles	88	172	26	42	6	2	2	14	11	4	.244	.293	.337
1994	Los Angeles	82	84	16	23	4	0	4	12	8	1	.274	.344	.464

ERIC WEDGE / Boston Red Sox / Designated Hitter/Catcher | $16

A 27-year-old right-handed slugger, once had a promising career as a catcher, but arm injuries have made him a DH. A product of the Red Sox system, he went to Colorado in the expansion draft, was hurt most of the 1993 season, then returned to Boston as a free agent. He can hit like Mike Stanley if he ever gets a chance to show it.

YEAR	TEAM/LEVEL	G	AB	R	H	2B	3B	HR	RBI	BB	SB	AVG	OBP	SLG
1992	Boston	27	68	11	17	2	0	5	11	13	0	.250	.370	.500
1993	Colorado	9	11	2	2	0	0	0	1	0	0	.182	.182	.182
1994	Pawtucket AAA	77	255	44	73	14	0	19	59	51	0	.286	.406	.565

BILL WEGMAN / Milwaukee Brewers / Starting Pitcher $25

Big right-hander, is fifth on the Brewers' all-time wins list, with 76. His ERAs over the last four years are 2.84, 3.20, 4.48, and 4.51, plus his ERA last year was 6.18 over the last six weeks. This is not to say that he won't pitch well in '95, as he already had three comebacks, and he's only 32. I just wouldn't count on him.

YEAR	TEAM/LEVEL	G	IP	W-L	PCT	HITS	SO	BB	ERA
1992	Milwaukee	35	262	13-14	.481	251	127	55	3.20
1993	Milwaukee	20	121	4-14	.222	135	50	34	4.48
1994	Milwaukee	19	116	8-4	.667	140	59	26	4.51

WALT WEISS / Colorado Rockies / Shortstop $31

The rap on Weiss for many years was that he couldn't stay healthy. Weiss was Oakland's shortstop from 1988 to 1992, but he was hurt almost 50 percent of the time. Healthy the last two years, he's hit over .250 for the first time(s), and also drawn a lot of walks. The Rockies made him their leadoff man, which is not recommended by central casting.

YEAR	TEAM/LEVEL	G	AB	R	H	2B	3B	HR	RBI	BB	SB	AVG	OBP	SLG
1993	Florida	158	500	50	133	14	2	1	39	79	7	.266	.367	.308
1994	Colorado	110	423	58	106	11	4	1	32	56	12	.251	.336	.303
1995	*Projected*	*141*	*479*	*57*	*117*	*15*	*2*	*2*	*38*	*69*	*9*	*.244*	*.339*	*.296*

BOB WELCH / Oakland Athletics / Starting Pitcher $14

Declared free agency in October. He was 0-5 as a starting pitcher last year, 9.53 ERA, then moved to the bullpen and pitched better (3-2, 4.67). This would not encourage me to believe that Welch can still pitch at 38, but then, it is well established that I don't think like a general manager. He's won 211 games.

YEAR	TEAM/LEVEL	G	IP	W-L	PCT	HITS	SO	BB	ERA
1992	Oakland	20	124	11-7	.611	114	47	43	3.27
1993	Oakland	30	167	9-11	.450	208	63	56	5.29
1994	Oakland	25	69	3-6	.333	79	44	43	7.08

BOB WELLS / Seattle Mariners / Right-handed Pitcher $18

Plagued by injuries, has had a sore shoulder several times, and Tommy John surgery on his elbow in 1992. When healthy, he's almost always been effective, both as a starter and a reliever. He was called up by the Phillies early in the season, then claimed on waivers by the Mariners in July. He'll be around, but is probably too fragile to be a closer.

YEAR	TEAM/LEVEL	G	IP	W-L	PCT	HITS	SO	BB	ERA
1994	Reading AA	14	19	1-3	.250	18	19	3	2.79
1994	Two Teams AAA	17	46	3-4	.429	61	30	15	5.24
1994	Philadelphia & Seattle	7	9	2-0	1.000	8	6	4	2.00

DAVID WELLS / Detroit Tigers / Starting Pitcher $24

A weighty left-hander with a legitimate fastball, good control, and strong pitching instincts. He had his elbow scoped last April, and at season's end was pitching extremely well. He's kind of a fat John Smiley—a fine pitcher, really, but stuck working for the Tigers because people don't feel they can count on him. Capable of winning 16-18 games.

YEAR	TEAM/LEVEL	G	IP	W-L	PCT	HITS	SO	BB	ERA
1992	Toronto	41	120	7-9	.438	138	62	36	5.40
1993	Detroit	32	187	11-9	.550	183	139	42	4.19
1994	Detroit	16	111	5-7	.417	113	71	24	3.96

TURK WENDELL / Chicago Cubs / Starting Pitcher/Flake $17

Idiosyncratic right-hander, put in a fine season at Des Moines, but pitched poorly in his major league time. Sinker/slider type, fastball in 86-89 range, good control. He's 28 years old and has 605 innings in the high minors, so if he's going to have a major league career its time to get on with it. Could make the rotation. Grade C prospect.

YEAR	TEAM/LEVEL	G	IP	W-L	PCT	HITS	SO	BB	ERA
1993	Chicago	7	23	1-2	.333	24	15	8	4.37
1994	Iowa AAA	23	168	11-6	.647	141	118	28	2.95
1994	Chicago	6	14	0-1	.000	22	9	10	11.93

BILL WERTZ / Cleveland Indians / Relief Pitcher $17

Also pitched four innings for the Indians, not shown below. Wertz is a very big right-hander, 6-6, 220 pounds, a Cleveland native, durable, throws a heavy fastball and a good slider, has pitched well everywhere since 1990, including with the Indians in '93. I don't know why Hargrove sent him out last year. He's 40-25 in the minors, 2.99 career ERA.

YEAR	TEAM/LEVEL	G	IP	W-L	SAVES	HITS	SO	BB	ERA
1993	Charlotte AAA	28	51	7-2	0	42	47	14	1.95
1993	Cleveland	34	60	2-3	0	54	53	32	3.62
1994	Charlotte AAA	44	66	4-3	1	53	60	34	3.14

DAVID WEST / Philadelphia Phillies / Left-handed Pitcher $21

Started the year in the bullpen, but moved to the rotation in late May after a meteor wiped out most of the other starters. He made 14 starts, going just 4-6 but with a 3.16 earned run average, holding hitters to a .187 batting average. He's always had good stuff, but it's foolish to bet on a pitcher with 61 walks in 99 innings.

YEAR	TEAM/LEVEL	G	IP	W-L	SAVES	HITS	SO	BB	ERA
1992	Minnesota	9	28	1-3	0	32	19	20	6.99
1993	Philadelphia	76	86	6-4	3	60	87	51	2.92
1994	Philadelphia	31	99	4-10	0	74	83	61	3.55

JOHN WETTELAND / Montreal Expos / Closer $73

Wetteland's 1993 season was very possibly the best season by a reliever in the history of baseball. He was slowed by a sore hamstring in '94, and wasn't quite as effective, but was still among the better relievers in the league. Throws his fastball almost every pitch, rarely throws anything else. There is every reason to expect him to be good again in '95.

YEAR	TEAM/LEVEL	G	IP	W-L	SAVES	HITS	SO	BB	ERA
1992	Montreal	67	83	4-4	37	64	99	36	2.92
1993	Montreal	70	85	9-3	43	58	113	28	1.37
1994	Montreal	52	64	4-6	25	46	68	21	2.83

LOU WHITAKER / Detroit Tigers / Second Base $32

Sparky Anderson last year never started a left-handed hitter against a left-handed pitcher, not even once. Whitaker, playing second against right-handers, hit .300 for the first time since 1983, and rang up the highest slugging percentage of his career. It was the 13th straight season his slugging percentage has been in the .400s. Turns 38 in May, defense may be slipping.

YEAR	TEAM/LEVEL	G	AB	R	H	2B	3B	HR	RBI	BB	SB	AVG	OBP	SLG
1993	Detroit	119	383	72	111	32	1	9	67	78	3	.290	.412	.449
1994	Detroit	92	322	67	97	21	2	12	43	41	2	.301	.377	.491
1995	*Projected*	*123*	*409*	*61*	*107*	*20*	*2*	*10*	*53*	*69*	*3*	*.262*	*.368*	*.394*

DEVON WHITE / Toronto Blue Jays / Center Field $40

The Blue Jays' disappointing season makes all of their players pale a little, and White did not play quite as well as he had in '93. His on-base percentage slipped by 28 points, and he stole only 11 bases. In 1993 he had six outfield assists and three errors; last year he had six errors and three assists. He is among the best center fielders in baseball.

YEAR	TEAM/LEVEL	G	AB	R	H	2B	3B	HR	RBI	BB	SB	AVG	OBP	SLG
1993	Toronto	146	598	116	163	42	6	15	52	57	34	.273	.341	.438
1994	Toronto	100	403	67	109	24	6	13	49	21	11	.270	.313	.457
1995	*Projected*	*147*	*611*	*97*	*156*	*28*	*5*	*16*	*56*	*45*	*32*	*.255*	*.306*	*.396*

GABE WHITE / Montreal Expos / Left-handed Starting Pitcher $19

Young left-hander, throws fastball with decent velocity, good curve and change. After a consistently successful minor league career (42-25) he was called to the majors in late May, and put in the rotation. He didn't pitch well, but this isn't surprising. Grade B prospect, will probably come around with more major league experience.

YEAR	TEAM/LEVEL	G	IP	W-L	PCT	HITS	SO	BB	ERA
1993	AA and AAA	22	140	9-3	.667	118	108	34	2.44
1994	Ottawa AAA	14	73	8-3	.727	77	63	28	5.05
1994	Montreal	7	24	1-1	.500	24	17	11	6.08

RICK WHITE / Pittsburgh Pirates / Reliever/Starter $23

White was working his way through the minors as a starting pitcher, reaching Triple-A in late 1993. A spring training surprise in '94, he was the Pirates' closer in April, and pitched brilliantly for a while. He lost that job, but was put into the starting rotation in July, and had 2.22 ERA through five starts. No Cy Young candidate, but looks OK.

YEAR	TEAM/LEVEL	G	IP	W-L	SAVES	HITS	SO	BB	ERA
1993	Carolina AA	12	69	4-3	0	59	52	12	3.50
1993	Buffalo AAA	7	28	0-3	0	25	16	8	3.54
1994	Pittsburgh	43	75	4-5	6	79	38	17	3.82

RONDELL WHITE / Montreal Expos / Outfielder $34

We can't be 100 percent sure, but there is every possibility that White is as good a player as the three brilliant outfielders who have been blocking his path. The departure of Walker and/or Grissom will probably allow him to play. I would expect him to hit .280 or better with power and speed. Doesn't throw well. Just 23 years old.

YEAR	TEAM/LEVEL	G	AB	R	H	2B	3B	HR	RBI	BB	SB	AVG	OBP	SLG
1993	Montreal	23	73	9	19	3	1	2	15	7	1	.260	.321	.411
1994	Montreal	40	97	16	27	10	1	2	13	9	1	.278	.358	.464
1995	*Projected*	*151*	*556*	*88*	*163*	*30*	*5*	*16*	*76*	*36*	*20*	*.293*	*.336*	*.451*

WALLY WHITEHURST / San Diego Padres / Starting Pitcher $15

Has opened the last two seasons in the Padres' rotation, and has pitched OK at times, but a strained rotator cuff and a bone spur on his elbow have taken him out in mid-season. With the development of the Padres' other young pitchers, he may not be back in the rotation, which may be in his best interests. Good pitcher within sharply defined limits.

YEAR	TEAM/LEVEL	G	IP	W-L	PCT	HITS	SO	BB	ERA
1992	New York (N)	44	97	3-9	.250	99	70	33	3.62
1993	San Diego	21	106	4-7	.364	109	57	30	3.83
1994	San Diego	13	64	4-7	.364	84	43	26	4.92

MARK WHITEN / St. Louis Cardinals / Right Field $36

He may have lost his best season to the strike. He wasn't going to match his home run and RBI totals of '93, but almost everything else was headed for a career high. A true switch hitter, hits just as well left as right. Runs well, makes many errors in the outfield but compensates with good range, exceptional arm. Is 28 years old.

YEAR	TEAM/LEVEL	G	AB	R	H	2B	3B	HR	RBI	BB	SB	AVG	OBP	SLG
1993	St. Louis	152	562	81	142	13	4	25	99	58	15	.253	.323	.423
1994	St. Louis	92	334	57	98	18	2	14	53	37	10	.293	.364	.485
1995	*Projected*	*149*	*532*	*80*	*139*	*21*	*4*	*18*	*75*	*65*	*16*	*.261*	*.342*	*.417*

MATT WHITESIDE / Texas Rangers / Relief Pitcher $19

Seemed to be on his way to big money two years ago, but has slipped into reverse. His basic pitches are a sinking fastball and a slider. The Rangers have pushed him to develop an offspeed pitch, and I honestly believe that has messed him up. In any case, his control, which was excellent two years ago, has not been as good recently.

YEAR	TEAM/LEVEL	G	IP	W-L	SAVES	HITS	SO	BB	ERA
1992	Texas	20	28	1-1	4	26	13	11	1.93
1993	Texas	60	73	2-1	1	78	39	23	4.32
1994	Texas	47	61	2-2	1	68	37	28	5.02

DARRELL WHITMORE / Florida Marlins / Outfielder $15

Athletic outfielder, fast and strong, left-handed hitter. He's 26 years old and not a great prospect. He failed a major league trial in '93, and hit .283 at Edmonton last year, which is not impressive. Will battle Conine, Sheffield, Carr, Everett, and Nigel Wilson for playing time in the Marlins' outfield. I would project him as a fifth outfielder.

YEAR	TEAM/LEVEL	G	AB	R	H	2B	3B	HR	RBI	BB	SB	AVG	OBP	SLG
1993	Florida	76	250	24	51	8	2	4	19	10	4	.204	.249	.300
1994	Florida	9	22	1	5	1	0	0	0	3	0	.227	.320	.273
1995	*Projected*	*88*	*207*	*24*	*52*	*10*	*1*	*5*	*23*	*13*	*5*	*.251*	*.295*	*.382*

BOB WICKMAN / New York Yankees / Reliever $28

Moved to the bullpen full-time, and responded with his best season, limiting hitters to a .213 batting average. Throws a sinking fastball and a hard slider, gets ground balls, and is effective against both right- and left-handers. Led the American League in game appearances, with 53. Only 26, he has made the transition to the majors now, and is just entering his best years.

YEAR	TEAM/LEVEL	G	IP	W-L	PCT	HITS	SO	BB	ERA
1992	New York	8	50	6-1	.857	51	21	20	4.11
1993	New York	41	140	14-4	.778	156	70	69	4.63
1994	New York	53	70	5-4	.556	54	56	27	3.09

RICK WILKINS / Chicago Cubs / Catcher $26

His true level of ability is halfway between his Bill Dickey stats of 1993 and his Bob Uecker stats of '94. He should platoon, because a) he can't hit left-handers (.222 lifetime with no power), b) few catchers play every day, and c) how hard is it to find a right-handed hitting catcher? Has one of the best throwing arms in the league.

YEAR	TEAM/LEVEL	G	AB	R	H	2B	3B	HR	RBI	BB	SB	AVG	OBP	SLG
1993	Chicago	136	446	78	135	23	1	30	73	50	2	.303	.376	.561
1994	Chicago	100	313	44	71	25	2	7	39	40	4	.227	.317	.387
1995	*Projected*	*145*	*458*	*58*	*115*	*22*	*1*	*17*	*57*	*54*	*2*	*.251*	*.330*	*.415*

BERNIE WILLIAMS / New York Yankees / Center Field $41

He has become a very solid center fielder, comparable to Devon White. In 1994 he was *clearly* better than White. He's probably not as fast as Devon, but he is fast, matches White's power, and gets on base much more (.384 to .313 last year). Good arm, good work habits. A much better hitter right-handed. Tends to start slowly.

YEAR	TEAM/LEVEL	G	AB	R	H	2B	3B	HR	RBI	BB	SB	AVG	OBP	SLG
1993	New York	139	567	67	152	31	4	12	68	53	9	.268	.333	.400
1994	New York	108	408	80	118	29	1	12	57	61	16	.289	.384	.453
1995	*Projected*	*153*	*601*	*93*	*167*	*33*	*4*	*15*	*74*	*74*	*18*	*.278*	*.357*	*.421*

BRIAN WILLIAMS / Houston Astros / Starting Pitcher $15

Like Matt Whiteside, he is going steadily backward. The batting average against him last year was .343, .397 by left-handed hitters (62 for 156). He throws hard, and has good action on several other pitches. But he was rushed to the majors with very little minor league experience. He needs to go back to the minors and learn to pitch.

YEAR	TEAM/LEVEL	G	IP	W-L	PCT	HITS	SO	BB	ERA
1992	Houston	16	96	7-6	.538	92	54	42	3.92
1993	Houston	42	82	4-4	.500	76	56	38	4.83
1994	Houston	20	78	6-5	.545	112	49	41	5.74

EDDIE WILLIAMS / San Diego Padres / First Base $23

A prospect in the mid-1980s whose career degenerated due mostly to bad defense, Williams played semi-pro ball in '93, was spotted by a Padres scout, signed to a minor league contract, and recalled after hitting 20 homers in two months in Triple-A. He was the Padres' first baseman the rest of the season. I don't know about .330, but he can hit.

YEAR	TEAM/LEVEL	G	AB	R	H	2B	3B	HR	RBI	BB	SB	AVG	OBP	SLG
1994	Las Vegas AAA	59	219	48	77	12	1	20	54	24	0	.352	.417	.689
1994	San Diego	49	175	32	58	11	1	11	42	15	0	.331	.392	.594
1995	*Projected*	*129*	*415*	*55*	*116*	*21*	*0*	*17*	*66*	*31*	*0*	*.280*	*.330*	*.453*

GERALD WILLIAMS / New York Yankees / Outfield $20

Made the roster as a backup outfielder, and hit well enough that he may play a little more in '95. Used by Showalter at all three outfield positions, most often for late-inning defense in left, and had 77 percent of his at bats against left-handed pitching. I would not expect him to get beyond the platoon role, at least with the Yankees.

YEAR	TEAM/LEVEL	G	AB	R	H	2B	3B	HR	RBI	BB	SB	AVG	OBP	SLG
1993	New York	42	67	11	10	2	3	0	6	1	2	.149	.183	.269
1994	New York	57	86	19	25	8	0	4	13	4	1	.291	.319	.523
1995	*Projected*	*93*	*272*	*42*	*69*	*15*	*2*	*7*	*36*	*14*	*13*	*.254*	*.290*	*.401*

MATT WILLIAMS / San Francisco Giants / Third Base $81

You probably heard, I would guess, that in the simulated continuation of the season, Williams hit 62 homers. While the strike may have cost him his chance to be really, really famous, he is clearly the best third baseman in baseball. He doesn't have Mike Schmidt's speed or his plate discipline, and for this reason will decline with age more rapidly than Schmidt did.

YEAR	TEAM/LEVEL	G	AB	R	H	2B	3B	HR	RBI	BB	SB	AVG	OBP	SLG
1993	San Francisco	145	579	105	170	33	4	38	110	27	1	.294	.325	.561
1994	San Francisco	112	445	74	119	16	3	43	96	33	1	.267	.319	.607
1995	*Projected*	*156*	*608*	*92*	*157*	*24*	*3*	*38*	*105*	*40*	*4*	*.258*	*.304*	*.495*

MIKE WILLIAMS / Philadelphia Phillies / Starting Pitcher $14

He made eight starts for the Phillies after injuries decimated the rotation, and did little to show he is ready for a major league job. Doesn't throw real hard, has good control but no strikeout pitch. Pitched well in Triple-A in 1992 and 1993 (18-3, 2.65 in 29 starts), not so well last year (2-7, 5.79 in 14 starts). Limited future.

YEAR	TEAM/LEVEL	G	IP	W-L	PCT	HITS	SO	BB	ERA
1992	Philadelphia	5	29	1-1	.500	29	5	7	5.34
1993	Philadelphia	17	51	1-3	.250	50	33	22	5.29
1994	Philadelphia	12	50	2-4	.333	61	29	20	5.01

MITCH WILLIAMS / Released / Ex-closer $13

I thought he would recover from the World Series debacle. Instead, he was traded to Houston, pitched very poorly, was demoted from the closer role, complained about it, and was released. He's lost some velocity, and he's not exactly Bob Tewksbury or Charlie Leibrandt. He now says he wants to come back, and some team will probably give him a chance to try.

YEAR	TEAM/LEVEL	G	IP	W-L	SAVES	HITS	SO	BB	ERA
1992	Philadelphia	66	81	5-8	29	69	74	64	3.78
1993	Philadelphia	65	62	3-7	43	56	60	44	3.34
1994	Houston	25	20	1-4	6	21	21	24	7.65

WOODY WILLIAMS / Toronto Blue Jays / Reliever $21

A utility pitcher, usually comes in when the game is out of hand, and occasionally pitches middle relief when the rest of the bullpen needs a rest. He has an adequate fastball and a pretty good breaking pitch, usually pitches above the belt. Good athlete, 28 years old, a 28th-round draft pick in 1988. Nobody expects much from him, but he might surprise us.

YEAR	TEAM/LEVEL	G	IP	W-L	SAVES	HITS	SO	BB	ERA
1992	Syracuse AAA	25	121	6-8	1	115	81	41	3.13
1993	Toronto	30	37	3-1	0	37	24	22	4.38
1994	Toronto	38	59	1-3	0	44	56	33	3.64

MARK WILLIAMSON / Baltimore Orioles / Reliever $19

Williamson hurt his elbow in 1992, and is still trying to reestablish himself. His 4.01 ERA, while it may not be impressive, was almost a run better than the American League norm (4.80). He made a couple of starts just before the strike, and he wasn't awful. He's 35 years old, and it wouldn't take much of a slump to finish his career.

YEAR	TEAM/LEVEL	G	IP	W-L	SAVES	HITS	SO	BB	ERA
1992	Baltimore	12	19	1-0	1	16	14	10	0.96
1993	Baltimore	48	88	7-5	0	106	45	25	4.91
1994	Baltimore	28	67	3-1	1	75	28	17	4.01

CARL WILLIS / Minnesota Twins (Released) / Middle Reliever $17

There used to be a pitcher called Line Drive Nelson, who was called that because everything he threw up there came rocketing back at him. Willis, after three fine seasons in the Twins' bullpen, became Line Drive Willis. His career may not survive the experience. He also allowed 25 inherited runners to score, helping to inflate the ERAs of Minnesota starters.

YEAR	TEAM/LEVEL	G	IP	W-L	SAVES	HITS	SO	BB	ERA
1992	Minnesota	59	79	7-3	1	73	45	11	2.72
1993	Minnesota	53	58	3-0	5	56	44	17	3.10
1994	Minnesota	49	59	2-4	3	89	37	12	5.92

DAN WILSON / Seattle Mariners / Catcher $21

Threw out 32 percent (22/69) of runners attempting to steal, ranking fifth in the league. That is basically all that he does well. He made nine errors behind the plate, which led the American League. He's never going to hit. He's Junior Ortiz—a competent enough backup catcher, if your number-one catcher doesn't get hurt. I wouldn't trade Matt Merullo to acquire him.

YEAR	TEAM/LEVEL	G	AB	R	H	2B	3B	HR	RBI	BB	SB	AVG	OBP	SLG
1993	Cincinnati	36	76	6	17	3	0	0	8	9	0	.224	.302	.263
1994	Seattle	91	282	24	61	14	2	3	27	10	1	.216	.244	.312
1995	*Projected*	*107*	*330*	*27*	*79*	*18*	*1*	*3*	*31*	*29*	*1*	*.239*	*.289*	*.327*

TREVOR WILSON / San Francisco Giants / Starting Pitcher $15

Lost the entire 1994 season to shoulder surgery. Wilson had the tools to be an effective pitcher: a live arm, pretty good control, some measure of intelligence. But like many pitchers, he could never stay in the rotation long enough to put it all together. Even if he eventually returns to pitch effectively, there's no reason to think that he will stay healthy.

YEAR	TEAM/LEVEL	G	IP	W-L	PCT	HITS	SO	BB	ERA
1992	San Francisco	26	154	8-14	.364	152	88	64	4.21
1993	San Francisco	22	110	7-5	.583	110	57	40	3.60
1994	San Francisco			(On Disabled List)					

DAVE WINFIELD / Released / Designated Hitter $19

The only player left who played in the Nixon administration, he is apparently determined to stick around and play under President Gingrich, too. The Twins traded him to the Indians during the strike, but the Indians have released him, and it is unclear where he'll get a job. He can still hit a lefty well enough to be useful (.306 with .526 slugging, 1992-94).

YEAR	TEAM/LEVEL	G	AB	R	H	2B	3B	HR	RBI	BB	SB	AVG	OBP	SLG
1992	Toronto	156	583	92	169	33	3	26	108	82	2	.290	.377	.491
1993	Minnesota	143	547	72	148	27	2	21	76	45	2	.271	.325	.442
1994	Minnesota	77	294	35	74	15	3	10	43	31	2	.252	.321	.425

BOBBY WITT / Oakland Athletics / Starting Pitcher $22

Continues to show flashes of brilliance, surrounded by long periods of utter ineffectiveness. He seemed to be making progress in '93, but fell into his old habits last year, walking more men and enjoying it less. He's not really a *bad* pitcher, 91-96 in his career; he's just maddeningly inconsistent. I don't imagine he'll ever change.

YEAR	TEAM/LEVEL	G	IP	W-L	PCT	HITS	SO	BB	ERA
1992	Two ML Teams	31	193	10-14	.417	183	125	114	4.29
1993	Oakland	35	220	14-13	.519	226	131	91	4.21
1994	Oakland	24	136	8-10	.444	151	111	70	5.04

MARK WOHLERS / Atlanta Braves / Relief Pitcher $26

Has one of the best arms in the world, but is having trouble getting beyond that. His 95-mph fastball paralyzes right-handed hitters (.218 career average, has given up only one home run ever to a right-handed hitter), but he needs more equipment to work on the lefties. He's still a **Grade A prospect,** but he could be the new Calvin Schiraldi.

YEAR	TEAM/LEVEL	G	IP	W-L	SAVES	HITS	SO	BB	ERA
1992	Atlanta	32	35	1-2	4	28	17	14	2.55
1993	Atlanta	46	48	6-2	0	37	45	22	4.50
1994	Atlanta	51	51	7-2	1	51	58	33	4.59

TONY WOMACK / Pittsburgh Pirates / Infielder $12

Remember Larry Lintz, anybody? Same kind of player. A 25-year-old infielder, left-handed hitter, extrememly fast and a good glove, but no offense to speak of. His future, if he has one, is as a utility infielder/pinch runner. At this point, he's unlikely to break the Mendoza line, but could steal 25 bases a year as a pinch runner.

YEAR	TEAM/LEVEL	G	AB	R	H	2B	3B	HR	RBI	BB	SB	AVG	OBP	SLG
1993	Pittsburgh	15	24	5	2	0	0	0	0	3	2	.083	.185	.083
1994	Buffalo AAA	106	421	40	93	9	2	0	18	19	41	.221	.253	.252
1994	Pittsburgh	5	12	4	4	0	0	0	1	2	0	.333	.429	.333

BRAD WOODALL / Atlanta Braves / Left-handed Pitcher $18

A left-handed starter, Woodall emerged from obscurity by pitching exceptionally well his first full season in Triple-A. He might join the Atlanta staff as a long reliever/sixth starter, or could be used as trade bait. Excellent command, doesn't throw particularly hard, and has a history of arm trouble. Grade B prospect, has been compared to Tom Glavine.

YEAR	TEAM/LEVEL	G	IP	W-L	PCT	HITS	SO	BB	ERA
1993	AA & AAA	18	111	7-7	.500	102	83	40	3.81
1994	Richmond AAA	27	186	15-6	.714	159	137	49	2.42
1994	Atlanta	1	6	0-1	.000	5	2	2	4.50

TIM WORRELL / San Diego Padres / Starting Pitcher $10

Pitched well his first two starts in '94, but his elbow exploded in his third start, and he will be re-building his career for several years. Before the injury, he threw in the 90s with a good slider and good control, like his brother. Unlike his brother, he doesn't have a lot of experience to fall back on if he loses his best fastball.

YEAR	TEAM/LEVEL	G	IP	W-L	PCT	HITS	SO	BB	ERA
1993	Las Vegas AAA	15	87	5-6	.455	102	89	26	5.48
1993	San Diego	21	101	2-7	.222	104	52	43	4.92
1994	San Diego	3	14	0-1	.000	9	14	5	3.68

TODD WORRELL / Los Angeles Dodgers / Relief Pitcher $21

Still throws hard, but remains fragile. His arm was healthy in 1994, but he lost time to a strained muscle in his rib cage. When he did pitch he struck out more than a batter per inning, had good control, and limited hitters to a .235 average. On the other hand, he blew eight saves, and his earned run average after July 1 was 7.50.

YEAR	TEAM/LEVEL	G	IP	W-L	SAVES	HITS	SO	BB	ERA
1992	St. Louis	67	64	5-3	3	45	64	25	2.11
1993	Los Angeles	35	39	1-1	5	46	31	11	6.05
1994	Los Angeles	38	42	6-5	11	37	44	12	4.29

RICK WRONA / Milwaukee Brewers / Catcher $9

Defensive catcher, holding on to a career by the skin of his teeth. Has been a Triple-A catcher since 1988, getting occasional major league time to cover injuries. In 1994 he played six games with the Brewers, going 5-for-10 with a homer, four doubles, and three RBI. It was a fluke; he can't really hit. Will hang around as home plate insurance.

YEAR	TEAM/LEVEL	G	AB	R	H	2B	3B	HR	RBI	BB	SB	AVG	OBP	SLG
1992	Nashville AAA	40	118	16	29	8	2	2	10	5	1	.246	.282	.398
1993	Nashville AAA	73	184	24	39	13	0	3	22	11	0	.212	.260	.332
1994	New Orl. AAA	59	179	22	45	8	3	1	21	7	2	.251	.293	.346

ANTHONY YOUNG / Chicago Cubs / Starting Pitcher $12

Was pitching fairly well for the Cubs, beginning to regain confidence, when he turned his elbow into Rice Krispies. He's since had the Tommy John surgery. This is a tough thing for any pitcher to overcome, and Young will miss all or most of 1995. It is impossible to know how good he will be when he comes back. Career record now 9-41.

YEAR	TEAM/LEVEL	G	IP	W-L	PCT	HITS	SO	BB	ERA
1992	New York	52	121	2-14	.125	134	64	31	4.17
1993	New York	39	100	1-16	.059	103	62	42	3.77
1994	Chicago	20	115	4-6	.400	103	65	46	3.92

ERIC YOUNG / Colorado Rockies / Left Field/Second Base $23

Young started the season on the Rockies' bench, with Roberto Mejia at second and Howard Johnson in left field, but won more playing time as the season progressed. Could be regular LF with Johnson's release.

Has far better leadoff skills than the Rockies' leadoff man, Walt Weiss. He hit .309 (career) in Mile High Stadium, could be hurt by the move to the new park.

YEAR	TEAM/LEVEL	G	AB	R	H	2B	3B	HR	RBI	BB	SB	AVG	OBP	SLG
1993	Colorado	144	490	82	132	16	8	3	42	63	42	.269	.355	.353
1994	Colorado	90	228	37	62	13	1	7	30	38	18	.272	.378	.430
1995	*Projected*	*133*	*416*	*60*	*116*	*16*	*4*	*5*	*42*	*48*	*30*	*.279*	*.353*	*.373*

ERNIE YOUNG / Oakland Athletics / Outfielder $16

Like Troy Neel and Mike Bordick, he arrives in Oakland with few press notices, but looks like he can play. Drafted in 1990 out of a small college in Illinois, Young is an excellent athlete, has power, runs average or better, will take a walk. He's 25; because of injuries it took him three years to get out of A Ball. Grade B prospect.

YEAR	TEAM/LEVEL	G	AB	R	H	2B	3B	HR	RBI	BB	SB	AVG	OBP	SLG
1994	Huntsville AA	72	257	45	89	19	4	14	55	37	5	.346	.427	.615
1994	Tacoma AAA	29	102	19	29	4	0	6	16	13	0	.284	.370	.500
1994	MLE	101	341	53	100	19	2	15	60	37	3	.293	.362	.493

GERALD YOUNG / St. Louis Cardinals / Outfielder $15

Like Jerome Walton, who has had a similar career, he breathed a little life into a dried tuber by hitting .300 in 41 major league at bats. He's 30, very fast, has often played well in the minors, and once played well in the majors, a long time ago. A switch hitter and a good defensive outfielder, needs to hit .260 to have a job.

YEAR	TEAM/LEVEL	G	AB	R	H	2B	3B	HR	RBI	BB	SB	AVG	OBP	SLG
1992	Houston	74	76	14	14	1	1	0	4	10	6	.184	.279	.224
1993	Colorado	19	19	5	1	0	0	0	1	4	0	.053	.217	.053
1994	St. Louis	16	41	5	13	3	2	0	3	3	2	.317	.364	.488

KEVIN YOUNG / Pittsburgh Pirates / First Base/Third Base $18

Looked like a potential star two years ago, but has played himself way out of the picture, and will have to struggle now even to save a career as a reserve. He's capable of hitting .280 or better, but has been given every opportunity to do it, and hasn't so far. I would expect him to stay at Buffalo until he earns another chance.

YEAR	TEAM/LEVEL	G	AB	R	H	2B	3B	HR	RBI	BB	SB	AVG	OBP	SLG
1993	Pittsburgh	141	449	38	106	24	3	6	47	36	2	.236	.300	.343
1994	Pittsburgh	59	122	15	25	7	2	1	11	8	0	.205	.258	.320
1994	Buffalo AAA	60	228	26	63	14	5	5	27	15	6	.276	.327	.447

EDDIE ZAMBRANO / Chicago Cubs / Outfielder/First Base $19

Zambrano was advertised as being able to crush a lefty, and he did, earning a little more playing time as the season went on. Of course, the Cubs have a new manager (the Cubs *always* have a new manager), so his good work may go for naught if he struggles in spring training. Slow, but has strong arm and gives 100 percent effort on defense.

YEAR	TEAM/LEVEL	G	AB	R	H	2B	3B	HR	RBI	BB	SB	AVG	OBP	SLG
1993	MLE	133	445	71	118	25	1	22	85	40	6	.265	.326	.474
1994	Chicago	67	116	17	30	7	0	6	18	16	2	.259	.353	.474
1995	*Projected*	*91*	*251*	*37*	*69*	*15*	*1*	*11*	*43*	*29*	*3*	*.275*	*.350*	*.474*

GREGG ZAUN / Baltimore Orioles / Catcher $14

Rick Dempsey's nephew, an exceptional defensive catcher in his own right, throws well and handles pitchers unusually well. He hit .306 at Double-A in 1993, but didn't hit at Triple-A in '94. Switch-hitter, short, not much power but uses his small strike zone to good advantage. He's not going to take Hoiles' job, but will have a career as a backup catcher.

YEAR	TEAM/LEVEL	G	AB	R	H	2B	3B	HR	RBI	BB	SB	AVG	OBP	SLG
1993	MLE	100	322	27	85	11	1	2	38	22	2	.264	.311	.323
1994	Rochester AAA	123	388	61	92	16	4	7	43	56	4	.237	.337	.353
1994	MLE	123	375	48	79	12	2	6	34	44	2	.211	.294	.301

TODD ZEILE / St. Louis Cardinals / Third Base $38

He's stabilized as a pretty good player, hits for an OK average, draws some walks, hits with moderate power in a tough park. His fielding improved dramatically last season, his fielding percentage moving from .922 to .960, with a higher double play rate and improved range. He's 29 now, unlikely to improve further. He's not Matt Williams, but hits cleanup for the Cardinals.

YEAR	TEAM/LEVEL	G	AB	R	H	2B	3B	HR	RBI	BB	SB	AVG	OBP	SLG
1993	St. Louis	157	571	82	158	36	1	17	103	70	5	.277	.352	.433
1994	St. Louis	113	415	62	111	25	1	19	75	52	1	.267	.348	.470
1995	*Projected*	*160*	*578*	*80*	*152*	*31*	*2*	*18*	*86*	*76*	*5*	*.263*	*.349*	*.417*

ALAN ZINTER / Detroit Tigers / First Base $12

A former first-round pick of the Mets, Zinter was traded to Detroit for fellow failed phenom Rico Brogna. A switch-hitting ex-catcher, now a first baseman/designated hitter, with good power and the ability to draw walks, but he's 27 years old and struck out 185 times in Triple-A last year (so you can see why the Tigers wanted him).

YEAR	TEAM/LEVEL	G	AB	R	H	2B	3B	HR	RBI	BB	SB	AVG	OBP	SLG
1993	Binghamton AA	134	432	68	113	24	4	24	87	90	1	.262	.386	.502
1993	MLE	134	417	55	98	20	2	18	70	61	0	.235	.333	.422
1994	Toledo AAA	134	471	66	112	29	5	21	58	69	13	.238	.344	.454

BOB ZUPCIC / Chicago White Sox / Outfield $14

Picked up by Chicago to take Mike Huff's place as the right-handed reserve outfielder, he played well in the field (as he always has) but didn't hit, putting his career in jeopardy. His .276 average as a rookie (1992) will get him at least one more chance, but he probably will not hit enough to stay in the majors, even as a fifth outfielder.

YEAR	TEAM/LEVEL	G	AB	R	H	2B	3B	HR	RBI	BB	SB	AVG	OBP	SLG
1992	Boston	124	392	46	108	19	1	3	43	25	2	.276	.322	.352
1993	Boston	141	286	40	69	24	2	2	26	27	5	.241	.308	.360
1994	Chicago	36	92	10	18	4	1	1	8	4	0	.196	.227	.293

LONG SHOTS

ROBERTO ABREU / Houston outfielder   **$14**
Left-handed line drive hitter, looks good but a year away.

JUAN ACEVEDO / Colorado pitcher   **$15**
17-6 at Double-A, excellent control, Grade A prospect

MANNY ALEXANDER / Baltimore shortstop   **$9**
Has made zero progress in the last two years

ANDY ALLANSON / San Francisco catcher   **$4**
Still runs well for a 225-pound catcher

MARCOS ARMAS / Oakland outfielder   **$6**
Tony's little brother, a wild swinger who sometimes connects

RICH AUDE / Pittsburgh first baseman   **$9**
230-pound line drive hitter, Grade D prospect

JIM AUSTIN / New York Yankees   **$8**
Journeyman reliever with a chronic neck injury

BOB AYRAULT / Florida reliever   **$5**
Non-prospect, won't make the roster if the strike ends

BRETT BACKLUND / Pittsburgh starting pitcher   **$9**
Once a hot prospect, 5-13 at Double-A in 1994

KEVIN BAEZ / Baltimore infielder   **$7**
No threat to the memory of Rich Dauer

CORY BAILEY / Boston reliever   **$10**
Triple-A closer, so-so stuff, could make the roster

JEFF BALLARD / Pittsburgh reliever   **$8**
If they settle the strike, his career is probably over

MARC BARCELO / Minnesota pitcher   **$15**
Big right-hander, throws in the 90s and throws strikes

BRIAN BARNES / Los Angeles reliever   **$10**
Little left-hander from Expos, still trying to find himself

SKEETER BARNES / Detroit utilityman   **$4**
Played well but released, career probably over

RICH BATCHELOR / St. Louis reliever   **$8**
Minor league veteran, looking for an opening

ALLEN BATTLE / St. Louis outfielder   **$10**
Speedy singles hitter, 26 years old, Grade D prospect

TREY BEAMON / Pittsburgh outfielder   **$15**
20-year-old singles hitter, looks great for 1996

ERIC BELL / Houston pitcher   **$10**
31-year-old minor leaguer, can actually pitch if gets a chance

MIKE BIRKBECK / Atlanta pitcher   **$13**
Veteran triple-A star, could help some teams in the majors

FRANK BOLICK / Pittsburgh third baseman   **$10**
Awkward minor league vet with good secondary averages

RODNEY BOLTON / White Sox pitcher   **$11**
53-27 in the minors, blew his only shot at the rotation

TOM BOLTON / Baltimore pitcher   **$5**
Pitched well for Boston in 1990, has run out of chances

RICKEY BOTTALICO / Philadelphia reliever   **$14**
Phillies' top pitching prospect, needs a little work

DENIS BOUCHER / Expos pitcher   **$9**
27-year-old lefty finesse pitcher, limited stuff

JIM BOWIE / Oakland first baseman   **$9**
Left-handed line drive hitter, 30; could star in a scab league

BILLY BRENNAN / Cub pitcher   **$4**
Only a scab league could get him back to the major leagues

ROD BREWER / Seibu Lions (Japan)   **$6**
Was pinch hitter for Cardinals, may look to come back

GREG BRILEY / out of work   **$3**
Unless he pulls an Oddibe, career appears to be over

BERNARDO BRITO / Minnesota outfielder   **$10**
Has now hit 278 minor league homers, most at Triple-A

HUBIE BROOKS / pinch hitter   **$1**
Released in July, career appears to be over

TERRY BROSS / Cincinnati reliever   **$8**
Right-handed Lee Guetterman, has pitched well in Triple-A

JARVIS BROWN / Atlanta outfielder   **$9**
Pinch runner/defensive sub who played for SD in '93

J. T. BRUETT / Cleveland Indians   **$9**
A left-handed Jarvis Brown

DUFF BRUMLEY / Texas pitcher   **$7**
Regarded as a prospect despite 5.51 ERA at Oklahoma City

MIKE BRUMLEY / infielder   **$8**
Still hanging in there at 32, looking for another chance

GREG BRUMMETT / Boston Red Sox pitcher   **$8**
Pitched for Giants, Twins in '93; back in the minors now

SCOTT BULLETT / Cub center fielder   **$6**
Speedy singles hitter, will swing at anything

ENRIQUE BURGOS / Kansas City left-hander   **$12**
Throws BBs, may be close to getting back to majors

TERRY BURROWS / Texas reliever   **$7**
Left-hander, good movement on his fastball, nothing else

CHRIS BUSHING / Cincinnati pitcher   **$6**
Throws 90, can't stay healthy long enough to finish his skills

JAMES BYRD / Milwaukee outfielder   **$1**
A minor league .219 hitter.

STANTON CAMERON / Pittsburgh outfielder   **$10**
Career minor leaguer, as good as some of the guys in the majors

MIKE CAMPBELL / Padres right-hander   **$7**
One-time prospect from the Mariners, 31, could pitch a little

WILLIE CANATE / Toronto outfielder   **$6**
Pinch runner/defensive outfielder, still young and may develop

CASEY CANDAELE / Cincinnati infielder   **$9**
Still banging around AAA, hoping for a few innings in the majors

OZZIE CANSECO / Milwaukee outfielder   **$7**
Returned to the minors in '94, but didn't hit

RAMON CARABALLO / Atlanta infielder $6
A minor league Joey Cora

PAUL CAREY / Baltimore first baseman $10
Big left-handed power hitter, could help a team off the bench

PEDRO CASTELLANO / Colorado third baseman $9
As long as Charlie Hayes is around, you'll never hear of him

NORM CHARLTON / Philadelphia reliever $10
Missed 1994 after elbow surgery, probably will come back

MIKE CHRISTOPHER / Detroit reliever $10
31-year-old finesse pitcher, deserves a chance in the majors

TONY CLARK / Detroit first baseman $11
6-8 left-hander with awesome power, slowed by injuries

ROYAL CLAYTON / Yankee reliever $7
Royce's older brother, no prospect but always wins

BRAD CLONTZ / Atlanta pitcher $13
Side-armer with control and a nasty slider, Grade B prospect

CRAIG COLBERT / Cleveland catcher $5
One-time prospect, bouncing listlessly around the minors

CRIS COLON / Cub third baseman $6
Now 26, doesn't know the strike zone from his mother-in-law

MIKE COOK / Mets reliever $6
Has been effective in Triple-A—since 1986

SCOTT COOLBAUGH / Cardinals third baseman $9
Had his best minor league season in '94

RON COOMER / Dodger third baseman $12
Trapped in minors, but as good a hitter as Zeile or Caminiti

MARTIN CORDOVA / Twins $12
No defense, but could hit .300 in the majors

TIM COSTO / Reds slugger $7
230-pounder without a position, almost out of chances

HENRY COTTO / Yomiuri Giants (Japan) outfielder $9
Good defensive outfielder, may be looking for a ticket back

JEFF DARWIN / Seattle pitcher $6
Danny's brother, was in the majors in '94 through a fluke

DOUG DASCENZO / Mets outfielder $8
Still in the minors if anybody needs him

JACK DAUGHERTY / Toronto outfielder $5
Released by Colorado a year ago, was a bench player at Syracuse

BUTCH (WARM FRONT) DAVIS / Texas outfielder $9
Now has 1649 hits in the minor leagues

GLENN DAVIS / Kansas City first baseman $10
A big year at Omaha may indicate that he's finally recovered

MARK DAVIS / relief pitcher $1
Released by San Diego last May, wouldn't expect him back

DREW DENSON / White Sox first baseman $9
A minor league Cecil Fielder/Frank Thomas type

JOHN DeSILVA / right-handed pitcher $6
One-time Tiger prospect, still bouncing around Double-A

ORESTES DESTRADE / first baseman $9
230-pound first baseman, released by Florida in May

JAMIE DISMUKE / Cincinnati first baseman $9
.245 hitter with some power, a challenge for Chris Berman

STEVE DIXON / Cardinals reliever $8
Closer at Louisville for two years, but marginal prospect

ROB DUCEY / Texas outfielder $8
Turns 30 in May; I still believe he can play a little

DAVE EILAND / Yankees pitcher $8
5-14 in the majors, but a proven winner at Columbus

CECIL ESPY / Outfielder $5
Speedy switch-hitting center fielder, been around forever

MARK ETTLES / Padres pitcher $6
28-year-old Australian, Grade D prospect, rag arm

PAUL FARIES / Giants infielder $7
Now 30, not playing as well as he did five years ago

MONTY FARISS / Florida infielder $9
Failed a trial as Texas shortstop, would be OK fifth OF

JOHN FARRELL / Cleveland pitcher $6
Still trying to come back, .350 winning percentages in Triple-A

HUCK FLENER / Toronto pitcher $7
A prospect last year, lost most of '94 to an injury

PAUL FLETCHER / Philadelphia starter $5
8-21 at Triple-A over the last two years

STEVE FOSTER / Giants reliever $5
Missed '94 after shoulder surgery, Giants claimed on waivers

JAY GAINER / Rockies first baseman $4
Thick-set left-handed hitter, can't play

JEFF GARDNER / Expos second baseman $9
Minor league veteran, had a shot with San Diego in '93

BOB GEREN / catcher $1
Out of baseball for a year, might return in emergency

BENJI GIL / Texas shortstop $10
Grade A prospect a year ago, played poorly at Oklahoma City

DAN GLADDEN / Yomiuri Giants (Japan) outfielder $3
Hit .259 in Japan, will be 38 in mid-season

LARRY GONZALES / Angels catcher $5
Big RHB, the Angels don't believe in him

TOM GOODWIN / Royals outfielder $7
Speed merchant, defensive outfielder who doesn't hit much

KEITH GORDON / Reds outfielder $7
Big right-handed hitter, runs and has power, wild swinger

MARK GRANT / reliever $1
Had trials with six teams (1984-93), may be out of baseball now

MARK GRATER / reliever $1
Had some good years in the Cardinals system

KEN GREER / Mets reliever $6
No prospect, pitched one inning in the majors in '93

KIP GROSS / pitcher $2
Went 6-11 with the Nippon Ham Fighters (Japan) in '94

KELLY GRUBER / third baseman $1
Injuries drove him out of baseball in mid-'93

LEE GUETTERMAN / Mariners reliever $9
Had outstanding '94 at Calgary, wants one more bite of the apple

DAVID HAAS / Tigers pitcher $2
Still battling arm troubles

DONALD HARRIS / Texas outfielder $5
Can play defense and has power, but will never hit

HILLY HATHAWAY / San Diego pitcher $6
Made Angels' rotation in '93, last year 2-9 at Las Vegas

ERIC HELFAND / Athletics catcher $4
The A's like him, but he's never going to hit enough to play

CESAR HERNANDEZ / outfielder $5
Defensive outfielder/pinch runner, had a shot with Cincinnati

KEVIN HIGGINS / Padres catcher $4
Weak left-handed hitter, minor league vet, had a shot in '93

AARON HOLBERT / Cardinals infielder $10
Appears to be the Cardinals shortstop of the future

BRAD HOLMAN / Mariners pitcher $3
Battling arm injuries, had 11.17 ERA at Calgary in '94

MARK HOLZEMER / Angels pitcher $6
Still reeling from his shot at the Angels rotation in '93

SAM HORN / first baseman $5
Released by Yankees, would be superstar in a scab league

CHARLIE HOUGH / retired pitcher   NO VALUE
Retired because of degenerating hip

KENT HRBEK / Twins first baseman   NO VALUE
Retired. Similar players: Vic Wertz, Boog Powell, Rudy York.

KEITH HUGHES / outfielder $1
Quit baseball in '94 after failing to earn a real shot.

MIKE HUMPHREYS / Yankee outfielder $5
Has spent four years at Columbus, will move on in '95

BRUCE HURST / retired pitcher   NO VALUE
Retired last June after a couple of seven-plus ERAs

BUTCH HUSKEY / Mets third baseman $7
Stock has dropped after a miserable year at Norfolk

JEFF HUSON / Rangers infielder $8
Spent all of '94 in Triple-A, may re-surface sometime

JEFF INNIS / Padres reliever $10
Back in the minors, but the same pitcher he's always been

DION JAMES / outfielder $3
Hit .257 with little power for Chunichi Dragons (Japan)

MIKE JAMES / Angels pitcher $6
Right-hander from Dodgers system, good arm, slow progress

DOMINGO JEAN / Astros pitcher $6
Wasted 1994 due to arm injury, pitched only 19 innings

DOUG JENNINGS / Cincinnati first baseman $9
Outstanding minor league hitter, will bounce up again

ERIK JOHNSON / Giants infielder $4
Can't play at all, but the Giants call him up occasionally

JOEL JOHNSTON / relief pitcher $8
Had trials with KC and Pittsburgh, has lost the strike zone

TIM JONES / Indians infielder $7
Played parts of six seasons with St. Louis

TERRY JORGENSEN / Portland infielder $6
Former Twins prospect, has played for Portland since 1990

KEITH KESSINGER / Reds shortstop $4
Still shows few signs of being a major league hitter

JOHN KIELY / Tigers pitcher $4
Has had arm troubles since posting 2.13 ERA for '92 Tigers

PAUL KILGUS / Cardinals pitcher $1
Shoulder surgery last spring has probably ended his career

JOE KLINK / left-handed reliever $1
Released by the Marlins last spring, career is probably over

JOE KMAK / Mets catcher $4
No prospect, 31-year-old catcher who runs but doesn't hit

MARK KNUDSON / right-handed pitcher   NO VALUE
Hasn't been sighted in a year and a half; assume he has retired

BRIAN KOELLING / Reds second baseman $8
Minor league Mark Lemke, will play if Boone gets hurt

TOM KRAMER / Reds pitcher $8
Went 7-3 for Cleveland in '93, went back to minors anyway

RICK KRIVDA / Orioles pitcher $11
Left-hander who was 9-10 at Rochester, Grade C prospect

STEVE LAKE / backup catcher $1
Out of the game, released by Cincinnati a year ago

TOM LAMPKIN / Giants catcher $6
Spent '94 in minors, will be up and down for next five years

TIM LAYANA / Expos reliever $4
One-time prospect in Yankees' system, almost out of baseball

DEREK LEE / Expos outfielder $12
Capable 28-year-old outfielder, can't get a job, could hit .270

MARK LEONARD / Giants outfielder $14
One of the best hitters trapped in the minors

BRIAN LOONEY / Expos starter $9
Brian Barnes type, small lefty, had unimpressive '94 at Ottawa

LARRY LUEBBERS / Cubs pitcher $7
Finesse pitcher, pitched for Cincy in '93, Grade D prospect

MITCH LYDEN / Marlins catcher $3
Veteran non-prospect, power is his only weapon

KEVIN MAAS / Reds first baseman $10
Now in the minors, still has 25-home run power

BOB MacDONALD / lefty reliever $8
Pitched 68 times for Tigers in '93, wasn't effective

LONNIE MACLIN / Cardinal outfielder $7
A minor league Dave Gallagher, fourth outfielder at Louisville

CARLOS MALDONADO / Oakland pitcher $5
Trying to harness his fastball, had 6.69 ERA at Tacoma

MARK MARINI / Indians outfielder $10
Very promising hitter, Indians have no reason to rush him

ORESTE MARRERO / Expos first baseman $5
I sure hope he *enjoys* playing in the minors

BILLY MASSE / Yankees outfielder $7
Member of the 1988 Olympic team, has never played in the majors

KEVIN McGEHEE / Orioles starter $8
Consistently good minor league starter, looking for a chance

TIM McINTOSH / Twins catcher $8
Converted outfielder from Brewers, good hitter for a catcher

JIM McNAMARA / Yankees catcher $2
Glove man, couldn't hit a baby in the butt with a fly-swatter

JEFF McNEELY / Red Sox outfielder $6
A prospect last year, had absolutely awful season at Pawtucket

HENRY MERCEDES / A's catcher $3
Similar to Jim McNamara, Triple-A catcher who can't hit

LUIS MERCEDES / Giants outfielder $5
Singles hitter; his time has arrived but he hasn't

HENSLEY MEULENS / Outfielder $6
Hit 20 home runs for Chiba Lotte Marines, might return

SAM MILITELLO / right-handed pitcher $2
Free-fall from super-prospect status has ended in his release

KEITH MILLER / Utility player $7
Released by Kansas City after two years of injuries

PAUL MILLER / Pirates pitcher $6
6-5, 225-pound right-hander, career is going nowhere

JOE MILLETTE / Marlins shortstop $5
28-year-old shortstop from Phillies system, will never hit

GINO MINUTELLI / Indians reliever $5
Left-handed pitcher with good control, a longshot for a career

DAVE MLICKI / Indians starter $10
Trying to come back from shoulder surgery, looking good

DENNIS MOELLER / Royals reliever $5
Left-handed finesse pitcher, failed starter, no fastball

CHARLIE MONTOYO / Phillies second baseman $9
Has .412 career OBP, once drew 156 walks in a season

OSCAR MUNOZ / Twins starting pitcher $9
Grade C prospect, had 5.88 ERA at Salt Lake City in '94

GLENN MURRAY / Red Sox outfielder $7
Runs like a Deer, strikes out like another one

TITO NAVARRO / Mets shortstop $7
Out of the picture for now, will re-emerge in time

ROD NICHOLS / Royals pitcher $5
The Loss Machine

JERRY NIELSEN / White Sox pitcher $5
Pitched for Yankees ('92) and Angels ('93), no prospect

RAFAEL NOVOA / free agent pitcher $5
Left-hander, went 6-10, 5.24 ERA for Iowa

JOHN O'DONOGHUE, JR. / Orioles pitcher $6
He'll never be the pitcher that his father wasn't either

BOBBY OJEDA / left-handed pitcher NO VALUE
Released by the Yankees last May

GREG OLSON / Catcher $7
A 1990 All-Star, released by the Braves and Mets last year

JOHN ORTON / Braves catcher $2
Hit .123 at Richmond

MIKE PAGLIARULO / Third baseman $3
Didn't help the Seibu Lions (Japan)

RICK PARKER / Mets outfielder $7
32-year-old defensive outfielder, Dave Gallagher type

JEFF PARRETT / Royals reliever $7
Trying to come back from a detached ligament

KEN PATTERSON / lefty reliever $3
Had elbow surgery in April, is now in the free agent market

DAN PELTIER / Rangers outfielder $9
Decent left-handed pinch hitter, pushed aside by Rusty Greer

WILLIAM PENNYFEATHER / Reds outfielder $3
He's a great athlete, but he's never going to be a ball-player

GENO PETRALLI / Backup catcher $2
Released by Texas a year ago, still wants to play

GUS POLIDOR / middle infielder $1
Out of baseball, may still be playing in Venezuela

SCOTT POSE / Brewers outfielder $9
A Steve Finley type, probably can play a little

TED POWER / free agent reliever $1
39 years old, missed the '94 season after shoulder surgery

CURTIS PRIDE / Expos outfielder $9
A prospect a year ago, but had poor season at Ottawa

HARVEY PULLIAM / Padres outfielder $5
The Pulliam express is about five years behind schedule

JAMIE QUIRK / Royals catcher NO VALUE
As long as he's alive, I figure there's a chance he'll return

KEN RAMOS / Astros outfielder $9
27 years old, no power, has career OBP in the minors of .396

DENNIS RASMUSSEN / Royals pitcher $6
Ancient left-hander, still pitching well in the minors

JEFF REARDON / reliever NO VALUE
39, released by the Yankees last May after posting 8.38 ERA

KEVIN REIMER / Fukuoka Daiei Hawks (Japan) $9
Hit .298 with 26 homers; can't field in Japanese, either

JEFF RICHARDSON / Cardinals second baseman $7
A minor league Jody Reed

ERNEST RILES / Angels infielder $8
One of the better backup infielders who is looking for work

MARC RONAN / Cardinals catcher $4
Triple-A backup catcher, hits left-handed but can't hit

RICO ROSSY / Royals infielder $8
31 years old, a capable enough backup infielder

BILL SAMPEN / Angels reliever $5
Probably stuck in the minors from now on

TRACY SANDERS / Mets outfielder $7
In his third organization at age 25, his status has slipped

NELSON SANTOVENIA / Royals catcher $1
Hit .166 at Omaha; professional career is probably over

MACKEY SASSER / Padres catcher $2
Released by the Mariners, was a Double-A backup last year

JEFF SCHAEFER / A's infielder $5
There'd be a place for him if teams could carry 20 infielders

SCOTT SCUDDER / Pirates pitcher $4
Had 5.62 ERA at Buffalo—a pitcher's park

MIKE SHARPERSON / Cubs infielder $9
Not a bad player, has spent most of career in minors, now 33

LARRY SHEETS / outfielder $1
Released by Seattle a year ago

BEN SHELTON / Pirates infielder $4
A first baseman who hits like a shortstop

KEITH SHEPHERD / Red Sox pitcher $5
Dropped to A Ball at age 26, career will recover sometime

DARRELL SHERMAN / Rockies outfielder $6
Released by San Diego, trying to get re-established

TOMMY SHIELDS / middle infielder NO VALUE
Announced his retirement in October

ZAK SHINALL / right-handed pitcher $1
Apparently not in organized ball in '94; I've lost him

JOE SIDDALL / Expos catcher $4
A backup at Ottawa, hit .173 in '94

DUANE SINGLETON / Brewers outfielder $6
22-year-old Mike Felder–Dave Gallagher type, might develop

JOE SLUSARSKI / Phillies pitcher $3
He's getting progressively worse

AARON SMALL / Blue Jays pitcher $11
A Big Small right-hander, Double-A swing man, pitching well

MARK SMITH / Orioles outfielder $7
Big right-handed hitter, probably won't hit enough

ROGER SMITHBERG / A's reliever $9
Triple-A set-up man; should have been lefty if he wanted a job

KURT STILLWELL / Reds infielder $7
Not yet 30, trying to re-start his career

WILLIAM SUERO / Pirates second baseman $6
Glove man, failed to stick with the Brewers

PAUL SWINGLE / Angels pitcher $2
Missed '94 with a shoulder injury, can't pitch anyway

BRIEN TAYLOR / Yankees airhead $5
Look for him sometime in the next millennium

SCOTT TAYLOR / Red Sox pitcher $1
Injured or something—didn't pitch in '94

TIM TEUFEL / infielder NO VALUE
Gone

GARY THURMAN / White Sox outfielder $9
Minor league Chuck Carr

BRIAN TRAXLER / Fukuoka Daiei Hawks (Japan) $6
Hit .263 in Japan, 15 homers, 62 RBI

GEORGE TSAMIS / Mariners pitcher $4
A modern Jerry Don Gleaton

GREG TUBBS / Pirates outfielder $6
Little leadoff man, has 1267 hits in the minors, now 32

JULIO VALERA / Angels pitcher $8
Trying to come back from blowing out his elbow, slow progress

TY VAN BURKLEO / Rockies first baseman $4
Big power-hitting first baseman, a poor man's Sam Horn

GUILLERMO VELASQUEZ / Red Sox first baseman $3
Singles hitter, good glove, no future

QUILVIO VERAS / Mets second baseman $10
Switch-hitting Dominican, good leadoff man skills

Tim WAKEFIELD / Pirates pitcher   **$6**
Back in minors, getting his knuckles beat in

Jim WALEWANDER / Angels infielder   **$2**
The same future as any 34-year-old minor league pinch runner

Chico WALKER / minor league legend   **$2**
Now playing in Mexico, career probably over

Todd WALKER / Twins second baseman   **$15**
First-round pick in 1994, from LSU; looks like a hitter

Dan WALTERS / Padres catcher   **$1**
Didn't play in '94; may be out of baseball

John WEHNER / Pirates third baseman   **$12**
Hit .303 at Buffalo; career may come back to life

Mickey WESTON / Rockies pitcher   **$4**
Makes Doug Jones look like Roger Clemens

Derrick WHITE / Marlins first baseman   **$5**
A big strong guy with no power, released by Expos

Kevin WICKANDER / Indians reliever   **$1**
Shaken by death of Steve Olin, was out of baseball in '94

Curtis WILKERSON / Expos infielder   **$1**
Major league career is probably over

Jerry WILLARD / Mariners catcher   **$7**
He's 35 and overweight, but he can hit

Craig WILSON / Rangers infielder   **$5**
Light-hitting third baseman, released by the Royals a year ago

Nigel WILSON / Marlins outfielder   **$8**
Had another strikeout- and injury-plagued season

Steve WILSON / Brewers reliever   **$6**
Supposed to have great stuff, blew several chances with LA

Willie WILSON / outfielder   **$1**
Released by the Cubs on May 16, led the Reagan years in hits

Ted WOOD / Expos outfielder   **$7**
Gary Varsho-, Dave Gallagher-type. Supply exceeds demand.

Tracy WOODSON / Cardinals third baseman   **$5**
Released by three organizations in a year, back with Cards

Eric YELDING / Cubs outfielder   **$6**
Great speed, nothing else to sell

Dmitri YOUNG / Cardinals first baseman   **$9**
Kevin Mitchell's body, Gerald Perry's power

Pete YOUNG / Red Sox pitcher   **$7**
Chubby ex-Expo, pitched poorly at New Britain in '94

HIGHEST-VALUED PLAYERS BY POSITION

CATCHER

Mike PIAZZA	$84
Chris HOILES	$66
Ivan RODRIGUEZ	$64
Darren DAULTON	$52
Mickey TETTLETON	$39
Mike STANLEY	$38
Javy LOPEZ	$37
Sandy ALOMAR	$36
Mike MACFARLANE	$36
Dave NILSSON	$36
Terry STEINBACH	$36
Todd HUNDLEY	$34

FIRST BASE

Frank THOMAS	$98
Jeff BAGWELL	$94
Fred MCGRIFF	$80
Gregg JEFFERIES	$66
Rafael PALMEIRO	$65
Mo VAUGHN	$59
John OLERUD	$58
Will CLARK	$53
Hal MORRIS	$47
Cliff FLOYD	$46
Cecil FIELDER	$44
Andres GALARRAGA	$44

SECOND BASE

Roberto ALOMAR	$92
Carlos BAERGA	$84
Chuck KNOBLAUCH	$69
Craig BIGGIO	$67
Delino DESHIELDS	$57
Jeff KENT	$45
Bret BOONE	$44
Bip ROBERTS	$40
Carlos GARCIA	$37
Joey CORA	$36
Pat KELLY	$36
Jeff FRYE	$35

THIRD BASE

Matt WILLIAMS	$81
Robin VENTURA	$68
Travis FRYMAN	$67
Bobby BONILLA	$50
Ken CAMINITI	$44
Charlie HAYES	$43
Jim THOME	$40
Edgar MARTINEZ	$39
Todd ZEILE	$38
Scott COOPER	$34
Wade BOGGS	$33
Dean PALMER	$32

SHORTSTOP

Barry LARKIN	$73
Wil CORDERO	$70
Jay BELL	$68
Cal RIPKEN	$48
Mike BORDICK	$45
Ozzie SMITH	$38
Andujar CEDENO	$36
Jeff BLAUSER	$34
Greg GAGNE	$34
Kevin STOCKER	$34
Ozzie GUILLEN	$32
Omar VIZQUEL	$32

LEFT FIELD

Barry BONDS	$100
Albert BELLE	$86
Juan GONZALEZ	$80
Joe CARTER	$70
Moises ALOU	$70
Jeff CONINE	$57
Kevin MITCHELL	$53
Tim RAINES	$46
Brady ANDERSON	$42
Ron GANT	$41
Rickey HENDERSON	$40
Al MARTIN	$37

CENTER FIELD

Ken GRIFFEY, Jr.	$99
Kenny LOFTON	$85
Marquis GRISSOM	$77
Rick LANGFORD	$61
Steve FINLEY	$52
Lenny DYKSTRA	$49
Shane MACK	$49
Devon WHITE	$46
Brett BUTLER	$44
Roberto KELLY	$43
Derek BELL	$40
Lance JOHNSON	$35

RIGHT FIELD

Larry WALKER	$78
Kirby PUCKETT	$75
Jay BUHNER	$73
Tony GWYNN	$70
Ruben SIERRA	$66
Manny RAMIREZ	$65
Tim SALMON	$62
Raul MONDESI	$54
Gary SHEFFIELD	$53
Sammy SOSA	$53
Paul O'NEILL	$52
Dave JUSTICE	$43

DESIGNATED HITTERS AND UTILITY PLAYERS

Jose CANSECO	$64
Tony PHILLIPS	$60
Paul MOLITOR	$59
Julio FRANCO	$40
Danny TARTABULL	$38
Bob HAMELIN	$37
Chili DAVIS	$35
Brian HARPER	$34
Troy NEEL	$34
Greg VAUGHN	$34
Harold BAINES	$27
Mariano DUNCAN	$27

RIGHT-HANDED STARTERS

Greg MADDUX	$96
Jose RIJO	$78
David CONE	$78
Roger CLEMENS	$75
Ken HILL	$74
Jack MCDOWELL	$74
Mike MUSSINA	$72
Doug DRABEK	$70
Andy BENES	$68
Kevin APPIER	$68
Alex FERNANDEZ	$68
Pedro J. MARTINEZ	$57
Pete HARNISCH	$51

LEFT-HANDED STARTERS

Randy JOHNSON	$83
Tom GLAVINE	$78
Jimmy KEY	$65
Steve AVERY	$62
Mark LANGSTON	$55
Chuck FINLEY	$53
Wilson ALVAREZ	$51
Jeff FASSERO	$46
Danny JACKSON	$43
John SMILEY	$38

SET-UP MEN

Mel ROJAS	$38
Gil HEREDIA	$35
Mike JACKSON	$35
Johnny RUFFIN	$34
Jeff BRANTLEY	$32
Hector CARRASCO	$29
Darren OLIVER	$29
Mark EICHORN	$28
Scott RADINSKY	$28
Bob WICKMAN	$28
Mark ACRE	$27
Paul ASSENMACHER	$27
Eric PLUNK	$27
Bill RISLEY	$27
Billy TAYLOR	$27

CLOSERS

Rod BECK	$76
John WETTELAND	$73
Jeff MONTGOMERY	$59
Trevor HOFFMAN	$55
Roberto HERNANDEZ	$54
Lee SMITH	$47
Randy MYERS	$46
Rick AGUILERA	$44
Bobby AYALA	$41
Doug JONES	$41
Tom HENKE	$39
Mike FETTERS	$37
John FRANCO	$37
John HUDEK	$37

PROSPECTS

Derek JETER	$40
Alan BENES	$37
Carlos DELGADO	$36
Alex GONZALEZ	$35
Charles JOHNSON	$34
Armando BENITEZ	$34
Jeff CIRILLO	$34
Shawn GREEN	$34
Ray DURHAM	$32
Willie GREENE	$32
Chipper JONES	$31
Albie LOPEZ	$31
Antonio OSUNA	$31
Jimmy HAYNES	$29
Scott RUFFCORN	$29
Billy ASHLEY	$28
Marc NEWFIELD	$28
Bill PULSIPHER	$28